Programming in SAP APO

Programming in SAP APO

Ankush Agrawal
Project Lead-SCM-APO
Asia Pacific Global Delivery
IBM India Private Limited

McGraw Hill Education (India) Private Limited
NEW DELHI

McGraw Hill Education Offices

New Delhi New York St Louis San Francisco Auckland Bogotá Caracas
Kuala Lumpur Lisbon London Madrid Mexico City Milan Montreal
San Juan Santiago Singapore Sydney Tokyo Toronto

McGraw Hill Education (India) Private Limited

Published by McGraw Hill Education (India) Private Limited
P-24, Green Park Extension, New Delhi 110 016

Programming in SAP APO

ISBN (13 digits): 978-1-25-905884-4
ISBN (10 digits): 1-25-905884-0

Vice President and Managing Director: *Ajay Shukla*
Publishing Manager—Professional: *Mitadru Basu*
Editorial Researcher—Computing: *Irene Rajalingam*
DGM—Sales and Business Development—Professional: *S Girish*
Deputy Marketing Manager—Science, Technology and Computing: *Rekha Dhyani*
General Manager—Production: *Rajender P Ghansela*
Manager—Production: *Reji Kumar*

Typeset at Tej Composers, WZ 391, Madipur, New Delhi 110 063 and printed at Sanat Printers, 312 EPIP, HSIDC, Kundli, Sonepat, Haryana.

Cover Printer: Sanat Printers

Cover Designer: Mukul Khattar

Cover Image: © Sergey Nivens—Fotolia.com

RXAYCRXODLBAX

To

my father
Late Sh. Sunder Shyam Agrawal
like whom I always want to become, the
legendary life he live, in the hearts of people

and

my beloved son Aarav
whom I always want to spend time with and to my mother,
her all the time blessings made me to achieve this milestone of my life

FOREWORD

Do you know APO? Are you aware of MySAP.com components? Do you know how MySAP.com component works and interacts with each other? Do you have the skill sets of Advance ABAP which covers LiveCache, portals, CRM, SRM. etc. etc. these types of questions now days all technical consultants like me have to face when SAP world is exploring every day. Just knowledge of normal ABAP keeps them out of the market and brings a question in front of themselves "If I don't know APO, I don't know where I am and what I am doing for years and years".

APO abbreviation for Advanced Planning and Optimization, and was originally a SCM-Supply Chain Management component of MySAP.com that was introduced by SAP only a few years ago. Today, APO is spreading its wings in almost all industries like Automobile, Consumer Goods, Food & Beverages, Steel, Oil & Gas and many more.

As a key ingredient of SAP SCM, APO leverage supply chain planner with components that support forecasting and planning within and along the supply chain. The modules within APO includes: Supply Chain Cockpit, Demand Planning, Supply Network Planning, Global Available to Promise, Transportation Planning/Vehicle Scheduling, Service Parts Planning, and Production Planning Detailed Scheduling.

According to SAP, APO can also help organizations to share information with customers in real time. In particular, SAP APO supports intercompany collaborative processes, such as vendor-managed inventory (VMI) and the voluntary inter-industry commerce standards collaborative planning, forecasting, and replenishment processes. In turn, in APO 7.0, SAP has improved characteristics-based cross-location planning – a more detailed level of planning.

Global Organizations eager to improve the processes and reduce costs, Organizations uses SCM-APO to streamline the planning process which reduces planning overhead and improves forecast accuracy and helps in reducing inventory.

The latest version of SAP APO, 7.0, went live in the fourth quarter of 2008 and became globally available in 2009, customers planning to upgrade to 7.0 from a previous version must have at least version 4.1, which now went out of mainstream support and into extended support. Customers having earlier release such as 3.1, will need to upgrade it to at least 4.1 before moving to 7.0

If you are in SAP world, then its time to get yourself involved into MySAP.com world if you are still not the part of advance components of SAP like APO, you must take the time out to become acquainted with the concepts, technical topics and programming style of APO, covered in this book. This book will help the readers with enough knowledge to understand programming concepts of APO.

Dr. Ankush Agrawal

PREFACE

"Don't take rest after your first victory, because if you fail in second, more lips are waiting to say, that your first victory was just a luck".

In this book ***"Programming in SAP APO"***, all readers will find something to learn. For those who are experienced APO technical consultants, experienced R/3 consultants, consultants who has experience in R/3 but new to APO, consultants new to R/3 and new to APO and also to the Functional consultants who wants to understand the technical aspects of APO. This book will help readers to understand the concept in easiest way and will increase their knowledge to the higher level.

This is not just a reference book, it is loaded with full technical experiences which I came across during my journey in APO as technical consultant and later-on as SME. As presently we do not find much documentation on APO technical side hence during my experience on the APO projects, I used to prepare notes on lots of discussions with some of the fantastic consultants I came across during various APO projects, with whom I have had the pleasure of working with.

My Indian and European colleagues always opened for discussions on the subject and later when I became the SME of the subject the knowledge I collected during the APO implementations was requested by my new teammates and colleagues, there the idea clicked to convert the raw notes to a publications, where my personal attention not required and readers can gain knowledge using my experience.

Here in the book I tried to use most easy examples and at the same time the most useful literature which makes is much understandable subject. In the initial chapters the book also covers the conceptual documentation on APO, which I always feel useful for technical consultants otherwise knowledge was always limited to programming without knowing "what exactly this program is doing, in business".

DR. ANKUSH AGRAWAL

ACKNOWLEDGEMENTS

Publication of book on niche skills like *"Programming in SAP APO"* would not have been possible without the support of family, friends and colleagues. First of all I want to thanks Tata McGraw-Hill for approving my concept and giving me opportunity to write this book and share my knowledge with my colleagues and SAP world. I am delighted to work with IBM India Pvt. Ltd. A fantastic company to work with, IBM always supports its employees and extends its liberty to explore new dimensions of new products. Here I also want to thank my manager Somnath Dey who always supported and encouraged me to complete the subject and for permitting me to work on the book along with my organization's work. Also to Devraj Bardhan, my German colleague and manager for giving the idea to convert the notes to a professional look of a published book and who constantly promoted this project, keeps on following-up and ensured that the idea of the book became reality.

I would like to give sincere thanks to all my colleagues specially Neha Nath, one of the outstanding APO technical consultants in IBM for her superb proofreading and help by contributing with suggestions and examples throughout shaping my ideas in the form of book.

Finally to God for everything "said/unsaid".

Dr. Ankush Agrawal

CONTENTS

1

INTRODUCTION TO SAP SUPPLY CHAIN MANAGEMENT (SCM)

1.1 DEFINITION OF SUPPLY CHAIN MANAGEMENT (SCM)

The terminology *Supply Chain Management* (SCM) refers to the inter-enterprise practice of coordinating the flows of material and information along the entire logistics series (or supply chain), throughout the entire business process chain or procurement process chain.

The purpose of SCM is to arrange the whole process—from raw materials procurement to end-customer sales—in a method that optimizes time and financials. It ultimately involves intensified cooperation between all the companies/individuals involved in a supplier-customer relationship. The structure in large process or service industries having kind of relationship is usually more complex than a supply chain, as most suppliers have multiple customers, and most customers have multiple suppliers.

Therefore, the term *Supply Networks Planning* is also used. However, integrated information-processing systems are required to manage this level of complexity. Initially we will more discuss about the concept of Supply Chain Management and gradually we will move towards SAP APO.

1.2 SCM APPLICATION COMPONENTS WITH SOME DEFINITIONS

- *Advanced Planning and Optimization (APO):* Plan for Demand, Supply, Replenishment, Production, Distribution and Transportation across organization Supply Chain network.
- *Supply Network Collaboration (SNC):* Collaboration with suppliers and customers for control and monitor replenishment of products efficiently.
- *Extended Warehouse Management (EWM):* Flexible, automated support of logistics processes (goods movement, stock management) within warehouse or organization premises.
- *Forecast & Replenishment (F&R):* Optimize internal logistics of retail companies, focus on replenishment.
- *Service Parts Planning (SPP):* Providing planning capabilities specific to service parts and analytics, monitoring functions to identify weak spots of

the supply chain and plan the entire supply chain for service part. In today's environment service parts also plays vital role same as the finished products.

- *Event Management (EM):* Monitor critical situations through capture of events within the business and partners for better business rules.

Along with the planning of the supply chain, optimization is key area to be take into consideration like what is the best process or method for the supply chain which saves cost, inventory, time etc. hence the application of an optimization model in an organization requires the development of an optimization modeling system. A key element in such a system is the supply chain decision database, which is derived from, but significantly different than, the organization's corporate databases. It is constructed from aggregate descriptions of the organization's products, customers and vendors. It contains

- Direct and indirect cost relationships
- Sub-models of production, transportation, warehousing and inventory management
- Cost and capacity information about commodities, parts, products offered by suppliers/vendors
- Order information and forecasts of demand for finished products

To understand the subject better, I am exploring some of the concepts on SCM here, later the book will focus on technical part of SCM-APO only and as and when require I will take you through the insight of other components of SCM which I think is required to make one understand the concept.

1.3 WHAT IS THE SAP SCM-APO?

SAP Advanced Planning and Optimization (APO) is the planning component of mySAP.com SCM, the supply chain management solution provided by SAP. SAP's venture into the advanced planning solution market was with the name ***SAP SCM-APO***. SAP APO is used to make strategic, tactical and operational decisions and supports the business users in performing the following planning activities:

1.4 MODULES OF SCM-APO

- Demand Planning (DP)
- Supply Network Planning (SNP)
- Production Planning (PP)
- Detailed Scheduling (DS)
- Deployment
- Transport Load Builder (TLB)
- Transport Planning and Vehicle Scheduling (TP/VS)
- Global Available-to-Promise (gATP)

Modules of SAP APO will be described in details later in the specific chapters.

1.5 SCM PROCESSES

The focus of this book is more on SCM-APO technical building blocks and programming techniques in APO still the SCM processes within a organization is little explained here. The possibilities of collaboration with customers and suppliers and the according processes are mentioned as well, as I have experience in the area of SCM implementations in automobile industries henceforth my examples might be more related to automobile industries but there is big potential for other sectors of various process companies.

From an organization's point of view a Supply Chain usually consists of

- Customers
- Distribution Centers (DCs) or Regional Distribution Centers (RDCs)
- Plants and
- Suppliers

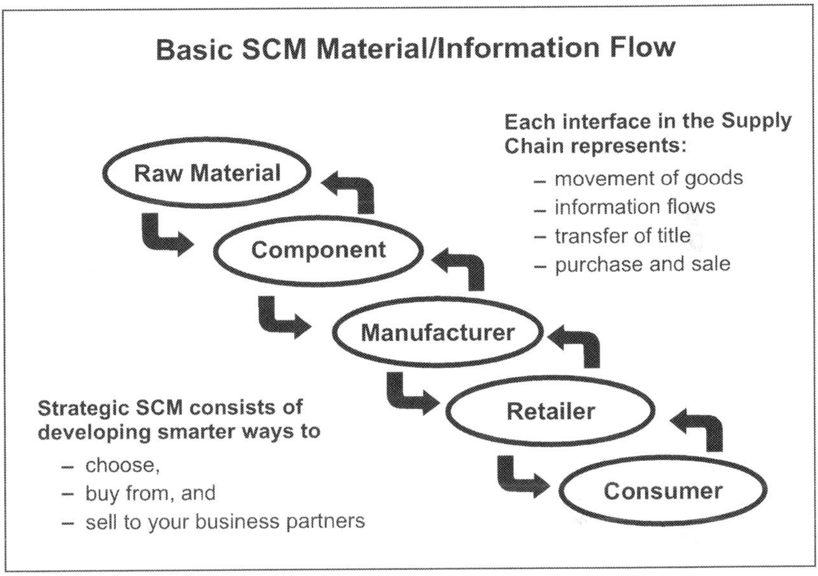

Figure 1.1 The basic flow of supply chain

There might be several levels for distribution (e.g. Regional and local DCs) or several levels of production, if one plant produces the input material for another plant. Another characteristic of a supply chain is whether sourcing alternatives exist.

Multiple sourcing is common for suppliers, and in many cases alternatives exist for production and distribution as well. Common variants in the distribution are direct shipments from the plant to the customer instead from the local DC, depending on the order size and supplier area network. The most common supply chain processes cover the areas:

- Demand planning

- Order fulfillment (Sales and Transportation Planning)
- Distribution (Distribution Planning, Replenishment, VMI)
- Production (Production Planning, Detailed Scheduling, Production Execution) and
- External procurement (Purchasing, Subcontracting).

In cases of multiple sources for internal procurement an integrated approach for distribution and production planning may be favorable for the supplier as well as for the customer.

There can be more complex supply chain process where there could be multiple suppliers to one supplier and they could supply to multiple plants. Multiple plants can have more than one DC or RDC (Distribution Centre or Regional Distribution Centre) and can have multiple retailers or sales unit to support various customers.

The difference between distribution planning and replenishment is that the purpose of distribution planning is to circulate the demand in the network to the producing (or procuring) locations. Therefore distribution takes place from short-term to medium-term or even long-term and requires subsequent processes, whereas Replenishment is concerned in the more operative task how to fulfill the demands within the network.

According to the different levels of the supply chain partners, time horizons and processes, APO consists of different modules (the modules are described in later chapters) with different levels of detail.

Supply chain management (SCM) is the oversight of materials, information, and finances as they move in a process from supplier to manufacturer to wholesaler to retailer to final consumer, It is a flow of material/cash/information, the flow is described graphically in Figure 1.2. Supply chain management involves coordinating

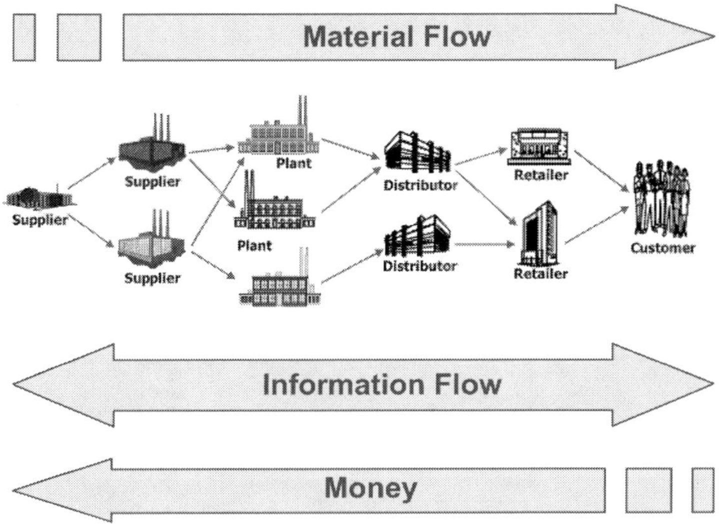

Figure 1.2 Complex flow of supply chain

and integrating these flows both within the companies and among companies. The ultimate goal of any effective Supply Chain Management system is to reduce inventory with the assumption and the application that products are available when needed i.e. zero or minimum inventory, many organizations implement several parallel projects to reduce their inventory cost, one of the most common and know is ***JIT – Just In Time***. As a solution for successful Supply Chain Management, sophisticated software systems with Web interfaces are inline with open source architecture which promises to provide part or all of the SCM service for companies.

Supply chain management flows can be divided into three main flows, it can be called with different names of process (terminologies can be different but process is same) :

- The product flow
- The information flow
- The finances flow

The product flow includes the movement of goods from a supplier to a customer, as well as any customer returns or service needs. The information flow involves transmitting orders and updating the status of delivery. The financial flow consists of credit terms, payment schedules, invoices, and consignment and title ownership arrangements.

1.6 ACTIVITIES OF SUPPLY CHAIN MANAGEMENT

Supply chain management is a cross-function approach including managing the movement of raw materials into an organization, certain aspects of the internal processing of materials into finished goods, and the movement of finished goods out of the organization and toward the distributer or towards the final customer. As organizations struggle to focus on core competencies and becoming more flexible, they reduce their ownership of raw materials sources and distribution channels. These tasks are increasingly being outsourced to other entities (or to the vendors or to the companies having core business in the field), that can perform the activities better or more cost effectively as they are the master of the subjective business. The effect is to increase the number of organization's involved in satisfying customer demand, while reducing management control of daily logistics operations. Less control and more supply chain partners led to the creation of Supply Chain Management concepts. The purpose of Supply Chain Management is to improve trust and collaboration among supply chain partners, thus improving inventory visibility and the speediness of inventory movement.

An organization's Supply Chain Management efforts start with the development and execution of a long-term supply chain strategy. Among other things, this strategy should:

- Identify what supply chains the organization wants to compete in, in-line with the long term organization's goal

- Help managers understand how the organization will provide value to the supply chain and continuous improvements to the process
- Guide the selection of supply chain partners, including suppliers, subcontractors, transportation providers, and distributors

As organization matured up to understand what supply chains they compete in, it is often valuable to map the physical flows and information flows that make up these supply chains. From these maps, organizations can begin to understand how they add value, and what information is needed to make the supply chain work in the most effective and efficient way possible

Several models and techniques have been proposed for understanding the activities required to manage material movements across organizational and functional boundaries. The SCM Model proposed by the Global Supply Chain Forum (GSCF).

Supply chain strategies require a total systems view of the linkages in the chain that work jointly, efficiently to create customer satisfaction at the end point of delivery to the final customer. As a consequence costs must be lowered throughout the chain by extracting out unnecessary costs and focusing on adding value. Throughput efficiency must be increased, bottlenecks removed and performance measurement must focus on total systems efficiency and equitable reward distribution to those in the supply chain adding value. The supply chain system must be more focused and responsive to customer requirements.

Strategic Activities Mostly these activities and decisions related to these activities are taken from higher management and the activities are in-line with organization level goals.

- Strategic network optimization, including the number, location, and size of warehouses, distribution centers and facilities.
- Strategic partnership with suppliers, distributors, and customers, creating communication channels for critical information and operational improvements such as cross docking, direct shipping, and third-party logistics.
- Product design coordination, so that new and existing products can be optimally integrated into the supply chain, load management
- Information Technology infrastructure, to support supply chain operations.
- Where to make and what to make or buy decisions
- Align overall organizational strategy with supply strategy

Tactical Activities This level mostly worked at department level where mainly HOD can take the decision.

- Sourcing contracts and other purchasing decisions.
- Production decisions, including contracting, locations, scheduling, and planning process definition.
- Inventory decisions, including quantity, location, and quality of inventory.
- Transportation strategy, including frequency, routes, and contracting.

- Benchmarking of all operations against competitors and implementation of best practices throughout the enterprise.
- Milestone payments

Operational Activities Activities at operation level, a day to day decisions and work process.

- Daily production and distribution planning, including all nodes in the supply chain.
- Production scheduling for each manufacturing facility in the supply chain.
- Demand planning and forecasting, coordinating the demand forecast of all customers and sharing the forecast with all suppliers.
- Sourcing planning, including current inventory and forecast demand, in collaboration with all suppliers.
- Inbound operations, including transportation from suppliers and receiving inventory.
- Production operations, including the consumption of materials and flow of finished goods.
- Outbound operations, including all fulfillment activities and transportation to customers.
- Order promising, accounting for all constraints in the supply chain, including all suppliers, manufacturing facilities. Distribution centers and other customers.
- Performance tracking of all activities.

1.7 OBJECTIVES OF SCM

Implementing any solution always have specific cause behind it and the traditional objective of supply chain management is to minimize total supply chain cost to meet fixed and given demand. This total cost may be comprised of a number of terms and factors including:

- Raw material and other acquirement costs
- In-bound shipping costs
- Facility investment costs
- Direct and indirect production costs
- Direct and indirect distribution center (DC) costs
- Inventory management costs
- Inter-facility transportation costs
- Out-bound transportation costs

In building a model for specific planning problems, we might decide to evaluate only a portion of the organization's entire supply chain and associated costs. One can disagree that total cost minimization is an inappropriate and timorous objective for the firm to pursue when it analyzes its strategic and tactical supply chain plans. Instead, the organization should look for to maximize net revenues where

$$\text{net revenues} = \text{gross revenues} - \text{total cost}$$

If demand is fixed, the implication is that gross revenues from meeting it are also fixed, and therefore, that the organization will maximize net revenues by minimizing total cost.

Objection to focusing only on cost control when using an optimization model for strategic or tactical planning is that the spectrum provides insights into product costs that should be exploited to increase net revenues by suitable adjustments in sales. For example, when planning for next year, information provided by a spectrum about the marginal costs of products delivered to various markets could be used to change the projected sales plan. The organization's sales department would be instructed to push products in markets with the highest margins, possibly at the expense of products in markets with low margins if total manufacturing capacity is limited.

The difficulty with trying to model decisions affecting demand management, even in the unassuming way we just described, is that it requires the commitment of marketing department of team, who generally feel uneasy with quantitative analysis. Moreover, once commit to including marketing and sales decisions in a model, it is difficult to decide on the scope that can be considered. However, integration of supply chain and demand management is an area of growing interest in many organizations.

Similarly, supply chain and demand management decisions are closely linked to corporate financial decisions, especially when planning the organization's strategy. Moreover, optimization models for exploring financial decisions linked to the corporate balance sheet, such as yearly changes in fixed assets and equity or dividends paid, have been proposed by academics for over years, although not yet widely applied. Since these models can be seamlessly integrated with supply chain models, financial managers have recently become more interested in pursuing their implementation and use.

Of course, an organization will also be concerned with non-monetary objectives, such as customer satisfaction and services, product variety, quality, and time, even some of the organization's more focus on their brand value in market. Some managers in organizations even suggest that cost or revenues are relatively unimportant and that the organization should focus instead on time, product variety, or other attributes of their business to achieve competitive advantage. Such recommendations are misleading since the organization exists to earn profits and which is also the ultimate goal of the organization, no one wants do a business of losses. From an analytic perspective, it is not necessary to choose one objective over another. Instead, optimization models can assist management in evaluating the tradeoffs or benefits among objectives.

1.8 CONSEQUENCES OF NOT BUILDING AN EFFICIENT SUPPLY CHAIN NETWORK

- Reduced service and satisfaction level to customers
- Increased inventory levels

- Inefficient allocation of resources
- Increased transportation costs
- Decrease in market share and position
- Decrease in profit
- Decrease in employee satisfaction

The books emphasis mainly on APO architectural design and programming but taking all readers into consideration, like:-

Experienced SAP APO technical users

Experienced R/3 technical users

Users having R/3 experience but new to SAP APO

Users new to R/3 and new to SAP APO

APO Functional and many more.....

Me too as a technical person, I think it will be beneficial to explore some more facts of SAP which will be helpful to the users who directly entering to SAP APO or to the experienced R/3 users to refresh their knowledge. The SAP architecture is described in Chapter 2 in details.

2

SAP TECHNICAL OVERVIEW AND SYSTEM ARCHITECTURE

In this chapter we will discuss more about the detail of SAP like how it helps organization to achieve the desired results, the components of the SAP system and will explore the technical aspects of the product and how it is integrated with other components, still the architecture of SAP will be covered in later chapters also.

2.1 ADMINISTRATING GLOBAL BUSINESS CHALLENGES

In today's demanding and competitive business environment, organizations are fighting hard to meet strategic goals, earn profitability and ensure regulatory compliance. At the same time, organizations require the flexibility to stimulate growth through differentiation, transformation and innovation while cutting the cost and maintaining operational control.

Process or Service industries need an ERP (Enterprise Resource Planning) solution that helps them in addressing the following challenges:

- Simple and all time access to all the applications and information. Services employee need to complete their daily tasks and to take the paramount business decisions. Should be a single system to get information rather than checking 10 legacy system and which also raise question on information consistency.
- Straightforward and open end collaboration with partners, vendors and customers. A common platform should be used where all the elements of the process chains can talk on same platform and can share information.
- Flexible and cost effective IT architecture that facilitate the fast adaptation of business processes to changing needs. IT architecture should be easy to maintain and must have functionality for open end communications with vendors, customers and within various location of the company or it should talk on common language across the globe.
- Incremental addition of new technologies, functions and processes without adversely affecting underlying technology or previous IT investments.
- Less complex IT environments, streamlined business processes and faster and measurable returns on investments as known as **ROI**.

With competition growing rapidly and increasing day by the day, cost reduction in business operations and making available the products to the customers, as per their requirement, come into foremost area of concern. Maintaining a flawless supply chain across all its operations thus becomes absolutely necessary for any business to exists in the competitive world.

Importance of supply chain management need not be over emphasized as it has become the cutting edge of business, after product quality and manufacturing capabilities of any business firm.

Information Technology is now playing major role in any of the organization growth, in today's world we cannot even think of any organization without IT setup or investments in IT. Organizations looking for the benefits by involving information technology:

- **Lower Inventory Investments:** Consolidated view of inventory including the optimum inventory at each point of sale. Also ensures that stock can be transferred to & fro from one point of sale to another in at short notice. This lowers investment and increases the return.
- **Increase of ROI:** Identify non-moving stock across the chain, transfer them to where they are selling and/or return them. Also, identify and return non-moving stock at purchase value to avoid any loss on non-moving stock return. Such effective stock transfers coupled with purchase returns increase the ROI.
- **More Stock Visibility:** Continuous stock audit based on ABC classification of items instead of periodic full stock verification helps to identify mismatch between physical stock and system stock early. Such continuous stock audit helps to lower the blocked stock and increase the visibility of the stock.
- **Best Purchase:** As organization increases their requirements, the volume of purchase goes up. This allows better negotiating leverage. Combining this with the analysis of sales, purchase and inventory data, allows source products from the cheapest and best. Vendor comparison also plays vital role in the profit making decisions.
- **Lower Operating Cost:** Optimal utilization of man power, optimal utilization of store space, effective inventory management etc. leads to lower operating costs. Optimal utilization of the service line results in lower down time or change over time of the service line.
- **Centralized Financial Control:** As business moves to a model of depositing the entire receipts/collections with the supply chain and all payments are can be visualized centrally, it reflects the better financial control over business.
- **Scam Prevention:** Real-time/Periodic upload and validating the data at any given point of sale prevents any tampering with data at any specific point of sale. This builds better awareness among sales, staff and prevent fraud.

- **Item Normalization:** Helps in providing a standardized, complete and accurate data across both the retailer and wholesaler for the material master. Item normalization helps to analyze the data more accurately and provide high quality reports.

MySAP.com ERP meets all of above challenges and offers advances multiply options of integration capabilities with the support of SAP NetWeaver platform. It is loaded with a wide-range of functions, global reach, personalized information access and reporting and industry orientation. It allows users to incrementally add functionality as needed for customer relationship management, product life-cycle management and the entire *Supply Chain*. All of these capabilities make mySAP.com ERP the most complete ERP solutions in today's market. SAP as an ERP solution captured more than 70% business in the ERP world and almost all the major companies are running on SAP ERP and the market percentage share is increasing every day.

To create a good IT infrastructure requires some awareness of the business functionality is required and it is being addressed in this book. The server, storage and network infrastructure solutions are now more focused on SAP business application software and now a day designed keeping SAP in mind or designed specifically to run SAP.

The preference and configuration of these software components plays an important role for the hardware configurations and ongoing IT operations needed. There are operating system, database, and server platform dependencies of these software solutions that may impact the performance including sizing, availability, and total cost of ownership of the IT hardware infrastructure. Thus, some introduction to SAP's business software solutions is useful and is presented here for the readers of this book.

Figure 2.1 mySAP components

2.1.1 MySAP.com

MySAP.com ERP is the world's most complete Enterprise Resource Planning (ERP) solution, providing organization with the strategic insight, ability to differentiate, increased productivity and flexible they need to be successful in the competitive market. With the mySAP.com ERP solution, SAP has evolved its vision of increasing efficiency within an organization to a next-generation ERP solution, automating End-To-End business processes and extending those processes beyond the enterprise to the entire business ecosystem by incorporating customers, partners and suppliers. In addition, mySAP.com ERP helps drive innovation and supports future growth of the organizations. SAP come with pre configured and pre implemented package which any organization just has to implement as per their requirement and mySAP.com also provides flexibility to the organization to do the customization and can configure or can do custom development in the software, this feature make SAP unique and different from other software where only executable can be received and every time organization has to pay extra to get the desired functionality.

MySAP.com ERP is enriched by the SAP NetWeaver platform, an innovative interaction and application platform that enable change and integration management. SAP NetWeaver supports new cross-functional business processes and helps to lower the total cost for the ownership by reducing the need for custom integration and by offering complete life-cycle management for the solution. It is also foundation for Enterprise Services Architecture further to service-oriented business solutions.

SAP NetWeaver is loaded with Mobile Infrastructure (MI) which will be the future of the Information Technology. A person can access the SAP applications, can access the vendor's, customer's, company's account sitting anywhere and take the real-time decisions for more profitable business. Mobile Applications (Apps) directly linked and can talk with SAP and information flows using mobile infrastructure.

2.2 THE mySAP.com WORLD

SAP has been traditionally involved in helping customers modernize their back-office operations by integrating business processes, mostly with its standard Enterprise Resource Planning (ERP) software solution called SAP R/3.

The traditional SAP R/3 ERP system offers transaction and reporting functionality in the areas of financial, logistics, and human resource applications, enabling the exchange of data between a organization's various business units or divisions.

The standard business process fits all approach of SAP R/3 often required business process reengineering to meet the business needs. Because this could only address a limited portion of the market's needs.

SAP began offering industry-specific solutions and extended ERP solutions, including the following.

Supply Chain Management

Managing supplier relationships with multiple organizations in supply chain. It is a separate component of mySAP.com with a choice to user to implement or not.

Customer Relationship Management

Managing the distributors, resellers, and customers with Customer Relationship Management solutions.

Business Intelligence

Managing the knowledge-assets with Business Intelligence.

Industry-specific solutions which provide additional functionalities related to a particular nature of businesses with more coverage of entire business chain.

2.3 mySAP.com INDUSTRY SOLUTIONS

SAP also offers a large number of industry-specific solutions for a wide range of industries such as automobile, oil and gas, banking, healthcare, retail, and utilities. The mySAP.com ***Industry Solutions (IS)*** consists of modified and extended standard SAP R/3 modules, providing industry-specific business processing functionality. The technical architecture of IS configurations is identical to standard SAP R/3 systems. Because of these modifications, Industry Solutions are incompatible to each other and to the standard SAP R/3 system in most cases.

Developed by dedicated expert groups within SAP, every IS has its own release schedule. Due to the modifications, standard maintenance (hot) packages are not always possible to apply to an IS system. Therefore, a separate setup is often recommended for each Industry Solution, interconnected by ALE to a standard SAP R/3 or other system.

However, these systems can be consolidated onto the same physical server, for example, of retail.

The business process modeled is the collection of daily sales data from the stores into a company's central headquarters system, called the point-of-sales (POS) upload. Then a replenishment planning calculation is executed by the user, which generates resupply orders and delivery notes for the shipment and re-calculate the store inventory. The POS upload and replenishment planning are very intense processes that require special care in the hardware-sizing of the SAP system.

SAP IS components covers most of the industries and the list is increasing day by day, might be within the time when I am writing this book and the publication, readers will find some more additions to the list.

Aerospace and Defense	Life Sciences
Automotive	Media
Banking	Mill Products
Chemicals	Mining
Consumer Products	Oil and Gas
Defense and Security	Professional Services
Engineering, Construction and Operations	Public Sector
Healthcare	Retail
High Tech	Telecommunications
Higher Education and Research	Transportation and Logistics
Industrial Machinery and Components	Utilities
Insurance	Wholesale Distribution

Figure 2.2 SAP-Is components

In traditional ERP world, organization's prime priority is on getting their own in-house business processes under control and integrated Business communication (such as placing orders or transferring financial data), within an organization it happens usually with SAP's Application Link Enabling protocol (ALE). Business communication with other partners usually happened with Electronic Data Interchange (EDI). This ALE or EDI communication was with known and established business partners, because these links had to be set up for each business channels.

In any case, these ERP systems were not as open to the outside world as the Internet has now enabled.

Yet, implementation step needed before exposing the in-house business processes to the outside Internet world.

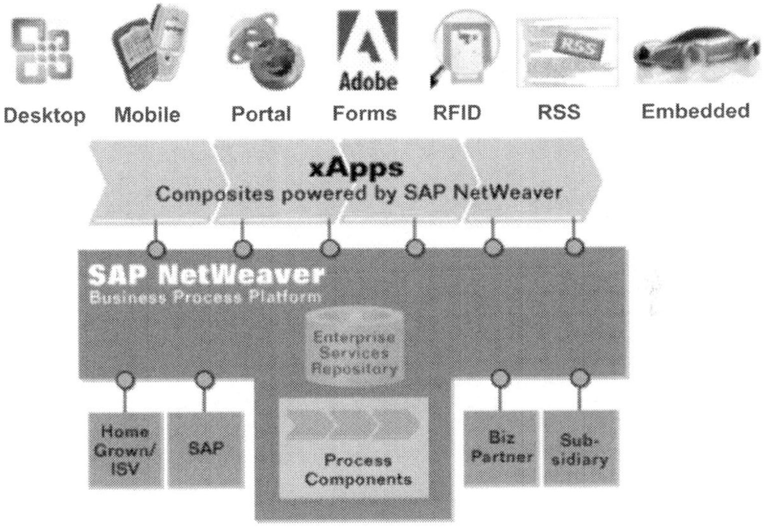

Figure 2.3 SAP NetWeaver integration

More complex business requirement/functionality leads to more complex infrastructures. To faultlessly access all of the services now available both internally and on the Internet, some middleware chain is needed to fasten everything together. The mySAP.com offers a personalized environment to help navigate across all the application functions and services needed to perform business tasks. The facility made the SAP ERP which was earlier limited to one organization or to organization's premises now open to the world and all parties like customers, vendors etc. can interact with SAP.

2.4 THE mySAP.com WORKPLACE

The mySAP.com Workplace provides an intranet portal that supplies users with role-based, personalized web access to all systems, functions and services that they require to accomplish their tasks i.e. for which they are authorized to do. For example, a user can enter a purchase order in SAP R/3's Materials Management and display a list from BI - Business Intelligence without having to perform separate logons to each system. The security is managed by the mySAP.com Workplace system's Single Sign-On concept.

The screen is adapted to the user's role in the organization and at the workplace. These services and information may actually be provided by a number of different systems (SAP or others).

Users perform roles to participate in particular business scenarios (for example, create sales order or create purchase order) that are provided by numerous mySAP.com components and external systems. The mySAP.com Workplace provides the user with an integrated, personalized working environment that offers access to all the functions and information required accomplishing the tasks related to his specific role.

The role determines the visual appearance of a user's mySAP.com Workplace. It is used to structure the Launch Pad and the display of the Mini-Apps. A user's role determines the transactions, information, and services that user may access via the mySAP.com Workplace.

The Launch Pad can have more than one role (composite roles) for the specific user. To implement the mySAP.com Workplace, the desktop PCs need a compatible HTTP browser, and then at least one mySAP.com Workplace Server is needed, as well as the mySAP.com Workplace Middleware.

2.5 THE BUSINESS APPLICATION COMPONENTS

The mySAP.com business applications consist of the following components (valid at the time when I am writing this book, however, more are planned to be added):

- The ERP core components—SAP Financials (FI), Logistics (LO), Human Resources Management (HR), and Industry Solutions (IS)
- Business Intelligence solutions, such as Business Information Warehouse (BW), Knowledge Warehouse Management (KM), Strategic Enterprise Management (SEM), and Corporate Finance Management (CFM)
- Supply Chain Management solutions, such as SAP Advanced Planner and Optimizer (APO), Logistics Execution System (LES), Business-to-Business Procurement (BBP), and Environment, Health and Safety (EHS)
- Customer Relationship Management solutions, such as Internet Sales Scenarios, Mobile and Field Sales and Service, the Customer Interaction Center, Employee Self Service (ESS), and others.

The conventional SAP R/3 ERP system is an online transaction processing system (OLTP). Earlier the SAP R/3 system was also used for functionality where the architecture of an OLTP system was not ideally appropriate. For example, reporting as well as logistic and production planning were considered the domain of ERP systems. Algorithms such as Material Requirements Planning (MRP) or Distribution

Requirements Planning (DRP) were executed in SAP R/3. As the planning process was extended to the complete supply chain, relational database structures could not easily provide the performance required for planning across large and complex networks of plants, distribution centers, customers, and suppliers.

The MRP run for a large organization would load up the SAP R /3 system extensively. Therefore, SAP developed extended ERP solutions called the ***Business Intelligence (BI)*** *and the* ***Advanced Planner and Optimizer (APO)*** *for logistics and production planning. These are separate applications optimized for managing and analyzing huge amounts of data. Each can be a stand-alone application but still has tight integration to SAP R/3, one of their primary advantages. Although these products were introduced as part of SAP's New Dimensions initiative, they are now components of the larger mySAP.com business applications offering.*

Middleware components like Internet Transaction Server (ITS) and Business Connector deploy a non-SAP kernel and have no database. Mixed components like Advanced Planner & Optimizer (APO) with an SAP R/3 based kernel, a relational database, and some specialized components, such as the SAP APO LiveCache (LiveCache is the most important concept in APO and later chapters of this book will only focus on LiveCache).

2.6 MIDDLEWARE

Middleware programs provide messaging services so that different applications can communicate to each other. The systematic binding of different applications, often through the use of middleware, is known as ***Enterprise Application Integration (EAI)***.

The mySAP.com Middleware provides a generic gateway between the common Internet protocol and the SAP protocol. The middleware components consist of the Internet Transaction Server (ITS), the Business Connector (BC), and the DCOM Connector.

- The Internet Transaction Server (ITS) is responsible for transforming SAPGUI screens into HTML pages that can be displayed in a common web browser.
- The Business Connectors convert IDocs (Intermediate Document) to the XML format, supporting BAPI (SAP's Business Application Programming Interface) and ALE scenarios. SAP IDocs can be converted to structured documents with direct access to each single field. The SAP Business Connector Server contains the mySAP.com Portal Connector that enables bi-directional communication between SAP systems and the other systems.
- The SAP DCOM Connector integrates SAP components written in ABAP with COM components written in Visual Basic, Visual C++, or Visual J++.

2.7 WORKPLACE MIDDLEWARE

The Internet Transaction Server (ITS) is responsible for transforming SAPGUI screens into HTML pages that can be displayed in a common web browser. SAP ITS is composed of the Application Gateway (AGate), the Web Gateway (WGate), and a common web server. One ITS instance per mySAP.com application component is required and implemented. The simplest ITS configuration is a single-host installation with the web server, WGate, and AGate installed on one hardware.

However, due to security issues, the components should be split between two computers (dual-host installation). The WGate is a small program that runs on the same system as the web server. The SAP Business Connector (BC) converts the proprietary RFC format to the eXtensible Markup Language (XML), the de-facto standard for Internet business community collaboration.

Vendors without an SAP R/3 system who want to sell over the mySAP.com Marketplace need to license the Business Connector from web Methods (www.webmethods.com). In general, the mySAP.com Marketplace is hosted and operated by SAP. However, organizations that wants to implement their own need a dedicated mySAP.com Marketplace system.

2.8 SAP R/3 SYSTEM—THE ERP BACKBONE

SAP's R/3 System sets the standard for the development of modern enterprise requirement's applications i.e. a multilingual, multinational client/server technology that meets all business requirements for scalability, portability, openness and high performance.

The SAP Enterprise Resource Planning (ERP) system, SAP R/3, is built as an integrated system where all functionality necessary to run an enterprise's operations is provided by one system. The main benefits of this approach are the workflow and seamless integration of the different business processes within an organization. The integration is what ensures the consistency of the business information.

SAP R/3 is delivered to a customer with selected standard process turned on, and many other optional processes and features turned off. In the core implementation of SAP R/3 there are more than 12,000 tables which controls the way the processes are executed. Configuration is the process of adjusting the settings of these tables to get SAP runs the way any specific organization wants it to.

SAP functionality included is truly enterprise specified: Financial Accounting, Logistic General, Human Resource. Each of these, in turn, consists of multiple submodules. All of these modules are tightly integrated. As the tables have 2 types of data. 1st which is organization's data i.e. business data and 2nd is control data which is used as configuration data for this business data, this configuration data decides how this business data should be visible to the user.

The modules are dedicated to the business functions in an enterprise or an organization. The core modules include hundreds of business processes to address the needs of an enterprise.

For instance, Financial Accounting includes general ledger, accounts receivable etc., Management Accounting includes cost centers, profitability analysis etc., logistics includes general logistics, material management, sales and distribution, plant maintenance, production planning, quality management, project Systems etc. All modules are available on the installation media, customers has a choice to decide what modules should be implemented as per their process requirements or as per their business expansion requirements.

2.9 THE SAP SYSTEM LANDSCAPE

Every SAP implementation project goes through deployment phases of some sort to fulfill the business needs or as per the organization nature of business and the way how the organization does the business. There are several types of systems used to implement a project. These should at least be dedicated software deployment layers, if not on physically separate servers:

- *Training, Evaluation, and Sandbox Systems*—used for user training, gaining experience in mySAP.com and trial for feasibility studies for customer-specific requirements, usually small systems with small databases.
- *Development System (DEV)*—for customization of the mySAP.com systems and development of new components and functionality, usually small systems with small data in databases. It can be on different operating system and hardware platform, however, similar operating system ease the maintenance.
- *Test and Quality Assurance System (Test/QA)*—enables extended testing of development done in DEV environment and also to test the upgrades/ transports prior to implementation in the production system. These tests can cover OS upgrades, SAP upgrades and patches, new system drivers, interface setups, and so on. These are smaller than the production system but in a ratio that allows forecasting the performance impact. The data used is a copy of the production system to run/tests with real, large quantities of data. The testing in QA environment is like a pre-production test.
- *Production System (PROD)*—system with live data for production use on which organization is running its business.

The Change and Transport System (CTS) transports configuration changes as well as upgrades, patches, and newly developed components or programs in a controlled manner between the layers of the system landscape (i.e., from DEV to Test /QA to PROD). This requires a file share facility available to all of the systems within the SAP landscape.

The normal SAP project starts with a development system to setup, configure and sometimes customize SAP software for a particular company's business processes.

A test system is used to verify the development code before going into production. In some cases, a separate integration system is used to consolidate the changes of multiple development teams. Most of the mySAP.com application components (SAP BW, SAP APO, etc.) use development, test, and production systems in the complete landscape.

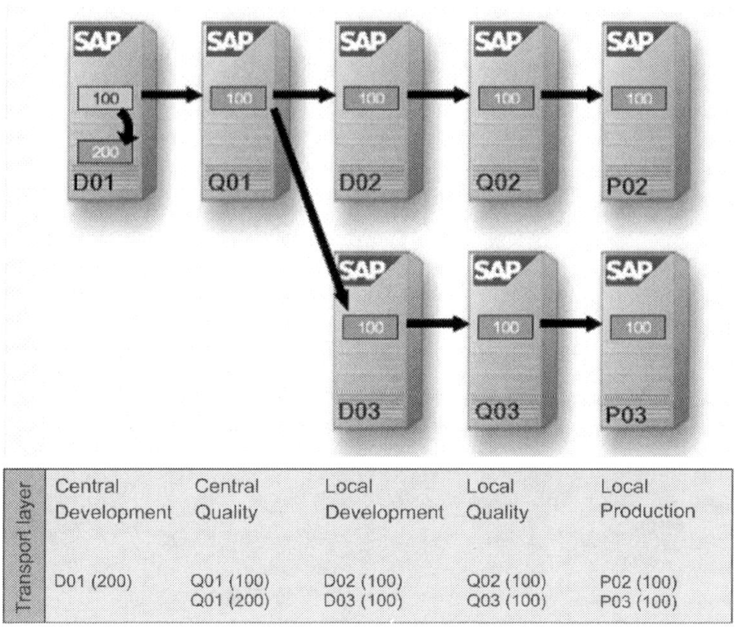

Figure 2.4 SAP system landscape

The minimum recommended configuration is a three-system landscape. However, due to budgetary restrictions sometimes a different setup can be chosen.

Development and Test /QA systems can be combined on one server with different client setup. In any case, it is still useful to have a minimum of three logically separate systems, although there may be lesser physical servers.

2.10 SAP R/3 PLUG-INS

Plug-In is the general terminology SAP has introduced for the interfaces between the mySAP.com business applications (like APO, CRM, SRM, BBP, etc.) and the standard SAP R/3 system. They are add-ons, like packages, to the standard SAP R/3 system to provide extractors for transaction and master data and are essential to enable the tight integration needed. For example, the **SAP APO Plug-In,** also known as ***Core Inter Face (CIF),*** extracts from SAP R/3's complex data set only those objects that are needed in SAP APO's data structures for individual planning and optimization processes. In addition to initial data provision, the SAP R/3 Plug-In also guarantees an incremental delivery of relevant data changes to SAP APO which is also termed as ***change pointers***. A similar situation applies to the SAP BW Plug-In, which enables the extraction of data from SAP R /3 to build the InfoCubes in an efficient manner.

The SAP R/3 Plug-Ins are constantly enhanced to ensure that the integration between a given SAP R/3 standard release and the latest version of mySAP.com application components works also for the new functionality which is keeps on increasing.

2.11 MULTI-TIER COMPUTING ARCHITECTURE

The SAP R/3 system is structured in a three-tier client/server architecture from a software point of view, with each tier having a distinct function. In this architecture, the presentation tier provides the interface to the user, the application tier processes the business logic, systems and the database tier stores the business data. The SAP system architecture supports heterogeneous environments and provides a high degree of system scalability and flexibility. With the Internet as middleware, SAP systems are now considered to be structured in a multi-tier architecture.

The presentation tier, typically installed on a desktop, provides the SAP Graphical User Interface (SAP GUI). The interface is also available through a web browser. In this case, an additional middleware tier transforms the SAP GUI DIAG protocol into HTTP. The access is via TCP/IP and consumes very little network bandwidth. Essential for WAN links, SAP has the lowest network bandwidth demand of all ERP solutions.

The application tier executes the business logic, responsible for processing client transactions, print jobs, running reports, coordinating access to the database, and interfacing with other applications - the center part of the SAP R/3 system. Because the application logic can be executed in parallel, the workload can be distributed between multiple servers if the system load exceeds the capacity of a single machine, this is known as load balancing in ERP terminology.

Running process in parallel can be at program level where multiple instance of the program is created and at server level where load balancing is introduced where load on one server is distributed to other server.

We will not discuss about server load balancing as it is more over hardware concept but yes parallel processing of programs is discussed in later chapters of this book.

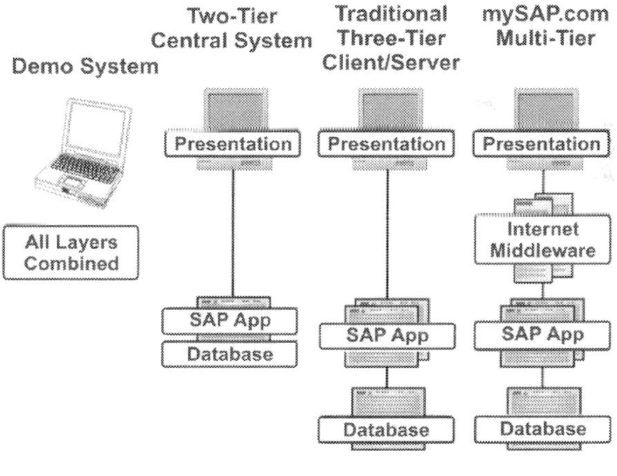

Figure 2.5 SAP 3 tier architecture

The *database tier*, it stores both the business-generated data and also the SAP application programs, which are loaded into the SAP application servers from the database at runtime. SAP supports several database platforms, so the customer is free to determine the hardware vendor. All business and application data associated with a single SAP system is located in one database. Therefore, the server executing the database is the component with the highest demands on reliability, availability, and performance and ultimately determines the scalability of the entire SAP system.

Depending on system workload and available computing power or the hardware sizing done during the initial stage of the implementation of SAP, the software tiers are executed on separate servers or consolidated onto same servers. The presentation tier is always considered distributed to the user's workplace. Development and test systems, as well as small production systems, commonly consolidate database and application instances onto one server (central system or two-tier). Large productive installations typically deploy a separate database server and multiple application instances on separate servers for increased scalability.

2.12 THE SAP KERNEL ARCHITECTURE

There are two very important terms to differentiate for SAP systems: kernels and releases.

The SAP release is the collection of business programs, usually written in ABAP (Advance Business Application Programming), that are stored in the relational database. These ABAP programs are the business and functional logic of the relevant SAP system which moves over designed to fulfill one business operational need or requirement. They are independent of the underlying operating system and server platform.

The SAP kernel, on the other hand, is a collection of executables and tools that enable the SAP system to process the business logic. The group of SAP kernel processes started or stopped as a whole is called an *SAP instance*. Each SAP system can install multiple instances, typically one instance per server box. There are several situations, however, where it makes sense to run multiple instances per single server box.

Each SAP instance consists of one dispatcher and multiple work processes. The dispatcher distributes requests to free work processes.

Some of the terms which I think a technical person should know are mentioned here, each term can be explained in one chapter but I am moreover giving here the definitions of the terms which make the reader understand about the architecture and the how technically SAP works. I will keep the main focus of this book to SAP APO and programming in APO, just highlighting some of the key definitions here.

- *Dialog work processes* are responsible for carrying out the online user transaction load. A dialog process can handle the requests of several users. However, a sufficient number of dialog processes must be available to prevent user requests from waiting for a free dialog process. At least two dialog work processes are required for each SAP R /3 instance. Related to load balancing for the servers.

- *Batch work processes* carry out background tasks that don't require an online response, for example, data loading from a file or processing of huge volume of data. Related to Batch Data Communication.
- *Update work processes* perform the actual updates to the database, asynchronously to the dialog and batch processes. Related to synchronous or asynchronous updated.
- *Spool work processes* support print spooling. More than one spool process is carried per SAP R /3 instances. Related to printing in huge data volume.
- *Gateway work process* provides communication between applications on the same or on an external system. Only one gateway process is needed per SAP R/3 instances. The work processes described fit in to the SAP application instance, of which there can be many in one single SAP system. Related to external communications.
- *The enqueue* server and the enqueue table help to manage the locks on database updates to guarantee data consistency as seen from the business process level, even across database transactions. i.e. same data cannot be processed by more than one use concurrently. Relation to data/table locking.
- *The message process* is responsible for communication between the various application servers. Users logging on to the system are assigned (by the message process) to the application server with the lowest load. However, this load distribution mechanism is at logon time only. If an application server goes down, the message process routes the new logon requests to the remaining application servers, providing a basic level of availability.

If an application server is running more than one SAP instance, there is one dispatcher for every instance but still only one message and enqueue server with the central instance. If the server is running more than one central instance (i.e. multiple SAP systems), there is a dispatcher for every instance together with a message and enqueue server for each central instance.

Although SAP software is generally independent of any one particular relational database management system (RDBMS), i.e. we can choose any RDBMS as SAP supports all RDBMS and it has open source architecture, there are some important software architecture concepts that apply to each database.

Just like SAP software, each RDBMS has a kernel, or a set of executables that enable the database application to run. These kernel files are compiled specifically for each server OS platform.

- The actual data stored in the database is logically stored as rows within relational tables. Physically, however, the data is stored in data files on disks, configured with a file system or as raw disks. Changes to the data are tracked by a log writer process and stored in log files, any time these log files can be accessed or read to check and do a deep dive into the issues. At the specified point of time, the changes stored in the log files are flushed out to the database data files by the database writer process.

- Transactions that are being processed but not yet committed as final are stored in the database rollback (or equivalent) tables or table areas (spaces). If a transaction aborts for any reason, the database can then be rolled back to a consistent state (previous state). It always helps to make the data consistent.
- Data needed for temporary use, such as for table joins are written onto the disks in temporary storage. To access data quickly index tables are used to reference the actual data. Indexing is basically the sorting of the data in the table using certain key fields. Often, logs, roll, temp, index, and data areas are each kept on separate disks for performance reasons.
- Scalability - with increased system load caused by a growing number of users, the number of application servers per component can be extended accordingly. Separate servers need to be added for SAP APO (LiveCache) and ITS (AGate, WGate) due to architectural and security reasons.

2.13 SAP LOGICAL UNIT OF WORK (LUW)

The Open SQL statements INSERT, UPDATE, MODIFY, and DELETE allows program database changes that extend over several dialog steps. Even if a database commit is not explicitly programmed, the implicit database commit that occurs after a screen has been processed concludes the database LUW.

LUW helps to guarantee database integrity. When an LUW has been successfully concluded, the database is once again in a correct state. If, however, an error occurs within an LUW, all database changes made since the beginning of the LUW are cancelled and the database is then in the same state as before the LUW started. The concept plays a vital role in keeping the data consistent.

An LUW Begins

- Each time the transaction started
- When the database changes of the previous LUW have been confirmed (database commit) or
- When the database changes of the previous LUW have been cancelled (database rollback)

An LUW ends

- When the database changes have been confirmed (database commit) or
- When the database changes have been cancelled (database rollback)

The diagram shows the individual database LUWs in a typical screen sequence: A transaction can have multiple screens and the LUW is triggered at every screen change it tracks the sequence of screens.

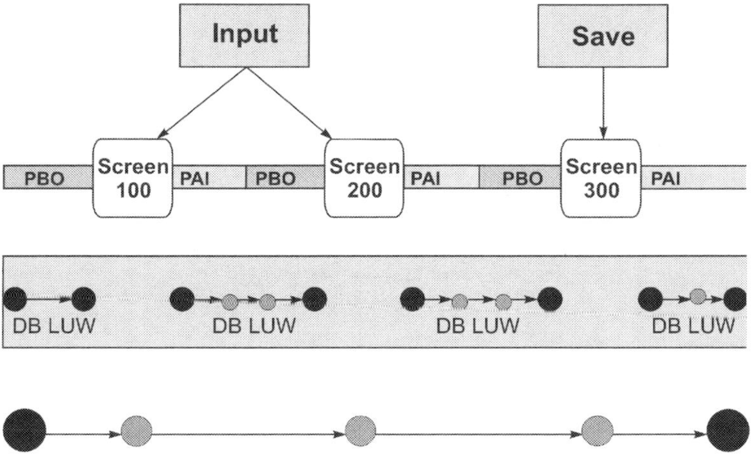

Figure 2.6 SAP logical unit of work

A database LUW is a non-separable sequence of database operations. At the beginning and end of the LUW, the database is in consistent state.

The database LUW is either fully carried out by the database system, or is not carried out at all. A database LUW is opened with every dialog step and by a database commit of the previous database LUW.

The database LUW is closed with a database commit. It is only in the commit that the data is written to the database (after which it can no longer be reversed). Before the database commit, one can undo the changes using a database rollback. Here, the database is reset to the status that it had before the first change was made to the current database LUW.

Data that has been written to the database permanently with a database commit cannot be rolled back. Database LUW allows encapsulating logically related actions from a business process. For example, when transferring sums of money in financial accounting, one has to deduct an amount from one account and then add it to another account. Before and after the process, the data is consistent, but in between the two steps, it can be inconsistent.

Till now we have discussed the general architecture of SAP, in next chapters will be more focused on SAP SCM-APO. We will discuss APO first (more in terms of APO modules) then we will discuss the APO architecture and programming in APO.

3

SAP APO FUNCTIONAL OVERVIEW

3.1 ADVANCED PLANNER AND OPTIMIZER (APO)

The SAP *Advanced Planner and Optimizer* (APO) combines sophisticated and intelligent planning algorithms, object-oriented data structures, and memory-resident optimization databases to address complex planning problems and optimize the best possible solution. SAP APO production planning (MRP runs) and shop-floor detailed scheduling support the generation of feasible production plans across multiple plants.

Production Planning (MRP) in SAP R/3 is limited to only the data in the SAP R/3 system with fewer optimization techniques and more over limited to one location. Distribution and transportation planning or planning in APO provide a wider range of assessment in the term of planning and order fulfillment, it considers warehouse and transportation constraints, creates optimal shipment, allocates inventory and vendor managed inventory. Global Availability To Promise (GATP) provides a multi-level, rule-based availability checking that considers allocations, production, transportation capacities, and costs in a global environment.

The Supply Chain Management provides a configurable, graphical user interface for maintenance of extended supply chain models (plants, distribution centers, etc.), factory layout (machines, storage locations, etc.), schedules, exceptions, and many more. We will here explore the terms used in SCM-SAP APO and try to make users familiar hence if used later, users will be well aware of the terminologies.

Forecast in **APO Demand Planning** (DP) based on aggregated historical data from R/3 or Business Information Warehouse (BW) system. "*Administrator Workbench*" of APO is used to upload this aggregated historical data from the R/3 or BW system. Demand Planning in APO is used to generate planned independent requirements for make-to-stock planning. There are two type of planning or production lines –make-to stock and make-to-order.

Sales orders and planned independent requirements are the starting point for **Supply Network Planning** (SNP) and **Production Planning and Detailed Scheduling** (PPDS) in APO. Existing storage location stock data is also included in planning. Sales orders are created in the R/3 system (in the Sales and Distribution module), but the availability check (also known as the Available-To-Promise (ATP) or Global

Available-To-Promise (GATP) check) can be made in APO. In APO, the sales orders are then offset against the planned independent requirements depending on the APO configuration and settings. While creating sales order in R/3 ATP check is triggered which checks the material availability in APO.

Supply Network Planning (SNP) is a tool for non-detailed planning along the entire supply chain on a short to medium-term basis. It is used to generate stock transfer orders (for stock transfer planning) between the distribution centers and plants, to directly generate planned orders (for planning in-house production), and to generate purchase requisitions (for planning external procurement) in the production plant for the longer term.

In **Production Planning and Detailed Scheduling** (PPDS) however, generation of planned orders and purchase requisitions takes place directly in the production plant primarily over the short-term horizon.

3.2 WHAT IS THE DIFFERENCES BETWEEN SAP R/3 AND APO

Often the question arises that what is the difference between R/3 and APO. Or if MRP run is available in R/3 then why APO is required of why to implement APO. Some of the key areas are highlighted as follows.

SAP R/3 is used for single plant planning and execution only, it is not possible to do cross plant planning in SAP R/3. For cross plant planning APO is used but after planning in APO one have to send the planning results to R/3 for execution because execution is not possible in APO.

SAP APO stands for Advanced Planner and Optimizer, which is one area of SCM and application component of mySAP.com products. Its is designed to provide solutions for companies in Demand planning, network design, supply network planning, production planning and global available to promise, transportation and scheduling. All the functionality is executed in most optimized way.

In SAP R/3 executing of production orders or purchase orders, material withdrawal and costing takes place, whereas in APO only planning can be performed, Sales Orders are only created in SAP R/3 whereas in APO it is not created. In APO planning is done for the critical materials using MRP type X0.

Apart from above APO will consider capacity constraints while production planning in R/3 will not consider capacity constraints and plan as a whole.

3.3 PROCESS FLOW IN APO

- APO starts with Demand Planning where Statistical Forecasting based on previous Sales and updates from Customer Demand i.e. Sales Order create "Demand Triggers" for subsequent Supply Planning. It is the processing and analyzing of historical data.
- Supply Network Planning considers the demand triggers and takes into account the delivery schedule of raw materials and production cycles to determine the net requirements and plan for replenishment. Also it allows distribution planning of products based on rules.

- Production Planning and Detailed Scheduling is focused primarily on In-house Production but can also be used for external procurement order generation.
- Global ATP is used for Order Promising with advanced rules for product availability check and creates suitable production orders.
- APO is designed to improve strategic forecasts and production plans, quotations, schedules and product shipping by real-time integration.

We will now discuss in detail about the individual modules of APO.

3.4 DEMAND PLANNING

The result of the demand planning process is the establishment of independent requirements which will trigger the planning activities as distribution, production and procurement planning. Usually a sales forecast is the key input to the demand plan. This sales forecast is consolidated and checked regarding plausibility, probably checked against a statistical forecast and corrected according to the experience of the planner before releasing it for the subsequent planning steps.

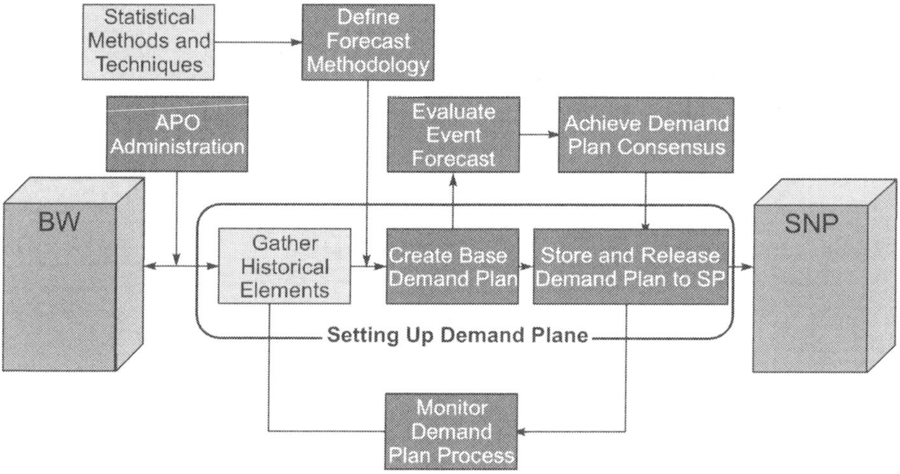

Figure 3.1 Demand planning process flow

In APO the planning levels are represented by '*characteristics*', the granularity of time corresponds to the '*time bucket*' and the data is linked to '*key figures*'. Aggregation and Disaggregation (drill down) of the data according to the characteristics is one of the main advantages to a simple spreadsheet. Though data is maintained on all levels, it is always stored on the most detailed level (with each characteristic having a value) to keep the planning consistent and detailed.

Both the characteristics and the key figures are technically represented by '*InfoObjects*'. These InfoObjects contain the data format definition, the name of the characteristic, the key figure plus other property specific data. The InfoObjects are maintained with the *transaction code RSD1*, we have a detailed chapter on InfoObjects, hence we will discuss InfoObjects later in this book.

3.4.1 Characteristics, Key Figures and Structure Overview

The display of the data and the planning is performed in planning books. Time Series for the Characteristic Combinations are generated Historical Data.

A ***planning book*** is the consolidate view of the status and is always linked to a planning area which contains the key figures. For the defined characteristic value combinations time series are created for each key figure of the planning area. These time series contain the actual data, so that the planning book serves to display the time series view/results of the planning area. The planning area itself is connected to a basic planning object structure, where the relevant characteristics are defined.

Historical data is stored in an *InfoCube* (which contains both characteristics and key figures) and loaded into the planning area. ***InfoCube*** concept in APO is same as of InfoCubes of BI and can be directly linked to BI InfoCubes. The characteristics for planning are defined in the planning object structure. The characteristics 9ALOCNO and 9AMATNR (these are the characteristics terms assigned in APO) correspond per default to the location and the product master in SNP and PPDS, which are used for the release of the demand plan. It is nevertheless possible to use other characteristics for the correspondence.

If there are levels on which the data is only displayed and no planning is performed, it is possible to model these levels as navigation attributes instead of characteristics. Navigation attributes have a reference to a characteristic, but are not part of the key for the data access. The advantage of the navigation attributes is that their values can be changed very frequently and easily without the necessity to realign any data. They are therefore very well suited to represent entities with more frequently changing values, for example the assignment of a planner to a product. In anticipation of only a handful of attributes are used, no performance restrictions are expected. For the standard characteristics 9ALOCNO and 9AMATNR it is not allowed to use navigation attributes as planning is performed on these characteristics.

Time Buckets

In Demand Planning there are two types of time bucket profiles, the storage bucket profile (*transaction code /SAPAPO/TR32*) and the planning bucket profile (*transaction code /SAPAPO/TR30*). The data of the planning area is mandatorily stored in the storage bucket profile, where on the other hand the planning bucket profile is used to display the data in the planning book. In the planning bucket profile only those period types (month, week, etc.) can be used that are also defined in the storage bucket profile. Therefore, if more than one time bucket is going to be used for planning or display, these have to be included in the storage bucket profile. For consistency reasons the data is stored on the lowest level.

Create Characteristic Value Combinations

Characteristic value combinations are created using the *transaction code /SAPAPO/MC62*. There are basically two ways to create the CVCs, either interactively or automatically from an InfoCube. Since manual creation of CVCs is rather tiresome and time consuming, the generation of the CVCs from an InfoCube is the usual preferred way. If an according entry exists in the InfoCube (e.g. a sales order), the CVC is created. It is also possible to create the time series in the *LiveCache*.

Add New Characteristic Value Combinations

When a new product is launched, planning is required for a CVC before any historical data is available. Therefore it is not possible to generate the Demand Planning CVC from the InfoCube. A common procedure for this case is to maintain these CVCs in a excel sheet, load the data into a separate InfoCube and generate these CVCs from the InfoCube. The advantage to the manual maintenance is the better overview of the created CVCs. If the CVC contains a new characteristic value, the according text is maintained as the master data for the InfoObject with the *transaction code RSDMD.*

3.5 PLANNING BOOK AND INTERACTIVE PLANNING

3.5.1 Planning Book

The planning book is the main screen for Demand Planning where the data is displayed, entered and processed – where interactive planning takes place. With the *transaction code /SAPAPO/SDP94* (one of the most important and most used transaction code in APO) the planning book is accessed. Figure 3.2 shows a planning book with the main features, that is

- The key figures displaying the data and
- The characteristics to select the data (planning levels).

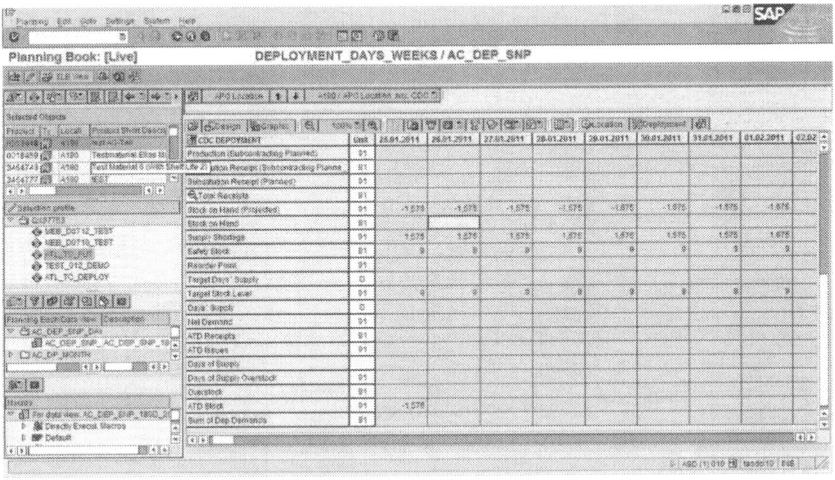

Figure 3.2 Planning book

Data Selection

To access the data in the planning book, the data has to be loaded explicitly from the LiveCache according to the range for the characteristic values specified in the selection screen, specified by user. A selection contains the version, the characteristic for display and the restriction of the data. These selections are saved with a unique name and assigned to the data view and the user. These assignments are managed with the *transaction code /SAPAPO/MC77*.

Create Planning Book

Planning books are created with a reference to a planning area using the *transaction code /SAPAPO/SDP8B*. In the planning book the desired key figures are selected and loaded as a subset of the key figures of the assigned planning area as well as the desired characteristics as a subset of the characteristics of the linked planning object structure. Each planning book contains one or more data views, where the key figures of the planning book are further restricted and grouped. If many key figures are in the planning book for different planning tasks, the data views help to keep a clear view of the key figures. In the data views the sequence of the key figures, the time buckets and the time horizons into the future and into the past are maintained.

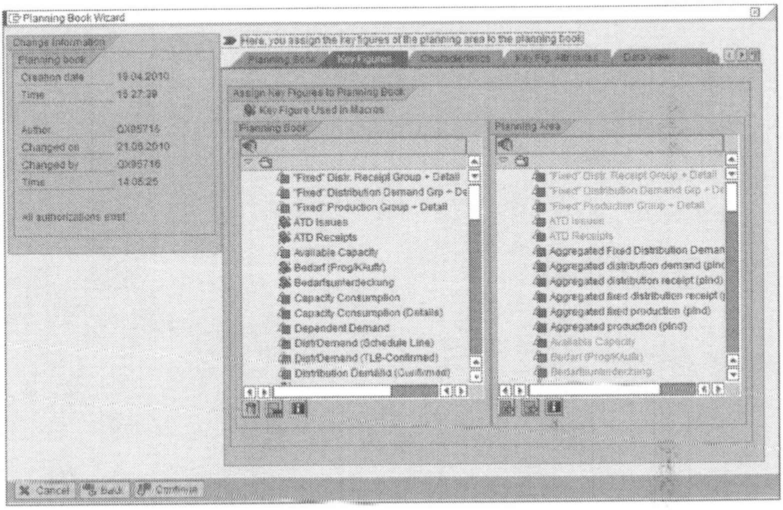

Figure 3.3 Key figure overview

3.5.2 Order Fulfillment Overview

Order fulfillment contains the processes related to the customer from order taking, availability check and confirmation to the shipment to the customer. The sales order entry is performed in R/3 and the ATP check is carried out in APO during the sales order entry. Backorder processing is performed in APO – usually as a batch job – and the results are sent as updates to the sales order to R/3. The deliveries are created in R/3. Again the ATP check is performed in APO. The transportation planning is performed in APO based on the deliveries and sends shipments back to R/3. The sales order might be placed a considerable time or an approximate time before the requested delivery date or with the request for immediate delivery. The sales order might be changed several times before it is actually delivered. Each time the sales order is changed, a new ATP check is carried out.

The first step towards execution is the creation of the delivery. At this point of time an ATP check is carried out again – usually with a much more restricted scope (i.e. stock only). The deliveries (and other documents as stock transfer orders and returns) are grouped to a shipment for transport. The shipment is a document which has a link to the included documents but does not replace them, that is the reason a shipment is not relevant for planning and does not reflects in the product view.

3.6 SUPPLY NETWORK PLANNING

3.6.1 Master Data for Distribution Planning

The supply chain network is defined by locations (termed as plants in R/3) and transportation lanes. The master data is focuses on locations, transportation lanes, calendars and transport resources.

3.6.2 Supply Network Planning (SNP)

- Mid-range Replenishment and Distribution planning across the supply chain
- Combined capacity and material planning
- Based on Supply Chain Model and on Master Data derived from execution system
- Bucket rather than continuous planning
- Requirement specific

3.6.3 Supply Network Planning Process

- Creation of Master Data
- Creation of Supply Chain Model
- Release of the Demand Plan to Supply Network Planning

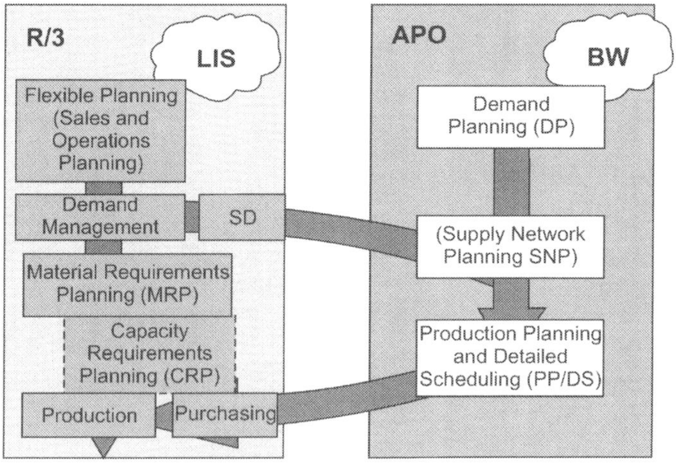

Figure 3.4 SNP process flow

- Supply Chain Model Setup
- Run SNP Heuristic / Optimizer
- Choosing Planning Method
- Release SNP Constrained Plan to DP
- Convert SNP Order to PPDS Order
- Receives PPDS Inputs
- Deployment of Available Receipts to Destination Locations
- Transport Load Building to create Replenishment Orders

Transportation Lanes

The transportation lane defines the material flow between locations and is the prerequisite for any stock transfer. Maintained by *transaction code /SAPAPO/SCC_TL1*.

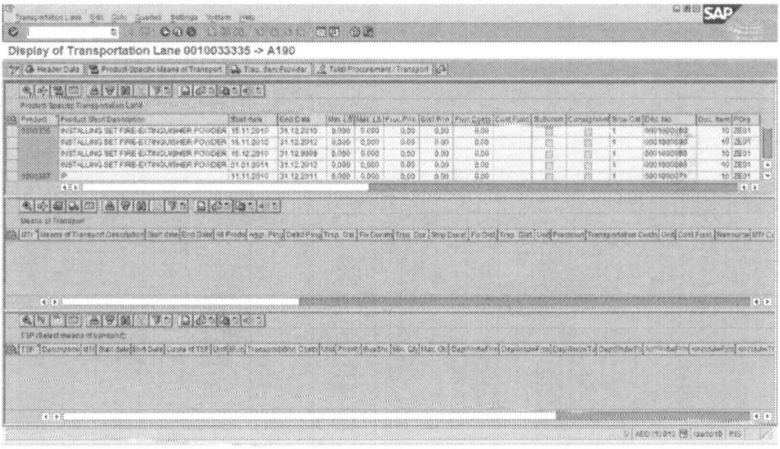

Figure 3.5 SNP transport distributions lane

Transportation Lane contains the three views '*product*', '*Distribution Planning transport*' and '*product specific means of transport*'. In the 'product' view the transportation lane is limited to the products and the lot sizes. It is even possible to lock a transportation lane, if it should temporarily not be used for distribution planning.

In the 'means of transport' view one or more transport methods (e.g. truck or plane or rail) are assigned to the transportation lane. On transport method levels the transport duration, the transport calendar, and the cost for the transport method. Choosing any one and assign as the transport resource. The TLB profile for transport load building is maintained on this level as well. Though it is not a mandatory field, without a transport method it is not possible to create a stock transfer order. Transport methods are selected by the planning applications according to their ability to procure in time, their costs and - if the SNP optimizer is used - the available capacity of the transport resource. Only if a distribution receipt is created manually, it is possible to select the transport method.

We will later discuss about how to change transportation lane programmatically.

SNP Heuristic

The SNP heuristic is the preferred tool for distribution planning without production planning. The SNP heuristic calculates planned stock transfers to cover the demand quantity taking the safety stocks, the lot sizes and the transport duration into account - but not the capacity. Therefore the result is simple to explore, but the distribution plan might not be feasible. As the result of the SNP heuristic in the worst scenario a delay due to transport durations is possible, but no shortage.

Planned Stock Transfers

For the scheduling of stock transfer orders the interval for goods issue, transport and goods receipt is taken into consideration. Goods issue and goods receipt are maintained in the product master in days (used by both SNP and PPDS), while the transport duration is maintained in hours. Each of these durations is represented by an own activity in the stock transfer order. For their scheduling the transport calendar and the shipping calendars of the target and the source location are taken into consideration.

Stock in Transit

After the goods issue has been posted in the source location, the goods are shipped to the target location. To reflect this change in the status of the stock transfer, the stock transfer order can be replaced by a purchase order memo. The pre-requisite for this is that the configuration on R/3 side contains a vendor that is assigned to the source location and an info record, which in case will be there in most of the cases as R/3 is the basis of APO data and R/3 data will be available before APO transactions, just we have to confirm and check the consistency.

The procedure is driven by the stock transfer execution in R/3 starting with the creation of an outbound delivery in the source location. Differing from the creation of deliveries for sales orders, the deliveries for stock transfer orders are created with the *transaction code VL10B* in R/3. After picking, the goods issue is posted for the delivery with the *transaction code VL02N*. It is possible to configure the R/3 system to create an inbound delivery in the target location with the goods issue. Alternatively an inbound delivery can be created manually with the *transaction code VL31N* (the vendor that is assigned to the source location and the stock transfer order number are used as keys). For the goods receipt at the target location (*transaction code MIGO_GR*) the inbound delivery must be linked. The number of the inbound delivery can be found in the 'confirmation' view of the stock transfer order.

The usage of the inbound delivery in R/3 is the only way to model the stock in transit in APO. The usage of the '*stock in transit*' in R/3 is also integrated with APO, but it is not planning relevant, it does not reduce the stock transfer order and it does not contain any information about the planned receipt date.

Sourcing

In a multi-sourcing environment distribution planning decides from which source the demands are covered. Except for SNP optimization, which decides the sources based on total supply chain costs, either quota arrangements or priorities are used. If none of them are maintained, simply the first or default sourcing alternative is selected by the system.

Priorities

Sourcing according to priorities represents a clear preference from where to procure, and other sources are only used as an exception, it does comparison and results the most suitable choice. Accordingly SNP and PPDS heuristics will always choose the source with the higher priority. Different sources are only chosen manually. CTM however switches to alternative sources with a lower priority in case of capacity or material constraints. The priorities for sourcing are maintained in the transportation lane (*transaction code /SAPAPO/SCC_TL1*) as procurement priorities, where zero is the highest priority.

Quota Arrangements

If it is projected to source from multiple locations on a customary basis, quota arrangements have to be used (except for the SNP optimizer). Quota arrangements relate to the location and are created with the *transaction code /SAPAPO/SCC_TQ1*. For distribution planning the inbound quota arrangements are the significant ones (outbound quota arrangements are used for deployment). The specified products/materials are assigned to the quota arrangement, and the ratio of the sources is defined. If more than one transport method is assigned to the transportation lane, the SNP heuristic interprets the ratio of the location as for each transport method.

As an example, if there is a one to one quota arrangement defined between two sources and one of the transportation lanes contains two transport methods, the demands are divided by three, so that real ratio between the locations is two : one. The quota arrangements are used in a different way in the applications SNP heuristic and PPDS heuristic and at the same time differently in CTM.

3.7 REPLENISHMENT

3.7.1 Deployment Overview

If the supply chain behaves exactly as planned—that is neither change in the demand nor unpredicted deviations of the supply happen—deployment is not necessary or not required. Since we are in an imperfect world, both demand and supply will usually differ from the planned quantities when it comes to execution. If the demand exceeds the supply, it has to be decided which demands—in case of the supply chain network, which locations—will be covered and to what extent. This is exactly the scope of deployment.

Depending on the supply chain configuration these decisions are difficult and complex in nature. In a hierarchical, single sourcing structure a simple fair share rule is adequate. In a multi-sourcing structure however the decisions become more complex.

The basic idea of deployment is to convert planned stock transfers into confirmed stock transfers (confirmed distribution requirements receipts) according to the available supplies, the demands, the deployment strategy and the fair share rule. The available supplies are defined by the difference between the ATD (Available-To-Deploy) relevant receipts and issues.

The ATD-receipts and the ATD-issues are category groups which are assigned to the location master and to the location product master. If an entry exists for the location product then it is used on priority, else the entry from the location is taken. Stock usually in-line to the ATD-receipts, whether other receipt elements as production orders or purchase orders are included in the ATD-receipts as well depends on the business scenario or the organization setup and the configuration done by the functional users. Regarding the ATD-issues, deliveries and confirmed distribution requirements should be included in the scenario. Including sales orders means that they are prioritized over distribution requirements, since the available quantity for distribution is reduced by the confirmed quantity of the sales orders. On the same way, an exclusion of the sales orders means that the total available quantity is used for distribution, i.e. sales orders have the lowest priority. Depending on the categories in the check mode for deliveries for the ATP check, this leads either to a lower prioritization of the sales orders or to conflicts because quantities are planned one way in deployment but handled '*first come first serve*' for delivery. Having the ATD-quantity defined, it is distributed according to the deployment settings defined in the location product master.

Safety stock is ignored by deployment (at least by the deployment heuristic). Since safety stock is modeled in APO as a demand and not a supply element, this means that safety stock settings do not have any impact on the available quantity.

Deployment Heuristic

The deployment heuristic is a source location by source location approach to distribute the ATD quantities. Deployment is either carried out online in the interactive planning book or in the background with the *transaction code /SAPAPO/SNP02*. For each source location a separate background deployment planning run is required.

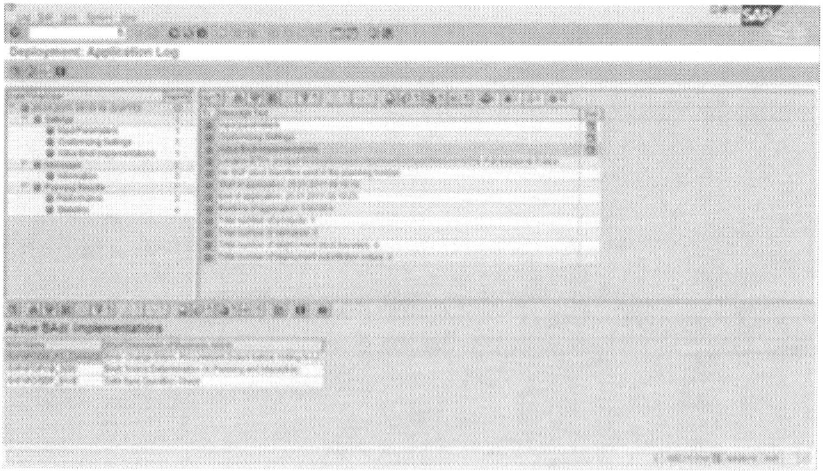

Figure 3.6 Deployment run

The focus of the deployment is the short term, therefore a distribution requirement that is close to today might 'steal' the ATD-quantities from a distribution requirement further somewhere in the future. This performance might not be as per expectation if both requirements are quite close to today. For this purpose the SNP checking horizon can be applied. The logic of the SNP checking horizon is to take all issues (e.g. deployment confirmed distribution requirements) into consideration before using the ATD-receipts for the deployment confirmation of new requirements.

Deployment Strategy

During the stock transfer i.e. whether stock is rather kept at the source or at the target location – is defined by the deployment strategy which is the organization's business decision. Available strategies are pull (blank), pull/push (P), push by demands (X), push by quota arrangement (Q) and push taking the safety stock horizon into account. The deployment strategy is maintained in the 'SNP2' view of the product master of the source location.

Distribution Order Categories

The deployment functionality requires distribution orders of the categories "AG" for receipt and "BH" for requirement, else no orders are selected. If deployment is performed after a CTM run, please check the categories are appropriate (*transaction code /SAPAPO/CTMCUST*).

Real-Time Deployment

Real-time deployment does not use the planned distribution orders of the last distribution planning run, but performs a SNP heuristic to determine the current requirements.

Means of Transport Selection

Deployment optimization creates always new orders with a new selection of the means of transport, deployment heuristic tries to use the same means of transport as the planned stock transfer if the bucket is the same, else it selects the means of transport as a new one.

3.8 DEPLOYMENT OPTIMIZATION

The main difference between the deployment optimization and the deployment heuristic is that the existing stock transfer requisitions are not taken into account but the distribution requirements and the ATD-quantities of the defined scope are re-calculated as a basis to create confirmed distribution orders according to the deployment settings i.e. configuration done by the functional consultant considering the business requirement. Since the sourcing decisions of the distribution planning are discarded by the deployment optimizer, the decision whether the heuristic or the optimization is used has an impact on the requirements for the distribution planning.

The deployment heuristic uses the distribution requirements calculated by the SNP heuristic, CTM or the SNP optimizer as a basis and does not take changes in the demand or the supply since the last planning run. The only exception is the use of the real-time deployment, which carries out a SNP heuristic for the relevant location products a new. For single-sourcing this is a suitable solution to deploy according to the actual demands, but for multi sourcing structures there are clear disadvantages compared to the deployment optimization because of the fix ratio of the requirements according to the quota arrangements.

The deployment optimizer is called with *transaction code /SAPAPO/SNP03*. The configuration or the architecture of the deployment optimization is similar to the SNP optimization. Both use the same objects for the optimizer profile, the cost profile and the cost settings. Accordingly the log file is displayed within the same transaction and with the *transaction code /SAPAPO/SNPOPLOG.*

During my experience in automobile industries, I came across entire custom solution for deployment, which we have created an interactive deployment with various features that are not available in standard deployment, which I explained fully in other chapters it also helps the user to understand the data handling in LiveCache..

3.9 PRODUCTION PLANNING DETAILED SCHEDULING (PPDS)

3.9.1 An Overview

- PPDS is the detailed planning application for in-house production and external procurement functions.
- Execution functions such as confirmations and goods receipt are performed in R/3 and planning part is performed in APO.
- Order and Operation Scheduling carried out in APO are concurrently transferred to R/3.
- R/3 supplies APO with both master and transaction data related for planning.
- Planning results are transferred from APO to R/3. If required, further planning is completed in R/3 e.g. if all of BOM components are not planned in APO.

3.9.2 PPDS Process Flow

- Planning critical products (for example, products with long replenishment times or products that are produced at bottleneck resources).
- Planning in a short-term time horizon with scheduling while taking order sequences into account.
- Generating a feasible production plan which includes the following improvements:
  - Reduced lead times and an increase of deliveries on time, leading to higher customer satisfaction.
  - Increased throughput of products based on a better coordination of resources.
  - Reduce cycle time, inventory and WIP.

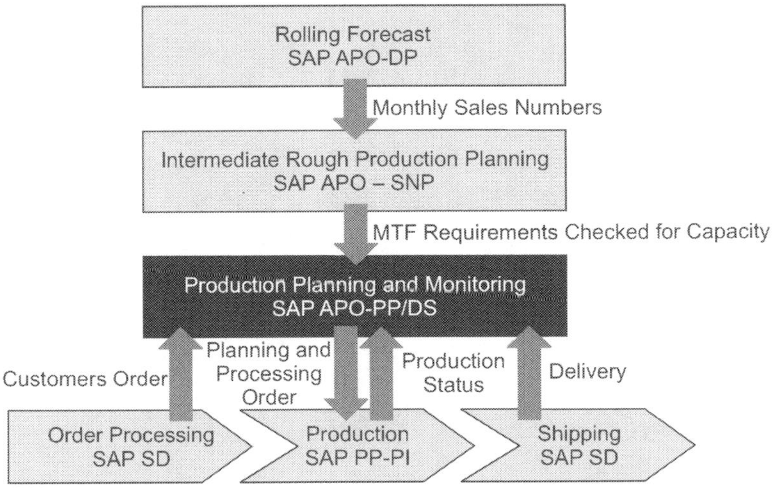

Figure 3.7 PPDS process flow

From the process point of view the production planning scenario consists mainly of the production planning itself i.e. the creation of planned orders represents purchase requisitions for the demand, the detailed scheduling to create a sequence for the orders which is sufficiently and the execution of the production order. In many cases it is desired to have at least a rough feasibility check of the production plan in the mid-term.

Occasionally there is an organizational differences between production planning i.e. the determination of the quantities which have to be produced (and externally procured) and the detailed scheduling, where the sequence of the orders and operations is determined. On the other hand if the scheduling tasks are more complicated, both processes are performed by the same organization. The detailed scheduling is usually only performed for the short term horizon. Traditionally both roles—production planning and scheduling are limited to the plant or location level. If a supply chain contains alternative production possibilities the process becomes more complex and usually an integrated distribution and production planning is required.

Depending on the business requirements it might be complimentary to create a tentative production plan for the mid-term or even long-term before the more detailed production plan. This approach represents the idea of a hierarchical planning, i.e. to plan with less detail for the future and has the benefits of avoiding unnecessary information and unnecessary system load and to have a tighter integration with the distribution planning. On the other side there is the downside of integrating two different detailed planning which should not be underestimated as huge resources are involved in that.

Requirements for the Production Plan

The requirement for production planning varies extensively. Some criteria for a good production plan are:

- To meet the exact demands
- High utilization of the resources
- To consider the resource capacities and the material availabilities
- Less efforts invested
- To minimize the stocks (produce Just-In-Time) and
- To minimize the WIP—Work-In-Progress.

The technical constraints, the number of orders and operations and the complexity of the material flow might lead to a very constraint plan. Especially in these cases the stability of the plan becomes area of concern. Small changes in the circumstances or scenarios (e.g. a delay in the production or an unexpected resource downtime) should not cause a complete re-planning and scheduling.

Dimensions for the Complexity of Production Planning

One measurement for the complexity of the production planning exists within the processes and process steps which are involved—a single production planning step and a simple scheduling heuristic for one BOM-level is less complicated than a global and a local production planning scenarios and more elaborate scheduling heuristics and a sequence optimization for several BOM-levels performed by different planners. The different responsibilities for the interaction between tentative production planning, detailed production planning and detailed scheduling are usually distinguished by multiple horizons and a kind of exception handling is used.

The area of expertise of production planning is that there is a second dimension for the complexity which is not or only to a much lower degree found in the other processes. This dimension is the complexity of the physical production process and its modeling for planning. Examples for the complexity are:

- Overlapping production (e.g. a continuous production of a product with a huge lot size and an overlapping packaging).
- Time constraints between production steps (within an order, e.g. a maximum duration between change over activities in steel mills because metal has to be processed before solidification)
- Processes which involve containers (e.g. health hazards in chemical, pharmacy or consumer industries)
- Alternative resources, secondary resources (e.g. for labor) and resource compatibility for alternative production sequences
- Sequencing of the processes and synchronization of the orders
- Parts (e.g. spare parts in automobile industry, a car can have 10 thousand of spare parts hence handling large number of products)
- Sequence dependent set-up
- Batch cleanliness for production.

The advantage of using PPDS compared to Production Planning in R/3 is the enhanced possibilities to create feasible plans - including sequence optimization. Its main challenges are due to the reflection of complex production structures and the variety of master data settings. In APO there are more options available to configure technical constraints of the productions process than in SAP R/3, and each limitation increases the complexity of the planning problem.

Order Cycle

The out come of the production planning step is planned orders which contain the detailed information about the dependent demands and the capacity requirement (in APO). Depending on whether the planned order was created by a SNP planning run or by a PPDS planning run, the planned order has different categories. Both are transferred to R/3 as planned orders just in the same way, but only the PPDS planned orders can be converted into production orders from APO.

If PPDS is used then the SNP planned order is either converted into a PPDS planned order or deleted by the PPDS planning run. The production order is reduced by the order confirmation and remains in APO until it is technically completed.

Production Planning Applications

APO offers different applications for production planning and detailed scheduling. Production Planning is supported by the modules SNP and PPDS with two different levels of detail. These are:

- Rough-cut and bucket-oriented planning (SNP) and
- Time-continuous planning (PPDS).

These two levels of requires a different set of production master data. If multiple resources are used, the properties for both PPDS and SNP are included in one object. Detailed scheduling with the purpose of creating a sequence for order execution is only supported by PPDS since SNP is limited to bucket-oriented planning and there is no sequence within a bucket.

3.9.3 Production Master Data Overview

The relevant master data for production planning are mainly the location, the product, the resource and the PDS representing the PPM. The PDS and the PPM describe both the operations and their capacity and component requirements for in-house production and procurement. The PDS and the PPM are alternatives and will be referred to as ‘plans’.

Resources

SNP and PPDS require a different view of the capacity – SNP in buckets, and PPDS as a time continuous capacity. Henceforth the resources for SNP and PPDS have dissimilar properties and are either different objects (bucket resources for SNP, single or multiple resources for PPDS) or combine both properties in one object (single-mixed or multi-mixed). In the capacity of the work center representing the resource in R/3 it is possible to control which resource type (single/multi, single/multi-mixed or bucket) shall be created in APO during CIF-transfer.

3.9.4 Resource for SNP

Since SNP is an application for bucket-oriented planning, the resources for SNP offer a specific capacity per time bucket—typically per day. The resources which are used in SNP for production planning are bucket resources, single mixed and multi mixed resources.

The bucket resource presents the capacity e.g. the amount of working hours per day of the resource which is used for the capacity consumption of the orders. For the scheduling of the orders the factory calendar is assigned to the resource. The capacity is defined in any unit of measure, and it is usually defined per day.

The standard capacity is defined in the resource master. The resources are maintained with the *transaction code /SAPAPO/RES01*. The resources are maintained per version or model independently. Only the version dependent settings are used for scheduling and capacity calculation. If resources are created in APO manually (i.e. not transferred via CIF), they are created model independently and have to be assigned to the relevant model manually.

PDS for SNP

On contradictory from the PPM for SNP, the PDS for SNP is transferred directly from R/3 and is not generated from the PPDS-PDS. The structure of the SNP-PDS is simpler than the structure of the PPDS-PDS. The construction of the SNP-PDS is used by the applications SNP, CTM and DP.

In a production version it is achievable to maintain routings for detailed and rough-cut planning. For the PDS transfer it is achievable to select from which routing the PDS will be generated (differing from the PPM transfer where always the routing for detailed planning was selected). This might be a organization's requirement option for the transfer of SNP-PDS. The PDS is displayed with the *transaction code /SAPAPO/CURTO_SIMU*.

PPM for SNP

To be specific and to be in more complex situation, the plan contains the information regarding the production process itself and the PPM is used to access the plan. To create an order, first a PPM is selected according to the product, the location, the validity and the lot size. This PPM is linked plainly to one plan. In the case of by-production one PPM for each output product is linked to the same plan. Mostly the plan is used for selection, but there are also cases in which only the PPM is used.

PPMs are created with the *transaction code /SAPAPO/SCC05*. SAP provides two reports to generate SNP-PPMs, with lot size margins (transaction) and */SAPAPO/PPM_CONV_310* without lot size margins (transaction). The generation of the PPMs is performed via creating a PPDS planned order. Some other common properties of these reports are:

- The input components are linked to the start of the first activity, the output product is linked to the end of the last activity
- Secondary resources in the PPDS-PPM are measured as additional secondary resources

- Order internal relationships and parallel sequences are modeled as additional secondary resources
- For components with limited validity

3.10 INTEGRATION TO PP-PI

The configuration of the recipe differs from the routing. Whereas in the routing most scheduling relevant information is assigned at operation level—work center, standard values and standard values for the secondary resources—the recipe contains operations and phases. The resources are mapped to the operation but the standard values are maintained at phase level. Each operation contains one or more phases. Secondary resources are defined or maintained in the detail view of the operation (secondary resources are separate resources, not an additional capacity of the work center) and the standard values are assigned in the detail of the secondary resource assignment.

3.11 INTEGRATION TO R/3

If no detailed planning (i.e. no PPDS) is used in APO, the planned orders are transferred directly to R/3, either immediately or periodically according to the settings in the *transaction code /SAPAPO/SDP110*. The order number of the R/3 planned order is received in APO (‘*key completion*’), but the order category is not affected by the transfer.

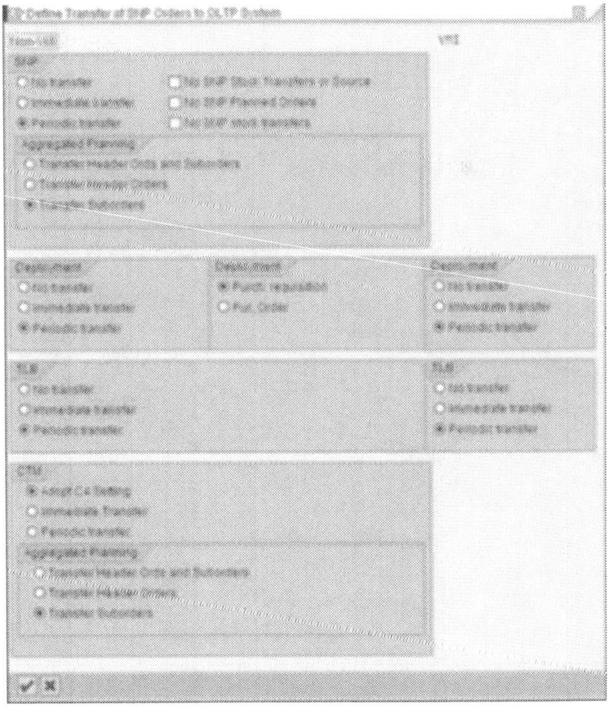

Figure 3.8 Order transfer settings

These planned orders are not fixed in R/3. They can be converted into production orders without any restrictions.

3.12 GLOBAL AVAILABLE TO PROMISE (GATP)

SAP GATP describes for **Global Available to Promise** and it is like promising to customer for their demand and delivery. Global ATP checks the entire network, product / material substitutions defined in the condition/rule and also production from alternative location based on the advanced functionality called rule based ATP.

During sales order entry in SAP R/3, the SAP SCM system is called in real time and the ATP check is performed in SAP APO. If the requested product is not available, the system automatically searches for the product in an alternative location or looks for a similar product using user-specific predefined rules.

3.12.1 GATP Overview

- Primary purpose of GATP is to promise Inventory to Sales Orders and Stock Transport Orders.
- Tight integration with R/3 Sales and Distribution for Availability Check during Sales Order creation
- Different possible Order Promising strategies include:
    - Product availability checking
    - Product allocation
    - Rules based ATP
    - Backorder processing
- In-house Production can be triggered by Capable to Promise (CTP) and Multilevel ATP (MATP)
- Fast response through use of LiveCache for ATP check

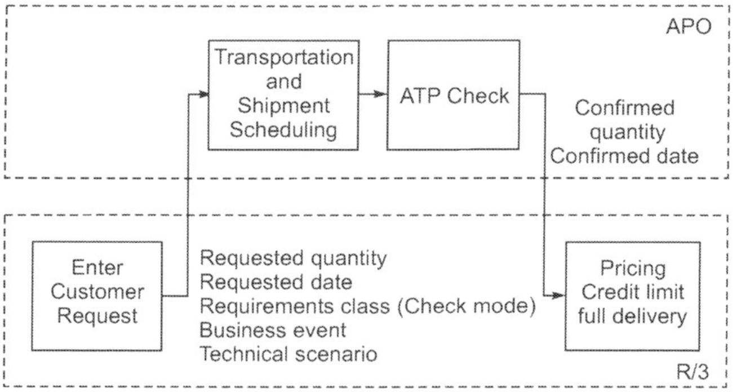

Figure 3.9 GATP process flow

ATP functionality is already available in SAP R/3 but it has following restrictions:

- Availability check in SAP R/3 is limited to single location
- Product substitution is manual
- ATP is limited to single material substitution

- No simulation

Global ATP uses the following basic methods:

- Product availability check
- Check against product allocations
- Check against the forecast

Usually ATP is works on at the existing or planned receipts. In a make-to-order environment there are no receipts per definition. The concept of an ATP check is therefore not to check whether there are receipts for the requested product but it checks whether there is enough available capacity to produce the product and whether the required components are available for further processing. APO does ATP checks using the following approaches, depending on the business requirements:

- Capable-To-Promise (CTP) allows to check for free capacity and optionally for available components as well based on simulative planned orders
- Multi-level ATP (ML-ATP) checks components according to the ATP settings based on infinitely scheduled simulative planned orders
- ATP check against allocations, where the allocations represent an aggregated capacity.

3.13 CAPABLE-TO-PROMISE

3.13.1 Steps within the CTP Process

There are multiple steps during a CTP check which involve both ATP and PPDS functionalities. First in ATP the requested date and the CTP quantity—requested quantity for CTP—are calculated and analyzed. The requested date for CTP is always the requested date of the sales order, while the CTP quantity might vary from the requested quantity of the sales order depending whether a product check is performed first. PPDS is triggered with this information and creates a simulative planned order according to the production restrictions and a simulative demand for the same quantity to prevent any demand element from using this planned order. PPDS is always creates planned orders for the requested quantity. PPDS returns with the availability date for the CTP quantity and ATP combines the confirmations from the ATP check with the PPDS result. After saving, the sales order is transferred to APO, the planned order status is changed from '*simulative*' to normal and the simulative demand is deleted from the system. The transactional simulation is used to create the required planned orders. If the planning task is complex, the required time span increases and therefore also the chances increases for required capacity is used by a parallel planning task (which is triggered by another CTP check).

3.14 MULTI-LEVEL ATP

3.14.1 Steps within the Multi-Level ATP Process

The multi-level ATP is to promise a customer request if the components for the product are available in time (i.e. taking the lead time to produce the finished product into account). Like CTP, multi-level ATP is triggered from the check instructions or from the rule and can be used in combination with the basis methods.

Scenarios for multi-level ATP are e.g. business areas where the finished products are assembled to order, e.g. cars, and the production capacity is not a bottleneck. In this case the availability of the cars depends on the availability of the components. When multi-level ATP is triggered, first the requested date and quantity is determined and passed on to PPDS. In PPDS the plan (PPM/PDS) for the finished product is exploded and a simulative planned order is created. The date of the dependent demands for the components is passed to ATP.

In the second step each component is checked according to the check instructions and the check control specified during configuration. The check instructions are determined by the check mode, which has to be maintained in the product master of each component. The business event is either taken from the customer request from R/3 or from the check instruction of the finished product (it is possible to maintain a separate business event for multi-level ATP in the check instruction). In the manner it is possible to choose a different scope of check for the components. If the components have a late availability, the availability of the finished product is calculated in ATP using correlations.

3.15 BACKORDER PROCESSING

The current availability circumstances might differ significantly from the planned one at the time of the sales order confirmation, the more the confirmed date is in the future. This means that the currently confirmed dates would not be confirmed any more. One main inspiration to resolve such a situation is to enhance or restore the visibility and the clearness of the planning situation. If it is clear that the confirmed dates can not be met, impractical requirement dates cause alerts for shortage or lateness and ambiguous goals for production planning and optimization. Nevertheless the first attempt has to be to cover the confirmed demands. Therefore the backorder processing must only be performed after the production planning is completed. A second point is that in many cases, especially when the lead time between placing an order and the requirement date is large, the customer should be keep informed about the delay. Whether information to the customer e.g. by sending a new confirmation date is required, depends on the sales order process. Sending confirmations to customers is a process entirely within sales in R/3, which can be triggered by a change in the confirmation dates. A new confirmation date however does not necessarily results a notification to the customer.

The basic idea of backorder processing is to carry out a new ATP check for a set of order items. Backorder processing can also be used to distribute quantities in case of shortage according to priorities. Backorder processing is usually performed in the background, but interactive backorder processing is also possible. The methods of the ATP check itself are the ones defined in the check instruction, with the only restriction that CTP can not be triggered (production planning should be finished before backorder processing starts). There are largely three categories of settings which manipulate the backorder processing. These are:

- The selection of the order items to be checked
- The sequence in which the check for the selected order items is carried out and
- The parameters for the check itself.

When calling backorder processing with the *transaction code /SAPAPO/BOP* the work-list is calculated using the assigned filter type and sort profile. The filter variant is either defined from there or assigned if variants already exist. It is possible to display the work-list with the *transaction code /SAPAPO/BOP_WORKLIST*. The main parameters for backorder processing are:

- New distribution
- Check of confirmation or request
- Read check mode and allocation procedure from product master
- Rule evaluation
- Cancel confirmation

3.16 TRANSPORT PLANNING AND VEHICLE SCHEDULING (TPVS)

SAP TPVS is designed to maintain and operate transportation across multiple enterprises, organizations and warehouse management systems, including end-to-end process steps that are executed by retailers, manufacturers, and logistics service providers. TPVS is to plan and optimize transportation process in detail. Goals of TPVS is to carry out the following:

- Optimized shipments considering Vehicle Resources
- Route Determination
- Transportation Service Provider selection
- Collaborative Transportation Planning

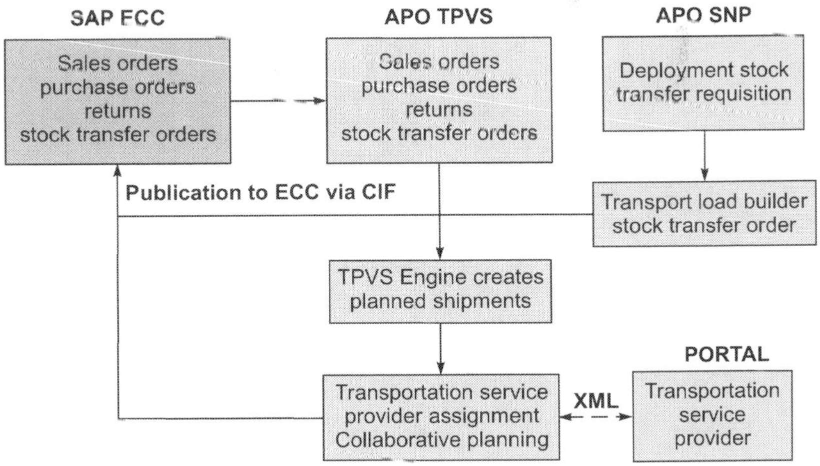

Figure 3.10 TPVS process flow

Input to TPVS engine is Sales Orders, Purchase Orders or Stock Transport Orders from SAP R/3 via CIF. Based on the availability and capacity of transport resources TPVS generates Transport Plan using advanced algorithms. The output of TPVS engine is planned shipments which are transferred back to SAP R/3 for execution further.

3.16.1 Transportation Request Processing

Transportation requests are the basis for the transportation planning and execution. Within SAP TPVS, transportation requests can be received, updated and confirmed. The processing of transportation requests pertains to their validation, error correction and confirmation. A transportation request represents a customer order to transfer goods from one location to another. It contains the business data sent by the customer including information on how the customer expects the handling of this request. It also contains the necessary information for the planning and execution of the transportation chain, that is the pick-up address, the delivery address, the quantities, product group being transported, expected delivery date window, expected pick-up date window and so on.

3.16.2 Planning and Executing Transportation Requests

Based on the transportation requests, next step is to create the shipments. For creating the shipments, SAP TPVS considers the detailed information like freight agreements, freight space capacity, resources (like drivers, vehicles, equipments etc.), and carrier availability at the same time. This process is known as Planning and Executing Transportation Requests.

SAP TPVS offers variety of tools to create and maintain the various planning processes like optimization, dynamic routing and scheduling and continuous move optimization. It also maintains and allows users to view planned as well as executed transportation dispatching and scheduling.

Till now I have explained in brief more the functional concept of SAP SCM-APO, from now onwards book will be more described as technical. I assume that readers should experience the transaction codes specified in this chapter, it will help the technical users to understand the transactions.

4 ARCHITECTURE OF APO

4.1 TECHNICAL ARCHITECTURE OF APO

The technical infrastructure for SAP APO is based on the SAP R/3 architecture (an SAP kernel, specialized modules, and a database) with two additional components: *LiveCache server* and *Optimizer servers*.

To provide the planning or ATP functions using a database with its data primarily on disk drives is not sufficient when huge amounts of data must be analyzed. In addition to an object oriented data model, extremely fast access to data is necessary to enable complex real-time scheduling calculations. Therefore, SAP developed a memory-based data structure optimized for SAP APO called ***LiveCache***.

Advanced **P**lanner and **O**ptimizer is a Supply Chain Management (SCM) application that consists of the following modules, which we discussed earlier also.

- Demand Planning (DP)
- Production Planning and Detailed Scheduling (PPS)
- Supply Network Planning and Developing (SNP)
- Global Availability to Promise (GATP)
- Transport Planning and Vehicle Scheduling (TPVS)

Key objectives, such as speedy data access and the bi-directional exchange of data between the Supply Chain application with the specific or multiple R/3 core modules FI, SD and HR, call for a new architecture that is somewhat different that R/3's current architecture.

The APO server, in the centre, consists of a standard R/3 system. The server is extended by tables that are specific to planning and BW analyses. It contains all of the necessary functions (transactions, reports, interfaces, etc.) for APO and BW in a multi-tier software model. APO uses key technology such as qRFC to communicate with the connected R/3 systems and connect the APO server to the so-called *LiveCache*.

LiveCache is a memory databasc that stores data in SAP DB's relational database. The application server processes talks to *LiveCache* in the same way that other SAP DB client applications talks, while at the same time maintaining a connection to the APO server's relational database. Speedy access is achieved by storing the relevant business objects and modification programs in main memory as COM objects. The programs, which are loaded into memory when the database is started, are stored on the *LiveCache* server in Dynamic Link Libraries (DLLs). Forecasts are stored in the APO system, however, the main transactional data in huge volume is stored in *Live-Cache*. In the event of a failure, the data that is stored in *LiveCache* can be recovered. However, such a recovery is very time consuming because the transactional data can only be retrieved from the R/3 systems where it is stored. When *LiveCache* is properly shutdown, the data is written to the SAP database, which is normally only run in DEMO mode (no logging).

The *Optimizer* is an external component that optimizes *LiveCache* by collecting and evaluating statistical data. Out of box situations, that occurs on the APO server or *LiveCache* will disturb the operation of R/3 applications on the systems. To ensure the system's continued high-availability, monitoring and timely corrective action are of meticulous importance.

The following components should be monitored:

- qRFC connections
- *LiveCache* (e.g. configuration, performance)
- SAP DB
- Optimizer
- Backup routines
- Consistency of the SAP Core Interface (CIF)

Optimal results are obtained by using both the REALTECH APO, and for special DB monitoring, the REALTECH SAP DB data collectors. Separate teams are formed to monitor the above mentioned activities to run business smoothly.

The following sections describe the main monitoring features:

4.2 APO CIF MONITORING

4.2.1 qRFC Ping

This connection test is dual in nature: First the availability of the connection to the APO clients is checked in the APO system itself, and then the external CIF connections (RFC lines) of the R/3 systems that are connected to APO are checked. The collector automatically recognizes all of the connections that needs to be tested and requests them periodically based on a user-definable interval. An alert is generated if the connection fails.

4.2.2 qRFC Queue State

A queue that is being processed can show a number of statuses. The collector checks if a queue has a failure status, in which case a red alert is generated.

4.2.3 qRFC Queue Length

The number of entries per destination queue provides a suggestion of the APO system's processing speed. If there are problems processing a queue, the jobs may be assigned to another queue. Threshold values that determine the number of queue entries that are required to generate a yellow or red alert are specified in a customization table. The collector is scheduled to run at user-definable intervals at the time of configuration.

4.2.4 qRFC Runtime

The runtime of a queue's job also provides an indication of the APO system's processing speed. If a queue's currently active job exceeds a pre-defined runtime (e.g. APO's upload program has stucked into an endless loop or the process has halted) a yellow or red alert will be generated based on the configuration. By default, a yellow alert is generated is the job's runtime exceeds 5 minutes and a red alert is generated if the job's runtime exceeds 15 minutes. Both of these threshold values are user-definable and done during configuration.

4.2.5 Consistency of the SAP Core Interface (CIF)

The collector checks the consistency of the SAP Core Interface. For the check, the data collector inspects the APO-specific tables for inconsistencies. If inconsistencies found, the data collector generates alerts providing detailed information about how many inconsistencies have been found and which logical systems (SAP R/3) are affected, etc.

4.2.6 Logging/Debugging

The collector checks the current logging and debugging settings of the user that is registered in the RFC connection for all CIF connections. Logging and debugging default values can be individually defined for every user. A alert is generated as soon as the actual value changed from the default.

4.3 LiveCache MONITORING

4.3.1 Heartbeat

LiveCache can have a number of statuses. *LiveCache* is working properly when it has a status of "WARM." By default, the status is checked every 5 minutes; however, this value is user definable. A red alert is generated if any other status then "WARM" is detected.

4.3.2 External Heartbeat

The collector uses an external program (DBMCLI) to periodically check if an SAP instance is able to access *LiveCache*. A red alert is generated when a failure occurs.

4.3.3 System Error Messages

At user-definable intervals, the collector reads the System Error Message log file. Every error message is reported as a alert. A customization table is used to suppress notification of specific error messages and how error messages evaluated.

4.3.4 Synchronous BAPI Logging and Archive Logging

A customization table is used to set the logging level (*"LiveCache logging switched off," "synchronous logging turned on"*) and the archive logging (ON/OFF) for each client. A red alert is generated as soon as the actual value deviates from the default.

4.3.5 Connection to LiveCache

The connection to *LiveCache* is checked according to the precised interval. In addition to the connection tests, the system also checks if the appropriate entries for LDA (primary connection for multi-connect) and LCA (secondary connection) are present in the DBCON table.

4.3.6 OMS Data Cache, Converter Cache

The Object Management System (OMS) stores and manages the business objects. The data blocks are stored in cache for rapid access, and the references to the physical blocks are stored in the SYSTEMDEVSAPCE. Storing the references enables to be accessed more quickly. After each run, the collector reports the actual OMS data cache usage values and hit ratio as well as the hit ratio for the converter cache. These values can be used for creating a performance graph.

4.3.7 Status Checks

The collector periodically checks the status of the following, all the below mentions activities are toggle i.e. ON/OFF:

- Database full
- Monitoring
- Monitoring and diagnose
- Vtrace

A red alert is generated as soon as the actual values diverge from the default.

4.3.8 Initialization Log File

The initialization log file is refreshed every time *LiveCache* is started and initialized. The collector searches the last log file for errors. The strings that the collector searches for in the log file are defined in a customization table. The "*" (wildcard) can be used in the string definitions. The alert threshold can be determined at the string level.

4.3.9 Functional Check/Simulation

A report is used to check *LiveCache*'s function ability. Test data is written to and read and deleted from the *LiveCache.* A red alert is generated if an error occurs during the simulation. The last erroneous log file is always saved so that analyses can be performed at any give stage.

4.3.10 Trace Level

The collector checks if at least one trace level is active in the system. A red alert is generated when an active trace level is found.

4.3.11 COM Routines

Application functions are implemented in *LiveCache* as C++/COM routines. These functions enable the objects to be modified directly in memory.

4.3.12 Runtime (COM Routines)

A COM routine's average runtime can provide an indication of the system's utilization. A customization table is used to define a COM routine's average response time. A red alert is generated when a defined response time is exceeded.

4.4 THE OPTIMIZER

4.4.1 Connection to the APO System

The collector checks if the RFC connection to the individual Optimizers is available. All of the configured and active Optimizers are checked. A alert is generated if one of the Optimizers cannot be reached.

4.4.2 Runtime

Optimizer is started manually and should only be active for a limited period so that it doesn't decrease system performance. An entry is maintained in the APO log file every time an Optimizer is started. The collector checks the age of the entries in the log table. A alert is generated if the entry in the log table is older than the specified value.

This does not essentially mean that the Optimizer is still active, but rather that the system could not delete the entry. Problems can occur and will not allow further entries, if an entry cannot be made due the reach of the maximum number (10 entries) for a specific Optimizer.

4.4.3 Application Log

The application log is periodically examined. A customization table is used to define a log file's selection criteria. The system uses the object, sub-object and problem class to determine if a yellow or red alert must be generated. The "*" (wildcard) can be used in the object and sub-object fields.

Till here we have discussed inner and outer system technical overview and system checks, now lets discuss more about the internal structure of APO, more on ***Live-Cache.***

Use of LiveCache memory resident computing technology enables forecasting, planning, and optimization functions to be executed in real time and very fast. The technology basis for LiveCache is SAP DB. This approach grants incredible performance and avoids slow disk access. SAP APO's LiveCache, made realistic by the current availability of high capacity main memory (RAM) at low prices, almost completely eliminates the need to copy data back and forth between hard disk and main memory during transactional data processing.

A large SAP APO system consists of one or more than one application servers, a database server, one separate server for LiveCache, also can be one stand-by server (active LiveCache server can be one only at any given point of time), and multiple optimizer servers executing the optimization algorithms. For smaller installations, database and application can be consolidated to one server and the optimizer software can be executed at the front-end PCs.

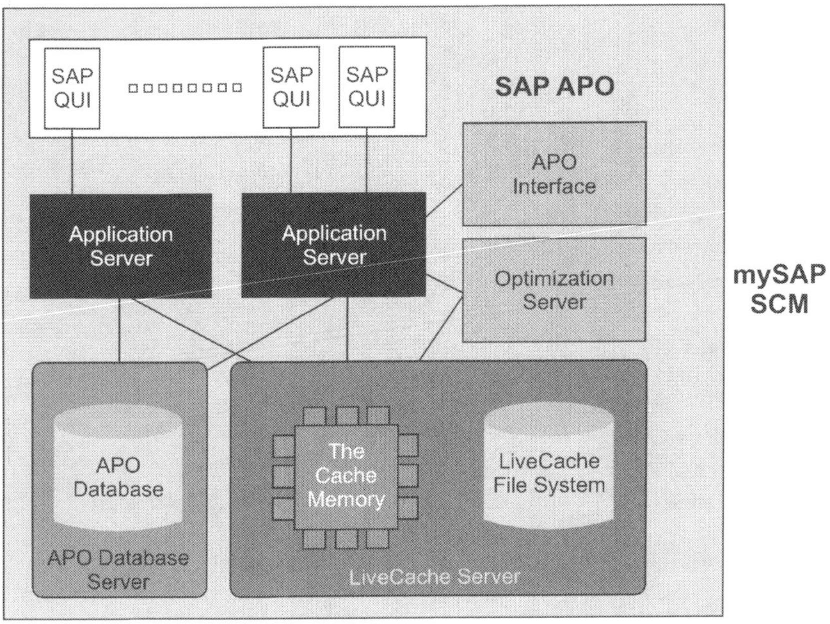

Figure 4.1 LiveCache in APO

For the LiveCache, nevertheless, a separate server is recommended due to the large memory demand. The biggest challenge for the SAP APO solution is using a LiveCache server that can address enough memory with level of fault-tolerance. As the entire data access in APO is dependent on LiveCache and it is the key of faster data retrieval and also for processing the huge volume of data hence large implementation of APO are more concentrated on LiveCache and to make over to the failure of LiveCache hence a standby LiveCache can also be introduced to the APO systems

The base of the standby LiveCache design is a fail-over system consisting of several (at least two) physically separated database server, each with their own copy of the database data files. Each instance maintains its own version of the data, but all instances must have concurrent access to a shared (common) online log. The online log is written by the primary and read by the secondary. The log is used to keep all instances in synchronization. Cluster software must be offered by the platform operating system to allow failover conditions to be recognized and to perform the actions necessary to trigger a failover, and redirect the client connections, moreover it is termed as switchover functionality.

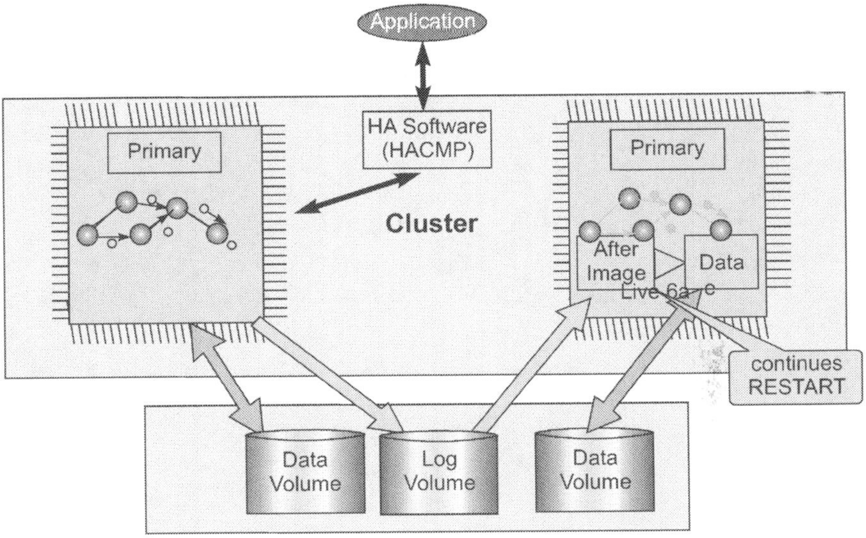

Figure 4.2 More complex LiveCache installations in large APO installations

It requires a close integration between the storage subsystem and the LiveCache as the LiveCache primary instance controls the data initialization of the standby server at storage system level. The supporting storage system must provide mirror image technology, simultaneous access to the log volume from multiple servers and provide a shared library which exports the control of the split mirror initialization and re-synchronization to application level, making it accessible to the LiveCache primary instance. The concept is used to make the LiveCache available all the time with zero failure and in worst case with fastest recovery.

4.5 HOW DATA IS STORED IN LiveCache

In APO transaction data is not stored in tables like R/3. To insert/view/check/extract transactional data from the APO system, one has to use standard BAPI or Function Modules. These BAPIs/FMs are available for different kind of data like sales orders, manufacturing orders, stocks, planned independent requirements, etc.

In LiveCache data is stored based on Time series and Order series. One can extract the data through BAPIs and standard Function Modules. LiveCache can store data in Order Objects (more relevant for DP and SNP) or Time series (more relevant for forecasting and ATP).

APO system has 2 databases APODB and LiveCache. LiveCache is also one of the databases used in APO system. Generally master data and some other data are stored in APODB. And some part of transaction data is stored in LiveCache. For APODB, normal database like Oracle, MSSQL, DB2, and MAXDB are used. For LiveCache, there are no options. LiveCache is one of the functions of MAXDB (Database comes with SAP).

If one has database conceptual knowledge, maybe he can get rough image of LiveCache (Compared to normal database), LiveCache has bigger data cache. So all data can be stored in data cache. Since most of the data is stored in data cache (it is better to be stored in data cache. Otherwise expensive disk access occur), APO application can access data speedily and very fast, LiveCache data is accessed by special routines that are called from function module start with */SAPAPO/OM**.

LiveCache is often called memory based database. But actually it also has database (disk). As same as other databases, database (disk) has all data and its copy is stored in data cache (memory).

The difference between other database and LiveCache is, it is recommended to store all the data in data cache. If most of the data is stored in LiveCache, this means data is on memory. Therefore LiveCache is called memory based database.

Some standard LiveCache data is viewable using standard transactions.

- /SAPAPO/OM19 LiveCache Browser
- /SAPAPO/OM16 Data Viewer

Detailed Transactions, Function Modules, BAPI's and tables are described in later chapters with examples and sample code for more specific explanation about handling LiveCache from ABAP.

4.6 THE SCM SYSTEM LANDSCAPE

4.6.1 Operational Landscape

SCM APO system architecture is based on R/3 architecture and having identical components as of SAP 3 tier architecture. Having SAPGUI on presentations server, APO Application Server with LiveCache and Database server.

APO is closely integrated with R/3 and BW for Master and transactional data as well as forecasting data. APO has ready to use Plug-Ins for other system by which APO can be directly integrated with R/3, BW etc.

4.6.2 SAP APO System

The SAP Advanced Planning and Optimization system facilitates the strategic, tactical, and operational planning processes.

APO consists of several software components: a relational database system (RDBMS) as in any R/3 system:

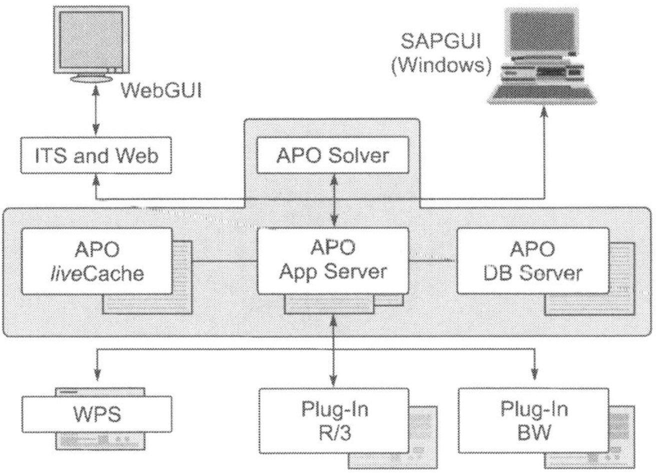

Figure 4.3 SAP APO 3 tier architecture

- APO Database
- SAP Web AS (or up to APO 3.1 an R/3 Basis)
- APO Application Programs
- LiveCache—A separate, very fast object-oriented SAP Database.
- COM routines—Application programs running in LiveCache
- Optimization Engines—A number of programs that execute elaborated optimization algorithms, these components can run on the same or on different servers.

Lets discuss the APO architecture in terms of transaction processing approach.

4.7 ON LINE TRANSACTION PROCESSING (OLTP) SYSTEM

Applications that support and manage transactions which involve high volumes of data are supported by OLTP system. OLTP is based on client-server architecture and supports transactions across networks. The On Line Transaction Processing system covers functionality for sales and distribution, material and inventory management, controlling, shop floor control, logistic execution, etc.

4.8 ON LINE ANALYSIS PROCESSING (OLAP) SYSTEM

Business data analysis and complex calculations on low volumes of data are performed by OLAP. An insight of data coming from various resources can be achieved by the user with the help of OLAP. An On Line Analysis Processing system, such as SAP Business Information Warehouse (BIW) or now a days refers as Business Intelligence (BI), provides cumulated historical data as a basis for future extrapolation purposes in APO's Demand Planning.

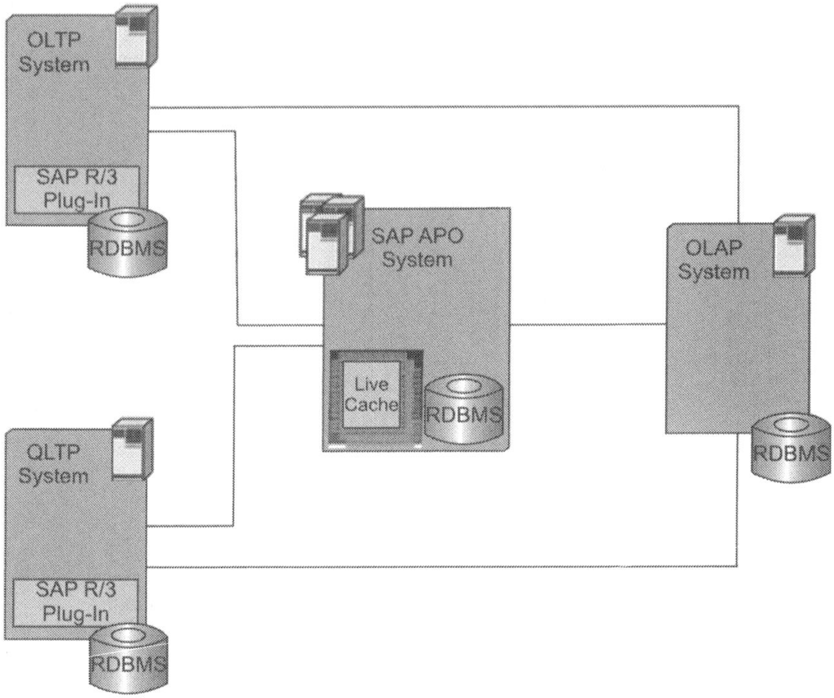

Figure 4.4 Transaction processing architecture of APO

Operationally APO consists of three parts: the database, the BW data and the LiveCache.

The BW data mart consists of InfoCubes and is technically the same as in the BW system. LiveCache (huge main memory) where the planning and the scheduling relevant data is kept to increase the performance for complex calculations. Though there is technically only one LiveCache per installation (there can be standby LiveCache but at a time one LiveCache can be in operational status), the data is stored in three different ways depending on the application:

- As a number per time period (month, week, day) and key figure (time series),
- As an order with a category, date and exact time (hour: minute: second) and
- As a quantity with a category and a date in the ATP time series.

We will refer to the components of the LiveCache as time series LiveCache, order LiveCache and ATP time series LiveCache.

Demand Planning uses a large amount of the BW functionality and relies on the InfoCubes as a data interface to any other system—R/3, BW or flat file. Therefore the historical data is always determined in an InfoCubes. For processing the data is written into the time series LiveCache. SNP and PPDS use mainly the order LiveCache, though SNP is able to access the time series LiveCache as well, since there are many structural similarities between DP and SNP. ATP at last relies only on the ATP time series LiveCache.

This method of data storage implies a certain redundancy, because orders are stored both in the order LiveCache and in the ATP time series LiveCache. The data model is however quite different, and the surplus data storage enables better performance for the applications. TPVS finally uses the order LiveCache to reference other orders. Figure shows how the APO modules use the LiveCache and the data integration for transactional data from R/3 and BW to APO.

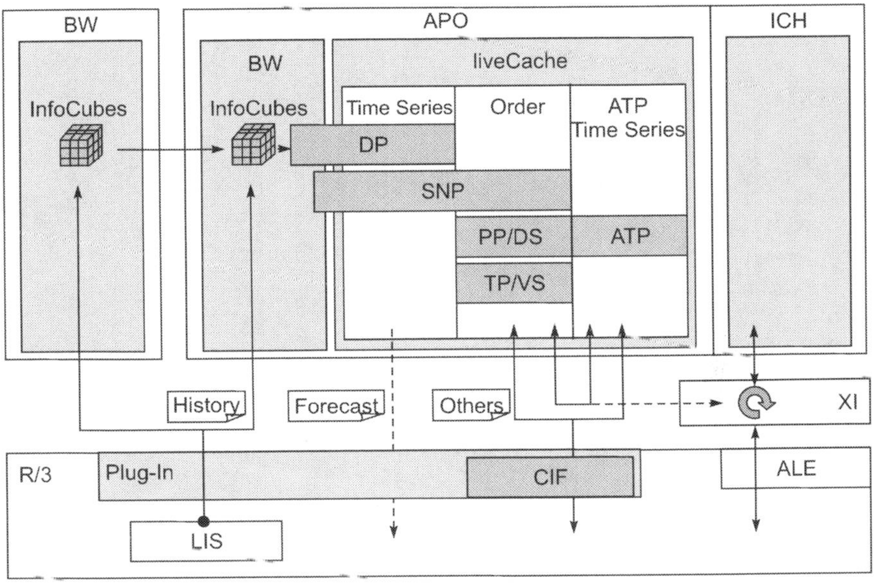

Figure 4.5 APO integration

The transactional data for planning purposes (planned orders and purchase requirements) are created in APO and should preferably remain in APO only to reduce the data load for the interface. In any case APO should only be used for planning. For data with a close link to the execution (sales orders and purchase orders) R/3 is the master. Historical data finally is stored in R/3 and in BW. For the integration of the transactional data and the data history with the Plug-In SAP provides an interface from R/3 to both to BW and APO. One part of the Plug-In is the ***Core Interface (CIF)***, we will discuss CIF in detail in later chapters. The other provides the interface to the BW structures. The integration of R/3 to the BW structures (whether in BW or in APO) relies on the info structures of the logistics information system (LIS) in R/3, where transactional data is stored for reporting purposes according to the defined selection criteria. These data are uploaded into an InfoCubes with periodic jobs.

A related logic applies to the data exchange between BW and APO (in both directions). In contrast to the periodic data upload to the BW part the CIF provides an event triggered online integration. For example with the update of the goods receipt an event is created which triggers the transfer of the updated stock situation to APO. This information creates two entries in APO: one as an order in the order LiveCache and one as an element in the ATP time series LiveCache.

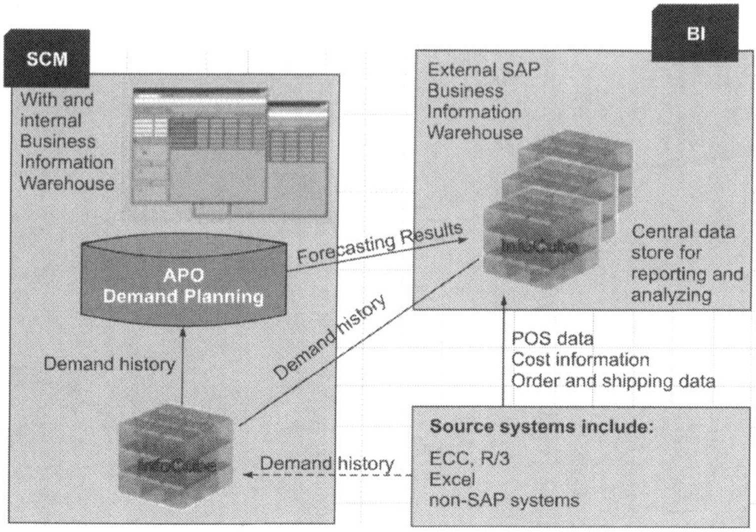

Figure 4.6 APO integration using InfoCubes

Some of the SCM-APO concepts are described here in brief and will be explained in detailed in separate chapters with the programming used in the concepts.

4.9 MACROS

Macro functionality supports the data processing from a simple addition of rows to more complex calculations using a set of standard functions. Even own coding can be applied in user function macros. The macros are defined specifically for each data view in the macro builder. The macro builder is accessed via the macro workbench with the *transaction code /SAPAPO/ADVM.*

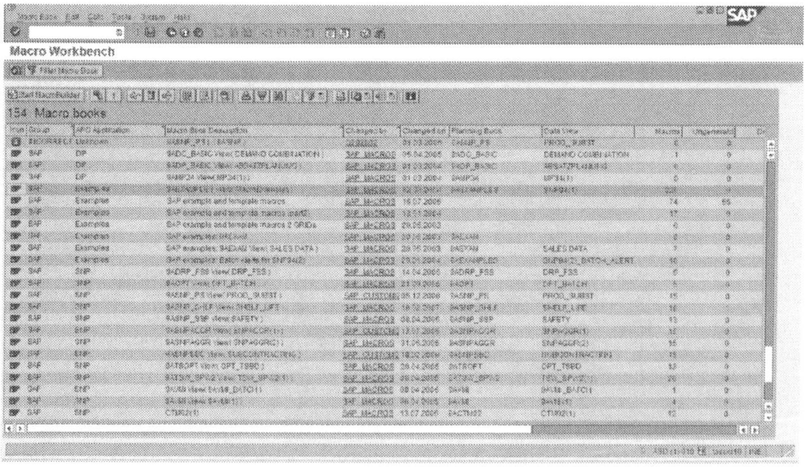

Figure 4.7 Macro workbench

Use advanced macros to perform complex calculations quickly and easily. Macros are executed either directly by the user in interactive planning or automatically at a predefined point in time during a background job.

The definition of macros is optional. There is no need to write macros from scratch, we can create custom macros by simply copy the standard macros and incorporate our logic. Some stock level and days supply macros are also delivered with the standard SNP planning books. One can create his own planning book for SNP using one of the existing books as a template (for reference), and copy the standard macros to the new book.

One can create an advanced macro either when creating or changing a planning book in Customizing, or in design mode of interactive planning. One can define a macro either for an entire planning book or for a specific data view.

4.9.1 Macro Execution

Macros are used in interactive planning by manual request from the planning book or triggered by events like the start of the interactive planning, the change of the level, the end of interactive planning or as a default macro. In these cases the macros process only the selected data on the current aggregation level. In general there is a difference whether a calculation is performed on the most disaggregated level or on an aggregated level and the result is disaggregated afterwards.

To create a macro the related elements (starting with the 'macro' element) are picked from the 'element' window on the top left by drag and drop. After the macro is defined, it has to be activated before it can be used. By default a macro is directly executable, unless it is inhibited within the macro definition. If the macro shall be executed at start of the interactive planning, when the level changes or after exit, the macro has to be assigned to the according events in the top right window by drag and drop.

Note that frequent execution of macros may affects the performance, therefore the assignment as default macro should be done carefully.

For more details in programming in Macro, please see Chapter 10.

4.10 BASICS OF ALERT MONITORING

Alerts notify the planner about situations which require his attention or interference. A shortage situation caused by higher demand due to increased sales or caused by production shortfall due to increased scrap is a typical example where an alert helps the planner to act as early as possible. Alerts are displayed either in the alert monitor as a stand alone application or are integrated into other planning functionalities. The alert monitor is called with the *transaction code /SAPAPO/AMON1*.

The alert monitor is prearranged into two parts: In the area left the objects for the alerts are selected. In the alert view right only those alerts for the objects are shown, which had been selected in the alert profiles and for which current alerts exist. The navigation becomes clearer after regarding the structure of the alert monitor configuration.

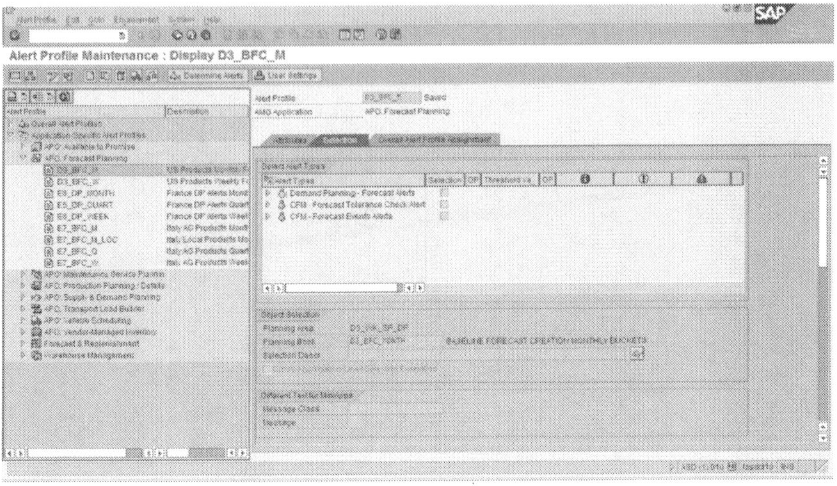

Figure 4.8 Alert monitor

4.10.1 Transaction Code/SAPAPO/AMON_SETTING

In the alert profiles the alert types and the objects for which the alerts should be displayed are selected and defined. Depending on the application different alert types and selection criteria are used. Usually it is recommended to choose alert types carefully since performance is an issue in alert monitoring.

To each alert there are lots of information—alert priority, alert type, product, location, target and actual value are only a few of them. The selection of the displayed information and their sequence are configured using the 'select layout' button in the header of the alert display box. In the menu bar of 'select layout' a new layout is created, in 'manage layout' it is set as a default. Non-default layouts have to be applied manually. In the alert monitor those alerts are displayed that were valid at the time the alert monitor was called. If the planning situation has changed in the meantime a refresh is necessary.

4.10.2 Alert Types

APO provides some standard alert types and allows for supply and demand planning to define own alert types. The alert types are selected per application area for the according profile.

Forecast Alerts

The alert types in the forecast alert profile are all related to the trespassing of forecasting limits. Consequently the prerequisites to use forecast errors are the selection of the errors in the unvaried forecast profile and the definition of the limits for the errors in the respective diagnosis groups.

SDP Alerts

SDP alerts are based on the planning book structure and the time series. These alerts are calculated using macros. Technically the two types of alerts, dynamic alerts and database alerts triggers in APO modules. In SNP and DP both dynamic and database alerts can be used, but especially for a larger data set it is not recommended to use dynamic alerts because of performance disadvantages. Database alerts are usually calculated by planning jobs and related to the planning situation at the specific point of time of the planning job. Database alerts are stored in the database. Therefore it is recommended first to delete the existing alerts before creating new ones.

4.10.3 Alert Handling

In order to help the planner to keep an overview of the alert situation it is possible to:

- Sort the alerts according to the specified column in ascending or descending order,
- Confirm the alert, that is to mark as checked (for example because its resolving is already triggered),
- Hide an alert, for example some exceptional constraints which are not configured in the system and
- Display hidden alerts again.

4.10.4 Sort Alerts Hide/Show Freeze

Another feature to support the planner in resolving the alert situations is the functionality to freeze the alerts. In this case any change is marked in the status column. This feature is especially helpful when calling the alert monitor in the transactional simulation mode from a PPDS application. This way it is possible to experiment with actions and see their impact on the alert situation.

Depending on this condition, it is possible to decide whether to save or not. With right mouse click on the alerts it is possible to branch into an application to resolve the alert. This functionality depends on the alert type.

There are three priorities for alerts

- Error
- Warning
- Information

For some alert types it is possible to set the priority depending on thresholds. Additionally the general priority of some alert types can be changed in customizing.

4.10.5 Alert Calculation in the Background

It is possible to send alerts regularly per batch job either to the SAP office workplace or to a specified e-mail address. These settings are maintained in the automatic messaging profile with the *transaction code /SAPAPO/AMONMSG* The actual sending of the alerts is triggered with the *transaction code /SAPAPO/AMONMSG_SEND.*

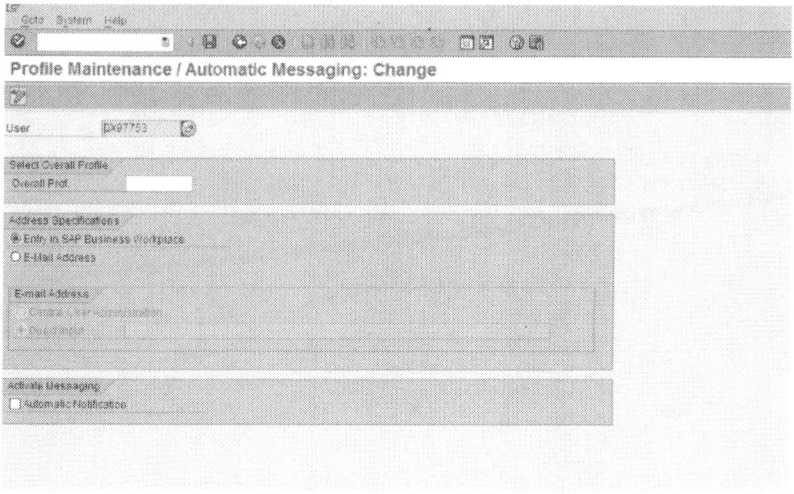

Figure 4.9 Alert scheduled in background

4.11 CORE INTERFACE (CIF)

4.11.1 Overview of the Core Interface

The SAP APO Core Interface (CIF) is used to transfer master and transaction data from one or more SAP R/3 systems to an SAP APO system and vice versa. The core interface (CIF) is the standard interface between R/3 and APO.

The CIF enables the integration of:

- Master data from R/3 to APO (one way only)
- Transactional from R/3 to APO and from APO to R/3 (both ways)

The CIF is delivered as part of the R/3 Plug-In, available for SAP R/3. The R/3 Plug-In is applied to the SAP R/3 system, thus enabling them to communicate with the mySAP.com components SAP APO, SAP CRM, SAP BW, SAP SRM, etc.

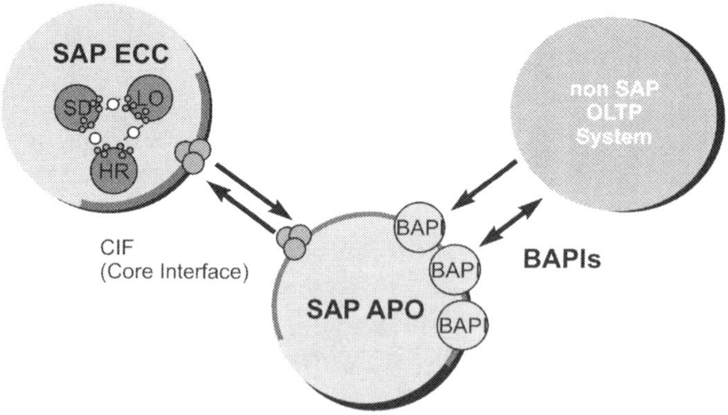

Figure 4.10 CIF as plug-in component

For SAP APO systems, the interfaces necessary for sending and receiving business data to and from R/3 are provided by SAP together with the SAP APO system in a single package. It is not necessary to apply an extra plug-in to APO.

The main objectives of the SAP APO CIF include determination of the source and the target system, provision of the APO with the relevant master and transaction data, transfer of data changes, and return of planning results from APO to the execution system.

Communication Method of CIF Queue

- The Communication Method of CIF Queue can be Inbound or Outbound
- With Inbound Queue
    - Calling system sends queues to the "entrance" (inbound) of target system allowing the receiving system to control system queue load
    - Scheduling of the LUW processes happen in receiving system
    - Results in better CIF performance even with high data volume
- With Outbound Queue
    - Calling system sends queues to target system without considering system load of receiving system
    - No scheduling of the LUW processes take place in the target system
    - Results in overloading of receiving system and CIF performance deterioration with high data volume

4.11.2 CIF Data Transfer from APO

- The system transfers Planning Data only of active planning version '*000*'.
- Product and location are assigned to the same business system group. In R/3 system, an active integration model exists for the respective material and plant.
- The application (for example the PPDS or the SNP) in the APO system creates an event. The event includes the Type of Change (Add, Change, Delete) and the Internal Order Number. The system sends the event to a module of integration module CIF (Core Interface) and stores it there temporarily.
- The system transfers the changes to the R/3 system at a certain time.

Generally, the system transfers changes as mentioned below:

- PPDS: Immediately (that is when the schedule in the APO system is saved)
- SNP: The system collects changes of the SNP and transfers them in blocks.
- Define in Configure Transfer to OLTP in Customizing *Transaction code / SAPAPO/C4*. In column 'Recording' one can define whether the system collects changes or not.
- If the system collects changes, it has to transfer all collected changes via *Transaction code /SAPAPO/C5* or by scheduling a job periodically using *report /SAPAPO/RDMCPPROCES*

The SAP APO CIF uses queued remote function calls (qRFCs) provided by SAP Technology to ensure the desired sequence and transactional security of data transmissions between SAP R/3 and SAP APO. With qRFCs, asynchronous data transfers between SAP APO and SAP R/3 are established, thus enabling business process steps to be completed in either one of the systems, without the need to wait until the data is actually transferred to the other systems. Nevertheless, there are a few exceptions, where synchronous calls are performed if immediate updates are necessary (for example, during ATP checks executed from SAP R/3 sales orders).

4.11.3 The SAP APO CIF Provides

- Integration models to specify which data is to be transferred between SAP R/3 and SAP APO
- Techniques for initial, incremental, and real-time data transfer between SAP R/3 and SAP APO
- Alerting (CIF Queue Alert) and monitoring tools (SCM Queue Manager) to supervise the CIF data transfer

The data sets (master and transactional data) required for APO planning processes are selected in an integration model. ***An integration model*** is exclusively defined by its application. Activation of a generated integration model starts the data transfer. The initial data supply loads planning-relevant data from an R/3 execution system to SAP APO. This applies to both master data and transaction data. After finishing the initial load, the system switches to incremental data transfer, where only the changed data is transmitted. The incremental transfer distinguishes between change transfer for master data and change transfer for transactional data.

Incremental transfers of master data are filtered and routed between APO and R/3 either periodically or, if necessary, immediately. The strategy for transferring master data is determined in Customizing. Either Business Transaction Events (BTE) are used to immediately notify CIF on changes to SAP R/3 master data (Material, Customer, and Vendor Masters) or ALE change pointer are recorded for the corresponding message types. Those pointers have to be processed regularly to notify APO of a changed master data situation. The ALE customizing settings for change pointers are needed for the transfer to be executed successfully.

To reflect the current planning situation as close to real time as possible, the incremental transfer of transaction data is event-driven. Within each transaction containing a change of a planning-relevant object in R/3 (such as production orders or sales orders), the change is sent to APO immediately.

The re-transmission of APO planning results into the R/3 execution system is result-based. All changes are distributed through a publish/subscribe mechanism. Depending on the application, the planning results are either extracted immediately and sent to the connected R/3 system (valid for PPDS) or published using a certain reports or transactions to be scheduled periodically (valid for SNP). These modes are the SAP standard settings delivered for those applications.

- Transfer changed SAP R/3 master data (Material, Customer, and Vendor masters) periodically via ALE change pointers, not immediately via Business Transaction Events (BTEs), if immediate updates of master data changes are not necessary.
- If possible, publish SAP APO planning results to R/3 periodically, not immediately.
- Set the PPDS settings in the Product master to Manual Planning or Automatic Planning in the Planning Run but not to Automatic Planning Immediately. Continuous data changes due to immediate automatic planning put a high load on CIF if the changed data is transferred to SAP R/3 immediately.

The SAP APO CIF uses queued remote function calls (qRFCs) to transfer data between the SAP APO and SAP R/3 systems. With this SAP Basis technology, all data is transferred with transactional consistency and serialized in the correct order.

By default, outbound qRFCs (on the sending system) are used. For high data transfer volumes, the CIF can be set up to use also inbound qRFCs, where consumption of system resources can better be controlled and the network load is restricted to a shorter period of time for each RFC.

The basis queue monitors can be accessed with transactions:

- *SMQ1* – outbound queues in the sending system
- *SMQ2* – inbound queues in the receiving system

With new qRFC versions, queue schedulers are used to control how queues are processed by the SAP systems, for example, which system resources may be used to process qRFCs.

The queue schedulers can be configured and monitored with transactions:

- *SMQR* – QIN scheduler for inbound queues
- *SMQS* – QOUT scheduler for outbound queues

CIF error handling ensures that all CIF queue entries are processed during the data transfer. This applies to transactional data only, master data and initial data transfer are exempted from CIF error handling. Faulty queues no longer lead to queue blocks. Instead, they are logged in post-processing records in the relevant target system for the data transfer. Then call these post-processing records at a later time point in CIF Post-processing (*transaction code /SAPAPO/CPP)*. Once the error has been corrected one can again send the objects to the relevant target system.

CIF error handling has to be activated explicitly in APO customizing *transaction code /SAPAPO/C2* and applies to transfers between SAP APO and the specified logical SAP R/3 system in both directions.

Early notification is required in order to resolve errors quickly. The CIF Queue Alert tools can be used for error notification (*transaction code /SAPAPO/CPPA*). The CIF application logs can be used to perform error analysis where reasons for errors are listed and described. To navigate to the CIF application logs, use the SCM Queue-Manager or the CIF post-processing.

The concept of CIF error handling and post processing is explained in detail in the CIF chapters where we will discuss CIF in details.

4.12 INFOOBJECTS

The terms InfoObjects, InfoSource, InfoCubes in APO are functionally and technically more over same as of BI, hence I am explaining them here with reference to BI objects.

Technically the APO-InfoCubes matches exactly with the BI-InfoCubes, i.e. it consists of dimensions, and a fact table. APO does not deliver any predefined planning scenarios, i.e. there are no sample InfoCubes which can directly be used. Templates are provided which includes the basic InfoObjects essential for the planning purpose on the APO. The name of this sample template-InfoCubes is *DP-REFER*.

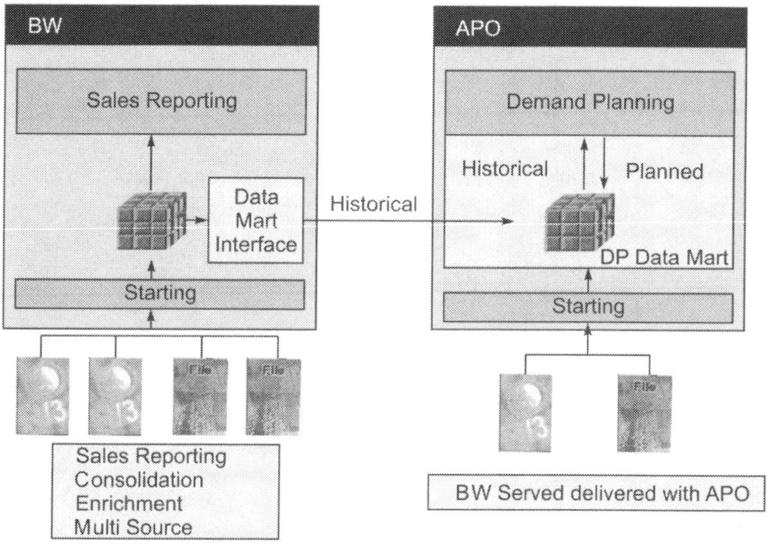

Figure 4.11 InfoCube integration between BI and APO

Master data and transaction data are called InfoObjects. They are used throughout the system to create structures and tables where data is stored. They enable information to be modeled in a structured form. They are also used to define reports to evaluate master and transactional data. InfoObjects are the most basic form of data and are the smallest available information modules or fields. These break into the following:

- Key Figures (ex. sales) – For data analysis and evaluations.
- Characteristics (ex. customers) – used to analyze key figures
- Time characteristics (ex. fiscal year)
- Units (ex. currency or amount unit)
- Technical characteristic (ex. request number)
- *Master Data Bearing Characteristics*

A characteristic is a master data in behavior if it specifies that table attributes, texts or hierarchies are linked to it to provide additional information. Enable master data bearing characteristics by selecting the appropriate checkbox for text.

Four tables are created when a master data bearing characteristic is created:

- Attribute tables
- Text tables
- SID tables
- Hierarchy tables
- *Compounding*

Compounding is the process of combining characteristics InfoObjects with another characteristic InfoObjects to ensure the ability to uniquely define values of the InfoObjects.

This tab determines whether or not the characteristics are to be compounded to other InfoObjects. One often needs to compound characteristic values to enable characteristic values to be uniquely assigned.

Attribute (InfoObjects)

These are characteristics or key figures that are used to describe characteristics in more detail. The characteristics cost center can be described in more detail with the profit center and person responsible information about the cost center. Like the compounding tab, attributes have their own tab on the characteristic. Attributes themselves are InfoObjects. Attributes can be defined as either:

- Display attributes
- Navigation attributes

If attributes are defined as navigational, they can be used to navigate in reporting. When a query is executed, the system does not distinguish between navigational attributes and characteristics for the InfoProvider.

DataSource

Replication is the process of accessing DataSource and mapping them to InfoProvider in BI.

InfoProvider

InfoProvider are objects into which data can be loaded. It is an object which queries can be created or executed. There are two types of InfoProvider.

- InfoCubes and Data Store Objects (which contain physical data)
- InfoObjects (characteristics with attributes) A characteristic can be an InfoProvider.

InfoCubes

An InfoCube is a multi-dimensional set of relational tables with a fact table in the middle and which is in accordance with the star schema. An InfoCube is the primary object used to provide historical data to APO DP. The goals are to design a warehouse is to ensure that most queries initially target this type of database object. They are designed to store summarized and aggregated data for long periods of time.

A Basic Cube is the foremost InfoProvider which will be used in conjunction with APO DP. An InfoCube consists of one fact table in which key figure values are stored. An InfoCube has a minimum of 4 dimension tables and a maximum of 16. There are two subtypes of InfoCubes:

- Standard (for pure read access)
- Real Time (optimized for direct update)
- *Virtual Provider*

A Virtual Providers is a data provider for which the transaction data is not saved. A Multi Provider is a type of data provider that combines data from several Info Providers and makes it available for reporting.

Data Store Object is an object that stores consolidated and cleaned transaction data on the lowest level (basic level). Data Store Objects often describes a consolidated data set from one or more InfoSources.

Info Set

This is a semantic view of a Data Store objects. Source systems provide data to the BI. (R/3, BIW, APO LiveCache, flat files, legacy). Data Sources subdivide the available data into a source system. The Data Sources are used to transfer master data and transaction data. Once the transfer structure has been replicated to SAP BI, create an InfoSource. An InfoSource is a quantity of InfoObjects that belong together and that contain all the information on a business process. Transfer rules connect the transfer structure to the communication structure. The structure where the InfoObjects are stored is called a communication structure.

InfoSource

Once a transfer structure has been replicated to SAP BI, create an InfoSource. An InfoSource is a quantity of InfoObjects that belong together and that contain all the information on a business process. The InfoSource may contain both transactional and master data. There are two types of InfoSource:

- InfoSource with flexible update
- InfoSource with direct update

InfoPackage

This is the BI object that contains all the settings directing how this data should be uploaded from the source system. The target of the InfoPackage is the PSA table tied to the specific DataSource associated with the InfoPackage. The InfoPackage placed between the Source System and the DataSource, the transformation occurs after the DataSource.

With the scheduling of an info package the data upload is triggered. The selections and parameters (e.g. check whether master data exists) for the data load and the scheduling parameters - immediately or planned as a job are set in the info package itself. Each data upload adds the data to the InfoCube. If data is required from more than one source (which is the usual scenario), the info packages have to be scheduled in a determined order after deleting the InfoCube content.

Info packages are created in the '*Info Source*' view. Each data upload is identified by a request number. To check whether the data upload was successful it is possible to branch into a monitor from the info package or with the *transaction code RSMO.*

From now onwards I will more concentrate on the programming in APO using the BAPIs and Function Modules in terms of reading/updating LiveCache and will touch the other concepts of APO.

5

CIF INTEGRATION MODEL

5.1 CORE INTERFACE (CIF)—OVERVIEW OF THE CORE INTERFACE

The core interface (CIF) is the standard interface between R/3 and APO for the order related applications PPDS, SNP and ATP. On R/3 side the '*Plug-In*' has to be implemented to use the CIF, on APO side it is always included.

The CIF enables the integration of:

- Master data from R/3 to APO (one way only)
- Transactional from R/3 to APO and from APO to R/3 (both ways)

The Core Interface (CIF) is responsible for the data exchange between SAP R/3 and SAP SCM (we are discussing here APO only) Systems. The CIF is a real-time interface that links SAP SCM with one or several SAP R/3 Systems. Only the data objects needed in the data structures in SAP SCM for the different planning and optimization processes are transferred from the complex data set of the SAP R/3 system into SAP SCM. The *Core Interface* guarantees both the initial data transfer and also the transfer of data changes within SAP SCM. The integration of SAP R/3 with the CIF interface is possible as of release 3.1I. Earlier releases or an R/2 System can be connected with BAPIs as Non-SAP ECC Systems.

The fundamental concept of the integration is to write events for each planning relevant change e.g. the creation of an order and use these as trigger for the transfer. Technically the transfer is performed via qRFC. Which objects (i.e. planned orders, stock, etc.) are transferred is controlled by the *Integration Models*, which could be regarded as the key concept of the CIF.

5.1.1 More on CIF

CIF is the standard method by which data is moved between SCM and R/3. The systems are "loosely coupled." Master data and transaction data must be transferred between the systems periodically only and in real time in few situations (such as GATP) where immediate interaction is necessary. However as SCM becomes increasingly transaction oriented (i.e. the areas outside of APO such EWM), the CIF being increasingly transactional real time. The CIF is both a frontend (GUI) and a container where multiple RFCs are batched into logical units of work that are collected for a data transfer using the *Core Interface (CIF)*. CIF has its own configuration *transaction (PIMG)* this is a highly recommended transaction to go into for managing the CIF, it is much more efficient and easier than searching in *SPRO*. However, it does not have any extra functionality over that of SPRO, it is just a specialized transaction to give access to all ECC CIF functionality.

One of the advantages of using SCM is that "CIF" over data from SAP ERP where it is maintained often as the system of record (although that certainly changes per implementation) the CIF always requires configuration and often some enhancements, however, it is the standard integration connect between SCM and SAP ERP. The integration includes:

From SAP ERP to SCM Master Data

- Plant
- Material Master
- BOM/PPM
- Schedule Agreement

Transaction Data

- Requirements (Purchase Requisitions)
- Planned Orders
- Production Orders
- Purchase Orders
- Confirmations

From SCM to SAP ERP Transactional Data

- Purchase Order
- Stock Transfer Order
- Production Order and Planned Order
- ATP Request

5.2 INTEGRATION MODELS AND DATA TRANSFER

There is also a dominant organization's principle the integration models should follow. SAP recommends the following to be performed, prior to IM:

- ATP Customizing
- Product Allocation Customizing
- Plants
- Characteristics and Classes
- Material Masters and Characteristics and Classes
- MRP Areas, Material Masters for MRP Areas, Characteristics and Classes
- Planning Product
- Availability Check

- Product Allocation
- Customer and Suppliers
- Work Centers
- PPM
- Schedule Agreement, Contracts, Purchase Info Records.

CIF uses a queuing system (like other middleware products) and comes with a consistency checking transaction that allows for the monitoring of the transfer.

The activation of an integration model leads to an initial transfer of master data and transaction data from SAP R/3 to SAP APO. Online transfer is released for transaction data. As standard, the integration models to be activated are compared with the integration models that are already active. In this way, the transfer restricts itself to difference, in other words, only data for filter objects that are not contained in any active integration models is transferred.

Before activating the CIF integration models, one has to do certain configuration settings.

5.3 CREATION OF INITIAL SYSTEM SETTINGS FOR DATA TRANSFER

The following sections should have been setup already through basis consultant. However, it has been explained here to give to detailed overview about the process how it works. This work has to be done before go into the CIF and start creating integration models. They are both on the SCM side and on the R/3 side. We will address the R/3 configuration first.

5.3.1 SAP ERP Side

The SAP R/3 side of the CIF is much bigger with more transactions and much more features. The first Name Logical Systems needs to be created in R/3 side.

SAP ERP SPRO – Implementation Guide – Integration with Other MySAP.com Components – Advanced Planning and Optimization – Basic setting for setting up the system landscape—Name Logical System.

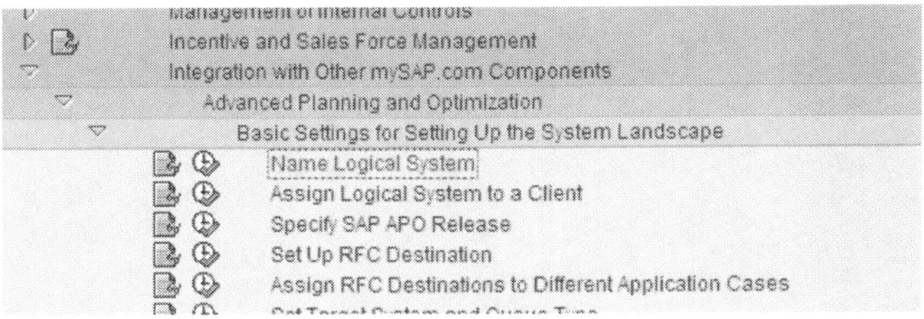

Figure 5.1 Define logical system in R/3

These setting are cross client setting hence one should take extra care.

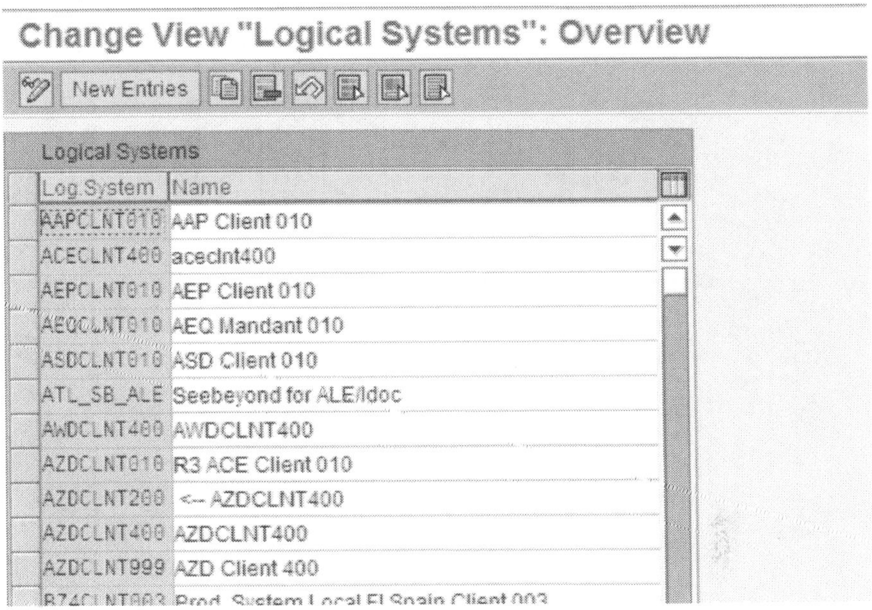

Figure 5.2 Maintain system information in R/3

5.3.2 Assigning to a Client

As more than one system can be connected to the One APO system hence client connection is required to be defined.

Figure 5.3 Assign clients to logical system in R/3

5.3.3 Setting up an RFC Destination

Transaction code SM59 is used to define RFC destination, it is technical path how system connect with other systems.

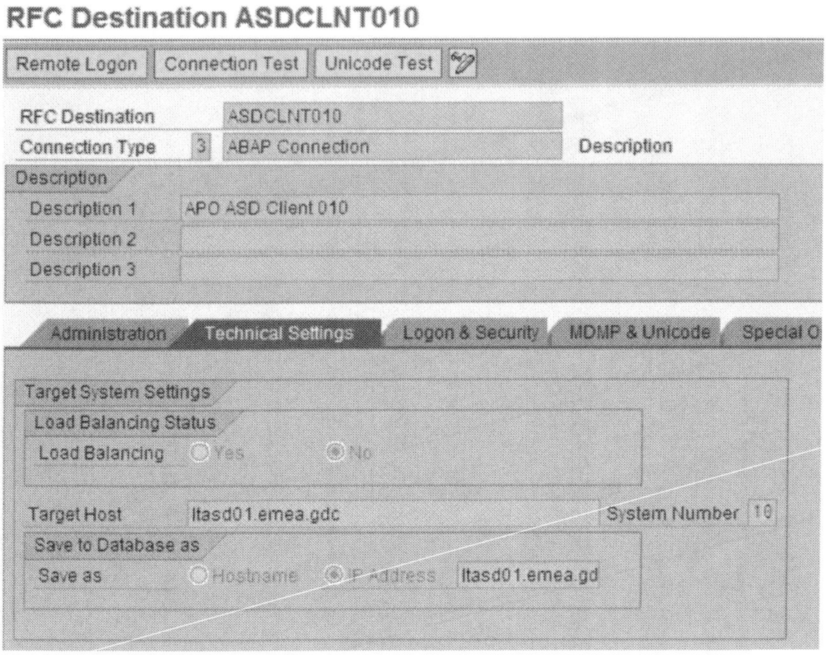

Figure 5.4 Create RFC destination in R/3

After the RFC destination has been created, assign it to application cases.

5.3.4 IMG Path – SPRO

SAP Customizing Implementation Guide – Integration with Other MySAP.com Components – Advanced Planning and Optimization – Basic setting for setting up the system landscape—Assign RFC Destination to Different Application Cases.

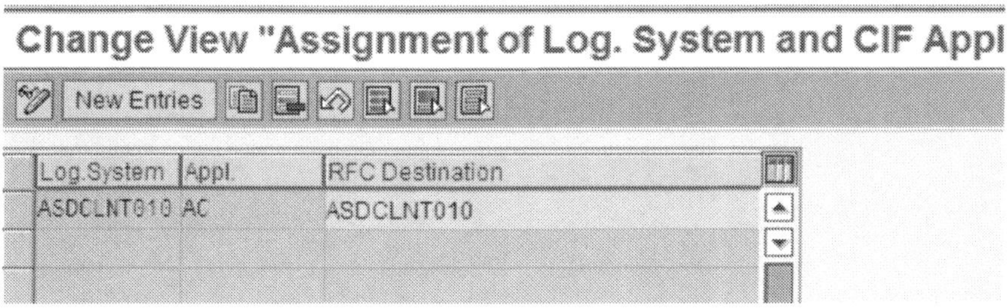

Figure 5.5 Define log system in R/3

Next is setting the target system model type. This is between transactional events, down or initial transfer active.

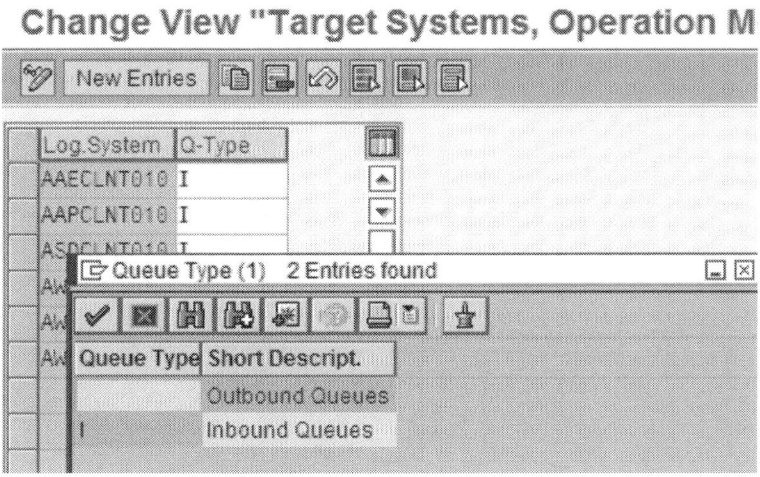

Figure 5.6 Transaction system type setting in R/3

There are other settings, such as setting number ranges, but the settings we discussed are the major ones for setting up the system. Now we will move on to the SCM side of the CIF.

5.3.5 SCM Side

Transfers happen between logical system names. Typical logical system names would be SCMCLNT400, ECCCLNT40. The logical names are first created with the program *SAPLBD41*.

5.3.6 IMG Path

SAP SCM Implementation Guide – Integration with SAP Components—Integration via Core Interface (CIF) – Basic Settings for Creating the System Landscape—Name Logical Systems.

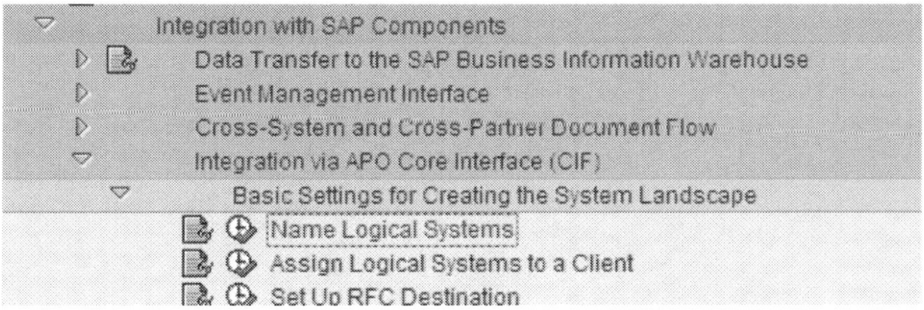

Figure 5.7 Define logical system in APO

Then the logical names assigned then to physical clients.

SAP SCM Implementation Guide – integration with SAP Components—Integration via Core Interface (CIF) – Assign Logical Systems to a Client.

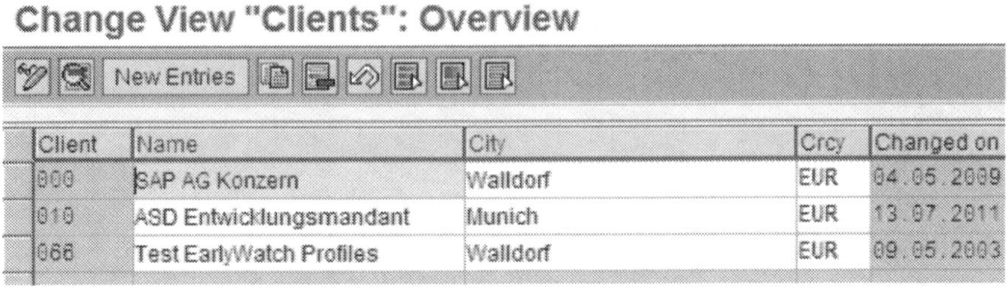

Figure 5.8 Assign clients in APO

5.3.7 Setting up RFC Destinations

Transaction code SM59, the way we created in R/3 same way we have to define the RFC destination APO.

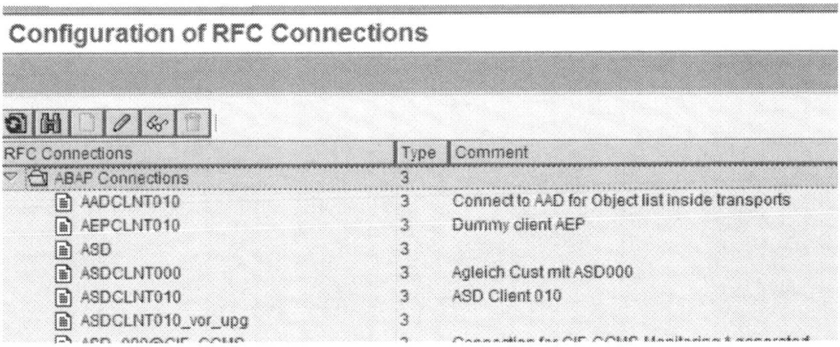

Figure 5.9 Setup RFC destination in APO

As a planning application, APO box can be integrated to multiple R/3 boxes, although the opposite would probably never happen. In these cases a master data issue comes up particularly with the material master. Integrating multiple R/3 systems and normalizing master data is one of the reasons for the application MDM. However, if MDM is not in the track, there are other ways of performing this normalization with customer exits.

5.3.8 IMG Path

SPRO – Integration with other SAP Components – Integration via APO core interface (CIF) – Basic Settings for creating the System Landscape – Maintain Business System Group.

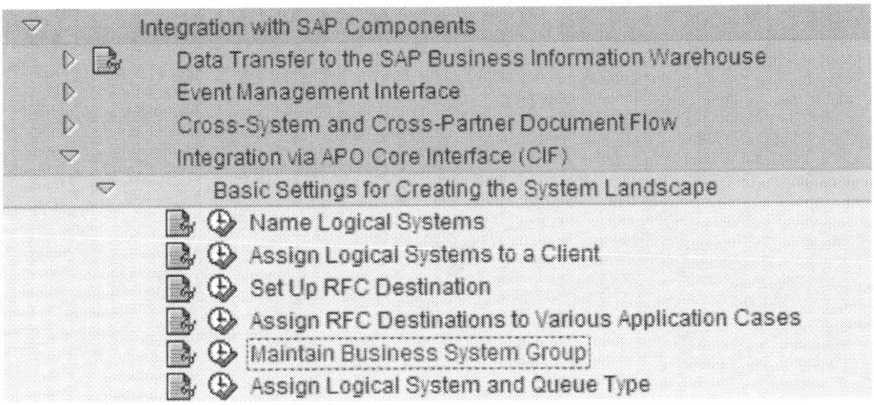

Figure 5.10 Define business groups

Also, Business System Groups (BSUs) allow to group physical systems. This allows a segmentation of their master data, within a single Planning Version and Model.

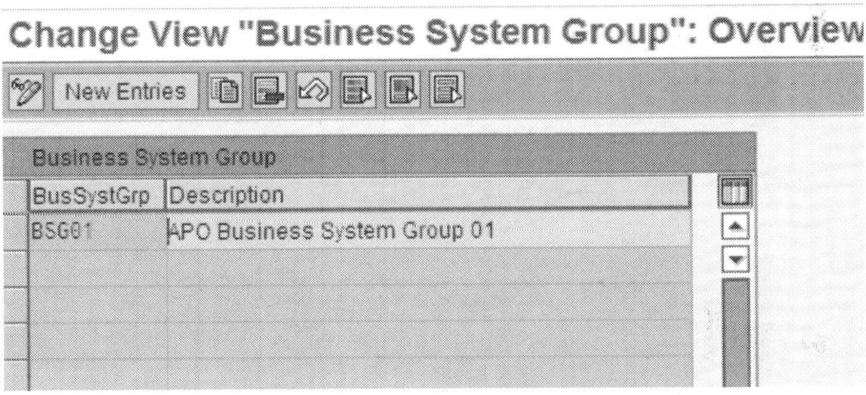

Figure 5.11 Define business groups

Of course another option is to create another Planning Version and Model for the second SAP ERP system data. Creating a BSG is easy. However the complexity comes with assigning the BSG to a logical system. Assignment is done by the following procedure.

5.3.9 IMG Path

SPRO – Integration with other SAP Components – Integration via APO core interface (CIF) – Basic Settings for creating the System Landscape – Assign Logical System and Queue Type.

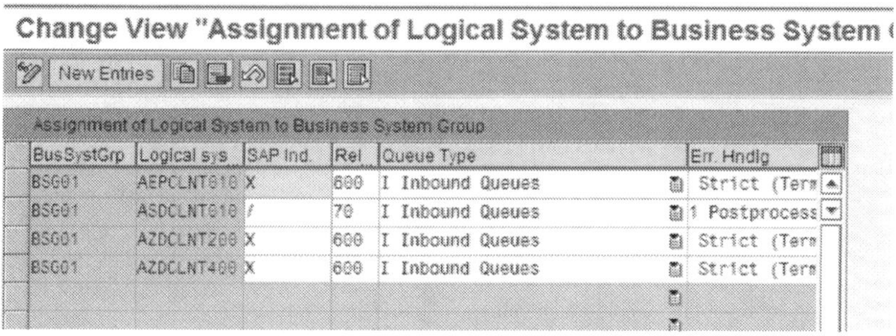

Figure 5.12 Assign business groups to logical system and queues processing types

On the other hand, a logical system can only be assigned to one BSG.

5.4 INBOUND VS. OUTBOUND QUEUES

One can choose either inbound or outbound queues. Inbound queues can handle a much larger data volume than outbound queues. What this means is that the receiving system controls the data transfer. The transfer between the two (inbound vs. outbound) takes place in R/3, (*Transaction code CFC1*).

5.5 IMPORTANT CIF TRANSACTIONS IN ECC

After the base transfer settings in *SPRO* have been initialized, the next step is to go to the CIF GUI. The CIF transactions can be conveniently segmented into those initiated from R/3 and those initiated from SCM. The integration models are created and activated in R/3.

The integration model is used for both the initial data transfer and the change (delta) transfer. *Transaction code CFM1.*

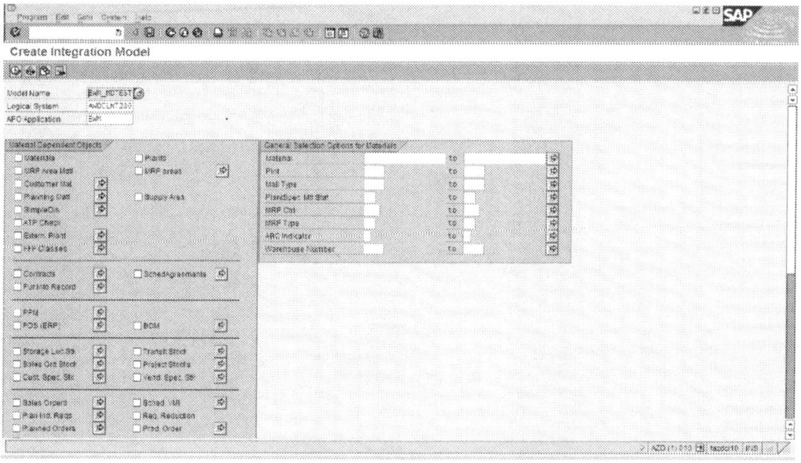

Figure 5.13 CIF integration model

Integration models (also called CIF-models) define which objects—master data or orders—are transferred to APO and whether the ATP check is carried out in APO. When APO sends orders to R/3, it is checked again whether an active integration model exists. The integration models are created on the R/3 side with the *transaction code CFM1* and activated with *transaction code CFM2*.

Objects

An integration model contains a set of objects, which are selected per object type and other selection criteria as object name etc. There are two groups of objects, the ones which are related to the material master, like all orders, and the ones which are material independent as resources and suppliers. APO. Another material dependent object is the control to perform the ATP check in APO. For the selection of the material dependent objects the restrictions for the material are taken into account first.

By generating the integration model the objects matching the selection criteria are read and assigned to the model. These objects—the content of the integration model—are displayed with the *transaction code CFM4*.

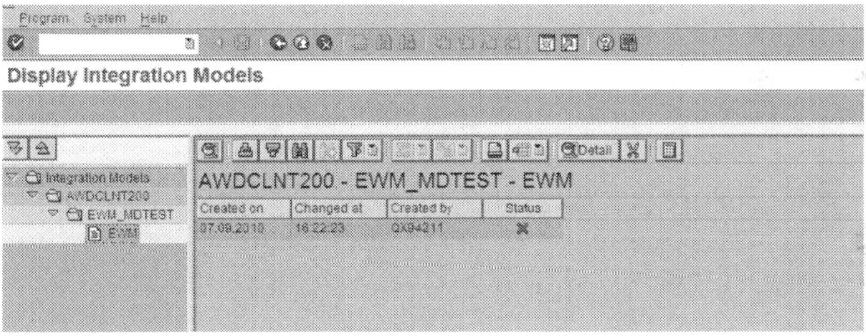

Figure 5.14 CIF integration model activate/deactivate

The key for the integration models consists of the name of the integration model, the target system, the application and its version. The name of the integration model and the application are chosen freely. The integration model receives a new version each time it is generated, independent whether its content has changed.

Data Transfer

The transfer of the data itself is triggered by activating the model with the *transaction code CFM2*. Now all objects of the integration model are transferred as long as they are not already part of an active integration model. Additionally those materials, customers, vendors and supply sources are updated, which are part of the model and have been changed (planning relevant changes).

Initial and Delta Transfer

To manage the transfer of new objects an integration model is usually generated periodically with the identical selection criteria. The content of the versions of this integration model however may differ. Since during transfer the CIF checks whether there is already an active integration model for an object, it is a difference whether the (older) active version is deactivated before activating the new version or not. If the older version is deactivated first, all objects within the new version of the integration model are transferred.

This procedure is called initial transfer. If the new version is activated without deactivating the old one first, only those objects are transferred which are not yet included in the old version.

This way of activating integration models is called *delta transfer*. Usually a periodical delta transfer is used for data integration, since the system load is much smaller this way.

5.5.1 Master Data Integration

Master data is typically one of the most crucial factors for the success of an implementation. For APO this means that two requirements have to be fulfilled:

- The master data in R/3 has to have a sufficient quality. If multiple R/3 systems are connected to APO, a synchronization of the master data is required.
- The master data has to be kept consistent between APO and R/3, else planning and execution drift apart and planning becomes the more inaccurate the higher the level of detail is, therefore mostly PPDS is affected here.

Master Data Maintenance Strategy for APO

Master data is only transferred in one way from R/3 to APO. There is no transfer or update of master data from APO to R/3.

In APO master data objects exist with and without correspondence to objects in R/3, and even those with correspondence (as the product master) usually have settings which do not relate to any setting in R/3. Generally it is recommend strongly to use R/3 as the master for master data maintenance whenever possible and rather transfer some settings via BAdI than to have an additional master data maintenance process in APO.

Change Transfer for Master Data

Change transfer is concerned with the transfer of changes in the master data objects on R/3 side which has already been transferred to APO before.

For the material master, the customer, the vendor and the supply source changes are transferred additionally in the normal delta transfer or separately with the *transaction code CFP1*.

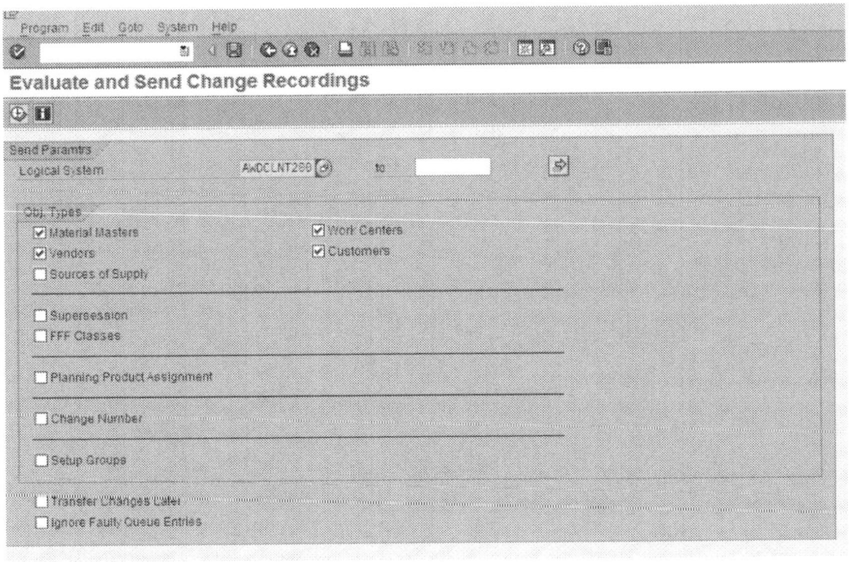

Figure 5.15 Activate delta changes

For the material master, the customer and the vendor it is also possible to define an online change transfer with the *transaction code CFC5*. This improves the consistency between the systems and reduces the workload for the periodical transfer as well.

A change of these objects is recognized if the field for the entry which has been changed is configured to create a change pointer. In the *transaction code BD52* it is possible e.g. for the material master to select the fields which trigger change pointers for the message type CIFMAT, but not all fields offer the option to create change pointers.

Deletion of Master Data

The integration of the master data deletion with respect to data locking from R/3 to APO is given for the material master and the production version. If a material is marked for deletion, the *report RCIFMTDE* sets the according product to 'externally planned' in APO. During the change transfer for PPMs with the *report RSPPMCHG* a PPM is deactivated if the according production version is locked in R/3. Of course each master data object can be deleted in APO as well. The dependencies to existing orders and to other master data objects have to be considered.

The system can transfer changes to APO-relevant master data (data contained in an active integration model) the material master, customer and vendor in real-time, (directly when updating a data change in the R/3 System) into the APO System.

Settings for this function can be done with *transaction code CFC9*. In real-time transfer, the system transfers the complete data record that has been changed directly to the APO System. (For several changes there are corresponding repercussions on the system performance). In the periodic transfer, the system collects and transfers the master data changes into the APO System, within a normal incremental data transfer. The incremental data transfer can finally be deactivated.

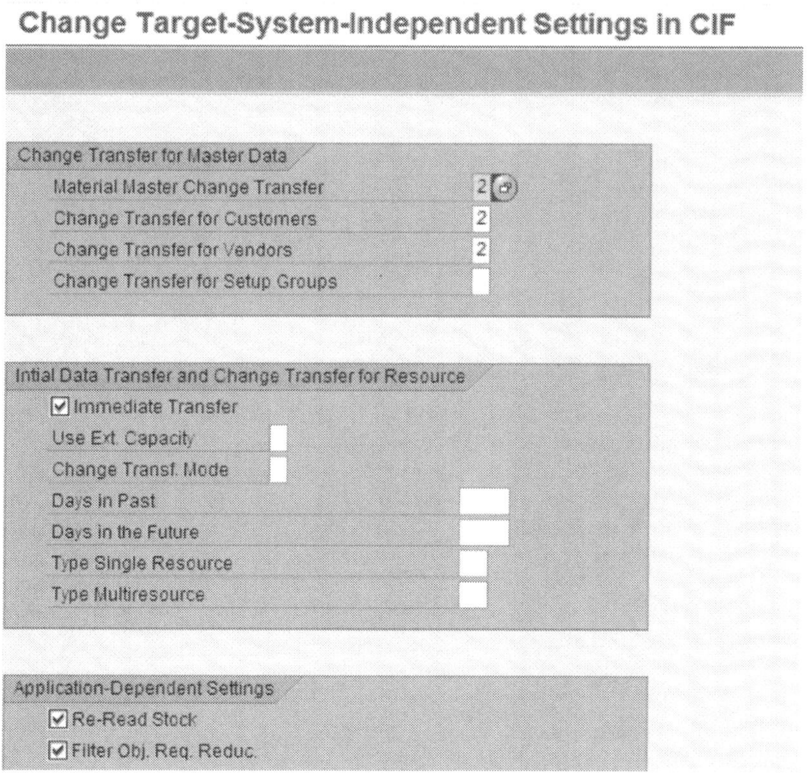

Figure 5.16 Change pointer settings

The incremental data transfer of master data can be controlled with *transaction code CFC9*. If the incremental data transfer is set to "*Business Transaction Event, immediately*", the processing takes place without using change pointers. If the incremental data transfer is set periodically, the change pointers are automatically activated.

5.5.2 Transactional Data Integration

In contrast to the master data transfer, the integration of the transactional data is working two ways, from R/3 to APO and from APO to R/3.

Transactional Data Transfer from R/3 to APO

From R/3 to APO there is usually one initial upload and from then onward a continuous online transfer of data changes. During the activation of an integration model for materials the flag in the field MARC-APOKZ ('APO-flag') is set. If the material is locked, this flag can however not be set, which causes that transactional data is not transferred from R/3 to APO. It is possible to correct the missing flag with the *report RAPOKZFIX*.

The runtime for a complete transactional data upload should be tested as early as possible, because this is an important constraint for the system recovery. The prerequisite for the data transfer from APO to R/3 is the maintenance of the publication types per location in the *transaction code /SAPAPO/CP1*. The default setting for the transfer of transactional data from APO to R/3 is '*immediately*' for PPDS orders and '*periodically*' for SNP orders.

These settings can be changed per user with the *transaction code /SAPAPO/C4* to periodical transfer ('*collect changes*') or to immediate transfer ('*do not collect changes*').

In the '*global parameters and default values*' setting using the *transaction code / SAPAPO/RRPCUST1*.

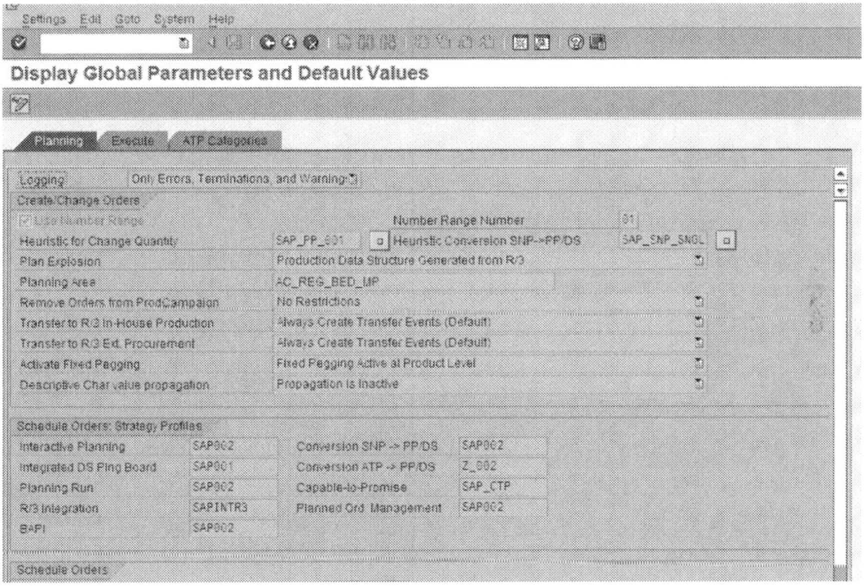

Figure 5.17 User setting

It is possible to inhibit the transfer of planned orders and/or of purchase requisitions to R/3 without the conversion indicator. These settings describe only the prerequisites on APO side to send the data from APO to R/3. On R/3 side furthermore an integration model has to be active for the order type and the according master data. If an order is transferred to R/3, the order number of the R/3 order is transferred back to APO.

5.6 ORGANIZATION OF THE DATA TRANSFER

The data transfer consists of the initial transfer, the delta transfer and the change transfer. Usually the integration models for the relevant master data are generated and activated in delta mode each night to transfer new objects to APO. To transfer changes in the purchasing conditions to APO, for the master data objects vendor, info record, scheduling agreement and contract a periodical initial data transfer is necessary. The changes within the master data objects are transferred either online according to the settings in the *transaction code CFC5* or periodically with the *report RCPTRAN4.*

Data Consistency

The consistency regarding the transactional data between R/3 and APO is checked with the CIF delta report from APO with the *transaction code /SAPAPO/CCR*. As a result both the objects missing in APO and those missing in R/3 are displayed. A transfer for both of them can be triggered to resolve the inconsistency. If there is no active integration model, the objects are displayed as missing in R/3.

Queue Monitoring

First some technical aspects of the data transfer are mentioned to understand the possible errors and the tools to monitor and correct them. It is possible to call a function from a different system using the RFC technique. The prerequisite for this is that the called function supports RFC and that the RFC connection is maintained in the RFC settings with the *transaction code SM59*.

To reduce the sensitivity to network problems, RFCs are usually sent as transactional RFCs (tRFC). For mass processing the concept of writing the tRFC requests into a queue and group them to logical units of work (LUWs) offers the advantage of processing the RFCs in the right sequence and considering the dependencies between LUWs.

For the communication the qRFC (queued RFC) requests are always sent from the outbound queue of the sending system to the inbound queue of the receiving system. Nevertheless there are two concepts of processing the qRFCs, depending whether the scheduling of the LUWs is performed by the sending or by the receiving system. The processing is done by the receiving system anyhow. These two concepts are referred to as '*outbound queue*' and '*inbound queue*', because this is where the scheduler is in charge and the information about the qRFCs are displayed. The outbound queue is displayed with the *transaction code SMQ1* and the inbound queue with the *transaction code SMQ2*.

Application Log for Error Processing

Application log is used to trace when (time), and what (data objects and integration model) was transferred by which user id. In addition, the application log provides a detailed error message when an application error occurred. As a prerequisite, logging must have been switched on. The setting of the logging mode takes place in SAP R/3 or SAP SCM (*transaction code CFC2* in SAP R/3 and transaction code */SAPAPO/C4* in SAP SCM).

The following settings are possible:

- Standard (only the headers of the data records are logged)
- Detailed (header and contents of the transferred data records are logged)

The detailed logging can quickly lead to large data quantities and therefore performance problems in the production operation. For this reason, it is recommended that use detailed logging only when the detailed data is actually needed, for example, in the implementation phase. The system does not delete the logs automatically.

To prevent extreme database load, it is also recommended to delete the logs periodically (also possible in background processing).

SCM Queue Manager for Error Processing in SAP SCM

The SCM Queue Manager is a tool that is only accessible via SAP SCM. This tool will allow an administrator to monitor all integration traffic, whether it will be outgoing data to SAP R/3, or an incoming availability check from an SAP CRM system.

Instead of evaluating the application logs in both systems (SAP R/3 and SAP SCM) separately when errors occur, the user can use the central SCM Queue Manager available in SAP SCM to monitor the queues and application logs in both systems. With the SCM Queue Manager, user can monitor both outbound and inbound queues. To monitor the inbound queues, set the corresponding switch when entered the *transaction code /SAPAPO/CQ*

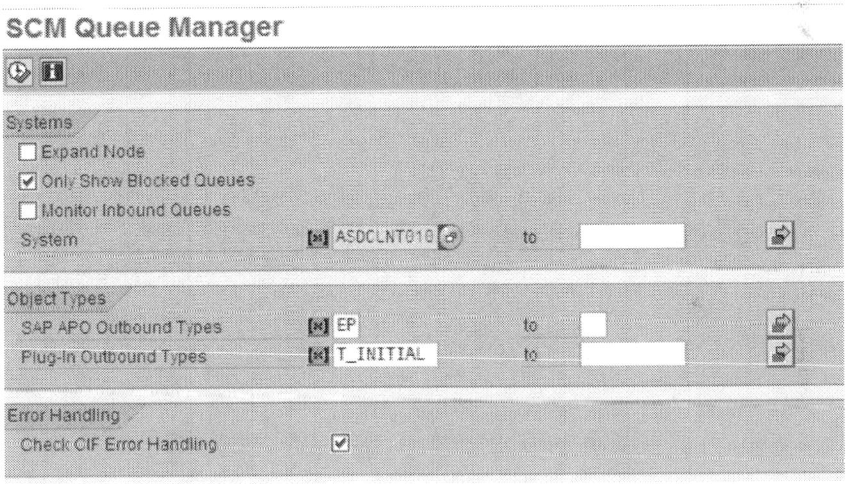

Figure 5.18 APO queue manager

SCM Queue Manager ask for remote login to the system with user name and password.

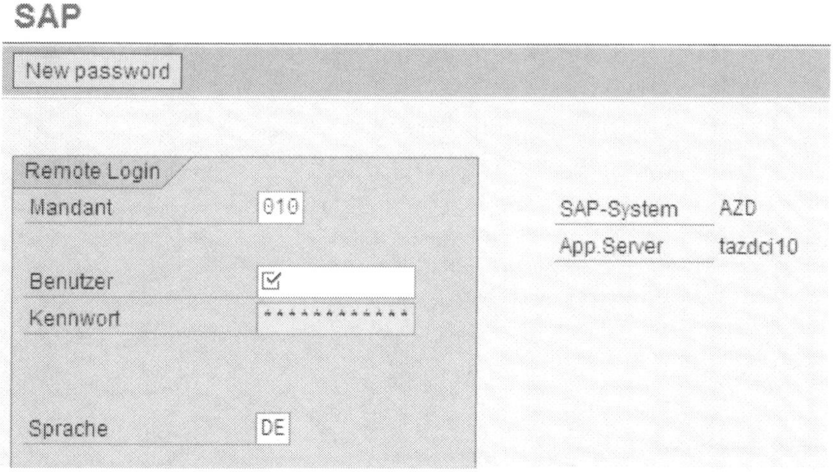

Figure 5.19 SAP remote login screen

Once get in to the remote system, one can view the detailed information about the queue.

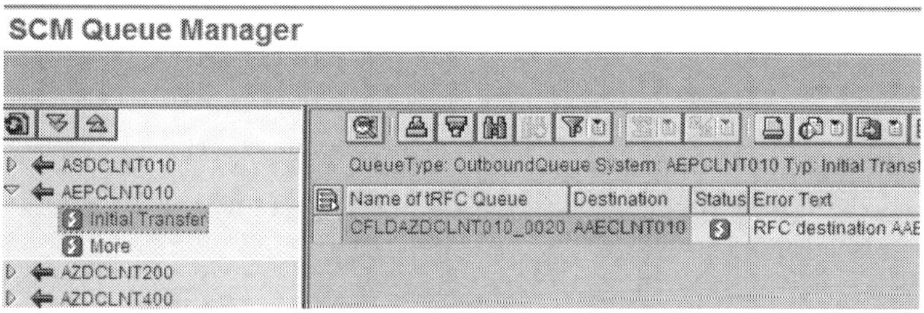

Figure 5.20 APO queue manager showing queues

In the SCM Queue Manager, transfer failures are indicated by red marks, whereas correct transfer channels have a green check mark. In this way, one can immediately recognize whether incorrect transfers exist. Any errors can be analyzed directly in the SCM Queue Manager and solved

CIF Cockpit

User or administrator can use the CIF cockpit to centrally monitor the data transfer between SAP APO system and all the connected SAP R/3 systems that takes place using SAP APO Core Interface (CIF).

The CIF Cockpit (*transaction code /SAPAPO/CC*) is a container for CIF background jobs, qRFC (remote function call, the CIF is a way of setting up remote function calls), CIF Comparison, etc.

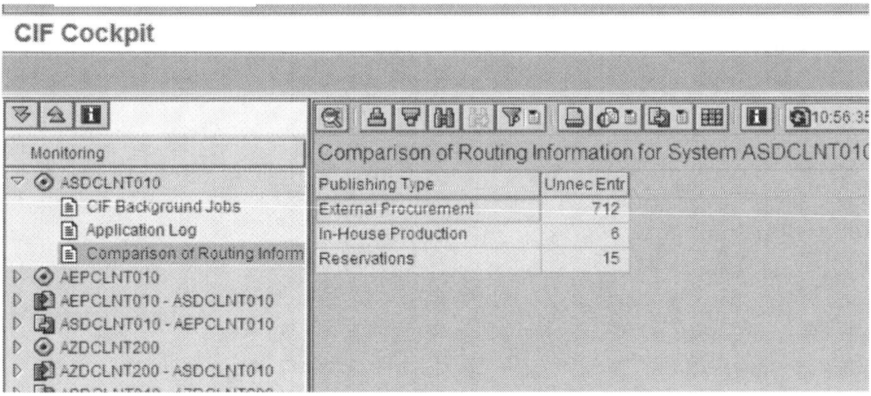

Figure 5.21 CIF cockpit

One can get a quick cross-system and cross-client overview of the following areas. Here one can find the following information:

- SAP APO system
- General information, for example, release
- CIF background jobs
- Entries in the application log
- Routing information
- SAPR/3 system
- General information
- CIF background jobs
- Entries in the application log
- Superfluous filter objects
- Inconsistent APO indicators
- Transfer from SAP APO system to SAP R/3 system
- CIF transfer
- qRFC
- Post Processing records
- CIF comparison/reconciliation of transaction data
- Transfer from SAP R/3 system to SAP APO system
- Comparison of routing information
- Integration model consistency
- Performance of each application

5.6.1 qRFC Alert for Error Processing in SAP SCM

The qRFC alert monitors all SAP SCM queues and the queues of the connected logical SAP R/3 systems. If there are queue errors or blocks, a message is generated from the status information and can be sent via SAP Office. All incorrect outbound queues are issued as a list.

5.7 CIF ERROR HANDLING

In earlier releases, qRFC errors could be a common problem, and this could lead to delays in recording critical information in either of the systems (serialization problems). As of SCM 4.0, organization can use new functionality called Post Processing. This new functionality will allows skipping the failed LUW and creating a post processing record in order to allow other LUWs to be recorded.

As a result of using post processing records the errors will disappear from the qRFC monitor and the qRFC alert. They will no longer be visible from *transactions code SMQ1 and SMQ2.*

The post processing functionality currently has some restrictions, and therefore, will not work with all data transfers. In SCM 4.0 post processing has the following restriction and therefore does not apply in the following situations:

- During initial loads
- Master data loads
- BAPI integration
- In the case of ABAP dumps or when LiveCache is not available
- If an object is locked in the target system, the entire LUW is flagged as a SYSFAIL, and will need to be monitored via the normal methods.
- Industry specific solutions
- TPVS: changes from SAP SCM to SAP R/3
- Descriptive Characteristics: transfer from SAP R/3 to SAP SCM, post processing is deactivated automatically
- Quota Arrangements: after transfer of errors with order related goods movements have occurred, the quota-allocated quantities of the corresponding sources of supply are not updated in SAP SCM.
- Planned independent requirements transfer between SAP SCM and SAP R/3.

If errors occur during the transfer from SAP R/3 to SAP SCM, CIF error handling ensures that serialization is avoided. If errors still occurs in the target system when the data is re-transferred from SAP R/3 to SAP SCM, serialization is again avoided. For new transfers, the sequence of RFCs (that is, the block formation) must be the same as in the qRFC LUW of the original transfer. This requirement leads to the following system behavior:

- Object for which a post processing record already exists to SAP SCM, but not from CIF post processing.

If the transfer proceeds without errors, the object is posted to the target system. The post processing record that already exists continues to exist and its processing status does not change if an error occurs in the transfer, a new post processing record is generated. The post processing record that already exists continues to exist and its processing status does not change.

When re-transfers occur from SAP SCM to SAP R/3, in this case, block formation can occur arbitrarily. This leads to the following system behavior:

- Object for which a post processing record already exists to SAP R/3, but not from CIF post processing. If the transfer proceeds without errors, the object is posted in the target system and the existing post processing record receives the status Obsolete (automatically set by system). If an error occurs in the transfer, a new post processing record is generated. The post processing record that already exists receives the status Obsolete (automatically set by system).

To support the new post processing functionality SAP has introduced 5 new transactions:

- /SAPAPO/CPP - CIF Post Processing (individual records)
- /SAPAPO/CPP1 - CIF Post processing (multiple records)
- /SAPAPO/CPP2 - CIF Post processing (display records)
- /SAPAPO/CPPR - CIF Post processing (archive records)
- /SAPAPO/CPPA - CIF Error Handling (alerts)

Post processing records that have been processed or that are set as obsolete are not deleted automatically by the system. To delete them, use *program /SAPAPO/ CIF_POSTPROC_REORG*. Only post processing records with the status Processed, Obsolete (set manually), or Obsolete (set automatically by system) can be deleted. To delete post processing records with the status *"Still to be processed"*, use this program to set them as obsolete and then can be deleted in a subsequent program run.

The reorganization program offers the following features:

Set post processing records as obsolete If need to set the set post processing records as Obsolete indicator, all post processing records that meet the selection criteria, have the processing status *"Still to be processed"*, and that are older than the specified number of days are assigned the status Obsolete (set manually).

Delete post processing records. Choose between two alternatives

If indicators to delete post processing records is set and to delete all post processing older records, than the system deletes all post processing records that meet the selection criteria and for which the status was set to Processed, Obsolete (set automatically by system), or Obsolete (set manually) in the time frame specified. The standard setting is 7 days.

Use the CIF post processing alert (*program /SAPAPO/CIF_POST- PROC_ALERT*) to check whether post processing records were generated during CIF error handling. One can also use it to specify that the originator of an error or the system administrator should receive a message when errors occur. This makes it easier to monitor the change transfer for transaction data.

From a technical perspective, in APO in most cases a lock collision will occur in LiveCache. Each transaction has to acquire a LiveCache lock for each object which has to be changed or deleted by that transaction. The LiveCache locks are by some means similar to conventional database locks. Most planning runs and CIF-updates are running in a so-called "*transactional simulation*". Changes are done provisionally within such a transactional simulation in LiveCache. Within a transactional simulation lock collisions can not occur, i.e. several parallel transactions can change an object simultaneously. After all appropriate changes are done the application program triggers a "*merge*" of the transactional simulation. This step merges all provisional changes performed within the transactional simulation into the operative data. To do so, the merge has to acquire a LiveCache lock for each object which has to be changed or deleted within that merge. The merge acquires all LiveCache locks right at the beginning of the merge. If one or several objects are locked by parallel transactions (usually by parallel merges) the merge will wait up to 20 seconds for these locks. If all needed locks are released within that time the merge starts to update, delete or create LiveCache objects as they have been updated, deleted or created during the transactional simulation. If the merge can not acquire all needed locks it terminates and returns an error to the calling application (CIF or a planning run or any other APO transaction.) Instead of merging a transactional simulation alternatively it could also be deleted. In that case all changes during the transactional simulation are discarded.

If a merge runs into a lock collision then the merge could be re-started (several times) as part of a retry-logic, as implemented in CIF, for instance. If after several retries the merge still can not acquire all locks the entry will remain in the CIF queue showing an error.

Planning runs usually do not have such a retry-logic. If the merge of a planning run can not acquire all needed locks the planning run might terminate completely or it might skip one object (like a product-location combination) and it will report an error.

5.8 CIF DEBUGGING

5.8.1 How to Debug APO Processing in ATP Checks

The ATP code is started in R/3 but processed in APO. If one places a breakpoint in APO with his user, debugging won't work because in APO the execution is done with the communications service user.

Place breakpoint before the call to the APO ATP function. The function name is *BAPI_APOATP_CHECK* and the call is in program *SAPLATPC*. Just search this program for the function and place a breakpoint in the call for the release of APO (or just put a breakpoint in each call). Then, when triggering the ATP in the sales order, the program stops in the BAPI. Step into the function and it will take the user into the debugging in the APO server.

5.8.2 Setting for Debug CIF Integration Models

To debug CIF integration models, setup required username in *transaction code CFC2*. Set the debug option to "*Debugging on and T/QRFC will only be recorded*".

Then, when integration models is executed, the transfer data will be kept in the queue and available for debugging with *transaction code SMQ1.*

In the next chapter also we will discuss about CIF, in that chapter we will also explore the enhancement of CIF.

6 CIF PROGRAMMING

6.1 CORE INTERFACE (CIF)

The *Core InterFace* (CIF) is the standard interface between R/3 and APO for the order related applications PPDS, SNP and ATP. On R/3 side the 'Plug-In' has to be implemented to use the CIF, on APO side it is always included.

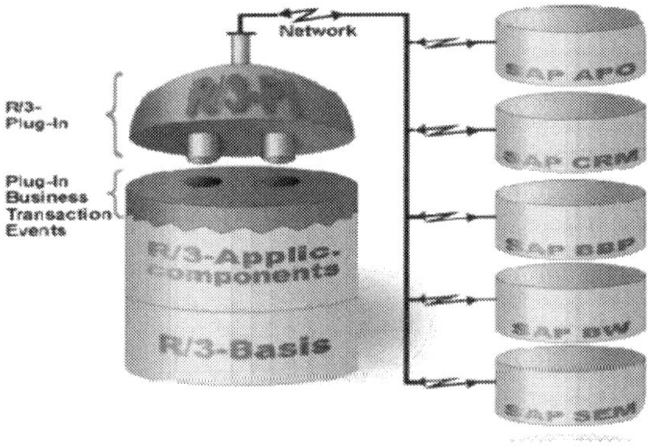

Figure 6.1 CIF plug-in at R/3 side and included in APO

6.1.1 CIF Data Transfer Technology

Data transferred in both directions (from R/3 to APO as well as from APO to R/3) by means of one or more queued Remote Function Calls (qRFC).

The function calls are buffered in the sending system and executed asynchronously in the same sequence they were called. This serialization is controlled by the use of identical queue names and is required to assure consistency.

Multiple qRFCs can be combined into a logical unit of work (LUW), whereby one LUW on the sender side results in one LUW on the receiver side.

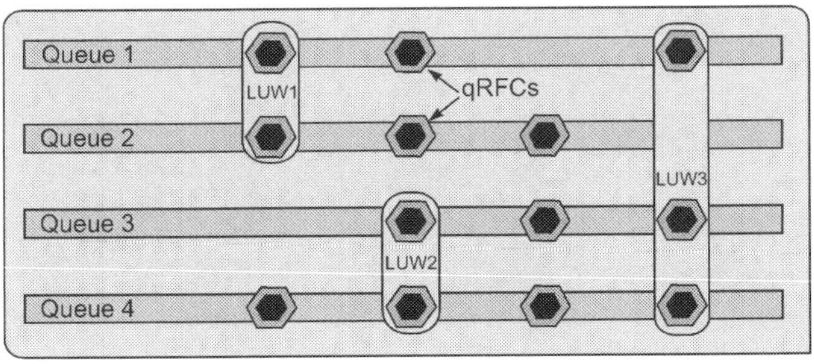

Figure 6.2 CIF qRFC with LUW

6.2 COMMUNICATION METHOD OF CIF QUEUE

The Communication Method of CIF Queue can be Inbound or Outbound which we have discussed in previous chapter also, here exploring more on that:

- With Outbound Queue
  - Calling system sends queues to target system without considering system load of receiving system.
  - No scheduling of the LUW processes take place in the target system
  - Results in overloading of receiving system and CIF performance deterioration with high data volume
- With Inbound Queue
  - Calling system sends queues to the "entrance" (inbound) of target system allowing the receiving system to control system queue load.
  - Scheduling of the LUW processes happen in receiving system
  - Results in better CIF performance even with high data volume

6.3 CHARACTERISTICS OF CIF

- Real-time interface and it guarantees data consistency in both the systems
- Communication layer to be applied to ECC to enable an exchange of data between SAP APO and R/3
- APO Core Interface connects APO to one or more R/3 or ECC systems
- CIF guarantees the Master/Transaction Data, data changes within SCM
- CIF has its own configuration transaction – *PIMG* along with *SPRO*
- Consists of set of transactions and programs for:
  - Interface definition
  - Data transfer
  - Data reconciliation and
  - Problem analysis and resolution
- CIF uses queuing system (like other middleware products) and comes with a consistency checking transaction that allows for the monitoring and analysis of the transfer

- In order to integrate two systems together, data mapping must take place. Data mapping includes matching up table/structure names and field names between systems. CIF Integration Models provide automatic data mapping between R/3 objects and the corresponding objects in APO.
- APO CIF is the communication layer to be applied to R/3 to enable integration of R/3 system with APO system. There is a similar communication layer which comes as a standard function in APO
- The basic idea of the integration is to write events for each planning relevant change e.g. the creation of an order and use these as trigger for the transfer. Technically the transfer is performed via qRFC. Which objects (i.e. planned orders, stock, etc.) are transferred is controlled by the integration models, which could be regarded as something like the master data of the CIF.
- In absence of standard interface for non SAP OLTP systems, custom development based on BAPIs/RFCs or ALE required to be developed. The development is in ABAP only.
- CIF Integration Models are used to transfer data from R/3 to APO. Integration Models used for
    - Initial data transfer
    - Changes (delta) transfer

6.4 WHY CIF

- APO is a separate system to SAP R/3
    - APO has been designed to work with SAP R/3 as well as other OLTP systems
    - APO has different hardware requirements compared to SAP ERP
    - CIF is tightly coupled between APO and R/3 system

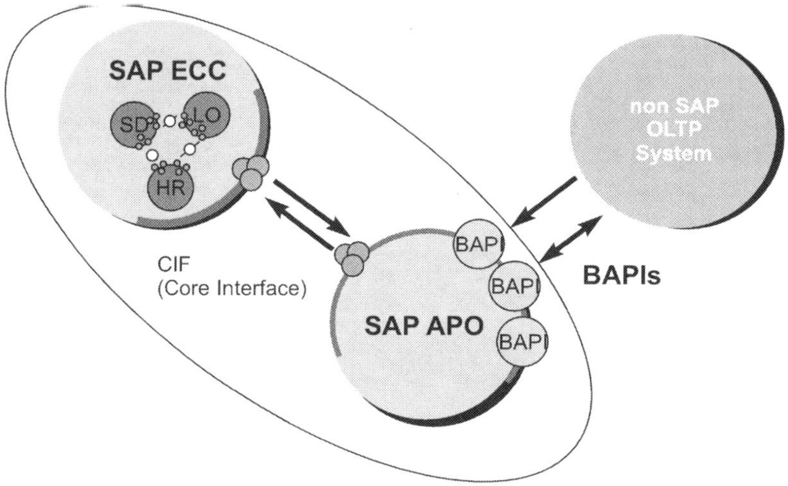

Figure 6.3 CIF integration with SAP APO

- No need to create custom interface, CIF is closely coupled with APO and a pre ready interface is already available in R/3 and APO.
  - Despite being separate systems, ECC and APO are commonly used together. SAP has therefore provided CIF as standard functionality

  The main roles of CIF are:
  - Initially supply APO with master and transactional data
  - Incrementally keep on supplying APO with transactional data, which we achieve using change pointers
  - Return planning results to R/3 system

6.5 IMPORTANT TRANSACTIONS IN R/3 TO SETUP CIF

CIF setup is described in detail in Chapter 5 as it is more over a configuration part

- Initial Mandatory Setup
  - Define Logical System — BD54
  - Assign Logical System to Client — SCC4
  - Specify SAP SCM Release — NDV2
  - Setup RFC Destination — SM59
  - Assign RFC Destination to app. cases — CFC7
- Additionally
  - Set Target System and Queue Type — CFC1
  - Set User Parameters — CFC2
  - Define Filter and Selection Block Size — CFC3
  - Determine no. Ranges for Parallelization — CFC8
  - Target-System-Independent Settings — CFC9

6.6 IMPORTANT TRANSACTIONS IN APO TO SETUP CIF

- Initial Mandatory Setup
  - Define Logical System — BD54
  - Assign Logical System to Client — SCC4
  - Setup RFC Destination — SM59
  - Assign RFC Destination to app. cases — CFC7
  - Maintain Business System Group (BSG) — /SAPAPO/C1
  - Assign LS to BSG and Queue Type — /SAPAPO/C2
- Additionally
  - Maintain Distribution Definition — /SAPAPO/CP2
  - Maintain Object-specific Setting — SPRO
  - Initiate Transfer of collected changes — /SAPAPO/C5
  - CIF Logging — /SAPAPO/C4

6.6.1 CIF Monitoring Transactions

- Monitor queues for queue blockages to keep ECC and APO data consistent
- On R/3 side
  - qRFC Monitor (*Transaction code CFQ1*)
  - Application Log (*Transaction code CFG1*)
- On APO side
  - qRFC Monitor (*Transaction code SMQ1*)
  - Application Log (*Transaction code /SAPAPO/C3*)
- Monitoring both centrally from within APO
  - SCM Queue Manager (*Transaction code /SAPAPO/CQ*)
  - qRFC Alert (*Transaction code /SAPAPO/CW*)
- In *transaction code SMQ2* (R/3 and APO) when Inbound Processing is activated:
  - See Inbound queues
  - Display queue entries (known as LUWs) and contents
  - Activate queues
  - Delete queues
  - Lock queues
  - Debug queues
- Use *transaction code SMQ1* in case Outbound Processing is activated

6.7 DATA-OBJECT-WISE QUEUE NAMING STANDARDS

• Initial supply	CF_ADC_LOAD
• Stock	CFSTK*
• Purchase orders and purchase requisition	CFPO*
• Planned orders/Production orders	CFPLO*
• Sales orders	CFSLS*
• Manual reservations	CFRSV*
• Confirmations	CFCNF*
• Planned independent requirement	CFPIR*
• Materials	CFMAT*
• Production campaigns	CFPCM*
• Master data for classes	CFCLA*
• Master data for characteristics	CFCHR*

6.8 CONSISTENCY BETWEEN APO AND LiveCache

- Although not directly related to CIF, consistency of data between APO database and LiveCache requires monitoring

- *Transaction code /SAPAPO/OM17* can be used to check for and resolve inconsistencies
- This activity should be carried out with users locked (no planning), no background consistency check is carried out and CIF activities are stopped.

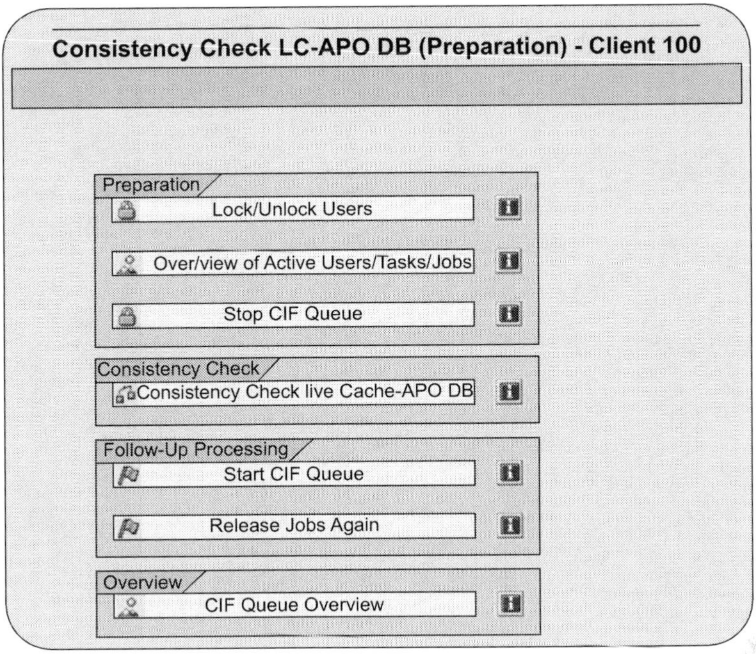

Figure 6.4 CIF consistency check

Steps to Follow – Data Transfer from R/3 to APO

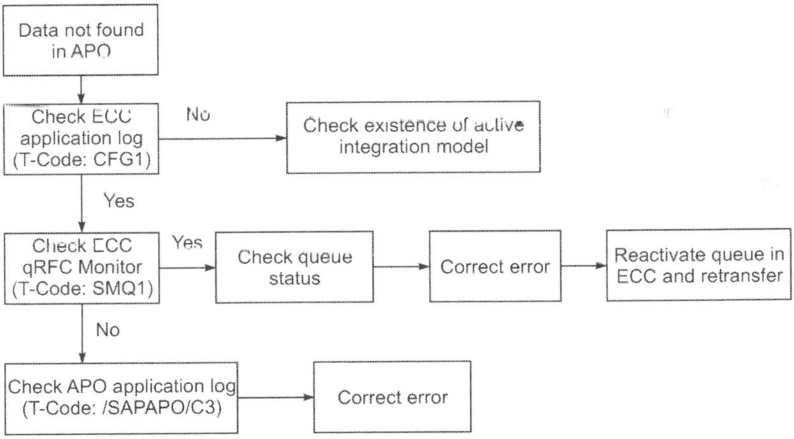

Figure 6.5 Data consistency check steps from R/3 to APO

Steps to Follow – Data Transfer from APO to R/3

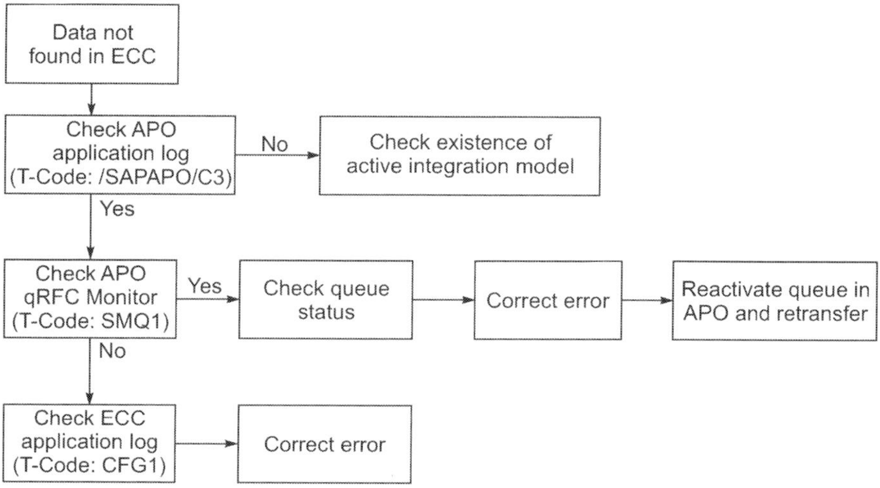

Figure 6.6 Data consistency check steps from APO to R/3

6.9 CIF ENHANCEMENTS OVERVIEW

CIF Enhancements are located in R/3 Customizing under

- *Integration with Other SAP Components → Advanced Planning and Optimization → Application-Specific Settings and Enhancements → Settings and Enhancements for In-House Production.Overview*

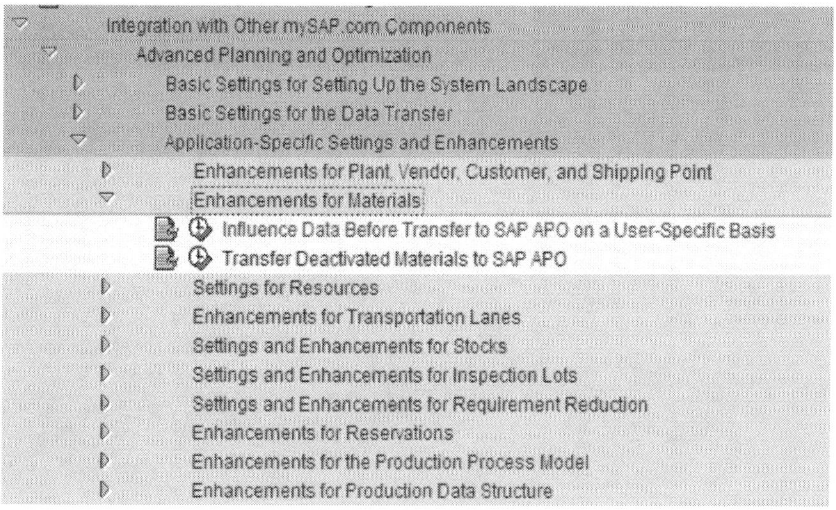

Figure 6.7 IMG for CIF enhancement

6.9.1 Incremental Data Transfer – ALE Change Pointers

The process of incremental data transfer reverts to the ALE change pointer. This change pointer selects the master data for the system to retransfer. When call up the transaction Incremental data transfer of master data (*Transaction code CFP1*), specify the logical target systems and the master data objects (material masters, vendors, sources of supply, customers), that have changes to be transferred.

Change pointers are used by the ALE message distribution. Changes to Master Data are recorded and given a change number (if they are in an active message type).

- Transaction BDCP
  - CIF Message types must be activated for change recording. *Transaction code BD50*
  - Activate Change Pointers. *Transaction code BD61*
  - The fields relevant to a message type to be selected. *Transaction code BD52*

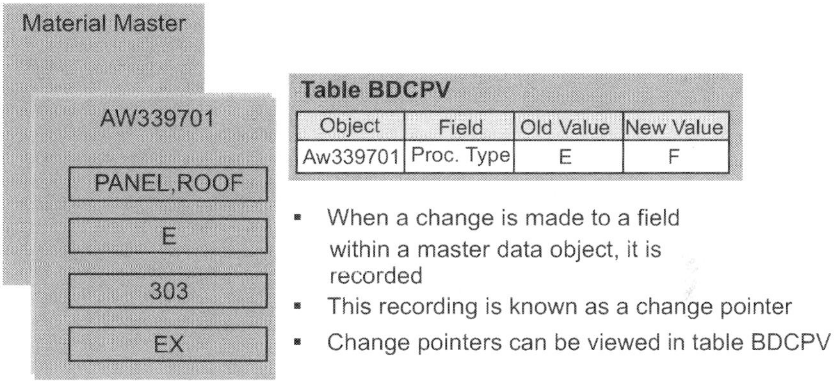

Figure 6.8 Change pointer concept

6.9.2 Processing Change Pointers

- *Transaction code CFP1* or *report RCPTRAN4* is run for
  - Material Masters
  - Vendors
  - Customers
  - Work Centres (if not immediate transfer)
- Change pointers are scanned

Table BDCPV

Object	Field	Old Value	New Value
AW339701	Proc. Type	E	F

Integration Model	Active	Data Object
MD_MAT NV (19/2/05)	X	AW338699
MD_MAT NV (19/2/05)	X	AW339701
MD_MAT NV (18/2/05)		AW339701

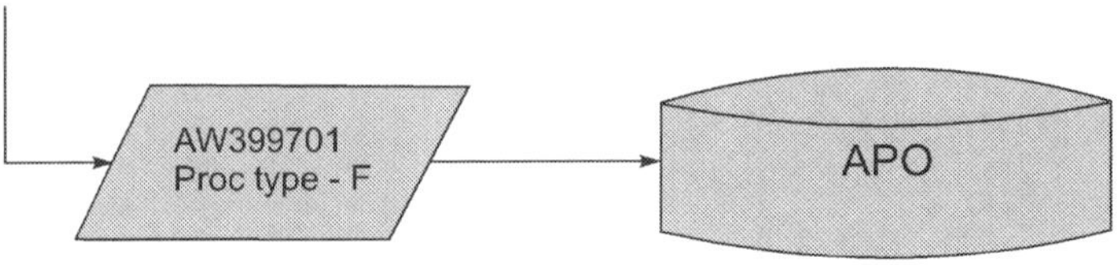

Figure 6.9 Change pointers old and new value comparison

- Check object for change pointer is in an active Integration Model
- Transfer corresponding Master Data change to APO

6.10 SYSTEM ADMINISTRATION RELATED TO THE APO CIF

6.10.1 Monitoring Activities

To optimize the performance of the data transfer between the APO and the connected R/3 OLTP systems and to prevent gathering of useless data in the systems, several reorganization jobs must be scheduled to run regularly.

6.10.2 Administration Jobs Related to Data Transfer (R/3)

To optimize the performance of the data transfer and monitoring, certain jobs must be scheduled on a regular basis in the R/3 system. These jobs are:

- **Delete application log** with *report RDELALOG*. If writing of application logs is enabled (R/3 *transaction code CFC2* or APO *transactions code /SAPAPO/C4 or /SAPAPO/C41*) – and this should be done in a production system for certain users and for problem analysis only – old logs must be deleted regularly. The job should run daily and delete logs older than 7 days.
- **Delete ALE change pointers** with *report RBDCPCLR*. If changes to master data are transferred periodically via ALE (as it is recommended), processed change pointers must be deleted regularly. After completing this, if the database

system on the R/3 side is Oracle, run *report RBDCPIDXRE* to reorganize the Oracle indexes on tables BDCP and BCDPS.

- **Delete old integration model versions** with *report RIMODDEL*. Every time an integration model is generated, a new version is created, distinguished by a timestamp. The old version is deactivated and the new one is activated. Old versions must be deleted regularly.

6.10.3 Administration Jobs Related to Data Transfer (APO)

To optimize the performance of the data transfer and monitoring, certain jobs must be scheduled on a regular basis in the APO system. These jobs are:

- **Delete application log** with *report /SAPAPO/RDELLOG*. Same as *report RDELALOG* in R/3.
- **Check processing of APO change pointers** with *report /SAPAPO/RDMCPPROCESS*. To verify that all change pointers created are processed, after publishing of planning results to R/3 run *report /SAPAPO/RDMCPPROCESS* without restricting the selection of orders and confirm that message "No change pointers were selected" is displayed. If change pointers remain unprocessed, contact the application support team to clarify whether these change pointers are necessary and why they are not processed.

  Deleting change pointers may cause inconsistencies, as the corresponding order changes are not transferred to R/3.
- **Deletion of R/3 data that are no longer required in APO** with *report /SAPAPO/SDORDER_DEL*. In SAP APO database tables, the tables expand with data from SAP R/3 documents. However, this data is no longer required; no corresponding information exists in LiveCache. In addition, the performance of the initial data supply or of other transfer processes with a huge data volume is affected negatively. The obsolete records need to be deleted regularly to control the size of certain tables (e.g. /SAPAPO/SDFIELD and /SAPAPO/POSMAPN) and to improve the performance of the Sales order updates on SAP APO side.

6.10.4 Administration Jobs Related to CIF Error Handling (APO)

The following is only valid as of SCM release 4.0:

Certain jobs must be scheduled on a regular basis in the APO system in order to optimize the performance of the data transfer and monitoring. These jobs are:

- **Delete old results of CIF delta report** with *report /SAPAPO/CIF_DELTAREPORT3_REORG*. As it is now possible to save the results of a Delta report run, it is necessary to delete outdated results from the database. The spool list from this report contains the number of records deleted.

- **Delete post-processing records** with *report /SAPAPO/CIF_POSTPROC_REORG*. Processed and obsolete post-processing records are no longer required and should be deleted. This report is used to do so. Non-deletion of these records will have an increasingly negative impact on CIF performance over the time. The deletion is a two-step process. Step first, run on outdated records that meet the selection criteria with the status *still to be processed* are set to status *obsolete (set manually)*. Step second, run on all processed and all obsolete records are deleted.

6.11 CIF ENHANCEMENT

To explain the programming in CIF, I will elaborate the concept using some examples, let me brief you first with the concept.

Within *transaction code /SAPAPO/MAT1* in APO there is a tab called 'Extra' where one can maintain the additional parameters to be passed from R/3. One can maintain the field description by going to

SPRO -> Advanced Planning and Optimization -> Master Data -> Maintain Freely Defined Fields.

Here one can see the other extra fields available in *transaction code /SAPAPO/MAT1*.

6.11.1 R/3 Outbound-APO Inbound Master Data Integration Models

One can modify/manipulate the master data sent from R/3 to APO either on the R/3 outbound (if want to capture some additional fields stored in R/3 tables) side before it gets to APO or on the inbound APO side (if want to capture some additional fields stored in APO tables) before it is saved to APO Product Master fields.

One can modify the Material Master data in R/3 before it is sent to APO in *Enhancement: CIFMAT01 (transaction SMOD in R/3).*

Function Module EXIT_SAPLCMAT_001

Include ZXCIFU01.

One can modify the Material Master data in APO before it stored in Product master via

Enhancement: APOCF005 (transaction SMOD in APO)

Function Module EXIT_/SAPAPO/SAPLCIF_PROD_001

Include ZXCIFUSERU08.

Additional Details

This user exit is used in Inbound Product integration model to control which fields on the product master are updated Value of space means field is not updated, value of 'X' means field is updated.

To prevent a field at material level from being updated, find the field name in table it_matkey then clear the corresponding flag for the field's name in it_matkeyx, missing the steps might results the not proper functioning of the requirement of the organization.

To prevent a field at material/location level from being updated, find the field names in it_matloc then clear the corresponding flag for the field's name in it_matlocx.

EXAMPLE 1

Requirement: Block transfer of the data to APO for those fields maintained in R/3 that are specified in the custom table.

Solution

To block the transfer of the field data we have to create an enhancement at R/3 side

- Enhancement - CIFMAT01
- Function Module - EXIT_SAPLCMAT_001
- Include - ZXCIFU01

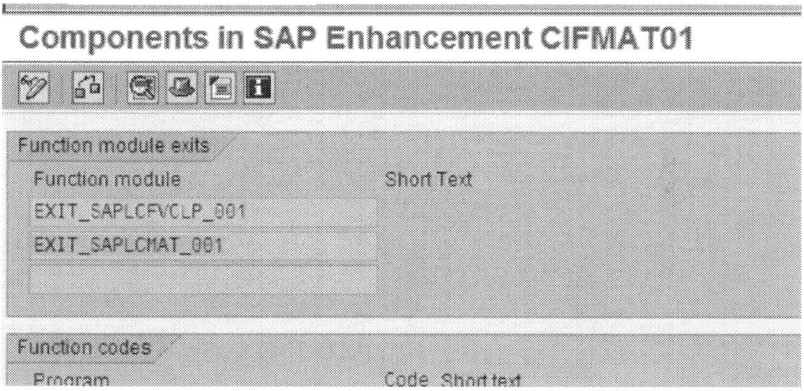

Figure 6.10 Change pointers old and new value comparison

This enhancement will stop the transfer to APO for certain fields from material master. The fields to stop/default transfer from R/3 to APO will be maintained in custom table in R/3 environment. The other changes will still transfer from R/3 to APO except the fields that are maintained in the custom table. This way the safety stock method will not be overwritten from R/3.

To Block the data during CIF, clear the field contents will overwrite the APO field data with blank values hence extension tables has to be replaced with space instead of 'X'.

Create Custom Table to maintain CIF Block fields 'ZXXXXXX' and create table maintenance.

loop the extension table (CT_CIF_MATKEYX, CT_CIF_MATLOCX, CT_CIF_MARMX, CT_CIF_MATTXTX, CT_CIF_MATVRX) if entry exists in 'ZXXXXXX'.

6.11.2 Remove 'X' from Extension Table

Sample code to block the field data transfer to APO.

```
DATA : li_cif    TYPE STANDARD TABLE OF zcif_XXXX    INITIAL
                 SIZE 0,
       lw_cif    TYPE zcif_XXXX.

* Field Symbol declaration
FIELD-SYMBOLS: <fs_cif_matlcx> TYPE cif_matlcx.

* Select the fields from the custom table
* As all fields are required hence select * is used
SELECT * INTO TABLE li_cif FROM zcif_XXXX.

LOOP AT li_cif INTO lw_cif.
   CASE LW_CIF-TBL_NM.
    WHEN 'CT_CIF_MATLOCX'.
       LOOP AT ct_cif_matlocx ASSIGNING <fs_cif_matlcx>.
        ASSIGN COMPONENT lw_cif-trg_field OF STRUCTURE
          <fs_cif_matlcx> TO <fs_field>.
        IF <fs_field> IS ASSIGNED.
            CLEAR <fs_field>.
            ENDIF.
        ENDLOOP.
       ENDCASE.
    ENDLOOP.
```

Same way loop all the CIF extension table.

EXAMPLE 2

R/3 remains the leading system for master data maintenance and sourcing. The update of the validity and generation of new procurement relationships in APO takes place via CIF. Therefore all required modifications on the procurement master data as such need to be implemented in the appropriate CIF user exit. The duration of validity of Sources of Supply is determined from the source list in R/3 and is reflected in APO in the particular procurement relationship.

Solution

During the activation of the Integration Model for Material Master field ZFIELD1_XXXX in table MARC is read and the corresponding Lead-Time value is written into field AT105 (additional Product-Attributes) in APO. *Function Module EXIT_SAPLCMAT_001* provides this functionality.

Also additional Material Master fields will be sent from MARC to APO Product Location Master table /SAPAPO/MATLOC, as will some standard fields in non-standard mappings, using this Function Module.

In R/3 custom include CI_MTLCCUS will be created to add field ZFIELD1_XXXX to contain the corresponding MARC data. This field will be filled in the include of the function module during CIF outbound processing. With BD52 we add the field marc-ZFIELD1_XXXX to create change pointer for t_mat.

Stepwise Details Process to Transfer Additional Data from R/3 to APO

1. Add custom include to MARC

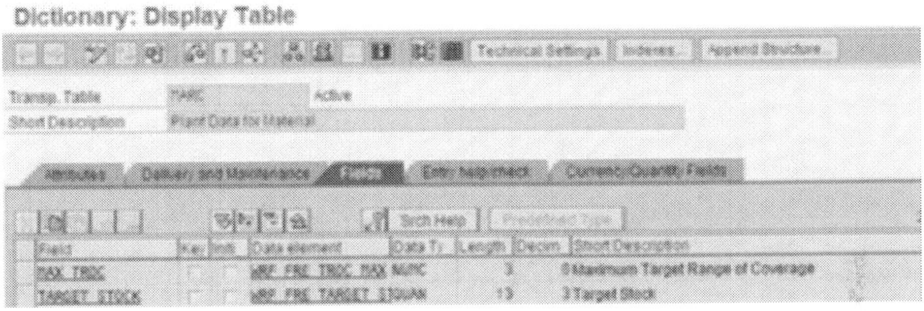

Figure 6.11 Append structure to standard table

2. Create Structure to add the fields to MARC table
3. Create Data Elements and Domain and add the fields to the newly created structure.
4. There are 2 ways to fill the data in the custom added fields in MARC
   (a) Add the field using screen enhancement or screen BADI implementation
   (b) Fill the fields from any specific report program of any other given logic

   Note: We are not covering the data filling to the fields as it is expected to know the terminologies here.
5. Create a project in *transaction code CMOD*
6. Implement the following user exit

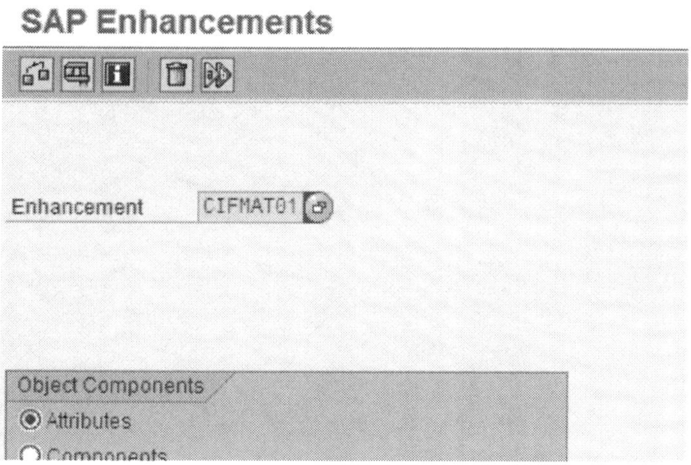

Figure 6.12 SAP enhancement - SMOD

- Enhancement - CIFMAT01
- Function Module - EXIT_SAPLCMAT_001
- Include - ZXCIFU01

7. In the include, write the following code (certain other checks and code should be written but I am not covering that here):

```
* Field Symbol declaration
FIELD-SYMBOLS: <fs_cif_matloc> TYPE cif_matloc.

LOOP AT ct_cif_matloc ASSIGNING <fs_cif_matloc>.
     <fs_cif_matloc>-AT105 = MARC-ZXXX.
ENDLOOP.
```

EXAMPLE 3

In some cases we need to pass some addition data to APO and that is not maintained in the standard tables like MARA/MARC. i.e. if we need to send some additional data from the custom table.

In this case as the CIF structures are mapped to standard table structures hence we need to enhance the structure of CIF. For the purpose SAP has provided 2 additional include structures to the CIFMAT01 enhancement where we can pas the additional data.

Before we CIF custom data to APO we need to decide where exactly this data should move in APO. One can move the data to APO custom table or to APO standard table.

If the data needs to be moved in APO custom table then creation of custom table should be done before and the data needs to be moved in standard table but in custom field then APO table needs to be enhanced first.

Here examples 1 and 2 contain the requirement of example 3 hence implementing both together make a solution for example 3.

6.11.3 Debugging CIF Inbound Processing User Exit

Debugging from R/3 to APO is required when one is CIFfing data from R/3 to APO and implemented used exits in APO side but not getting the desired results.

EXAMPLE 1

On user-exit *APOCF001* (Inbound processing: Location), if one have some problem in CIFfing the data. The data transfer from the source R/3 system to the destination APO system is triggered from this source R/3 system, while the user-exit is executed in the APO system. We need to debug the APO system but the triggering point is at R/3 side hence need to start debugging APO while into the R/3 system.

Solution

To debug CIF queues one need to set Debugging On, Recording of t/qRFCs (NOSENDS) for the CIF user id (whatever is the user id in RFC for transferring from R/3 to APO). The maintenance of this Debugging On is using *transaction code CFC2* in R/3 and *transaction code /SAPAPO/C4* in APO. Also mostly the CIF user id will be a system user—need to change it to Dialog user.

Then transfer location data through activation of integration model from R/3 to APO, the CIF queue should show up in *transaction code SMQ2*. Start debugging (/h) and then execute the CIF queue to get into the code.

Stepwise details process to debug the CIF queue from R/3 to APO

1. Maintain entries in *transaction code CFC2* and set the user as Debug = 'X' or 'R'.

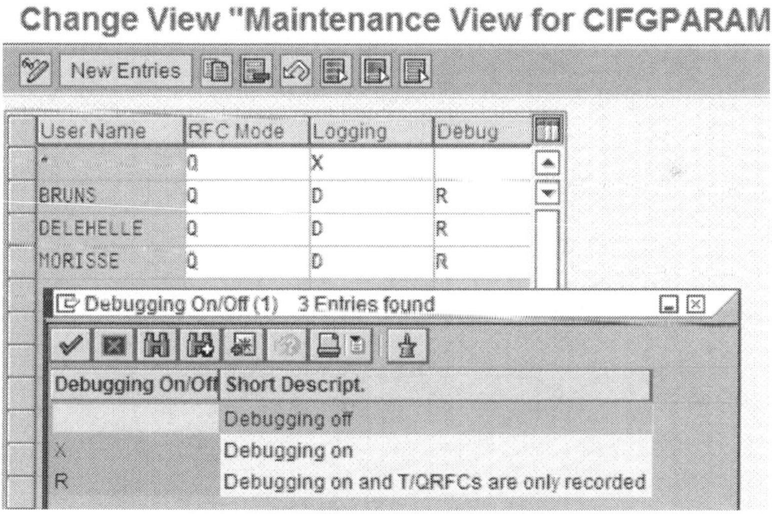

Figure 6.13 CIF – Debugging activation settings

2. Maintain the entries in *transaction code /SAPAPO/C4*, it will allow to debug APO system from R/3.

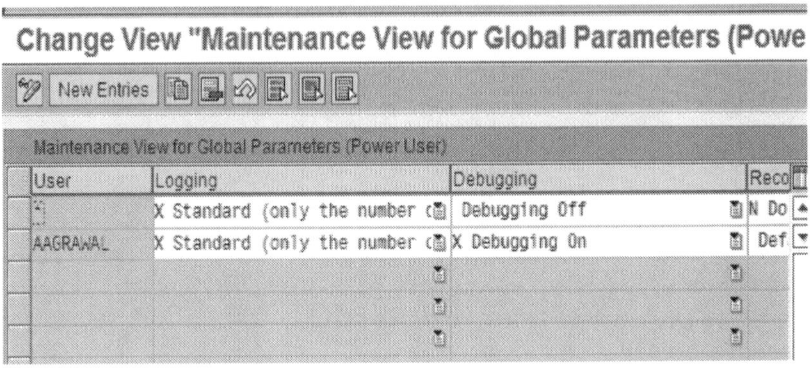

Figure 6.14 CIF – Debugging activation settings

6.11.4 How to Debug APO Processing done in ATP Checks

The ATP code is started in R/3 but runs in APO. If one places a breakpoint in APO with your user, debugging won't work because in APO the execution is done with the communications service user.

One must first place a breakpoint before the call to the APO ATP function. The function name is *BAPI_APOATP_CHECK* and the call is in program *SAPLATPC*. Just search this program for the function and place a breakpoint in the call for the release of APO (or just put a breakpoint in each call). Then, when triggering the ATP in the sales order, the program stops in the BAPI. Step into the function and the debugging in the APO server started.

6.11.5 How to Debug the CIF Integration Models without using Transaction Code CFC2

The function name in APO needs to be find out where this function is called in R/3. One can do it using one of the reports to search the source (*RPR_ABAP_SOURCE_SCAN, RSRSCAN1*) and place as a restriction the CIF function groups (to get this list search for the function groups with CIF in the description).

Place a breakpoint before in the function call. Then run the integration model and when the program stops, with another session, stop the CIF queues with function *TRFC_QOUT_STOP*. Then continue the execution. now go to the outbound queue (*transaction code SMQ1*) and run the function in debug mode.

6.11.6 CIF Comparison/Reconciliation

- When one performs CIF comparison/reconciliation of transaction data, it is recommended to already process the existing change pointers. In the result screen of the comparison one can see if change pointer still exist for individual inconsistency in the change pointer column. Until now one had to have found and processed the relevant change pointer in the transaction Publish Orders (*transaction code* /SAPAPO/C5).

To call the CIF comparison/reconciliation of transaction data, on the *SAP Easy Access* screen for *mySAP Supply Chain Management*, choose *Advanced Planning and Optimization → APO Administration → Integration → CIF Comparison/Reconciliation of Transaction Data → Execute Comparison/Reconciliation.*

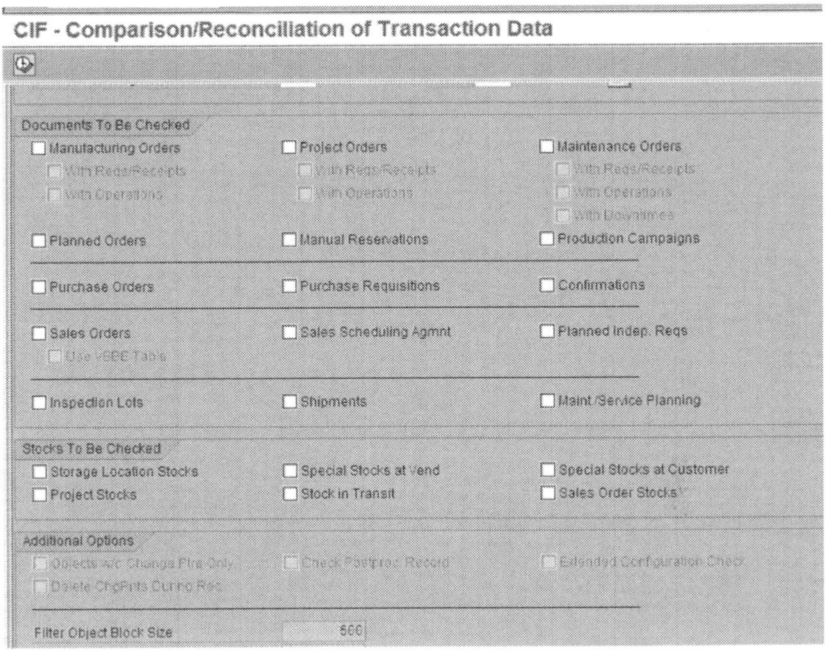

Figure 6.15 CIF – comparisons and reconciliation

Or use *transaction code - /SAPAPO/CCR*

These options will be activated once the profile in configuration is set using the transaction code.

- As of SCM 5.0 the change pointer push button is available to users in the result screen of the comparison. One can use this push button to directly process the change pointers. The system automatically deletes these change pointers after they have been processed. One can use this push button to delete the change pointers which are no longer relevant.
- If one rectify the inconsistency for which a change pointer exists using the comparison / reconciliation and not the change pointer push button, the change pointer remains although the inconsistency has been rectified. If one wants to make sure that the change pointer is deleted in this case also, set the deletion

of the change pointer during rectify indicator in the selection screen for the comparison/reconciliation. This indicator is not been set as default, user has to set this indicator manually.

6.11.7 Parallel Processing Option

- As of SCM 5.0, one can convert the data access for the CIF comparison/ reconciliation to parallel processing in the SAP APO system and R/3 system and can improve the performance which is one of the major point of consideration in processing huge volume of data.

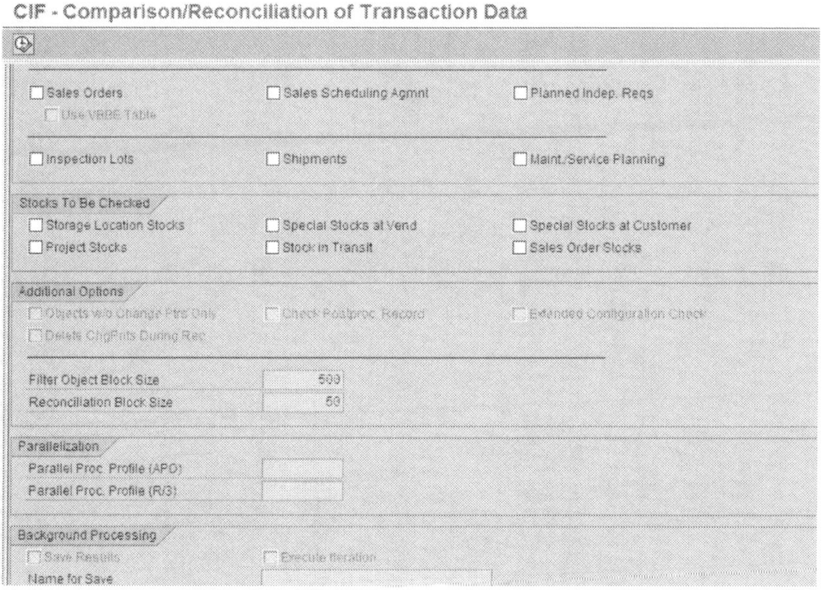

Figure 6.16 CIF – parallel processing settings

- Parallel processing is not activated by default.
- *Transaction code /SAPAPO/CCR_PAR* is used to define the parallel processing profile, this activity needs to be performed first.

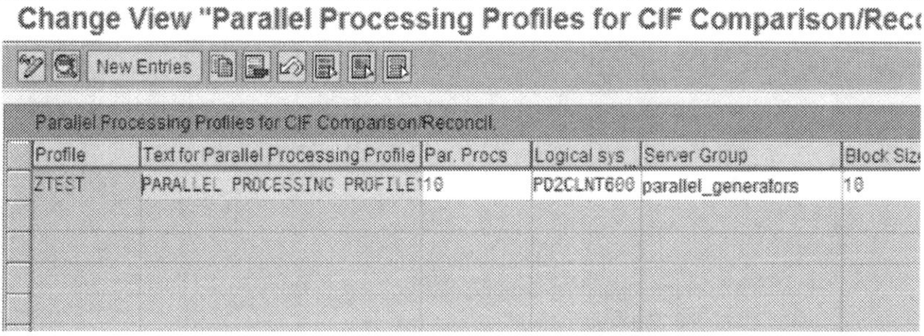

Figure 6.17 CIF – parallel processing profile

Parallelization for Production Data Structure (PDS) while transfer from R/3 to SCM is available in *transaction codes CFM2/CFM3*. This is to improve performance of PDS Master Data transfer.

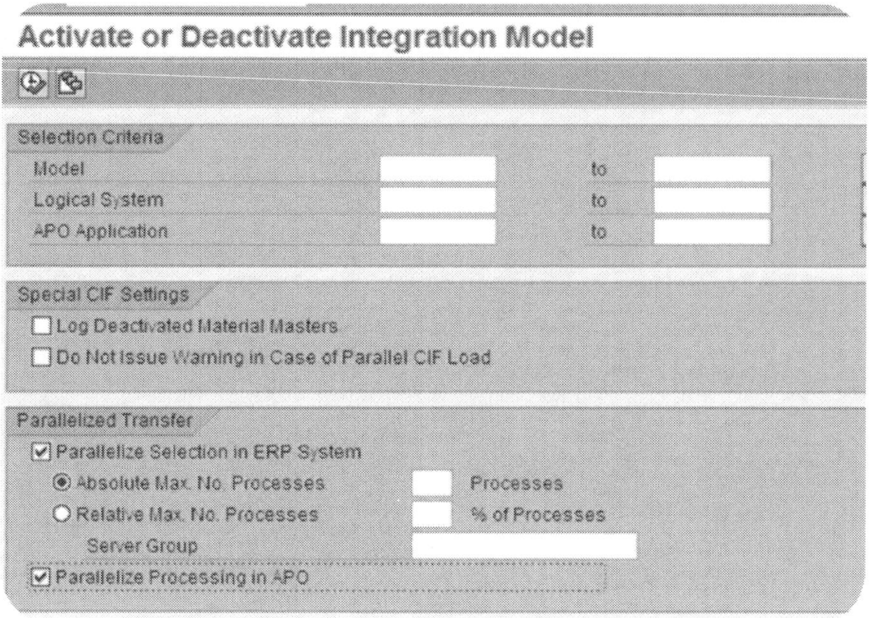

Figure 6.18 CIF – parallel processing setting

Some of the enhancement I am writing here with little explanation as covering all the enhancements will be very lengthy for this book.

Master Data Enhancements

- **APOCF001** - EXIT_/SAPAPO/SAPLCIF_LOC_001

  Inbound processing: Location
- **APOCF008** - EXIT_/SAPAPO/SAPLCIF_RES_001

  Inbound processing: Resource
- **APOCF005** - EXIT_/SAPAPO/SAPLCIF_PROD_001

  Inbound processing: Products
- **APOCF012** - EXIT_/SAPAPO/SAPLCIF_PPM_001

  Inbound processing: PPM

BAdI

PPDS PDS — /SAPAPO/CURTO_CREATE

SNP PDS — /SAPAPO/CURTO_SNP

/SAPAPO/CL_EX_CIF_IP

To control if and when the activity dates planned in SAP APO should be rescheduled, or if a change to the order quantity in SAP R/3 leads to a proportional change to receipt and requirement quantities.

6.11.8 Transaction Data Exits—SAP APO

- **APOCF032** - EXIT_/SAPAPO/SAPLCIF_TPSRC_001
  Inbound processing: Source of supply
- **APOCF011** - EXIT_/SAPAPO/SAPLCIF_STOCK_001
  Inbound processing: Stock
- **APOCF004** - EXIT_/SAPAPO/SAPLCIF_ORD_001
  Inbound processing: Production orders and planned orders
- **APOCF013** - EXIT_/SAPAPO/SAPLCIF_ORD_002
  Outbound processing: Production orders and planned orders
- **APOCF006** - EXIT_/SAPAPO/SAPLCIF_PU_001
  Inbound processing: Purchase order documents
- **APOCF010** - EXIT_/SAPAPO/SAPLCIF_SLS_001
  Inbound processing: Sales and distribution document

6.11.9 SAP R/3 Exits

Customer exits in SAP R/3 for the publication types:

- **CIFORD03** - To change orders that are transferred from SAP APO to SAP R/3 in R/3 inbound queue
- **CIFORD01** - Change Object Type and Order Data, Exit is used to change order data that is transferred from SAP APO to SAP R/3 and is already in SAP R/3 format in R/3 inbound queue
- **PPAPO002** - To influence the data that was transferred from SAP APO to SAP R/3 for a manufacturing order before it is transferred to the SAP R/3 manufacturing order
- **PPAPO008** - To manually influence the order type of a manufacturing order generated by conversion from SAP APO (customer exit EXIT_SAPLCOXT_002)
- **PPAPO004** - To force the re-explosion of a BOM (customer exit EXIT_SAPLCOXT_001)
- **PPAPO009** - To run own checks when components are added to a manufacturing order from SAP APO
- **PPAPO007** - To override checkbox fields for manufacturing orders on transfer from SAP APO to SAP R/3

- **CIFPUR01** - To change purchasing data from purchase requisitions, POs, scheduling agreement schedule lines (OLTP scheduling agreement), and confirmations/shipping notifications (for SAP APO and OLTP scheduling agreements)
- **CIFPUR02** - To change PO data from SAP APO before a purchase requisition, scheduling agreement schedule line, or a PO is created in the OLTP system

6.11.10 Additional Exits

Customer exits for orders and manufacturing orders in SAP APO.

- **APOCF020** - User-specific fields in the order interface (after posting in SAP LiveCache or to the database)
- **APOCFPIP** - Publication of in-house production orders (planned orders, manufacturing orders)

I insist users should explore more enhancements in CIF, it will give experience and confidence to handle difficult situations.

7 PROGRAMMING USING LiveCache

7.1 LiveCache

Planning and decision making for a organization's supply chain—from determining when the supplier should send or to create a detailed, long-term production schedule—involves analyzing large volume of data from the own business processes and from the partners along with the supply chain. In contrast to typical ERP data models, the demands on such planning systems require models designed to process large data in near real time.

Thus organizations often find themselves in a data-processing dilemma: for any tough planning solution to achieve acceptable performance under these circumstances, processing must be done timely where even the data volume is large. To get another performance boost, processing must be done on main memory. The first paradigm omits extra network round trips, the second one avoids unnecessary disk access. And then, of course, efficient backup and recovery of this critical data is key.

MySAP.com Supply Chain Management (SCM) offers a way out of this dilemma: SAP APO (SAP Advanced Planner and Optimizer) with *SAP LiveCache*. SAP APO increases the speed of transactions for supply chain planning many times over. Now, with the newest version of SAP LiveCache and SAP APO, SAP clients will continue to see high performance and availability, but will also find simpler and more powerful tools for full point-of-failure recovery of planning data.

7.2 HIGH PERFORMANCE AND UNIQUE POINT-OF-FAILURE RECOVERY

SAP APO offers planning functionality for strategic, tactical, and operational planning of supply chains. Combined with SAP LiveCache, it helps SAP customers respond to the data-processing challenges of supply chain planning.

Designed to improve the flow of information, SAP APO offers real-time and collaborative decision processes, advanced planning and optimization as part of the SAP system to cover long-term and short-term planning issues, such as supply network planning, demand planning, and production planning. SAP APO pulls data out of mySAP.com SCM solution and other applications and transforms and stores it to its own object-based and network-based data model, with its own representation in the database server. The system can either work off the SAP APO database server for more basic planning data, or off SAP LiveCache for high-performance, high-memory planning issues. Application servers can also handle multiple connections to the different databases (described in figure), meaning that multiple processes and applications can connect simultaneously with different systems during the same session, and can work on data in either SAP LiveCache or the SAP APO database server.

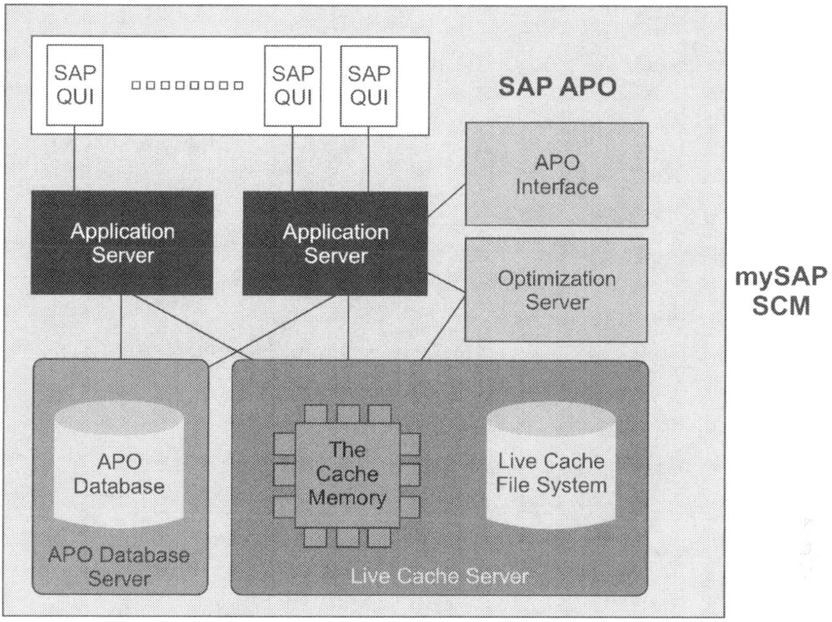

Figure 7.1 SCM LiveCache architecture

In APO transaction data is not stored in tables like SAP R/3. If one wants to view/check/extract transaction data then standard BAPI's or Function Modules should be used. These BAPI's/FM's are available for different kind of data like sales orders, manufacturing orders, stocks, planned independent requirements, etc.

SAP LiveCache is the database management system for SAP Advanced Planning and Optimization (SAP APO), the planning solution within mySAP.com SCM. SAP APO collects data from a variety of SAP R/3 instances and, where appropriate, from third-party systems. SAP LiveCache can help carry out resource-intensive planning activities, such as capacity leveling for a organization's plants, warehouses, and vendors. SAP LiveCache is not simply intermediate memory, as was originally planned. Given how quickly it can supply data, it is every bit as effective as a conventional Cache.

The SAP LiveCache technology is an object-based enhancement of the SAP Max-DB database system. It was developed for managing complex objects in applications in which large quantities of data must be constantly available and changeable. SAP LiveCache technology can be used with SAP applications only.

Properties of an SAP application with SAP LiveCache technology:

- With optimal configuration, all application data and objects are located in the working memory
- Multiple application servers are sharing the read/write cache
- Relational and object-oriented data modeling
- Data-intensive business logic is executed close to the application data
- All database functions are available

7.3 SAP LiveCache TECHNOLOGY

Technical System Landscape in addition to the SAP MaxDB database kernel which provides basic database functions such as saving, restoring, and transaction management, an SAP LiveCache database instance also comprises the following software layers:

- SAP LiveCache Applications (LCApps)
  The business logic is included in the SAP LiveCache kernel by using DB procedures (stored procedures). This removes much of the work that would otherwise be needed for communication and the transfer of data.

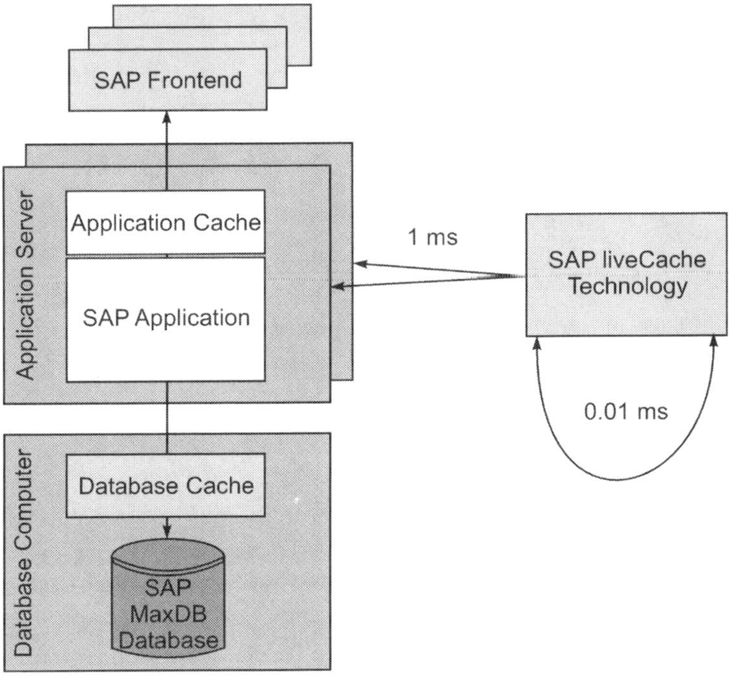

Figure 7.2 Data accessibility from LiveCache

- Object Management System (OMS): A large part of the application data in an SAP LiveCache database instance is managed in objects (OMS data). OMS data is managed in containers that are mapped to a persistent C++ class of the object type as object memory.

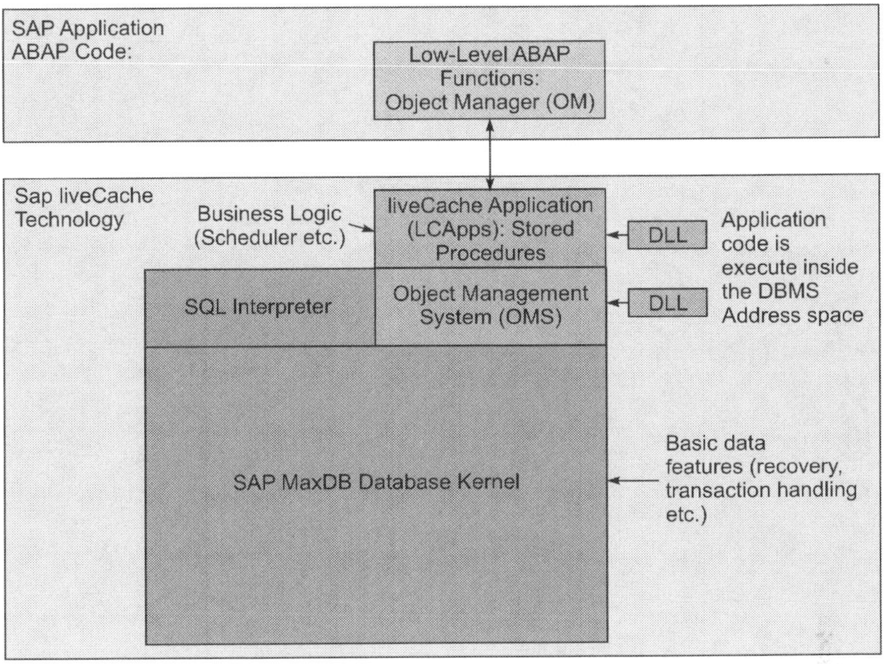

Figure 7.3 Technical architecture of APO LiveCache

7.3.1 Connection to LiveCache

The connection to LiveCache is checked according to the specified interval. In addition to the connection tests, the system also checks if the appropriate entries for LDA (primary connection for multi-connect) and LCA (secondary connection) are present in the DBCON table.

7.4 LiveCache CONCEPTS AND ARCHITECTURE

For the development of APO component a database system was needed which allows fast access to data organized in a complex network.

Applying conventional relational database management systems as data sources for the APO showed poor performance since disk I/O and the non-appropriate data description in the relational schema limited the performance.

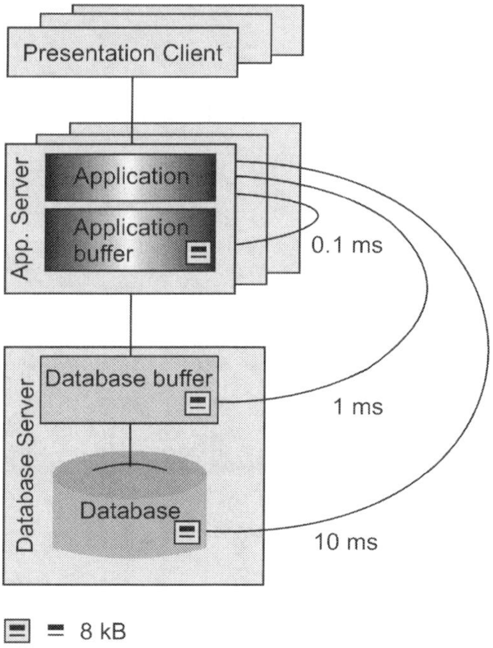

Figure 7.4 Response timings using SCM LiveCache

To read data from an application buffer which is in the same address space as the application takes 0.01 ms. Reading data from database takes about 1ms id corresponding record is already in database buffer and 10 ms if record must be read from hard disk before.

Working with an application having too small buffer to accommodate all required data causes huge data traffic between application and database buffer.

To overcome performance problems the LiveCache was introduced which is dedicated server tier for the main memory based temporary storage of volatile shared data.

7.5 WHAT IS LiveCache?

LiveCache is a program for high performance management of objects used by APO application programs (COM Routines). These objects called OMS objects include application data whose meaning is unknown to LiveCache. All objects ideally are located in main memory in the global data cache of the LiveCache - in the global data cache of the LiveCache, but may be swapped out to disk in case of memory shortage.

COM routines run as stored procedures in the address space of LiveCache and are called from APO ABAP programs which run on the APO application servers. Due to the fact that COM routines run in the address space of LiveCache, a direct access to OMS objects, and navigation over networks of OMS objects is very fast. Typical access time is less than 10 microseconds per object.

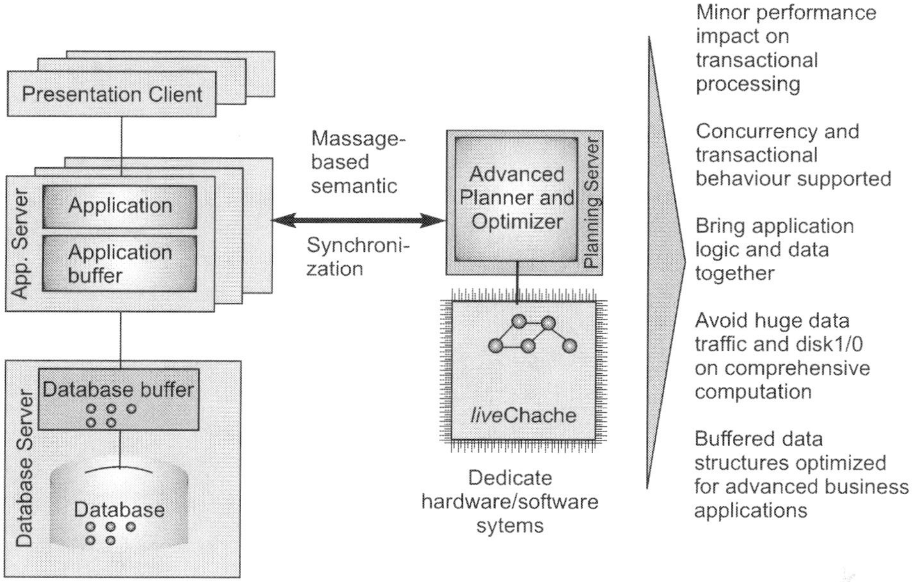

Figure 7.5 LiveCache flow

LiveCache provides classes and class methods to the COM routines to administrate their objects. Technically: COM routines inherit class methods from the LiveCache base classes to create, read, store and delete OMS objects.

LiveCache supports the application programs of implementing their own transaction and lock management. The application program is able either to commit or rollback all changes made on several objects in a business transaction.

LiveCache ensures the existence of OMS objects beyond the lifetime of COM routines. That's why LiveCache uses the term persistent OMS objects. When LiveCache is stopped or when a checkpoint is requested, all objects are stored on hard disks. The APO application uses a complex object orientated application model. This model is easier to implement by an object oriented programming than with the relational structures of a relational database. Therefore, LiveCache supports object oriented programming through providing adequate C++ methods/functions.

LiveCache provides the application with the concept of consistent views to isolate the data of an application from simultaneous updates by other users (reader isolation). COM routines are implemented in LiveCache as stored procedure.

Therefore the call of a COM routine from ABAP is quite simple through using EXEC SQL.

7.6 LiveCache ARCHITECTURE

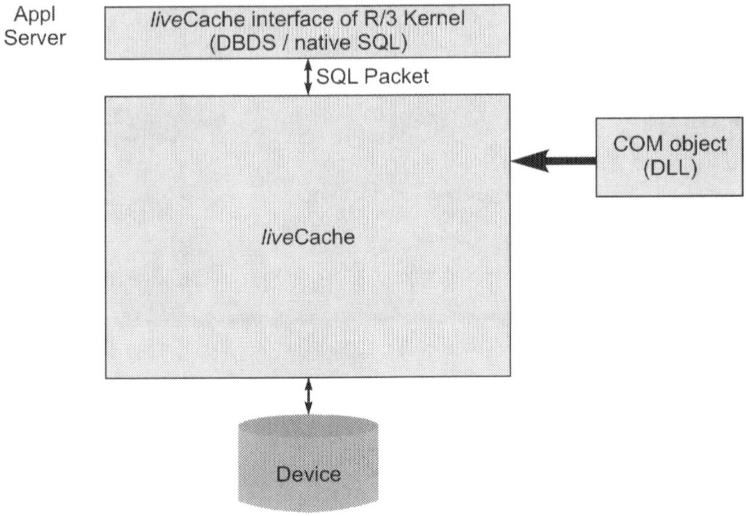

Figure 7.6 LiveCache as a separate server

ABAP Programs and the APO optimizers use native SQL for communicating through the standard SAP DB interface to LiveCache. LiveCache has an SQL interface that is used to communicate with the SAP instances. With native SQL, ABAP programs call stored procedures in the LiveCache that point to Component Object Model (COM) routines written in C++. An SQL class provides SQL methods to access the SQL data through the COM routines.

The COM routines are part of a dynamic link library that runs in the process context of the LiveCache instance. In the Windows NT implementation of LiveCache, COM routines and their interface are registered in the Windows NT Registry. For the Unix implementation, a registry file is provided by LiveCache. A persistent C++ class provides the COM routines with access to the corresponding Object Management.

System (OMS) data that is stored in the LiveCache.

COM Routines in APO are delivered in DLL libraries as SAPXXX.DLL and SAPXXX.LST on NT or as shared libraries SAPXXX.ISO and SAPXXX.LST on UNIX. The application specific knowledge is built into these COM routines based on the concept of object orientation.

7.7 LiveCache ADMINISTRATION TOOL

The LiveCache can be administered by

- *Transaction code LC10* in the SAPGUI
- Database Manager CLI (DBMCLI) command line interface

- Database Manager GUI (DBMGUI) graphical user interface for Windows NT/2000 only
- Web Database Manager (WEBDBM)

LiveCache, similar to the standard SAP RDBMS, can be administered within the SAP system. The SAP *transaction code LC10* makes it possible to monitor, configure and administer LiveCache.

The *transaction code LC10* applies the Database Manager CLI (DBMCLI) to administer the LiveCache. Therefore, it is obvious that all functionalities of an SAP System are still available without the *transaction code LC10* and could also be performed with the "*native*" database administration tool DBMCLI. In addition to the DBMCLI the administration tool DBMGUI is available, which is a graphical user interface to the LiveCache management client tool DBMCLI. While the DBMGUI works only on Windows NT/2000, running the WEBDBM requires only an internet browser and the DBMWebServer which can be installed anywhere in the net.

DBMCLI, DBMGUI and WEBDBM should not be used for starting or stopping the LiveCache, even if *transaction code LC10* itself calls DBMCLI for starting or stopping the LiveCache. They should only be used for changing LiveCache parameters, defining backup media and for LiveCache monitoring. That is because the *LC10* runs in addition to starting, stopping and initializing application specific reports. Moreover, it registers the COM routines each time the LiveCache is started.

7.8 LiveCache INTEGRATION INTO R/3 VIA LC10

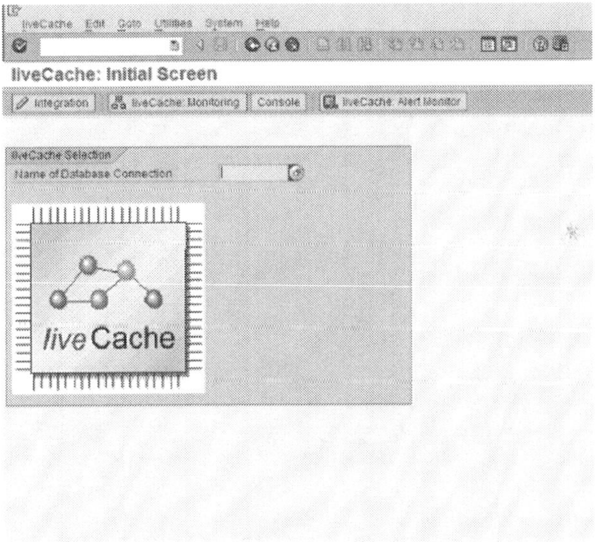

Figure 7.7 Integration of LiveCache

- *Transaction code LC10* introduces LiveCache specific administration functions within R/3 ($\geq$ 4.6D). It allows the administration of multiple LiveCache.

- *Transaction code LC10* identifies LiveCache via a connection name (in the example above it is LCA_LAPTOP) which need not to be the physical name of the LiveCache as it was installed on the LiveCache server.
- Integration Button
  - Creates and modifies new LiveCache connections
- Monitoring Button
  - Leads to the main screen of the *transaction code LC10*
  - LiveCache administration (stop, start and initialization of the LiveCache) and changing LiveCache configuration
  - Watch and analyze the LiveCache performance by the LiveCache administrator
  - Save and recovery of the LiveCache
- Console Button
  - Views the status of LiveCache tasks
- Alert Monitor Button
  - Reports error situations (LiveCache part of the *transaction code RZ20*)

7.8.1 LiveCache Integration – User Data

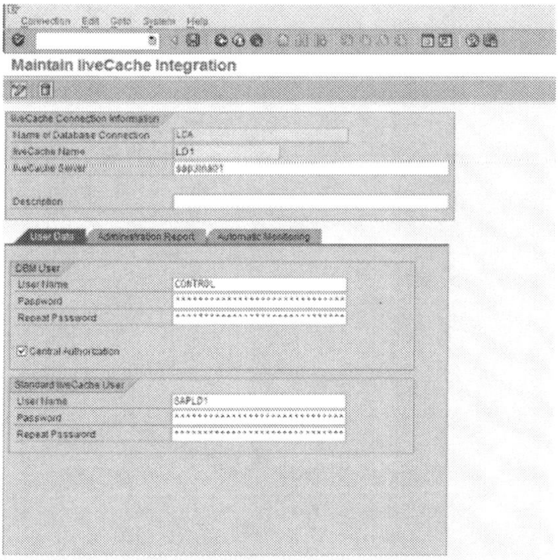

Figure 7.8 Settings for integration of LiveCache

Choose '*Integration*' on the initial screen of *transaction code LC10* to reach the integration screen.

The integration data are required for the multi-db-connection from an R/3 system to the LiveCache via NATIVE SQL. They are stored in tables DBCON and DBCONUSR on the RDBMS.

The '*Name of the database connection*' is used for a NATIVE SQL connection to an R/3 system. The '*LiveCache name*' is the name of the LiveCache database. It can be different from the name of the database connection.

The server name in the '*LiveCache server name*' is case sensitive. It must be the same as the output from the command 'hostname' on a DOS prompt or UNIX shell. The default user/password combinations are control for the DBM operator and R/3 for the standard LiveCache user. The APO application server has to be stopped and started again after changes of LiveCache connection information. This guarantees the R/3 system connects to the correct LiveCache instance. There are two possibilities to authorize a connection to the LiveCache:

De-central Authorization

- One have to authorize access to the LiveCache on each APO application server
- On each application server one has to start the dbmcli command (via *sm49):dbmcli –d <LiveCache name> -n <lc-server> -us <DBM user>,<DBM password>*

Central Authorization

- Central authorization data is stored in the APO database in table DBCONUSR
- This authorization is recommended and it is the default

7.8.2 LiveCache Integration - Administration Report

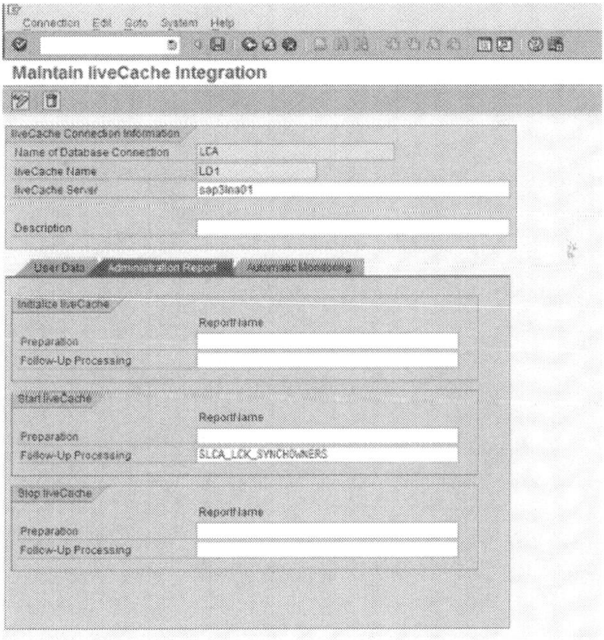

Figure 7.9 Settings for LiveCache

Execution of Application-specific Functions

To run an ABAP report automatically prior or after LiveCache start, stop and initialization, users can specify the report names in this section. The same report cannot be used more than once, unless a new name is used. The report names are stored in the table LCINIT within the APO database.

The *report /SAPAPO/DELETE_LC_ANCHORS* has to be executed each time after the LiveCache was initialized. This report is responsible for the reliability of the APO and the LiveCache data.

7.8.3 LiveCache Integration – User Data

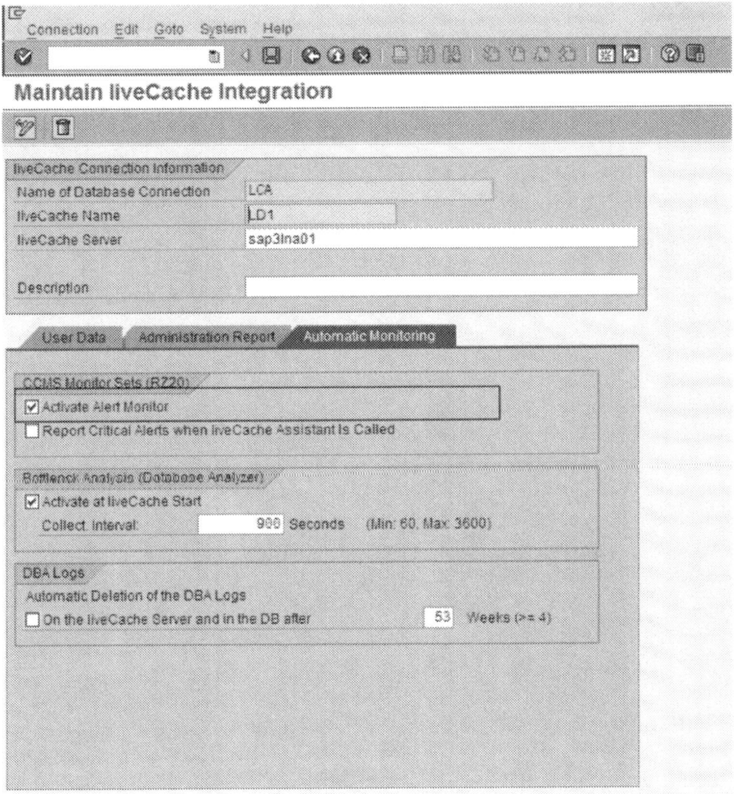

Figure 7.10 Settings for LiveCache – Name and server details

- When the alert monitor is activated a number of performance critical data (i.e. heap and device usage, cache hit rates) is collected periodically and displayed in the alert monitor which can be reached by pressing '*Alert monitor*' on the initial screen of the *transaction code LC10*.
- The alert monitor is activated by default if the LiveCache was installed by the standard installation tool (LCSETUP).

7.9 BASIC ADMINISTRATION

7.9.1 LiveCache Status

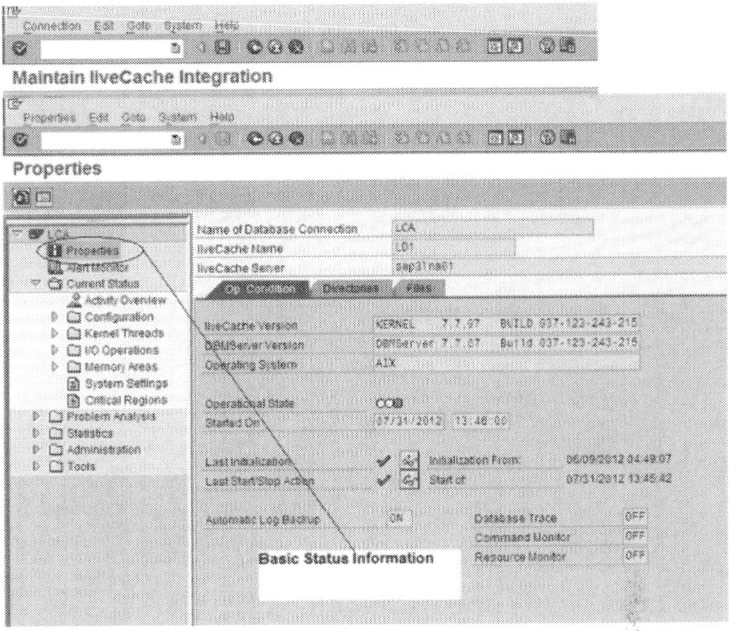

Figure 7.11 LiveCache details

- This is the initial screen of the *transaction code LC10* which can be reached by pressing '*LiveCache Monitoring*' on the initial screen of the *LC10*. It offers all services and information to administrate the LiveCache.
- Before this window appears, the R/3 system sends a request to the LiveCache about the status. The LiveCache name and LiveCache server information are stored in the table DBCON as described in previously. The remaining information displays the output from the status request. If the connection to a LiveCache is not available, error message is displayed.
- The left frame of the screen shows a tree which contains all information and services needed to administer the LiveCache. The tree branches with the most important information and services are opened by default.
- The right frame displays the details which belong to the activated branch of the service tree.
- Initially the window screen which belongs to the '*Properties*' icon is activated.
- The '*DBM server version*' displays the version of the database manager server which is responsible for the dbmcli communication to the LiveCache.
- The '*LiveCache version*' shows the LiveCache kernel build version.
- The traffic light at '*LiveCache status*' illustrates the operation mode of the LiveCache.

7.9.2 LiveCache Operation Mode

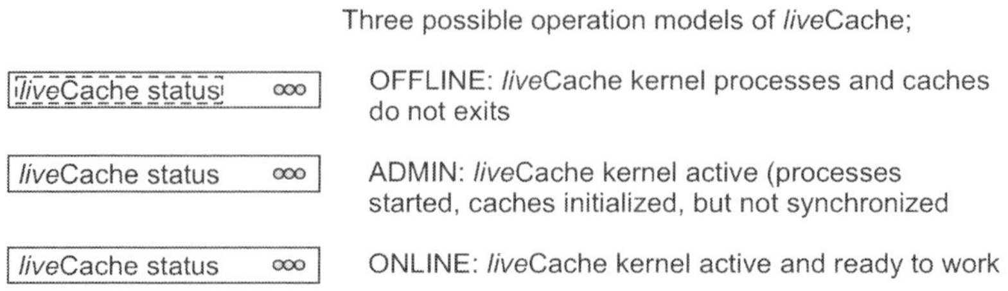

Figure 7.12 Status of LiveCache

There are three LiveCache operating modes:

OFFLINE: No LiveCache kernel processes are running, memory areas (caches) are not allocated. No user can use LiveCache.

ADMIN: The LiveCache kernel is active, but caches are not yet synchronized with the volumes. Users cannot connect to the LiveCache. Only the LiveCache administration user can connect and perform administrative tasks like restoring the database.

ONLINE: The LiveCache kernel is active and data and log information is synchronized between caches and volumes. Users can connect to the LiveCache.

7.9.3 Starting, Initializing and Stopping LiveCache

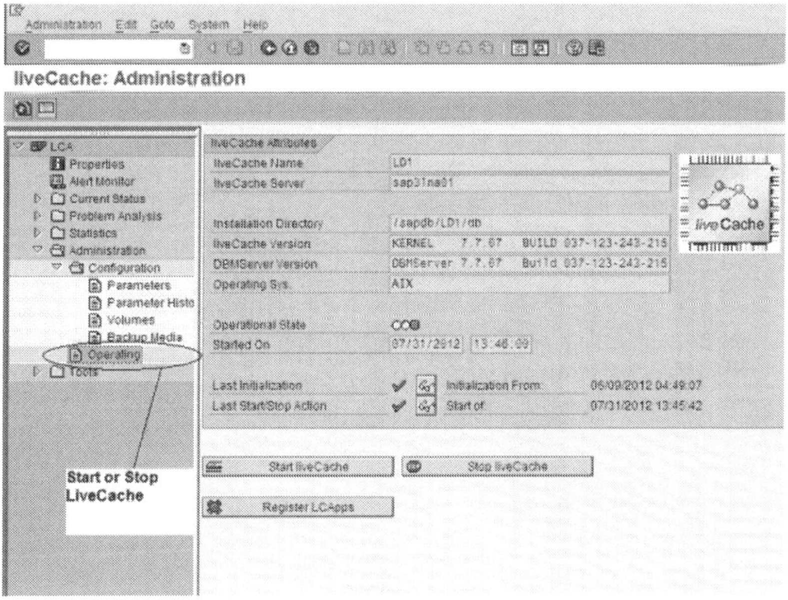

Figure 7.13 LiveCache functionality

To start, stop or initialize the LiveCache choose *Administration -> Operating* in the '*LiveCache Monitoring*' screen. There three buttons are available with the following meanings:

Start LiveCache

- starts the LiveCache into online mode. After the restart all data, committed before the last shutdown or crash, are available again.
- Initialize LiveCache deletes the complete contents of the LiveCache.
- Stop LiveCache shuts the LiveCache down into the offline mode.

Although starting, stopping and initializing the LiveCache is also possible with DBMGUI or DBMCLI, it is strongly recommended to use the *transaction code LC10*. First, LC10 calls up an APO specific report after starting the LiveCache instance. If the report does not run, accesses of work processes to the LiveCache may cause an error. Second, during stopping the LiveCache instance, *transaction code LC10* informs all work processes about this, which causes them to automatically execute a reconnect when accessing the LiveCache next time. If the LiveCache instance was stopped using DBMGUI or DBMCLI, a short dump occurs as soon as work processes try to access the LiveCache again after a restart.

Initialize LiveCache

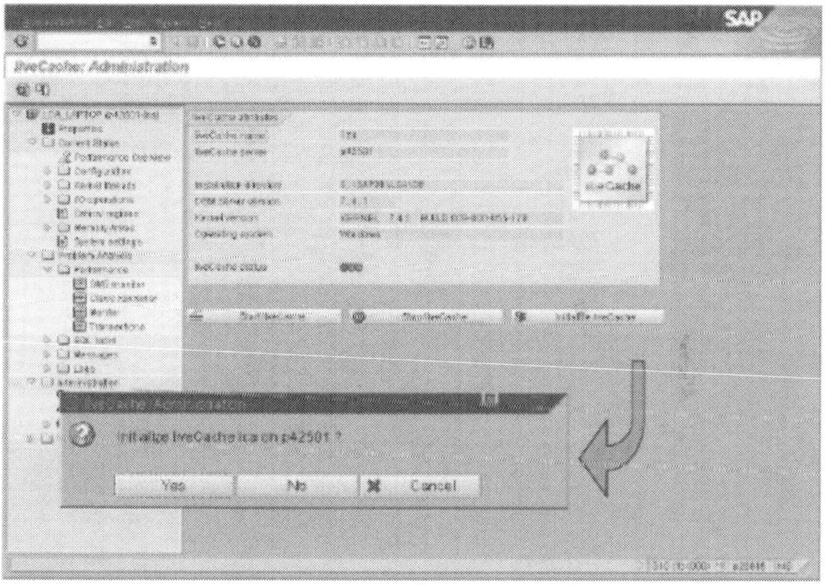

Figure 7.14 Initializing LiveCache

Initializing the LiveCache always formats the log volumes. If the data volumes do not already exist they are created and formatted. All LiveCache data will be lost after initialization, and it has to be loaded again via the APO system or via a recovery.

Program LCINIT.BAT with option init is used to initialize the LiveCache. The initialization process is logged in the log file LCINIT.LOG, which is automatically displayed at the end of the initialization process

7.9.4 SAP LiveCache and SAP APO's New Approach to Backup and Recovery

With such critical business data, backup and recovery is always a concern of organizations. SAP LiveCache's self-sufficiency in backup and point-of-failure recovery is one of the unique features that separate SAP APO from its competitors.

Until recently, SAP APO handled recovery through logging on the application level, together with switching log areas and SAP LiveCache check pointing. This required complex synchronization of processes during any restart of SAP APO and SAP LiveCache, and involved special treatment to recognize the point where users could return to their work. Furthermore, there was potential for slow-downs at the SAP LiveCache checkpoints during normal operation.

In the latest release of SAP LiveCache (7.4) delivered with SAP APO 3.1, administrators now have a simpler solution: new, encapsulated logging and recovery capabilities for the determined data in SAP LiveCache. In fact, the applications no longer have to deal with logging and recovery procedures at all.

Although the SAP APO and SAP LiveCache databases are independent, they are designed to ensure the consistency of data and transactions. Any open SAP APO transactions whose modifications have been rolled back during an SAP LiveCache restart will receive a return code, and will be undone by the application and thus the SAP APO database.

Notes: Some important transaction related to LiveCache

/SAPAPO/OM19	-	LiveCache Browser
/SAPAPO/OM16	-	Data Viewer
/SAPAPO/OM17	-	LiveCache consistency check (LC-APO DB) or Report /SAPAPO/OM_SYNC_LC_DB.
/SAPAPO/REST02	-	Internal Consistency Check for Resources
/SAPAPO/OM11	-	LiveCache Application log
/SAPAPO/ATPQ_CHKUSG	-	Internal Consistency Check for Product Allocations.
RSLVCBACKUP	-	LiveCache Backup in Background

Also, do check on these tables

/SAPAPO/BWEXDSRC APO	-	BW: Data Source - Extractor
/SAPAPO/BWEXTRAC APO	-	BW: Extractors for Transactional Data
/SAPAPO/BWEXTRFM APO	-	BW: Formula to Calculate a Key Figure
/SAPAPO/BWEXTRIN APO	-	BW: Dependent Extractors
/SAPAPO/BWEXTRMP APO	-	BW: Mapping Extractor Structure Field

Now onwards lets work on programming part of LiveCache, here I will explain about the data extraction, updation in LiveCache, as we discussed earlier that only BAPI's/FM's can be used to handle LiveCache.

EXAMPLE

The Master data object transformations of PPDS PPM to SNP PPM which exist in APO are required to be created in APO. The code below is for mass conversion and will avoid manual creation/change for each record in the system.

```
*&---------------------------------------------------------------*
*       Fetch PPDS PPM for selection criteria
*----------------------------------------------------------------

*    Get Activity Key from /SAPAPO/MODE
     SELECT actid                           "Activity key (GUID)
       INTO TABLE i_actid
       FROM /sapapo/mode                    "Mode
       FOR ALL ENTRIES IN i_resuid
       WHERE resid EQ i_resuid-resuid.     "Resource Id
     IF sy-subrc EQ 0.
*      Get Plan ID from /SAPAPO/PLANACT
       SELECT planid                        "Plan Id
         INTO TABLE i_planid
         FROM /sapapo/planact               "Planning Activities
         FOR ALL ENTRIES IN i_actid
         WHERE actid EQ i_actid-actid.     "Activity
       IF sy-subrc EQ 0.
*        Get List of PPDS PPM from /SAPAPO/V_PLMALO for seltn. criteria
         SELECT plannr                      "Plan
                pl_usage                    "Use of a Plan
                matnr                       "Product Number
                locno                       "Location
                planid                      "Int. plan number
         INTO TABLE i_plmalo
         FROM /sapapo/v_plmalo              "View for Search Help
                                            for PPM Maint

         FOR ALL ENTRIES IN i_planid
         WHERE pl_usage EQ c_p              "Use of a Plans
          AND  matnr    IN s_prod[]         "Product
          AND  locno    IN s_loc[]          "Location
          AND  planid   EQ i_planid-planid.
        IF sy-subrc NE 0.
```

```
*       No PPDS PPM found for Selection Criteria
        MESSAGE i038.
        LEAVE LIST-PROCESSING.
      ENDIF.
    ENDIF.
  ENDIF.

*&---------------------------------------------------------------*
*       Create SNP PPM
*----------------------------------------------------------------*

* Local data Declaration
  DATA : l_plan       TYPE bdc_fval,
         l_plan_gen   TYPE bdc_fval,
         lw_plmalo    TYPE ty_plmalo,
         lw_plan_gen  TYPE ty_plan_gen.

  IF i_plmalo[] IS NOT INITIAL.
    SELECT planid_org                            "Int. plan number
           planid_gen                            "Int. plan number
           plannr_gen                            "SNP Plan Number
      INTO TABLE i_plan_gen
      FROM /sapapo/plan_gen                      "PPDS to SNP/PPM
                                                 Generation
      FOR ALL ENTRIES IN i_plmalo
      WHERE planid_org = i_plmalo-planid.  "Int. plan number
   IF sy-subrc EQ 0.
     SORT i_plan_gen by planid_org.
     LOOP AT i_plmalo INTO lw_plmalo.
       READ TABLE i_plan_gen INTO lw_plan_gen
            WITH KEY planid_org = lw_plmalo-planid BINARY SEARCH.
      IF sy-subrc EQ 0 AND lw_plan_gen-plannr_gen IS NOT INITIAL.
        CLEAR : l_plan, l_plan_gen.
        l_plan     = lw_plmalo-plannr.
        l_plan_gen = lw_plan_gen-plannr_gen.

*       Create SNP PPM
        PERFORM sub_create_snp_for_ppds USING l_plan
                                              l_plan_gen.
      ENDIF.
     ENDLOOP.
   ENDIF.
  ENDIF.

  WAIT UP TO 10 SECONDS.
```

```
* SNP is changed after mode generation
* _01 is added so Data is fetched again to avoid data mismatch
  IF i_plmalo[] IS NOT INITIAL.
    REFRESH i_plan_gen.

    SELECT planid_org                              "Int. plan number
           planid_gen                              "Int. plan number
           plannr_gen                              "SNP Plan Number
      INTO TABLE i_plan_gen
      FROM /sapapo/plan_gen                        "PPDS to SNP/PPM
                                                   Generation
      FOR ALL ENTRIES IN i_plmalo
      WHERE planid_org = i_plmalo-planid.  "Int. plan number

*  SY-SUBRC check not required
  ENDIF.
FORM sub_create_snp_for_ppds USING p_plan      TYPE bdc_fval
                                   p_plan_gen TYPE bdc_fval.
 PERFORM sub_bdc_dynpro using '/SAPAPO/PPM_CONV_PPDS2SNP_310'
                               '1000'.
 PERFORM sub_bdc_field   using 'BDC_CURSOR'
                               'X_FLAG'.
 PERFORM sub_bdc_field   using 'BDC_OKCODE'
                               '=ONLI'.
 PERFORM sub_bdc_field   using 'S_PLAN-LOW'
                                p_plan.
 PERFORM sub_bdc_field   using 'STRT_GEN'
                                g_date.
 PERFORM sub_bdc_field   using 'BUCKET'
                               'W'.
 PERFORM sub_bdc_field   using 'PRIO'
                               'A'.
 PERFORM sub_bdc_field   using 'CNS_CALC'
                               '1'.
 PERFORM sub_bdc_field   using 'LTSIZEFR'
                               '3'.
 PERFORM sub_bdc_field   using 'MAXNR'
                               '01'.
 PERFORM sub_bdc_field   using 'X_FLAG'
                               'X'.
 PERFORM sub_bdc_transaction USING '/SAPAPO/PPM_CONV_310'.
ENDFORM.                  " SUB_CREATE_SNP_FOR_PPDS
```

The above code describes how to create SNP PPM, I have not covered the BDC structure or other data declarations, that I am assuming technical person should be aware of.

7.9.5 BDC - Batch Data Communication

To ensure data consistency in SAP system, we must not update SAP data directly from ABAP program. We must upload data through similar program flow compared to manual input by user. SAP thus provided BDC. BDC works by simulating the user input from transactional screen via an ABAP program. The program follows all program flow and do not bypass any of the standard SAP consistency checks, authorizations, update conjunction tables, etc.

EXAMPLE

Time phased rates (or material consumption) have to be maintained in APO (PPM) for planning in PPDS and SNP. The result based on time based PPM (Planned Order) have to be send to manufacturing so execution can be based on realistic data.

```
*&---------------------------------------------------------------*
*      Retrieve resource-ids and valid PPMS

*---------------------------------------------------------------*

* Local declarations
  CONSTANTS: lc_000 TYPE /sapapo/vrsioid VALUE '000',
             lc_1   TYPE char01 VALUE '1'.

  IF NOT i_resper IS INITIAL.
*   Fetch resource ids from table /sapapo/res_head
    SELECT resuid                            "resource id
        FROM /sapapo/res_head
        INTO TABLE i_resid
        FOR ALL ENTRIES IN i_resper
        WHERE  simversid  EQ  lc_000
        AND    simsessid  EQ  space
        AND    name       EQ  i_resper-resource_name.

    IF sy-subrc EQ 0.
      CLEAR w_resid.
      LOOP AT i_resid INTO w_resid.
*       Get PPMs for the resource ids
        CALL FUNCTION '/SAPAPO/PPM_GET_PLAN_FOR_RESID'
          EXPORTING
            iv_resid  = w_resid-resuid
```

```
          TABLES
            et_plan    = i_plan_tmp
          EXCEPTIONS
            not_found = 1
            OTHERS    = 2.
        IF sy-subrc EQ 0.
          APPEND LINES OF i_plan_tmp TO i_plan.
          REFRESH i_plan_tmp.
        ENDIF.
      ENDLOOP.
    ENDIF.
  ENDIF.

* Retrieve PPM components from view /sapapo/v_plmalo to re-
  strict the
* plans based on entered product and location combination
  SELECT planid                                         "plan id
         FROM /sapapo/v_plmalo
         INTO CORRESPONDING FIELDS OF TABLE i_ppm_comp
         FOR ALL ENTRIES IN i_plan
         WHERE plannr EQ i_plan-plannr
         AND   planid EQ i_plan-planid
         AND   state  EQ lc_1
         AND   matnr IN s_prod[]
         AND   locno IN s_locno[].

  IF sy-subrc EQ 0.
    SORT i_ppm_comp BY  planid.
  ENDIF.

*&---------------------------------------------------------------*
* Update time dependent parameters of PPMs
*----------------------------------------------------------------*

** Local BAPI declarations
  DATA: li_plan                      TYPE TABLE OF bapi10003plano,
        li_ppm                       TYPE TABLE OF bapi10003trprod,
        li_mode                      TYPE TABLE OF bapi10003modeo,
        li_logical_component         TYPE TABLE OF bapi10003compo,
        li_logical_component_save    TYPE TABLE OF bapi10003comp,
```

```
        li_logical_component_save_x  TYPE TABLE OF bapi10003compx,
        li_comp_product              TYPE TABLE OF bapi10003compalto,
        li_comp_product_tdpp         TYPE TABLE OF bapi10003tdppcompalto,
        li_trpmod                    TYPE TABLE OF bapi10003ppmmodelo,
        li_return_get_call           TYPE TABLE OF bapiret2,
        li_plan_guids                TYPE STANDARD TABLE OF bapi10003planids,
        li_ppm_model                 TYPE TABLE OF bapi10003ppmmodel,
        li_return                    TYPE TABLE OF bapiret2,
        li_operation                 TYPE TABLE OF bapi10003planopro,
        li_operation_save            TYPE TABLE OF bapi10003planopr,
        li_operation_save_x          TYPE TABLE OF bapi10003planoprx,
        li_activity                  TYPE TABLE OF bapi10003planacto,
        li_activity_save             TYPE TABLE OF bapi10003planact,
        li_activity_save_x           TYPE TABLE OF bapi10003planactx,
        li_comp_product_tdpp_save TYPE TABLE OF bapi10003tdppcompalt,
        li_comp_product_save         TYPE TABLE OF bapi10003compalt,
        li_comp_product_save_x       TYPE TABLE OF bapi10003compaltx.

** Local work area declarations
  DATA:    lw_plan_guids   TYPE bapi10003planids,
           l_guid_32       TYPE sysuuid-c.

  LOOP AT i_ppm_comp INTO w_ppm_comp.
*   Convert GUID to 32 char
    CALL FUNCTION '/SAPAPO/CIF_GUID_CONVERT'
      EXPORTING
        iv guid_c22        = w_ppm_comp-planid
      IMPORTING
        ev_guid_c32        =  l_guid_32
      EXCEPTIONS
        parameters_error = 1
        OTHERS           = 2.
      IF sy-subrc EQ 0.
        lw_plan_guids-plan_id = l_guid_32.
        APPEND lw_plan_guids TO li_plan_guids.
        CLEAR lw_plan_guids.
      ENDIF.
    ENDLOOP.

* Get logical system name
  CALL FUNCTION 'OWN_LOGICAL_SYSTEM_GET'
    IMPORTING
      own_logical_system              = g_log_sys
    EXCEPTIONS
      own_logical_system_not_defined  = 1
      OTHERS                          = 2.
```

```
  IF sy-subrc <> 0.
    MESSAGE ID sy-msgid TYPE sy-msgty NUMBER sy-msgno
            WITH sy-msgv1 sy-msgv2 sy-msgv3 sy-msgv4.
    LEAVE LIST-PROCESSING.
  ENDIF.

* Retrieve the PPM data using GET_LIST BAPI function
  PERFORM sub_get_ppm_data  USING     li_plan_guids
                            CHANGING  li_plan
                                      li_ppm
                                      li_operation
                                      li_activity
                                      li_mode
                                      li_logical_component
                                      li_comp_product
                                      li_comp_product_tdpp
                                      li_return_get_call
                                      li_trpmod.

*  Prepare change tables before save
   PERFORM sub_prepare_change_tables TABLES li_plan

                                   li_operation
                                   li_activity
                                   li_mode
                                   li_logical_component
                                   li_comp_product
                                   li_comp_product_tdpp
                                   li_trpmod
                                   li_operation_save
                                   li_operation_save_x
                                   li_activity_save
                                   li_activity_save_x
                                   li_logical_component_save
                                   li_logical_component_save_x
                                   li_comp_product_save
                                   li_comp_product_save_x
                                   li_comp_product_tdpp_save
                                   li_ppm_model.

*Update Time dependent parameters of PPMs
 PERFORM sub_ppm_tdpp_update TABLES li_operation_save
                                   li_operation_save_x
                                   li_activity_save
```

```
                                      li_activity_save_x
                                      li_logical_component_save
                                      li_logical_component_save_x
                                      li_comp_product_save
                                      li_comp_product_save_x
                                      li_comp_product_tdpp_save
                                      li_ppm_model
                                      li_return.

* Refresh local internal tables
  REFRESH: li_plan,
           li_ppm,
           li_mode,
           li_logical_component,
           li_logical_component_save,
           li_logical_component_save_x,
           li_comp_product,
           li_comp_product_tdpp,
           li_trpmod,
           li_return_get_call,
           li_plan_guids,
           li_ppm_model,
           li_return,
           li_operation,
           li_operation_save,
           li_operation_save_x,
           li_activity,
           li_activity_save,
           li_activity_save_x,
           li_comp_product_tdpp_save,
           li_comp_product_save,
           li_comp_product_save_x.

*&---------------------------------------------------------------*
*&     Form  SUB_CONV_DT_INTO_TSTAMP
*&---------------------------------------------------------------*
*     Convert date into timestamps
*----------------------------------------------------------------*
*     -->P_W_RESPER_START_DATE   Start Date
*     -->P_W_RESPER_END_DATE     End Date
```

```
*      <--P_L_START_TSTAMP        Start Timestmap
*      <--P_L_END_TSTAMP          End Timestamp
*----------------------------------------------------------------------*

FORM sub_conv_dt_into_tstamp  USING      p_w_resper_end_date TYPE datum
                              CHANGING  p_l_end_tstamp TYPE timestamp.

* Local constants declarations
  CONSTANTS: lc_000000 TYPE t VALUE '000000',
             lc_235959 TYPE t VALUE '235959'.

* Convert end date into timestamp
  CALL FUNCTION '/SAPAPO/DATE_CONVERT_TIMESTAMP'
    EXPORTING
      iv_date       = p_w_resper_end_date
      iv_time       = lc_235959
    IMPORTING
      ev_timestamp = p_l_end_tstamp.

ENDFORM.                    " SUB_CONV_DT_INTO_TSTAMP

*&---------------------------------------------------------------------*
*&      Form  SUB_GET_PPM_DATA
*&---------------------------------------------------------------------*
*       Retrieve the PPM data
*----------------------------------------------------------------------*
*      -->P_LI_PLAN_GUIDS        plan guid
*      <--P_LI_PLAN              plan
*      <--P_LI_PPM               ppm
*      <--P_LI_OPERATION         operation
*      <--P_LI_ACTIVITY          activity
*      <--P_LI_MODE              mode
*      <--P_LI_LOGICAL_COMPONENT  logical component
*      <--P_LI_COMP_PRODUCT       comp product table
*      <--P_LI_COMP_PRODUCT_TDPP  time dependent parameters
*      <--P_LI_RETURN_GET_CALL    return table
*      <--P_LI_TRPMOD             model
*----------------------------------------------------------------------*

FORM sub_get_ppm_data USING    p_li_plan_guids TYPE STANDARD TABLE
                      CHANGING p_li_plan TYPE tt_plan
                      p_li_ppm        TYPE tt_ppm
                      p_li_operation TYPE tt_operation
```

```
                    p_li_activity  TYPE tt_activity
                    p_li_mode               TYPE tt_mode
                    p_li_logical_component TYPE tt_logical_component
                    p_li_comp_product       TYPE tt_comp_product
                    p_li_comp_product_tdpp TYPE tt_comp_product_tdpp
                    p_li_return_get_call    TYPE tt_return
                    p_li_trpmod             TYPE tt_ppm_model.

* Local declarations
  DATA:  lw_return TYPE bapiret2,
         l_message TYPE string.

* -> call the get list bapi function
  CALL FUNCTION 'BAPI_PPMSRVAPS_GETLIST'
    EXPORTING
      logical_system     = g_log_sys
    TABLES
      plan_guids         = p_li_plan_guids
      plan               = p_li_plan
      ppm                = p_li_ppm
      operation          = p_li_operation
      activity           = p_li_activity
      mode               = p_li_mode
      logical_component  = p_li_logical_component
      comp_product       = p_li_comp_product
      comp_product_tdpp  = p_li_comp_product_tdpp
      return             = p_li_return_get_call
      ppm_model          = p_li_trpmod.

READ TABLE p_li_return_get_call
TRANSPORTING NO FIELDS WITH KEY type = c_e.
  IF sy-subrc EQ 0.
    LOOP AT p_li_return_get_call INTO lw_return WHERE type EQ c_e.
      CALL FUNCTION 'FORMAT_MESSAGE'
        EXPORTING
          id          = lw_return-id
          lang        = sy-langu
          no          = lw_return-number
          v1          = lw_return-message_v1
          v2          = lw_return-message_v2
          v3          = lw_return-message_v3
          v4          = lw_return-message_v4
```

```
        IMPORTING
          msg          = l_message
        EXCEPTIONS
          not_found = 1
          OTHERS     = 2.
      IF sy-subrc <> 0.
        CLEAR l_message.
      ELSE.
        w_output_tab-product = lw_return-message_v3.
        w_output_tab-message = l_message.
        APPEND w_output_tab TO i_output_tab.
        CLEAR w_output_tab.
      ENDIF.
      CLEAR lw_return.
    ENDLOOP.
  ENDIF.
ENDFORM.                              " SUB_GET_PPM_DATA

*&---------------------------------------------------------------*
*&       Form  SUB_PREPARE_CHANGE_TABLES
*&---------------------------------------------------------------*
*       Prepare  change table before saving
*----------------------------------------------------------------*

*      -->P_LI_PLAN               plan
*      -->P_LI_PPM                ppm
*      -->P_LI_OPERATION          operation
*      -->P_LI_ACTIVITY           activity
*      -->P_LI_MODE               mode
*      -->P_LI_LOGICAL_COMPONENT   logical component
*      -->P_LI_COMP_PRODUCT        comp product
*      -->P_LI_COMP_PRODUCT_TDPP   time dependent parameters
*      -->P_LI_TRPMOD  text        model
*      <--P_LI_OPERATION_SAVE      operation save table
*      <--P_LI_OPERATION_SAVE_X    operation save change table
*      <--P_LI_ACTIVITY_SAVE       activity save table
*      <--P_LI_ACTIVITY_SAVE_X     activity save change table
*      <--P_LI_LOGICAL_COMPONENT_SAVE  logical component save
*      <--P_LI_LOGICAL_COMPONENT_SAVE_X  logical component save change
*      <--P_LI_COMP_PRODUCT_SAVE         comp product save
*      <--P_LI_COMP_PRODUCT_SAVE_X       comp product save change
*      <--P_LI_COMP_PRODUCT_TDPP_SAVE    comp product save tdpp change
*      <--P_LI_PPM_MODEL                 return
```

```
*----------------------------------------------------------------------*
FORM sub_prepare_change_tables  TABLES   p_li_plan TYPE tt_plan
         p_li_operation          TYPE tt_operation
         p_li_activity           TYPE tt_activity
         p_li_mode               TYPE tt_mode
         p_li_logical_component  TYPE tt_logical_component
         p_li_comp_product       TYPE tt_comp_product
         p_li_comp_product_tdpp  TYPE tt_comp_product_tdpp
         p_li_trpmod             TYPE tt_ppm_model
         p_li_operation_save     TYPE tt_operation_save
         p_li_operation_save_x   TYPE tt_operation_savex
         p_li_activity_save      TYPE tt_activity_save
         p_li_activity_save_x    TYPE tt_activity_savex
         p_li_logical_component_save TYPE tt_logical_component_save
         p_li_logical_component_save_x TYPE tt_logical_component_savex
         p_li_comp_product_save   TYPE tt_comp_product_save
         p_li_comp_product_save_x TYPE tt_comp_product_savex
         p_li_comp_product_tdpp_save TYPE tt_comp_product_tdpp_save
         p_li_ppm_model              TYPE tt_ppm_model_save.

* Local work area declarations
  DATA: lw_operation_save_x          TYPE bapi10003planoprx,
        lw_activity                  TYPE bapi10003planacto,
        lw_activity_save_x           TYPE bapi10003planactx,
        lw_logical_component_save    TYPE bapi10003comp,
        lw_logical_component_save_x  TYPE bapi10003compx,
        lw_mode                      TYPE bapi10003modeo,
        lw_plan                      TYPE bapi10003plano,
        lw_ppm_model                 TYPE bapi10003ppmmodel,
        lw_comp_product_save_x       TYPE bapi10003compaltx,
        lw_comp_product_tdpp_save    TYPE bapi10003tdppcompalt,
        lw_operation                 TYPE bapi10003planopro,
        lw_activity_save             TYPE bapi10003planact,
        lw_logical_comp              TYPE bapi10003compo,
        lw_comp_product              TYPE bapi10003compalto,
        lw_trpmod                    TYPE bapi10003ppmmodel.

* Field symbol declarations
  FIELD-SYMBOLS: <fs_comp_product_tdpp> TYPE bapi10003tdppcompalt,
                 <fs_comp_product>      TYPE bapi10003compalto,
                 <fs_comp_product_x>    TYPE bapi10003compaltx.

* Local constant declarations
  CONSTANTS: lc_p   TYPE char01   VALUE 'P',
             lc_s   TYPE char01   VALUE 'S',
             lc_100 TYPE char03   VALUE '100'.
```

```
* Local variable declarations
  DATA:
        l_start_tstamp TYPE timestamp,
        l_end_tstamp   TYPE timestamp.

* Move the operation data
  p_li_operation_save[] = p_li_operation[].
  CLEAR lw_operation.
  LOOP AT p_li_operation INTO lw_operation.
    lw_operation_save_x-plan_number = lw_operation-plan_number.
     lw_operation_save_x-operation_number = lw_operation-opera-
tion_number.
     lw_operation_save_x-operation_number_extension = lw_opera-
tion-operation_number_extension.
     APPEND lw_operation_save_x TO p_li_operation_save_x.
     CLEAR lw_operation_save_x.
  ENDLOOP.

  CLEAR lw_activity.
  LOOP AT p_li_activity INTO lw_activity.
     lw_activity_save-plan_number = lw_activity-plan_number.
     lw_activity_save-operation_number = lw_activity-operation_
number.
     lw_activity_save-operation_number_extension = lw_activity-
operation_number_extension.
     lw_activity_save-activity = lw_activity-activity.
     lw_activity_save-scrap = lw_activity-scrap.
     lw_activity_save-activity_type  =  lw_activity-activity_
type.
     lw_activity_save-setup_flg = lw_activity-setup_flg.
     lw_activity_save-tdpp_flg = lw_activity-tdpp_flg.
     lw_activity_save-synchronization = lw_activity-synchroni-
zation.
     lw_activity_save-effectivity = lw_activity-effectivity.
     APPEND lw_activity_save TO p_li_activity_save.
     CLEAR lw_activity_save-effectivity.

     lw_activity_save_x-plan_number = lw_activity-plan_number.
     lw_activity_save_x-operation_number  = lw_activity-opera-
tion_number.
     lw_activity_save_x-operation_number_extension = lw_activi-
ty-operation_number_extension.
     lw_activity_save_x-activity = lw_activity-activity.
```

```
    APPEND lw_activity_save_x TO p_li_activity_save_x.
    CLEAR lw_activity_save_x.
  ENDLOOP.

  CLEAR lw_logical_comp.
  LOOP AT p_li_logical_component INTO lw_logical_comp.
     lw_logical_component_save-plan_number = lw_logical_comp-
plan_number.
     lw_logical_component_save-operation_number = lw_logical_
comp-operation_number.
     lw_logical_component_save-operation_number_exten-
sion = lw_logical_comp-operation_number_extension.
     lw_logical_component_save-activity = lw_logical_comp-ac-
tivity.
     lw_logical_component_save-log_component = lw_logical_comp-
log_component.
     lw_logical_component_save-io_indicator = lw_logical_comp-
io_indicator. "Mandatory in case of SNP plan
     lw_logical_component_save-consumption_mode = lw_logical_
comp-consumption_mode.
     lw_logical_component_save-relation_io_offset = lw_logical_
comp-relation_io_offset.
     lw_logical_component_save-io_offset = lw_logical_comp-io_
offset.
     lw_logical_component_save-io_offset_uom = lw_logical_comp-
io_offset_uom.
     lw_logical_component_save-io_offset_uom_iso = lw_logical_
comp-io_offset_uom_iso.
     lw_logical_component_save-io_duration = lw_logical_comp-
io_duration.
     lw_logical_component_save-io_duration_uom = lw_logical_
comp-io_duration_uom.
     lw_logical_component_save-io_duration_uom_iso = lw_logi-
cal_comp-io_duration_uom_iso.
     lw_logical_component_save-cp_date_to = lw_logical_comp-cp_
date_to. "Mandatory in case of SNP plan
    APPEND lw_logical_component_save TO p_li_logical_compo-
nent_save.
    CLEAR lw_logical_component_save.

lw_logical_component_save_x-plan_number = lw_logical_comp-
plan_number.
lw_logical_component_save_x-operation_number = lw_logical_
comp-operation_number.
lw_logical_component_save_x-operation_number_extension = lw_
logical_comp-operation_number_extension.
```

```
lw_logical_component_save_x-activity = lw_logical_comp-activ-
ity.
lw_logical_component_save_x-log_component = lw_logical_comp-
log_component.
APPEND lw_logical_component_save_x TO p_li_logical_component_
save_x.
CLEAR lw_logical_component_save_x.
ENDLOOP.

* Move comp product data
  p_li_comp_product_save[] = p_li_comp_product[].

CLEAR lw_comp_product.
LOOP AT p_li_comp_product INTO lw_comp_product.
  lw_comp_product_save_x-plan_number = lw_comp_product-plan_
number.
  lw_comp_product_save_x-operation_number = lw_comp_product-
operation_number.
  lw_comp_product_save_x-operation_number_extension = lw_comp_
product-operation_number_extension.
  lw_comp_product_save_x-activity = lw_comp_product-activity.
  lw_comp_product_save_x-log_component = lw_comp_product-log_
component.
  lw_comp_product_save_x-product_alt = lw_comp_product-prod-
uct_alt.
  lw_comp_product_save_x-date_to = lw_comp_product-date_to.
  lw_comp_product_save_x-tdpp_flg = c_x.
  APPEND lw_comp_product_save_x TO p_li_comp_product_save_x.
  CLEAR lw_comp_product_save_x.
ENDLOOP.

CLEAR lw_trpmod.
LOOP AT p_li_trpmod INTO lw_trpmod.
  lw_ppm_model-plan_number = lw_trpmod-plan_number.
  lw_ppm_model-ppm_number = lw_trpmod-ppm_number.
  lw_ppm_model-model = lw_trpmod-model.
  APPEND lw_ppm_model TO p_li_ppm_model.
ENDLOOP.

* Sort the internal tables
  SORT p_li_comp_product[] BY plan_number.
  SORT p_li_plan[] BY plan_number.
  SORT p_li_mode[] BY plan_number.
```

```
* Logic for TDPP update based on entries in table ZGPTS_
  RESPER starts here
  CLEAR lw_comp_product.
  LOOP AT p_li_comp_product INTO lw_comp_product.
    CLEAR lw_plan.
    READ TABLE p_li_plan INTO lw_plan WITH KEY plan_number = lw_
comp_product-plan_number BINARY SEARCH.
    IF sy-subrc EQ 0.
      CLEAR lw_mode.
      READ TABLE p_li_mode INTO lw_mode WITH KEY plan_num-
ber = lw_plan-plan_number BINARY SEARCH.
      IF sy-subrc EQ 0.
        CLEAR: w_resper.
        LOOP AT i_resper INTO w_resper.
" WHERE resource_name = lw_mode-resource.

      if w_resper-resource_name = lw_mode-resource.

* Convert date into timestamps for valid to check with TDPP entries
      PERFORM sub_conv_dt_into_tstamp USING  w_resper-end_date
                                      CHANGING  l_end_tstamp.

*       Check whether any TDPP entry exists
  READ TABLE p_li_comp_product_tdpp  TRANSPORTING NO FIELDS
      WITH KEY plan_number = lw_comp_product-plan_number
      operation_number = lw_comp_product-operation_number
      operation_number_extension = lw_comp_product-
      operation_number_extension-activity = lw_comp_product-
      activitylog_component = lw_comp_product-log_component
      DATE_VALID_TO = l_end_tsta
      product_alt = lw_comp_product-product_alt.

  IF sy-subrc EQ 0.
  LOOP AT p_li_comp_product_tdpp  ASSIGNING <fs_comp_product_tdpp>
      WHERE  plan_number = lw_comp_product-plan_number
      AND    operation_number = lw_comp_product-operation_number
      AND    operation_number_extension = lw_comp_product-opera-
             tion_number_extension
      AND    activity = lw_comp_product-activity
      AND    log_component = lw_comp_product-log_component
      AND    DATE_VALID_TO = l_end_tstamp
      AND    product_alt = lw_comp_product-product_alt.
```

```
* Update existing TDPP entries
  IF <fs_comp_product_tdpp>-date_valid_to LE l_end_tstamp.
    IF NOT lw_comp_product-prod_consump_var IS INITIAL.
      IF lw_plan-plan_usage EQ lc_p. "PPDS plan
* Follow PPDS logic
      <fs_comp_product_tdpp>-prod_consump_var = lw_comp_prod-
uct-prod_consump_var * ( w_resper-percnt_chg_ppds / lc_100 ).
      ELSEIF lw_plan-plan_usage EQ lc_s. "SNP plan
* Follow SNP logic
      <fs_comp_product_tdpp>-prod_consump_var = lw_comp_prod-
uct-prod_consump_var * ( ( w_resper-percnt_chg_ppds - w_resper-
percnt_chg_snp ) / lc_100 ).
      ENDIF.
    ENDIF.
    <fs_comp_product_tdpp>-use_prod_consump_var_flg = c_x.
    lw_comp_product_tdpp_save  =  <fs_comp_product_tdpp>.
    APPEND lw_comp_product_tdpp_save TO  p_li_comp_product_
tdpp_save.
    CLEAR: lw_comp_product_tdpp_save.
  ELSE.

*  Create new TDPP entries
  lw_comp_product_tdpp_save-plan_number  =  lw_comp_product-
plan_number.
  lw_comp_product_tdpp_save-operation_number  =  lw_comp_prod-
uct-operation_number.
  lw_comp_product_tdpp_save-operation_number_extension  =  lw_
comp_product operation_number_extension.
  lw_comp_product_tdpp_save-activity = lw_comp_product-activi-
ty.
  lw_comp_product_tdpp_save-log_component  =  lw_comp_product-
log_component.
  lw_comp_product_tdpp_save-product_alt  =  lw_comp_product-
product_alt.
  lw_comp_product_tdpp_save-use_prod_consump_var_flg = c_x.
  lw_comp_product_tdpp_save-prod_consump_var_uom  =  lw_comp_
product-prod_consump_uom.

* Mandatory in case of SNP plan
  lw_comp_product_tdpp_save-cp_date_to = lw_comp_product-date_
to.
  lw_comp_product_tdpp_save-date_valid_to = l_end_tstamp.
  IF NOT lw_comp_product-prod_consump_var IS INITIAL.
    IF lw_plan-plan_usage EQ lc_p. "PPDS plan
```

```
* Follow PPDS logic
     lw_comp_product_tdpp_save-prod_consump_var = lw_comp_prod-
uct-prod_consump_var * ( w_resper-percnt_chg_ppds / lc_100 ).
 ELSEIF lw_plan-plan_usage EQ lc_s. "SNP plan

* Follow SNP logic
    lw_comp_product_tdpp_save-prod_consump_var = lw_comp_prod-
uct-prod_consump_var * ( ( w_resper-percnt_chg_ppds - w_resper-
percnt_chg_snp ) / lc_100 ).
 ENDIF.
 APPEND lw_comp_product_tdpp_save TO p_li_comp_product_tdpp_
save.
 CLEAR: lw_comp_product_tdpp_save.
ENDIF.
ENDIF.
ENDLOOP.

ELSE.

*  Create new TDPP entries if TDPP entries do not exist
lw_comp_product_tdpp_save-plan_number = lw_comp_product-plan_
number.
lw_comp_product_tdpp_save-operation_number = lw_comp_product-
operation_number.
lw_comp_product_tdpp_save-operation_number_extension = lw_
comp_product-operation_number_extension.
lw_comp_product_tdpp_save-activity = lw_comp_product-activity.
lw_comp_product_tdpp_save-log_component = lw_comp_product-log_
component.
lw_comp_product_tdpp_save-product_alt = lw_comp_product-prod-
uct_alt.
lw_comp_product_tdpp_save-use_prod_consump_var_flg = c_x.
lw_comp_product_tdpp_save-prod_consump_var_uom = lw_comp_prod-
uct-prod_consump_uom.
lw_comp_product_tdpp_save-cp_date_to = lw_comp_product-date_
to. "Mandatory in case of SNP plan
lw_comp_product_tdpp_save-date_valid_to = l_end_tstamp.

IF NOT lw_comp_product-prod_consump_var IS INITIAL.
   IF lw_plan-plan_usage EQ lc_p. "PPDS plan

*  Follow PPDS logic
     lw_comp_product_tdpp_save-prod_consump_var = lw_comp_prod-
uct-prod_consump_var * ( w_resper-percnt_chg_ppds / lc_100 ).

ELSEIF lw_plan-plan_usage EQ lc_s. "SNP plan
```

```
*  Follow SNP logic
lw_comp_product_tdpp_save-prod_consump_var = lw_comp_product-
prod_consump_var * ( ( w_resper-percnt_chg_ppds - w_resper-
percnt_chg_snp ) / lc_100 ).
ENDIF.
APPEND lw_comp_product_tdpp_save TO p_li_comp_product_tdpp_
save.
CLEAR lw_comp_product_tdpp_save.
ENDIF.
ENDIF.
ENDIF.
ENDLOOP.
ENDIF. "read on table li_mode
ENDIF. "read on table li_plan "
ENDLOOP.

* Set the field TDPP_FLG to 'X'
loop at p_li_comp_product_save assigning <fs_comp_product>
     where tdpp_flg ne c_x.
<fs_comp_product>-tdpp_flg = c_x.
ENDLOOP.

* Set the field TDPP_FLG to 'X'
LOOP AT p_li_comp_product_save_x ASSIGNING <fs_comp_product_x>
     WHERE tdpp_flg NE c_x.
<fs_comp_product_x>-tdpp_flg = c_x.
ENDLOOP.

* Unassign the field symbols
UNASSIGN: <fs_comp_product>, <fs_comp_product_x>, <fs_comp_
product_tdpp>.

ENDFORM.                          " SUB_PREPARE_CHANGE_TABLES

*&---------------------------------------------------------------*
*&      Form  SUB_PPM_TDPP_UPDATE
*&---------------------------------------------------------------*
*       Update PPM TDPP entries
*----------------------------------------------------------------*
*      -->P_LI_OPERATION_SAVE      operation save
*      -->P_LI_OPERATION_SAVE_X    operation save change
*      -->P_LI_ACTIVITY_SAVE       activity save
*      -->P_LI_ACTIVITY_SAVE_X     activity save change
*      -->P_LI_LOGICAL_COMPONENT_SAVE  logical component save
```

```
*      -->P_LI_LOGICAL_COMPONENT_SAVE_X  logical component save change
*      -->P_LI_COMP_PRODUCT_SAVE          comp product save
*      -->P_LI_COMP_PRODUCT_SAVE_X        comp product save change
*      -->P_LI_COMP_PRODUCT_TDPP_SAVE     comp product save tdpp change
*      -->P_LI_PPM_MODEL                  model
*      -->P_LI_RETURN                     return
*----------------------------------------------------------------*

FORM sub_ppm_tdpp_update   TABLES
  p_li_operation_save            TYPE tt_operation_save
  p_li_operation_save_x          TYPE tt_operation_savex
  p_li_activity_save             TYPE tt_activity_save
  p_li_activity_save_x           TYPE tt_activity_savex
  p_li_logical_component_save    TYPE tt_logical_component_save
  p_li_logical_component_save_x  TYPE tt_logical_component_savex
  p_li_comp_product_save         TYPE tt_comp_product_save
  p_li_comp_product_save_x       TYPE tt_comp_product_savex
  p_li_comp_product_tdpp_save    TYPE tt_comp_product_tdpp_save
  p_li_ppm_model                 TYPE tt_ppm_model_save
  p_li_return                    TYPE tt_return_save.

* Local declarations
  DATA: lw_return                   TYPE bapiret2,
        lw_comp_product_tdpp_save   TYPE bapi10003tdppcompalt,
        l_message                   TYPE string.

* Check if there are some TDPP entries to update
  IF NOT p_li_comp_product_tdpp_save[] IS INITIAL.
* Sorting and deletion will be required when multiple en-
tries are selected from table ZGPTS_RESPER
SORT p_li_comp_product_tdpp_save BY operation_number plan_num-
ber operation_number activity log_component product_alt plan-
ning_version date_valid_to.

DELETE ADJACENT DUPLICATES FROM p_li_comp_product_tdpp_save COM-
PARING operation_number plan_number operation_number activity
log_component  product_alt planning_version date_valid_to.

* call BAPI-function to update the TDPP entries of PPMS
    CALL FUNCTION 'BAPI_PPMSRVAPS_SAVEMULTI_30A'
      EXPORTING
        logical_system       = g_log_sys
        commit_control       = c_e
```

```
    TABLES
      operation              = p_li_operation_save[]
      operation_x            = p_li_operation_save_x[]
      activity               = p_li_activity_save[]
      activity_x             = p_li_activity_save_x[]
      logical_component      = p_li_logical_component_save[]
      logical_component_x    = p_li_logical_component_save_x[]
      comp_product           = p_li_comp_product_save[]
      comp_product_x         = p_li_comp_product_save_x[]
      comp_product_tdpp      = p_li_comp_product_tdpp_save[]
      ppm_model              = p_li_ppm_model[]
      return                 = p_li_return[]
    EXCEPTIONS
      OTHERS                 = 1.

IF sy-subrc EQ 0.
  READ TABLE p_li_return TRANSPORTING NO FIELDS WITH KEY type = c_e.
  IF sy-subrc EQ 0.
    LOOP AT p_li_return INTO lw_return WHERE type EQ c_e.
      CALL FUNCTION 'FORMAT_MESSAGE'
        EXPORTING
          id        = lw_return-id
          lang      = sy-langu
          no        = lw_return-number
          v1        = lw_return-message_v1
          v2        = lw_return-message_v2
          v3        = lw_return-message_v3
          v4        = lw_return-message_v4
        IMPORTING
          msg       = l_message
        EXCEPTIONS
          not found = 1
          OTHERS    = 2.
      IF sy-subrc <> 0.
        CLEAR l_message.
      ELSE.
        w_output_tab-product = lw_return-message_v3.
        w_output_tab-message = l_message.
        APPEND w_output_tab TO i_output_tab.
        CLEAR w_output_tab.
      ENDIF.
      CLEAR lw_return.
    ENDLOOP.
```

```
* In case of error, rollback is committed by the BAPI it-
  self so no need to do explicitly

    ELSE. "success message

* Commit the data to database
    CALL FUNCTION 'BAPI_TRANSACTION_COMMIT'
          EXPORTING
            wait = c_x.

* Populate success records

*  BAPI does not return anything in case of success records
   LOOP AT p_li_comp_product_tdpp_save INTO lw_comp_product_tdpp_save.
     w_output_tab-plan_number = lw_comp_product_tdpp_save-plan_number.
     w_output_tab-product = lw_comp_product_tdpp_save-log_component.
     w_output_tab-date_valid_to = lw_comp_product_tdpp_save-date_val-
id_to.
     w_output_tab-prod_consump_var = lw_comp_product_tdpp_save-prod_
consump_var.
     w_output_tab-prod_consump_var_uom = lw_comp_product_tdpp_save-
prod_consump_var_uom.
     w_output_tab-message = 'Material consumption variable updat-
ed successfully'(002).
     APPEND w_output_tab TO i_output_tab.
     CLEAR w_output_tab.
  ENDLOOP.
  ENDIF. "read on table li_return
  ENDIF. "BAPI end of processing
     ELSE.
       MESSAGE i036. "No TDPP entries to be updated
       LEAVE LIST-PROCESSING. "leave program
     ENDIF. "check TDPP entries
  ENDFORM.                      " SUB_PPM_TDPP_UPDATE
```

7.10 USAGE OF PERIOD FACTOR

Period Factor maintained in the SNP PPM or Transportation Lane determines the Availability Date of a Receipt element within a time bucket (period). The system determines the exact availability date/time of the receipt elements within a period, by adding a time interval (that it gets by multiplying the period factor with the period length) to the start time of the period. For example enter a factor between 0 and 1, where 0 is the start of the period, 0.5 the middle, and 1 the end of the period. When calculating the availability date/time, the system takes into consideration all week-days, meaning that it does not take into consideration any days that have been defined as non-workdays in the calendars. Period Factor used is 0.71 = 7 x 0.71 = 4.97 or 5 days from optimizer of weekly bucket resulting in a Friday.

If Period Factor is not maintained in PPM or Transportation Lane then the User Period Factor indicator and the Period Factor value maintained in the Lot Size tab of the location-product combination is used. If this is not maintained a default value of 0.5 is used.

EXAMPLE

Set the source of supply to the order.

```
CALL FUNCTION '/SAPAPO/RRP_ORDER_SET_SOURCE'
  EXPORTING
    iv_ordid              = p_ordid
    iv_position_no        = '1'
    iv_line_no            = space
    iv_application        = space
    iv_trpid              = p_tgt_trpid
    iv_ttype              = space
  EXCEPTIONS
    order not changable = 1
    OTHERS              = 2.
```

7.11 RELEASE PROFILE

Release Profile is used to release timeseries data from DP to SNP/PPDS. One need to define the DP Planning Area and timeseries keyfigure the data in which is released and the SNP Category Type (typically FA) to which data is released. Maintain a Daily Buckets Profile it will define the number of working days (working days determined based on Shipping Calendar maintained for the location master) starting on and from the From Date if released online/interactively or that many workdays of the planning horizon when release of planning is executed and carried out in background. The Period Split (blank, 1 and 2) field in the SNP2 tab of location-product master determines how demand plan is released to SNP from DP (how bucketed data is disaggregated to the workdays).

EXAMPLE

Requirement is to convert the orders to Purchase orders in the system, it also covers the deletion of orders from LiveCache.

```
* Read Procurement Orders for Selection Criteria - With Characteristics
CALL FUNÇTION 'BAPI_POSRVAPS_GETLIST3'
  EXPORTING
    logical_system     = logical_system          "Logical System
    start_time         = start_time              "Start Time
    end_time           = end_time                "End time
    plng_version       = '000'
    io_node_selection  = 'I'
```

```
  TABLES
    product_selection   = product_selection       "Product
    location_selection  = location_selection      "Location
    order_selection     = order_selection         "Order Selection
    ordertype_selection = ordertype_selection     "Order Type Selection
    atpcat_selection    = atpcat_selection        "APO Category
    receipts            = receipts                "Receipts at RDC
    requirements        = requirements            "Requirements at CDC
    return              = return.                 "Return Table
* refresh internal table
REFRESH:  gt_poco_update[].
************************************************************************

LOOP AT requirements INTO gs_requirements2.
  IF  gs_requirements2-atpcat = 'EG'.
    CLEAR : lf_dat.
    lf_dat = gs_requirements2-requirement_date.
    IF lf_dat+0(8) LE lf_io_time .
      CALL FUNCTION 'GUID_CONVERT'
        EXPORTING
          iv_guid_c32    = gs_requirements2-ordid      "Order Id 32 bit
        IMPORTING
          ev_guid_c22    = gs_detail1-orderid          "Order Id 22 bit
        EXCEPTIONS
          no unicode_support_yet = 1
          parameters_error       = 2
          OTHERS                 = 3.
        CASE sy-subrc.
          WHEN 1.
*              MESSAGE i051.
          WHEN 2.
*              MESSAGE i052.
          WHEN OTHERS.
        ENDCASE.
* populate the detailed table for order deletion
        gs_detail1-date = lf_dat+0(8).                     "date
        gs_detail1-loc  = gf_loc.                          "location
        gs_detail1-quan = gs_requirements2-quantity.       "quantity
        APPEND gs_detail1 TO gt_detail1.
        CLEAR : gs_detail1.

      ENDIF.
    ENDIF.
  ENDLOOP.
```

```
*  Delete order from the LC !!
SORT gt_detail1 BY orderid.
DELETE ADJACENT DUPLICATES FROM gt_detail1 COMPARING orderid.
LOOP AT gt_detail1 INTO gs_detail1.
  CALL FUNCTION '/SAPAPO/RRP_LC_ORDER_DELETE'
    EXPORTING
      iv_ordid        = gs_detail1-orderid    "order id to be deleted !!
      iv_application = 'D'
      iv_flush        = space.

  CALL FUNCTION '/SAPAPO/OM_LC_COMMIT'
    EXCEPTIONS
      lc_connect_failed = 1
      lc_com_error      = 2
      lc_appl_error     = 3
      OTHERS            = 4.
  CASE sy-subrc.
    WHEN 1.
    WHEN 2.
    WHEN 3.
    WHEN OTHERS.
  ENDCASE.
ENDLOOP.
gt_poco_update_conv2[] = poco_update[].
***********************************************************************

LOOP AT gt_poco_update_conv2 ASSIGNING <fs_poco_update>.
  <fs_poco_update>-catfr = cf_bi.           "For tlb po at Loc1 side
  <fs_poco_update>-catto = cf_bf.           "For tlb po at Loc2 side
  <fs_poco_update>-kzfr = cf_9admddt.       "Key figure at Loc1 side
  <fs_poco_update>-kzto = cf_9atship.       "Key figure at Loc2 side
  <fs_poco_update>-mosta = cf_n.            "Type - New
  <fs_poco_update>-status = cf_2.           "Status will be 2
ENDLOOP.

IF gt_poco_update_conv2[] IS NOT INITIAL .
  CALL FUNCTION '/SAPAPO/MSDP_TD_TRANSFER_SET'
    EXPORTING
      iv_appl = 'SNP'
    CHANGING
      ct_poco = gt_poco_update_conv2.

  LOOP AT gt_poco_update_conv2 ASSIGNING <fs_poco_update>.
    <fs_poco_update>-catfr = cf_bi.
    <fs_poco_update>-catto = cf_bf.
    <fs_poco_update>-kzfr = cf_9admddt.
    <fs_poco_update>-kzto = cf_9atship.
    <fs_poco_update>-mosta = cf_n.         "New
```

```
    <fs_poco_update>-status = cf_2.          "Order Status = 2
    <fs_poco_update>transfer = cf_0.
  ENDLOOP.

*Create Order with new quantity
  CALL FUNCTION '/SAPAPO/TS_DM_TRANS_SET'
    EXPORTING
      iv_pareaid         = gv_pareaid
      is_write_options   = ls_write_options
      it_cols            = lt_cols_dm1
    CHANGING
      ct_poco            = gt_poco_update_conv2          "Poco Update
    EXCEPTIONS
      lc_com_error       = 1
      lc_appl_error      = 2
      OTHERS             = 3.
  IF sy-subrc <> 0.
    CASE sy-subrc.
      WHEN 1.
      WHEN 2.
      WHEN OTHERS.
    ENDCASE.
  ELSE.
    flag_conv = 'X'.
    poco_update_conv[] = gt_poco update_conv2[].
  ENDIF.
ENDIF.
```

7.12 PARALLEL PROCESSING

Parallel processing is a concept where execution can be done parallel to increase the speed and reduce the execution time. I am explaining here the concept of parallel processing also which can be coded along with the handling of LiveCache program to make the execution more fast.

Parallel Processing Technique allows the program to let them parcel out the work to be done to available dialog work processes in the SAP system and then collect the results. Parallel-processing is implemented with a special variant of asynchronous RFC. It's important to use only the correct variant for own parallel processing applications: the CALL FUNCTION STARTING NEW TASK DESTINATION IN GROUP keyword. Using other variants of asynchronous RFC circumvents the built-in safeguards in the correct keyword. Parallel processing is implemented in the application reports that are to run in the background.

7.12.1 Why to Implement Parallel Processing

Parallel processing can be very useful in the programs which handles huge volume of data, handling huge volume in a program does not only lead to very long execution time but also other leads to issue like run time error due to memory shortage (ST22) etc. It can be difficult to finish such jobs in the "night-time" that is available, especially if dialog users are spread across several time zones.

For our example of Ex-factory Price calculation Program

In a single transaction execution, program fetch Trigger Data, EA Prices, Special Discount prices, Product Hierarchy data, Customer PH Discount, Customer General discounts, Old Ex-factory data from database, each of these 7-8 tables may contain 3-5 millions of records each in real time scenario which mean we could have around 40 million records in internal tables of program before even the calculation of ex-factory price the outcome of this program makes this 40 million to much more higher since the Ex-Factory Price calculated based on these will be around 10-20 million based on time slices. Without implementing parallel processing in program to handle 50-60 million records, will leads to various issues like:

- Very Long time execution (Around 10 hours for 0.2 million outcome).
- Runtime Errors in ST22 (No more memory space available to extend Internal table.

To deal with these issues in current scenario, the best approach is to implement parallel processing in the program.

7.12.2 Pre-requisites to Implement Parallel Processing

- In the function module this attribute is specified in the *Remote function call supported* field in the function module definition (transaction SE37).
- The called function module may not include a function call to the destination "BACK.".
- The calling program should not change to a new internal session after making an Asynchronous RFC call. That is, one should not use SUBMIT or CALL TRANSACTION in such a report after using CALL FUNCTION STARTING NEW TASK.
- One cannot use the CALL FUNCTION STARTING NEW TASK DESTINATION IN GROUP keyword to start external programs.

7.12.3 How to Implement Parallel Processing

Step 1 Define the size of Data Packets for parallel processing.

Split the Total records of Original Input data which require parallel processing into separate data packets so that these data packets can be used for parallel processing.

Packets of size can be defined by 2 ways:

(a) Allow the User to decide for the size of Data packet (Block) for parallel processing through Selection Screen, by this way we would split the total records of Original Input data into the data packets of user defined value.

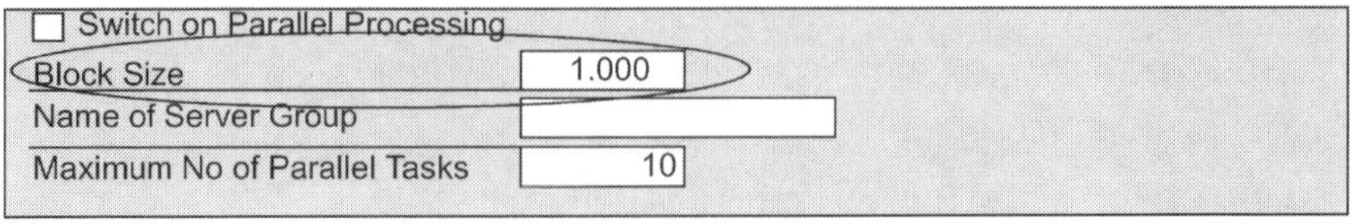

Figure 7.15 Parallel processing block size

The above screenshot shows that User can set the size of data packets by providing require value to Block size parameter. Currently 1000 records per Data packets are set.

(b) Find out how many work processes are available to more efficiently size the packets of data that to be processed.

Function module SPBT_INITIALIZE: Optional. Use to determine the availability of Resources for parallel processing.

```
CALL FUNCTION 'SPBT_INITIALIZE'
      EXPORTING
            group_name = RFC Server Group
      IMPORTING
            free_pbt_wps = lv_free_wps
```

Once we determine available free resources for parallel processing, into lv_free_wps, we can prepare Data packets using that as below Get the total number of records of Main Input table.

```
DESCRIBE TABLE IT_ALL_DATA LINES lf_tfill.
```

Split the total number of records by using available work processes

```
Data packet Size = CEIL (lf_tfill / lv_free_wps).
If Data packet Size = 0.
      Data packet Size = 1.
End if.
```

Once the size of Data packets is determine using preferred/required way of above two ways, proceed to Step 2.

(**Note:** For example shown this document, we have allowed user to define Data packets on selection screen)

Step 2 Create a RFC Function module which will be used as Processing Function module for all tasks in parallel processing. Create a Function module which must be Remote Enabled Function module, This RFC will contain all the require code which need to be executed parallel. Provide the Import, Export and Tables parameter as require for processing.

Once the Processing Function module is created, proceed to Step 3.

Step 3 Prepare data packets with the size define using Step 1.
Its time now to prepare Data packets which we would pass to Parallel Processing FM (Created in Step 2), we have already determined the size of these packets.

```
LOOP AT IT_ALL_DATA.
For First row of Internal table.
* Store the start index of the packet
lf_start_index = sy-tabix.
ENDIF.
* Add the record to the packet to be passed to the function
APPEND IS_ALL_DATA TO Packet_data.
* Increase number of records added to the packet.
lf_line_count = lf_line_count + .
IF lf_line_count GE Packet Size.
* Store the last index of the packet
lf_end_index = sy-tabix.
* Remove the records added to packet from original input table.
DELETE IT_ALL_DATA FROM lf_start_index TO lf_end_index.
```

LOOP over Original Input data for processing and once the records reached the limit of data packets size. Prepare the data packet with the records processed so far of Original Input data also delete the data packets records from Original Input data so that it could not be processed again. Now when we are ready with packets to process parallel, proceed to Step 4.

Step 4 Check the work process resources status, prepare task number before calling processing FM, we need to check if we have any resource availability problem of max number of parallel processes are already filled up (define of selection screen and used decided how many max number of parallel process resource at a time should be used to run program) also, increment task number.

```
* When only 1 job is suffering from unavailability of resource.
IF pf_res_problem = 1.
      WAIT UNTIL gf_received >= gf_sent UP TO '0.01' SECONDS.
      IF sy-subrc = 0.
            pf_res_problem = 0.
      ENDIF.
* When 2 jobs are suffering from unavailability of resource.
ELSEIF pf_res_problem = 2.
      WAIT UNTIL gf_received >= gf_sent UP TO '0.1' SECONDS.
      IF sy-subrc = 0.
            pf_res_problem = 0.
      ENDIF.
```

```
* When 3 jobs are suffering from unavailability of resource.
ELSEIF pf_res_problem = 3.
      WAIT UNTIL gf_received >= gf_sent UP TO '1' SECONDS.
      IF sy-subrc = 0.
            pf_res_problem = 0.
      ENDIF.
ENDIF.
* Wait until job slots are freed so that number of parallel running
* jobs don't cross sel. screen value of total number of parallel
  jobs
lf_dummy = gf_sent - pi_nmtsk.
IF gf_received <= lf_dummy.
      WAIT UNTIL gf_received > lf_dummy.
ENDIF.
* Increment the task number by 1.
taskname = taskname + 1.
```

Here gf_sent has been used to keep the status of Sent jobs while gf_received has been used for the status of Received jobs, gf_sent will be filled while calling the parallel processing FM (Step5) while gf_received will be filled when retrieving result from parallel processing FM (Step 6) later.

Once the resource status availability checked and no problem found, Proceed to step 5 to call Parallel processing FM.

Step 5 Call the Parallel Processing passing data packets Call the Processing Function Module with the data packets ABAP keyword CALL FUNCTION <function> STARTING NEW TASK <taskname> with the DESTINATION IN GROUP argument:

Use this keyword to have the SAP system executes the function module call in parallel.

Typically, place this keyword in a loop in which code to divide up the data that is to be processed into packets prepared it Step 3. Pass the data that is to be processed in the form of an internal table (EXPORT, TABLE arguments).

```
* Call the function module to process the input data packet
* in a separate task.
CALL FUNCTION 'Y_PARELLEL_TEST'
STARTING
NEW TASK taskname
DESTINATION
IN GROUP Server Group
PERFORMING
f_func_info_return ON END OF TASK
```

```
EXPORTING
      piv_input_data = Data Packet
EXCEPTIONS
      communication_failure = 1
      system_failure        = 2
      resource_failure      = 3.
```

Here is example, where data packets has been passed to parallel processing FM into Export parameter with Data packets Other important information's are:

Task name- Prepared in Step 4 Server Group- Server Group Name from Selection Screen or Default value f_func_info_return – This is a routine which will be used to retrieve results from parallel. Processing FM later in Step 6.

Step 6 Retrieve the Processing Function module outcome to receive the results from each parallel task once the processing task completes, below syntax can be used -

```
RECEIVE RESULTS FROM FUNCTION 'RFC_SYSTEM_INFO':
```

The CALL FUNCTION keyword (Step 5) triggers processing of form RETURN_INFO when each parallel processing task completes. RECEIVE is needed to gather IMPORTING and TABLE returns of an asynchronously executed RFC function module.

```
FORM f_func_info_return USING pf_taskname TYPE clike.
* Receive the result of the tasks created for parallel processing.
RECEIVE RESULTS FROM FUNCTION 'Y_PARELLEL_TEST'
IMPORTING
      pev_tr_data = lt_result
EXCEPTIONS
      communication_failure = 1
      system_failure        = 2.
```

Here is example; where data have been received from parallel processing FM Import parameter with lt_result.

For each data packets determined from Step 3, repeat the processing of Step 4 to Step 6 till all data for Original Input table have been processed. Once no more records in Original Input table are left for processing.

Step 7 Check the results have been returned from all parallel processing FM call for each data packets before processing further ABAP keyword WAIT: Required to wait for all of the asynchronous parallel tasks created with CALL FUNCTION to return.

```
WAIT UNTIL gf_active_calls = 0.
```

Here in example gf_active_calls is a variable which keeps the track between send Jobs (Parallel processing FM call- Step 5) and receive jobs (Receive Results from Parallel processing FM call – Step 6).

7.12.4 Error Handling and Parallel Task Tracking

Error handling in Parallel Processing can be done both at the time of Calling Processing FM for start parallel task also at the time of receiving result from the Processing FM at the end of task. In the example used for this Document Error handling has been done by Spool writing for all exceptions.

(a) While Calling Parallel Processing FM to initiate a parallel task–

```
CALL FUNCTION 'Y_PARELLEL_TEST'
STARTING
NEW TASK gf_taskname
DESTINATION
IN GROUP p_srvgp
PERFORMING
EXCEPTIONS
      communication_failure = 1
      system_failure        = 2
      resource_failure      = 3.
```

If any exception is raise, require action can be performed for the exception received.

Please refer to below spool log for an example.

(b) Receiving Result from Parallel Processing FM at end of task–

```
RECEIVE RESULTS FROM FUNCTION 'Y_PARELLEL_TEST'
EXCEPTIONS
      communication_failure = 1
      system_failure        = 2.
```

If any exception is raise, require action can be performed for the exception received.

Please refer to below spool log for an example.

7.12.5 Parallel Tasks Tracking

Status and progress of parallel tasks can be tracked using the Transaction Code SM66 which will display all parallel tasks running in the system.

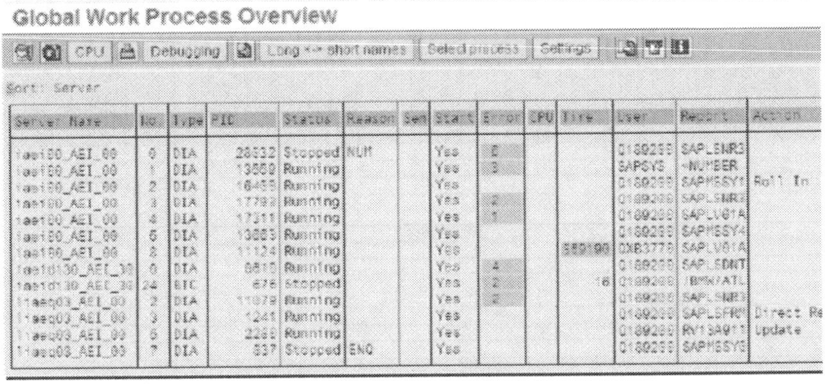

Figure 7.16 Server work processes

SM50 can also be used to analyze the Parallel Tasks status and progress.

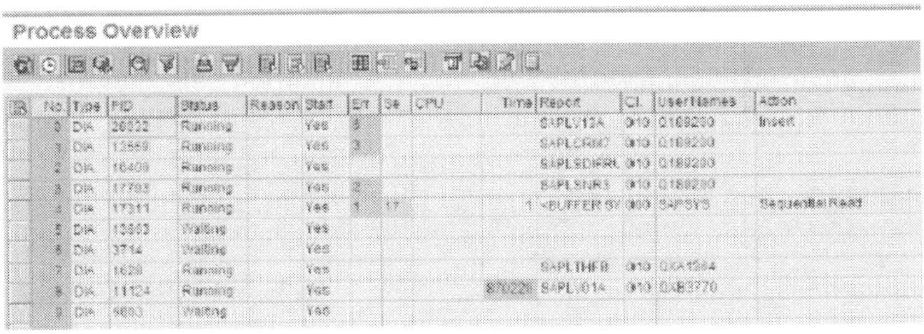

Figure 7.17 Server work processes

7.12.6 Benefits and Constraints of Parallel Processing

(A) Benefits

- Very fast execution time
- Allows handling of very huge data from a SAP program
- Minimize the runtime errors, for example - memory issues, data overflow etc.
- Very useful for long running programs

(B) Constraints

- There is no guarantee that data will be processed in a particular order in parallel processing or that a particular result will be available at a given point in processing.
- The data processing task that is to be carried out in parallel must be logically independent of other instances of the task. That is, the task can be carried out

without reference to other records from the same data set that are also being processed in parallel, and the task is not dependent upon the results of others of the parallel operations.

- Due to possibility of resources unavailability It is recommended (for performance and other reasons) to use an RFC group with sufficient resources for parallel processing of asynchronous calls only.
- Exception handling in parallel processing requires very good care so that require action can be taken for each parallel task's success or failure.

Here in this chapter I have covered much of the technical part in APO, explained how to access LiveCache data using function module, I suggest to use as much as function modules and BAPI's to explore more on the programming techniques in APO.

8

DEPLOYMENT

8.1 DEPLOYMENT CONCEPT

Deployment determines which requirements can be covered by the existing supply. If the produced quantities (supply and demand) match actual plans, then the result of Deployment is a confirmation of the supply network plan. If the available quantities are insufficient to cover the demand, the system makes adjustments accordingly, depending on whether to run the Deployment Heuristic or Optimization.

Deployment adjusts the stock transfers for short-term changes on both the supply and demand side. Deployment determines whether requirements can be covered by the existing supply or not. If the produced quantities match actual planned order, then the result of Deployment is a confirmation of the supply network plan i.e. confirmed planned order. If the available quantities are insufficient to cover the demand, the system makes adjustments accordingly.

8.2 DEPLOYMENT HEURISTIC

Deployment Heuristic calculates a replenishment plan for one product at one location. If the available quantities are less than the demand, the system uses fair share rules to determine the distribution plan. If the available quantities are more than the demand, the system uses push rules to determine the distribution plan.

- Calculates a replenishment plan for one product at one location
- Fair share (if ATD is less than the distribution demand planned at the supply location)
- Push (if ATD is more than the distribution demand planned at the supply location)
- Fair Share and Push rules are defined in the deployment profile

8.3 DEPLOYMENT OPTIMIZATION

The Deployment Optimization run calculates a replenishment plan for one product at all locations in the network. If the available quantities are insufficient to cover the demand, or there is more product available than demand, the system uses minimum cost flow optimization to determine an optimal distribution plan for the entire network simultaneously.

- Calculates a replenishment plan for one product at all locations in the network
- Minimum cost flow optimization

There are several deployment and allocation strategies:

- Fair share
- Push deployment
- Pull-push deployment
- Minimum cost flow optimization.

Different deployment strategies are used depending on the current situation. If demand exceeds supply, then a fair share allocation can be employed. If supply exceeds demand, than a push strategy is employed. When excess inventory exist, surplus stock must be distributed according to a different principle called push logic.

The pull-push deployment rules use demand and supply time fences to determine the deployment logic.

The pull horizon is on the demand profile and the push horizon is on the supply profile.

- Fair share rules are evoked when 'demand' exceeds 'supply' at the source location.
- 'Demand' refers to the sum of the 'Distribution Demand Planned' (Purchase Requisition) quantities within the Pull Deployment Horizon.
- 'Supply' refers to the sum of the order category quantities that form the order category group ATD receipts.

8.3.1 Process Flow and where Deployment Triggered

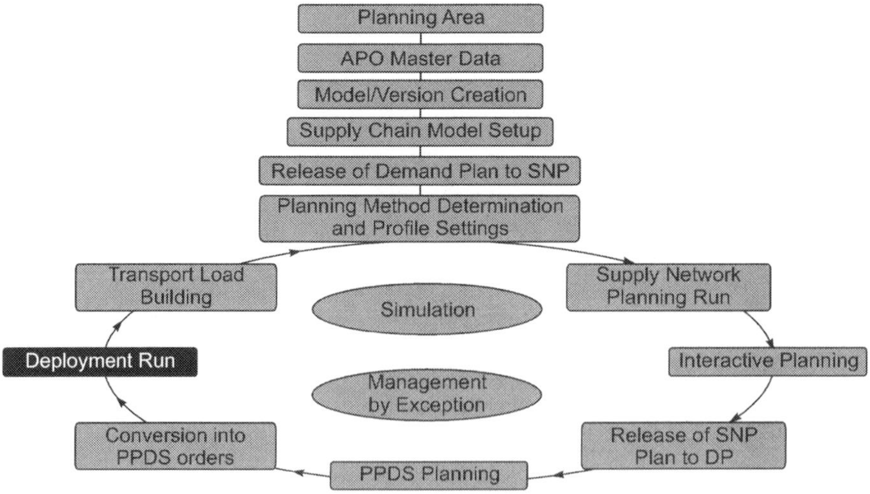

Figure 8.1 Process flow of SCM-APO

- Deployment determines which requirements (Distribution Demand Planned at the source location) can be covered by the existing supply.
- Existing Supply in this case is called 'Available to Deploy' or ATD.
- ATD is the net of ATD Issues (grouping of requirement elements) and ATD Receipts (grouping of receipt elements).
- ATD receipts and ATD issues are order category groups maintained in Location Master (SNP Tab). This is over-ridden by ATD Receipts and Issues maintained in Product Master (SNP2 Tab).
- If the produced quantities (supply and demand) match actual plans, then the result of Deployment is a confirmation of the supply network plan.
- If the available quantities are insufficient to cover the demand, the system makes adjustments accordingly.

The Standard SAP uses fair share rule and Push logic to deploy stocks from the manufacturing plants to various locations. Fair share rule is used when demand is greater than supplies. Push Logic is used when the supplies are greater than the demands from all the locations. Within the Push Logic there are different ways the system considers the demands and supplies.

- With pull/push distribution, the entire supply is distributed immediately to the demand locations to fulfill all demand within the pull deployment horizon. The demand dates specified at the demand locations are ignored in this instance. Any supplies that are greater than the demands within the Pull horizon are left at the manufacturing plant.
- With Push by demands, the supply is distributed immediately to the demand locations for the entire Deployment horizon to fulfill all demands. (The "pull" deployment horizon is ignored in this instance.) Any supplies that are greater than the demands within the Pull horizon are left at the manufacturing plant
- With Push by quota arrangement, the entire supply is distributed immediately according to the set quota arrangements for the demand locations. The demand situation at the destination locations is ignored in this instance.

Generally, Distribution Center has demand pulling stock from the manufacturing plants. When there is excess stock at the manufacturing plants because of the rounding values or due to over production, agenda will be to 'Push' the excess out of the door. In order to fulfill the business requirement to deploy all stock regardless of demand, copy of standard Pull/Push (Strategy "P") logic and deploy to all requirements within the Pull Horizon can be created or used. Then, for all excess supply, use the outbound quota arrangement. If there is no demand within the Pull deployment horizon, use the outbound quota arrangement to push the excess stock to demand plants that have a relationship with the supply plant (APO Transportation Lanes). If there is no quota arrangement, it leaves the excess stock at the manufacturing plant.

Example

A manufacturing planning process will produce more product than what is needed at the distribution plant. This will occur where there is a replenishment multiples related to manufacturing lot size i.e. replenish in multiple of 20,000 cases. The standard SAP logic will not deploy the added stock unless there is a DC demand within the Pull deployment horizon.

Example with figures: DC demand is 12,000 cases, manufacturing lot size is 20,000. There will be a STR for 12,000 to the DC. The remaining 8,000 will be kept at the manufacturing plant. Excess stock can occur 3 ways; SNP Heuristic round up to next lot size multiple, Plant Scheduler manually increases the Process Order Qty, or there is a production overrun.

In the case where there is a shortage of deployable inventory at the manufacturing plants Deployment uses APO standard fair share rule. The standard fair share rule is a 50/50 split of the supply orders to the demand orders from the DC.

Example: If 2 DC have orders for 50 each and the total available supply at the manufacturing plant is 80. So there is a difference of -20 at the manufacturing plants. The logic should be to split the available supply at the manufacturing plant equally to both the demand from the DC's. If there is only one DC with demand at the manufacturing plants then all the available supply should be allocated to that DC's.

Standard Deployment *program: /SAPAPO/RMSDPDEP*

Selection Screen:

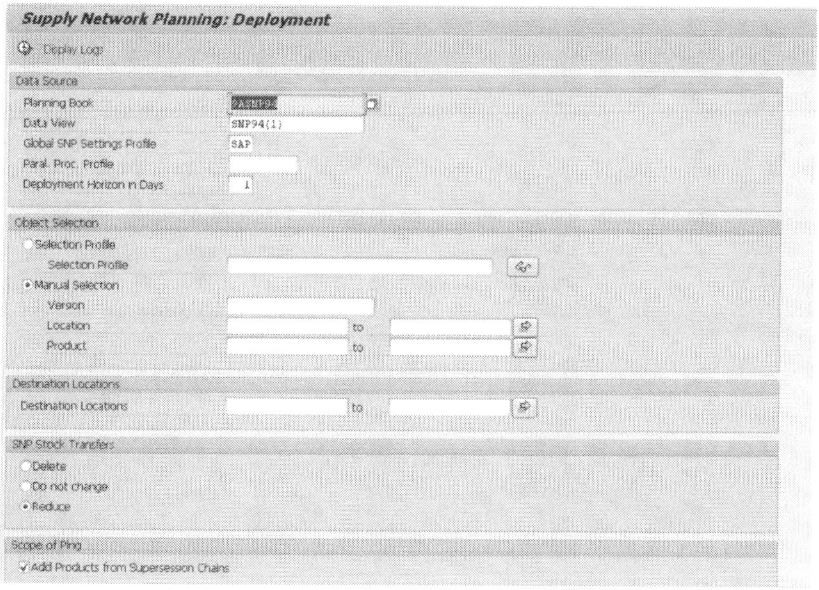

Figure 8.2 Deployment selection screen

As mentioned in selection screen, for executing deployment, we require prerequisites as mentioned below:

1. *Planning Book* – Deployment is run for the particular planning book which is given in selection screen

2. *Data View* – Deployment is run for the particular data view which is given in selection screen
3. *Global SNP Setting Profile* – Profile where to make settings for planning procedures in SNP heuristic or SNP optimizer.
4. *Parallel Proc. Profile* – This profile specifies how background jobs are split into parallel processes.
5. *Deployment Horizon in Days* – Indicates number of days the system considers during deployment calculation.
6. *Selection Profile or Manual Selection* – Can either specify selection profile or manual selection. Selection profile is already saved during interactive planning and that profile can be mentioned in screen for which deployment needs to be run.
7. *Destination Location* – If this selection field is used, deployment is carried out for specified destination location else deployment is carries out for all possible destination locations
8. *SNP Stock Transfers Processing* – Here to specify how the system proceed with the SNP stock transfers created during the Supply Network Planning run and the deployment stock transfers after the deployment run.
    - If "*Do not change" selected*, the system does not create any deployment stock transfers and does not reduce the existing SNP stock transfers. This option is for simulation purposes only. View the results in the log.
    - If "*Reduce" selected*, the system creates deployment stock transfers and reduces the SNP stock transfers accordingly.
    - If "*Delete" selected*, the system creates deployment stock transfers and deletes all the SNP stock transfers that fall within the planning period, regardless of whether or not they could be confirmed during the deployment run.

Figure 8.3 Setting to consider supersession in deployment

If this indicator is set, all products of a supersession chain are included in the selection and also planned as part of product interchangeability within *Supply Network Planning (SNP)*. This indicator is set by default.

If the indicator is **not** set, the system behaves as follows:

- **SNP planning run:** The system transfers a demand to a successor product (if necessary) by creating SNP substitution orders; however, it does not plan the receipt for the successor product. This type of planning does not provide correct results for the entire supply chain, since the system does not plan all products of the supersession chain.

- **Deployment:** Deployment does not consider any SNP substitution orders. If to carry out product interchangeability in deployment, must make sure that this indicator is set.

8.4 TECHNICAL DETAILS

Code sequence for deployment: How the deployment is executed technically is described here, i.e. the sequence executed behind the standard deployment or steps to follow if one has to create a custom deployment solution as per new requirement.

1. Check LiveCache availability
2. Fetch material and location id based on selection ID
3. Fetch material information based on material ID
4. Read model based on simulation version
5. Fetch source and destination location ID and location information based on location number
6. Fetch transportation lane information based on version id and material ID
7. Fetch information about current data view
8. Fetch start date from current data view
9. Get planning start date
10. Update master data queue based on planning version and planning area ID
11. Start deployment heuristic for multiple source location
12. Write log with error, success message and detailed information

Function modules used in deployment program is mentioned below, the function modules are explained in detail, later in the chapter:

- /SAPAPO/MSNP_BAS_CHECK_LC
- /SAPAPO/MSNP_BAS_VERSION2MODEL
- /SAPAPO/MSNP_MATERIAL_GET
- /SAPAPO/DM_MATERIAL_GET
- /SAPAPO/MSDP_MD_ARCMAT_GET
- /SAPAPO/MSDP_DEP_MULTI_SOURCE
- /SAPAPO/TS_LCM_QUEUE_REPORT
- /SAPAPO/TS_LCM_INITIALIZE
- /SAPAPO/MSNP_BAS_EXTERN_PDATE
- /SAPAPO/MSDP_SDP_GET_PLANSTART
- /SAPAPO/OM_ORDER_GET_DATA
- /SAPAPO/MSDP_TD_TRANSFER_SET
- /SAPAPO/TS_DM_TRANS_SET
- BAPI_PBSRVAPS_GETDETAIL2
- /SAPAPO/ATP_DISP_LC_SINGLE
- /SAPAPORRP_LC_ORDER_DELETE

- /SAPAPO/DM_ORDID_GET_ORDER
- /SAPAPO/RRP_SIMSESSION_LEAVE
- /SAPAPO/RRP_SIMSESSION_CREATE
- /SAPAPO/TS_PAREA_PAREAID_GET
- BAPI_POSRVAPS_GETLIST3

8.5 FUNCTION MODULES

/SAPAPO/MSNP_BAS_CHECK_LC: It checks whether LiveCache exists and displays dialog box if errors occurs in LiveCache

FUNCTION /SAPAPO/MSNP_BAS_CHECK_LC.

```
*"------------------------------------------
*"*"Lokale Schnittstelle:
*"  IMPORTING
*"     VALUE(IV_LCERR_MSG_BATCH) TYPE /SAPAPO/BOOLEAN DEFAULT 'X'
*"  EXPORTING
*"     VALUE(EV_LC_OK)
*"     VALUE(EV_OK)
*"------------------------------------------
```

Explanation

```
IMPORTING
  IV_LCERR_MSG_BATCH     =    'X'
EXPORTING
  EV_LC_OK               =    'X'
```

Check EV_LC_OK for availability of LiveCache

/SAPAPO/MSNP_BAS_VERSION2MODEL: It reads model for simulation version. This function module extracts model from database table /SAPAPO/APO01 based on version id.

FUNCTION /SAPAPO/MSNP_BAS_VERSION2MODEL.

```
*»----------------------------------------
*»*»Lokale Schnittstelle:
*»      IMPORTING
*»         VALUE(IV_VERSION) TYPE /SAPAPO/VRSIOID
*»      EXPORTING
*»         VALUE(EV_MODEL) TYPE /SAPAPO/C_MODELID
*»         VALUE(EV_VRSIOEX) TYPE /SAPAPO/VRSIOEX
*»      EXCEPTIONS
*»         VERSION_NOT_FOUND
*»----------------------------------------
```

Explanation

```
IMPORTING
     IV_VERSION     = <Version ID>
EXPORTING
   EV_MODEL         = <Model>
     EV_VRSIOEX     = <Planning Version>
```

/SAPAPO/DM_MATERIAL_GET: Function module extracts data like material information, material text, base unit of measure for particular material based on material id.

FUNCTION /SAPAPO/DM_MATERIAL_GET.

```
*"----------------------------------------
*"*"Local Interface:
*"  IMPORTING
*"    VALUE(IV_LANGU) LIKE  SY-LANGU OPTIONAL
*"  TABLES
*"    I_MATID_TAB STRUCTURE /SAPAPO/DM_MATERIAL_STR
*"    E_MATKEY_TAB STRUCTURE /SAPAPO/MATKEY OPTIONAL
*"    E_MATTXT_TAB STRUCTURE /SAPAPO/MATTXT_STR OPTIONAL
*"    E_MARM_TAB STRUCTURE /SAPAPO/MARM_STR OPTIONAL
*"    E_MATID_ERR_TAB STRUCTURE /SAPAPO/DM_MATERIAL_STR OPTIONAL
*"  EXCEPTIONS
*"   MATERIAL_NOT_FOUND
*"----------------------------------------
```

Explanation

```
IMPORTING
     I_MATID_TAB-MATID = <Material ID>
EXPORTING
     E_MATKEY_TAB      = <Matkey information like material num-
                         ber, product type, product attributes
                         etc.>
     E_MATTXT_TAB      = <Material Text>
     E_MARM_TAB        = <MARM table information like alternate
                         unit of measure, attributes of alter-
                         native UOM etc.>
```

/SAPAPO/MSDP_MD_ARCMAT_GET: Function Module reads transportation lanes for given product based on version or model. If version or model is not provided error is raised.

FUNCTION /SAPAPO/MSDP_MD_ARCMAT_GET.

```
*"----------------------------------------
*"*"Lokale Schnittstelle:
*"  IMPORTING
```

```
*"      VALUE(IV_VERSION) TYPE /SAPAPO/VRSIOID OPTIONAL
*"      VALUE(IV_MODEL) TYPE /SAPAPO/C_MODELID OPTIONAL
*"      VALUE(IV_VALFR) TYPE /SAPAPO/SNPTSTMP OPTIONAL
*"      VALUE(IV_VALTO) TYPE /SAPAPO/SNPTSTMP OPTIONAL
*"      VALUE(IT_ARCMAT) TYPE /SAPAPO/MSNP_ARCMAT_TAB OPTIONAL
*"      VALUE(IV_SNP12) TYPE C OPTIONAL
*"      VALUE(IV_INVALID_TOO) TYPE /SAPAPO/BOOLEAN DEFAULT SPACE
*"      VALUE(IT_ARC) TYPE /SAPAPO/MSNP_ARC_TAB OPTIONAL
*"      VALUE(IT_MATID) TYPE /SAPAPO/MATID_TAB OPTIONAL
*"   EXPORTING
*"      REFERENCE(ET_ARCMAT) TYPE /SAPAPO/MSNP_ARCMAT_TAB
*"      REFERENCE(ET_ARCMAT_INVALID) TYPE /SAPAPO/MSNP_ARCMAT_TAB
*"      REFERENCE(ET_MESSAGE) TYPE /SAPAPO/APOGRID_LOG_MSG
*"   EXCEPTIONS
*"      NO_MODEL_OR_VERSION
*"      ERROR
*"----------------------------------------
```

Explanation

```
IMPORTING
    IV_VERSION    = <Version ID>
    IV_MODEL      = <Model No>
    IT_ARCMAT     = <Material ID>
EXPORTING
    ET_ARCMAT     = <Material & Transporting Lane info>
```

For fetching Transporting Lane information based on material ID function module /SAPAPO/TR_TRM_GET and fetching source of supply and quota arrangement function module /SAPAPO/MSDP_MD_SOS_GET_ARRAY is called within function module /SAPAPO/MSDP_MD_ARCMAT_GET.

/SAPAPO/TR_TRM_GET: This FM reads means of transportation for the transportation lane. The means of transport for the transportation lane is read. The selection criteria can be start location, destination location, means of transport, or the start or end of the validity.

When the read takes place, the bucket transportation resource from the global means of transport entry (TRTYPE entry) is written to the corresponding entries of the means of transport, if the RESUID field is initial/blank.

FUNCTION /SAPAPO/TR_TRM_GET.

```
*"----------------------------------------
*"*"Local Interface:
*"   IMPORTING
*"      VALUE(I_VDREL_LOCFR) TYPE XFELD DEFAULT ' '
*"      VALUE(I_MODEL_FLD) TYPE /SAPAPO/C_MODELID OPTIONAL
```

```
*"     VALUE(I_VERSID_FLD) TYPE /SAPAPO/VRSIOID OPTIONAL
*"     VALUE(I_VALFR_FLD) TYPE /SAPAPO/SCC_VALFROMTSTMP OPTIONAL
*"     VALUE(I_VALTO_FLD) TYPE /SAPAPO/SCC_VALTOTSTMP OPTIONAL
*"     VALUE(I_AGGTPL_FLG) TYPE /SAPAPO/TR_AGGPLFLG OPTIONAL
*"     VALUE(I_DTLTPL_FLG) TYPE /SAPAPO/TR_DTLPLFLG OPTIONAL
*"     VALUE(I_BUFFER_FLG) TYPE XFELD OPTIONAL
*"  TABLES
*"     I_TRMID_TAB STRUCTURE /SAPAPO/S_TRMID OPTIONAL
*"     I_LOCFR_TAB STRUCTURE /SAPAPO/LOC_LOCID_STR OPTIONAL
*"     I_LOCTO_TAB STRUCTURE /SAPAPO/LOC_LOCID_STR OPTIONAL
*"     I_LOCFRNO_RTAB STRUCTURE /SAPAPO/LOCNO_RSTR OPTIONAL
*"     I_LOCTONO_RTAB STRUCTURE /SAPAPO/LOCNO_RSTR OPTIONAL
*"     I_TTYPE_TAB STRUCTURE /SAPAPO/S_TRATY OPTIONAL
*"     I_TTYPE_RTAB STRUCTURE /SAPAPO/TTYPE_RSTR OPTIONAL
*"     I_VTPRID_TAB STRUCTURE /SAPAPO/VT_PFR_IN OPTIONAL
*"     I_VTOSIDDEF_TAB STRUCTURE /SAPAPO/VT_OSID_IN OPTIONAL
*"     I_VTOSID_TAB STRUCTURE /SAPAPO/VT_OSID_IN OPTIONAL
*"     E_TRM_TAB STRUCTURE /SAPAPO/S_TRM OPTIONAL
*"     E_TRMC_TAB STRUCTURE /SAPAPO/S_TRMC OPTIONAL
*"----------------------------------------
```

Explanation

```
IMPORTING
    I_MODEL_FLD    = <Model>
    I_VALFR_FLD    = <Validity Start Timestamp>
    I_VALTO_FLD    = <Validity End Timestamp>
    I_LOCFR_TAB    = <Start Location>
    I_LOCTO_TAB    = <Destination Location>
    I_TTYPE_TAB    = <Means of Transport>
EXPORTING
    E_TRM_TAB      = <Means of Transport, Key for means of
                     transport, internal data part for means of
                     transport>
```

/SAPAPO/MSDP_MD_SOS_GET_ARRAY: Reads sources of supply from table TRPROD, TRPRODM/TRM and quota arrangement based on selection criteria model, destination location, start and end validity, material id and mean of transport.

FUNCTION /SAPAPO/MSDP_MD_SOS_GET_ARRAY.

```
*"----------------------------------------
*"*"Lokale Schnittstelle:
*"  IMPORTING
*"     REFERENCE(IV_MODEL) TYPE /SAPAPO/C_MODELID OPTIONAL
*"     REFERENCE(IV_VERSION) TYPE /SAPAPO/VRSIOID OPTIONAL
*"     REFERENCE(IV_VALFR) TYPE /SAPAPO/SNPTSTMP OPTIONAL
```

```
*"      REFERENCE(IV_VALTO) TYPE /SAPAPO/SNPTSTMP OPTIONAL
*"      REFERENCE(IT_MATID) TYPE /SAPAPO/MATID_TAB
*"      REFERENCE(IT_LOCFR) TYPE /SAPAPO/LOCID_TAB OPTIONAL
*"      REFERENCE(IT_LOCTO) TYPE /SAPAPO/LOCID_TAB OPTIONAL
*"      REFERENCE(IT_TRMID) TYPE /SAPAPO/T_TRMID OPTIONAL
*"      REFERENCE(IV_WITH_CONTRACTS) TYPE /SAPAPO/CHAR1 OPTIONAL
*"      REFERENCE(IV_BESKZ) TYPE /SAPAPO/BESKZ DEFAULT 'X'
*"      REFERENCE(IV_NO_QUOTA) TYPE /SAPAPO/CHAR1 DEFAULT ' '
*"      REFERENCE(IV_USEAGGRSOS) TYPE /SAPAPO/USEAGGRSOS DEFAULT ' '
*"      REFERENCE(IV_PAREAID) TYPE /SAPAPO/TS_PAREAID OPTIONAL
*"   EXPORTING
*"      REFERENCE(ET_SOURCES) TYPE /SAPAPO/SOURCES_TAB
*"      REFERENCE(ET_SOURCES_INVALID) TYPE /SAPAPO/SOURCES_TAB
*"      REFERENCE(ET_MESSAGES) TYPE /SAPAPO/APOGRID_LOG_MSG
*"   EXCEPTIONS
*"      INVALID_INTERFACE
*"      NO_MODEL_OR_VERSION
*"      ERROR_MASTER_DATA
*"----------------------------------------
```

Explanation

```
IMPORTING
     IV_MODEL    = <Model>
     IV_VERSION  = <Version>
     IV_VALFR    = <Validity Start>
     IV_VALTO    = <Validity End>
     IT_MATID    = <Material ID>
     IT_LOCFR    = <Source Location>
     IT_LOCTO    = <Destination Location>
     IT_TRMID    = <Means of Transport>
EXPORTING
     ET_SOURCES  = <Source of Supply, quota arrangement>
```

/SAPAPO/DM_MATMODS_GET: Function module fetches information of model assignment to material, location with selection criteria model, material and location. Database table used to fetch model assignment information in FM are /sapapo/v_matmod, /sapapo/v_mtlmod.

FUNCTION /SAPAPO/DM_MATMODS_GET.

```
*"----------------------------------------
*"*"Local Interface:
*"  IMPORTING
*"      VALUE(I_MODELID_FLD) TYPE /SAPAPO/C_MODELID
*"      VALUE(I_INIT_FLG) TYPE XFELD DEFAULT 'X'
*"      VALUE(I_SORT_FLG) TYPE XFELD DEFAULT 'X'
```

```
*"      VALUE(I_DEL_DUPL_FLG) TYPE XFELD DEFAULT 'X'
*"      VALUE(I_NO_FILL_BUFFER) TYPE XFELD DEFAULT SPACE
*"   TABLES
*"      I_MATNR_RTAB STRUCTURE /SAPAPO/MAT_NR_RSTR OPTIONAL
*"      I_LOCNO_RTAB STRUCTURE /SAPAPO/LOCNO_RSTR OPTIONAL
*"      I_LTYPE_RTAB STRUCTURE /SAPAPO/LTYPE_RSTR OPTIONAL
*"      I_PL_SNP_RTAB STRUCTURE /SAPAPO/PLANNER_SNP_RSTR OPTIONAL
*"      I_PL_PPS_RTAB STRUCTURE /SAPAPO/PLANNER_PPS_RSTR OPTIONAL
*"      I_PL_DEM_RTAB STRUCTURE /SAPAPO/PLANNER_DEM_RSTR OPTIONAL
*"      I_PL_TRA_RTAB STRUCTURE /SAPAPO/PLANNER_TRA_RSTR OPTIONAL
*"      I_EKGRP_RTAB STRUCTURE /SAPAPO/EKGRP_RSTR OPTIONAL
*"      I_BESKZ_RTAB STRUCTURE /SAPAPO/BESKZ_RSTR OPTIONAL
*"      I_SELGROUP_RTAB STRUCTURE /SAPAPO/RRP_SELGROUP_RSTR OPTIONAL
*"      I_OBJ_BASIS_TAB STRUCTURE /SAPAPO/OO_MODEL_OBJ_STR OPTIONAL
*"      E_MATMOD_TAB STRUCTURE /SAPAPO/MATMOD OPTIONAL
*"      E_MATMOD_BUFFER_TAB STRUCTURE /SAPAPO/MATMOD OPTIONAL
*"      I_PRIO_RTAB STRUCTURE /SAPAPO/PRIO_RSTR OPTIONAL
*"      I_VEGRP_RTAB STRUCTURE /SAPAPO/VEGRP_RSTR OPTIONAL
*"      I_MATKL_RTAB STRUCTURE /SAPAPO/MATKL_RSTR OPTIONAL
*"      I_ATT01_RTAB STRUCTURE /SAPAPO/ATX01_RSTR OPTIONAL
*"      I_ATT02_RTAB STRUCTURE /SAPAPO/ATX02_RSTR OPTIONAL
*"      I_ATT03_RTAB STRUCTURE /SAPAPO/ATX03_RSTR OPTIONAL
*"      I_ATT04_RTAB STRUCTURE /SAPAPO/ATX04_RSTR OPTIONAL
*"      I_ATT05_RTAB STRUCTURE /SAPAPO/ATX05_RSTR OPTIONAL
*"      I_AT101_RTAB STRUCTURE /SAPAPO/ATX01_RSTR OPTIONAL
*"      I_AT102_RTAB STRUCTURE /SAPAPO/ATX02_RSTR OPTIONAL
*"      I_AT103_RTAB STRUCTURE /SAPAPO/ATX03_RSTR OPTIONAL
*"      I_AT104_RTAB STRUCTURE /SAPAPO/ATX04_RSTR OPTIONAL
*"      I_AT105_RTAB STRUCTURE /SAPAPO/ATX05_RSTR OPTIONAL
*"----------------------------------------
```

Explanation

```
IMPORTING
     I_MODELID_FLD  = <Model>
     I_MATNR_RTAB   = <Material No.>
     I_LOCNO_RTAB   = <Location>
EXPORTING
     E_MATMOD_TAB   = <Model assignment to material & location
                      information>
```

/SAPAPO/TS_LCM_QUEUE_REPORT: In case planning version was not initialized in *transaction code /SAPAPO/MSDP_ADMIN* after master data changes were made, so newly created or deleted master data are captured through this FM.

FUNCTION /sapapo/ts_lcm_queue_report.

```
*"-----------------------------------------------------------
*"*"Lokale Schnittstelle:
*"   IMPORTING
*"      REFERENCE(IV_PAREAID) TYPE /SAPAPO/TS_PAREAID
*"      REFERENCE(IV_VERSION) TYPE /SAPAPO/VRSIOID
*"   EXCEPTIONS
*"      VERSION_NOT_INITIALIZED
*"      UPDATE_FAILED
*"-----------------------------------------------------------
```

Explanation

```
IMPORTING
     IV_PAREAID  =  <Planning Area ID>
     IV_VERSION  =  <Version ID>
```

Other Function Modules called inside to capture master data:

/SAPAPO/TS_LCM_UPD_SETTING_GET: Fetches update queue customizing setting.

FUNCTION /sapapo/ts_lcm_upd_setting_get.

```
*"-----------------------------------------------------
*"*"Local Interface:
*"   EXPORTING
*"      REFERENCE(EV_QUEUE_UPD) TYPE /SAPAPO/TS_QUEUE_UPD
*"      REFERENCE(EV_QUEUE_WAIT) TYPE /SAPAPO/TS_QUEUE_WAIT
*"      REFERENCE(EV_TS_AUTO_UPD) TYPE /SAPAPO/TS_AUTO_UPD
*"   EXCEPTIONS
*"      COULD_NOT_READ
*"-----------------------------------------------------
```

/SAPAPO/TS_DM_LOCK_UNLOCK: Used to lock and unlock planning area based on the criteria, planning area id, version id and lock flag. If lock flag is equal to "X" then lock the planning area else unlock the planning area.

FUNCTION /sapapo/ts_dm_lock_unlock.

```
*"-----------------------------------------------------------
*"*"Lokale Schnittstelle:
*"   IMPORTING
*"      VALUE(IV_PAREAID) TYPE /SAPAPO/TS_PAREAID
*"      REFERENCE(IV_VRSIOID) TYPE /SAPAPO/VRSIOID
*"      REFERENCE(IV_LOCK) TYPE AS4FLAG
*"   EXPORTING
*"      REFERENCE(EV_USER) TYPE EQEUNAME
*"      REFERENCE(ES_LOCK_STR) TYPE /SAPAPO/TS_LC_LOCK_STR
*"   CHANGING
*"      REFERENCE(CT_SELECTION) TYPE /SAPAPO/TS_IOBJ_SELECTION_TAB
```

```
*"  EXCEPTIONS
*"      ERROR
*"------------------------------------------
```

/SAPAPO/TS_LCM_INITIALIZE: Initialize planning area, create anchor, time-series.

FUNCTION /sapapo/ts_lcm_initialize.

```
*"----------------------------------------------
*"*"Lokale Schnittstelle:
*"  IMPORTING
*"      REFERENCE(IV_PAREAID) TYPE /SAPAPO/TS_PAREAID
*"      REFERENCE(IV_VERSION) TYPE /SAPAPO/VRSIOID
*"      REFERENCE(IV_FROMDATE) TYPE /SAPAPO/TSTR_STARTDATE OPTIONAL
*"      REFERENCE(IV_TODATE) TYPE /SAPAPO/TSTR_TODATE OPTIONAL
*"      REFERENCE(IS_LCM_OPTIONS) TYPE /SAPAPO/TS_LCM_OPTIONS
*"      REFERENCE(IT_KEYF_HORIZON_TAB)  TYPE  /SAPAPO/TS_KEYF_
        HORIZON_TAB
*"        OPTIONAL
*"  CHANGING
*"      REFERENCE(CT_KEYF_HORIZON_DEL)  TYPE  /SAPAPO/TS_KEYF_
        HORIZON_TAB
*"        OPTIONAL
*"  EXCEPTIONS
*"      AREA_INVALID
*"      INVALID_DATA_STATUS
*"      CUSTOMIZING_ERROR
*"      ERROR
*"      LC_CONNECT_FAILED
*"      NO_PERMISSION
*"----------------------------------------------
```

/SAPAPO/TS_LCM_DELTA_MASTER: Delta initialization is done to update master data changes.

FUNCTION /sapapo/ts_lcm_delta_master.

```
*"------------------------------------------
*"*"Lokale Schnittstelle:
*"  IMPORTING
*"      REFERENCE(IV_PAREAID) TYPE /SAPAPO/TS_PAREAID
*"      REFERENCE(IV_VERSION) TYPE /SAPAPO/VRSIOID
*"  EXCEPTIONS
*"      AREA_INVALID
*"      ERROR
*"      VERSION_NOT_INITIALIZED
*"      BAD_PERFORMANCE
*"----------------------------------------------
```

/SAPAPO/MSNP_BAS_EXTERN_PDATE: Used to fetch default start date from the data view.

FUNCTION /SAPAPO/MSNP_BAS_EXTERN_PDATE.

```
*»------------------------------------
*»*»Lokale Schnittstelle:
*»   IMPORTING
*»      VALUE(IV_FLG_DP) TYPE /SAPAPO/FLAG OPTIONAL
*»   EXPORTING
*»      VALUE(PDATE) TYPE  D
*»      VALUE(EV_USER_DATE) TYPE  C
*»------------------------------------
```

```
Exporting:     start date
               user date
```

/SAPAPO/MSDP_SDP_GET_PLANSTART: Used to fetch planning start date

FUNCTION /sapapo/msdp_sdp_get_planstart.

```
*"----------------------------------------
*"*"Lokale Schnittstelle:
*"   IMPORTING
*"      REFERENCE(IV_MVIEW) TYPE /SAPAPO/PB_MVIEW
*"      REFERENCE(IV_DVIEW) TYPE /SAPAPO/PB_DVIEW
*"   EXPORTING
*"      REFERENCE(EV_STARTDATE) TYPE  D
*"----------------------------------------
```

Explanation

```
IMPORTING
     IV_MVIEW        = <Planning Book>
     IV_DVIEW        = <Data View>
EXPORTING
     EV_STARTDATE    = <Start Date>
```

/SAPAPO/TS_LCM_INITIALIZE: Used to initialize planning area, create anchor and time series

FUNCTION /sapapo/ts_lcm_initialize.

```
*"----------------------------------------
*"*"Lokale Schnittstelle:
*"   IMPORTING
*"      REFERENCE(IV_PAREAID) TYPE /SAPAPO/TS_PAREAID
*"      REFERENCE(IV_VERSION) TYPE /SAPAPO/VRSIOID
*"      REFERENCE(IV_FROMDATE) TYPE /SAPAPO/TSTR_STARTDATE OPTIONAL
*"      REFERENCE(IV_TODATE) TYPE /SAPAPO/TSTR_TODATE OPTIONAL
*"      REFERENCE(IS_LCM_OPTIONS) TYPE /SAPAPO/TS_LCM_OPTIONS
*"      REFERENCE(IT_KEYF_HORIZON_TAB)  TYPE  /SAPAPO/TS_KEYF_
```

```
        HORIZON_TAB
*"          OPTIONAL
*"    CHANGING
*"        REFERENCE(CT_KEYF_HORIZON_DEL) TYPE /SAPAPO/TS_KEYF_
        HORIZON_TAB
*"          OPTIONAL
*"    EXCEPTIONS
*"        AREA_INVALID
*"        INVALID_DATA_STATUS
*"        CUSTOMIZING_ERROR
*"        ERROR
*"        LC_CONNECT_FAILED
*"        NO_PERMISSION
*"-----------------------------------------
```

/SAPAPO/TS_PAREA_SINGLE_GET: Used to read data for a planning area information like storage bucket profile, fiscal year variant, factory calendar, start and end date of DP/SNP time stream etc. using the selection criteria planning area ID.

FUNCTION /sapapo/ts_parea_single_get.

```
*"-------------------------------------
*"*"Local Interface:
*"    IMPORTING
*"        REFERENCE(IV_PAREAID) TYPE /SAPAPO/TS_PAREAID
*"        REFERENCE(IV_BYPASS_BUFFER) TYPE  FLAG DEFAULT FALSE
*"        REFERENCE(IV_ADD_INTERN_CHARS) TYPE /SAPAPO/FLAG DEFAULT ' '
*"        REFERENCE(IV_ADD_FRWK_CHARS) TYPE /SAPAPO/FLAG OPTIONAL
*"    EXPORTING
*"        REFERENCE(ES_AREAKO) TYPE /SAPAPO/TS_AREAKO_STR
*"        REFERENCE(ES_TSTR) TYPE /SAPAPO/SDPTSTR
*"        REFERENCE(ES_TSPLOBKO) TYPE /SAPAPO/TS_PLOBKO_STR
*"        REFERENCE(ET_PAPLOB) TYPE /SAPAPO/TS_PAPLOB_TAB
*"        REFERENCE(ET_PAREL) TYPE /SAPAPO/TS_PAREL_TAB
*"        REFERENCE(ET_CHARS) TYPE /SAPAPO/DM_INT_CHARS_TAB
*"        REFERENCE(ET_KEYFS) TYPE /SAPAPO/TBL_KEYFS
*"        REFERENCE(EV_SNP_PLAN) TYPE /SAPAPO/TS_SNP_PLAN
*"        REFERENCE(EV_SNP_PLAN_LP) TYPE /SAPAPO/TS_SNP_PLAN_LP
*"        REFERENCE(EV_CDP_FLAG) TYPE /SAPAPO/TS_CDP_FLAG
*"        REFERENCE(EV_DP_BOM) TYPE /SAPAPO/TS_DP_BOM
*"        REFERENCE(EV_KEYF_IC) TYPE /SAPAPO/AS400FLAG
*"        REFERENCE(EV_KEYF_OL) TYPE /SAPAPO/AS400FLAG
*"        REFERENCE(EV_KEYF_TS) TYPE /SAPAPO/AS400FLAG
*"        REFERENCE(EV_KEYF_TS_SNP) TYPE /SAPAPO/AS400FLAG
*"        REFERENCE(EV_KEYF_TSDM) TYPE /SAPAPO/AS400FLAG
*"        REFERENCE(EV_LOCPROD_HIER) TYPE /SAPAPO/RELID
```

```
*"      REFERENCE(EV_PPM_HIER) TYPE /SAPAPO/RELID
*"      REFERENCE(EV_RES_HIER) TYPE /SAPAPO/PARESHR
*"      REFERENCE(EV_LOCPROD_HSTRU) TYPE /SAPAPO/PALP_HRS
*"      REFERENCE(EV_PPM_HSTRU) TYPE /SAPAPO/PAPPM_HRS
*"      REFERENCE(EV_RES_HSTRU) TYPE /SAPAPO/PARES_HRS
*"      REFERENCE(ES_TSAREATE) TYPE /SAPAPO/TS_AREATE_STR
*"      REFERENCE(EV_SEASON_PLAN) TYPE /SAPAPO/SEASABLE
*"  EXCEPTIONS
*"       NOT_FOUND
*"--------------------------------------------
```

Explanation

```
IMPORTING
     IV_PAREAID  = <Planning Area ID>
EXPORTING
     ES_AREAKO   = <Planning Area Info>
     ES_TSPLOBKO = <Time Streams for DP/SNP>
```

/SAPAPO/MSDP_PAR_PROFILE_GET: Used to read dp/snp parallelization profile information based on parallelization profile name and application.

FUNCTION /sapapo/msdp_par_profile_get .

```
*"--------------------------------------------
*"*"Lokale Schnittstelle:
*"  IMPORTING
*"      REFERENCE(IV_PAR_PROFILE) TYPE /SAPAPO/SDP_PARALLEL_PROF_NAME
*"        OPTIONAL
*"      REFERENCE(IV_APPLICATION) TYPE /SAPAPO/SDP_PARALLEL_PROF_APPL
*"        OPTIONAL
*"  EXPORTING
*"      REFERENCE(ES_PAR_PROFILE) TYPE /SAPAPO/SDP_PAR_STR
*"      REFERENCE(ET_PAR_PROFILE) TYPE /SAPAPO/SDP_PAR_TAB
*"  EXCEPTIONS
*"      PAR_PROFILE_INVALID
*"--------------------------------------------
```

Explanation

```
IMPORTING
     IV_PAR_PROFILE  = <Parallelization Profile Name>
     IV_APPLICATION  = <Application>
EXPORTING
     ES_PAR_PROFILE  = <DP/SNP Parallel Processing Profiles with
                       Definitions>
```

/SAPAPO/TS_LCM_INVALID_CLEAR: Used to delete objects for version after error on first initialization based on selection criteria planning area ID, version ID.

FUNCTION /sapapo/ts_lcm_invalid_clear.

```
*"----------------------------------------
*"*"Lokale Schnittstelle:
*"  IMPORTING
*"     REFERENCE(IV_PAREAID) TYPE /SAPAPO/TS_PAREAID OPTIONAL
*"     REFERENCE(IV_VRSIOID) TYPE /SAPAPO/VRSIOID OPTIONAL
*"----------------------------------------
```

/SAPAPO/TS_LCM_QUEUE_UPDATE: Queue update, returns with status of the queue.

FUNCTION /sapapo/ts_lcm_queue_update.

```
*"--------------------------------------
*"*"Local Interface:
*"  IMPORTING
*"     VALUE(IV_ALWAYS_PARALLEL) TYPE /SAPAPO/BOOLEAN OPTIONAL
*"     REFERENCE(IV_BGPROC) TYPE  FLAG OPTIONAL
*"  EXCEPTIONS
*"     CANNOT_UPDATE
*"     BAD_PERFORMANCE
*"     ERROR
*"--------------------------------------
```

/SAPAPO/TS_PLOB_COUNT: It determines number of planning objects for the specified selection.

FUNCTION /sapapo/ts_plob_count.

```
*"-------------------------------------------
*"*"Lokale Schnittstelle:
*"  IMPORTING
*"     REFERENCE(IV_PLOBID) TYPE /SAPAPO/TS_PLOBID
*"     REFERENCE(IT_SELECTION) TYPE /SAPAPO/TS_IOBJ_SELECTION_TAB
*"       OPTIONAL
*"     REFERENCE(IT_GROUP_BY) TYPE /SAPAPO/TS_GROUP_BY_TAB OPTIONAL
*"  EXPORTING
*"     REFERENCE(EV_NUMBER_OF_PLOBS) TYPE  I
*"  EXCEPTIONS
*"     INVALID_INPUT
*"     INTERNAL_ERROR
*"-------------------------------------------
```

Explanation

```
IMPORTING
    IV_PLOBID           = <Planning Object ID>
    IT_SELECTION        = <Selection ID>
EXPORTING
    EV_NUMBER_OF_PLOBS = <No of planning objects>
```

/SAPAPO/TS_PAREA_KEF_HORIZ_SET: It calculates start date and end date for the key figures.

FUNCTION /sapapo/ts_parea_kef_horiz_set.

```
*"----------------------------------------
*"*"Lokale Schnittstelle:
*"  IMPORTING
*"     REFERENCE(IV_PAREAID) TYPE /SAPAPO/TS_PAREAID
*"     REFERENCE(IV_VERSIONID) TYPE /SAPAPO/VRSIOID
*"     REFERENCE(IV_START_DATE) TYPE /SAPAPO/TSTR_STARTDATE
*"     REFERENCE(IV_END_DATE) TYPE /SAPAPO/TSTR_TODATE
*"     REFERENCE(IV_GET_USER_SETTINGS) TYPE /SAPAPO/FLAG DEFAULT 'X'
*"     REFERENCE(IV_SHOW_DYNPRO) TYPE /SAPAPO/FLAG DEFAULT 'X'
*"     REFERENCE(IV_PROCESS_USER_SETTINGS) TYPE /SAPAPO/FLAG DEFAULT
*"        'X'
*"     REFERENCE(IV_NOT_ADJUST_HORIZONS) TYPE
*"      /SAPAPO/TS_KEF_HORIZ_NO_ADJUST OPTIONAL
*"  EXPORTING
*"     REFERENCE(EV_MIN_STARTDATE) TYPE /SAPAPO/TSTR_STARTDATE
*"     REFERENCE(EV_MAX_ENDDATE) TYPE /SAPAPO/TSTR_TODATE
*"     REFERENCE(EV_DIFFERENT_HORIZONS) TYPE /SAPAPO/FLAG
*"  CHANGING
*"     REFERENCE(CT_KEYF_HORIZON) TYPE /SAPAPO/TS_KEYF_HORIZON_TAB
*"      OPTIONAL
*"     REFERENCE(CT_KEYF_HORIZON_DEL) TYPE /SAPAPO/TS_KEYF_HORIZON_
       TAB
*"      OPTIONAL
*"  EXCEPTIONS
*"     INTERNAL_ERROR
*"----------------------------------------------
```

Explanation

```
IMPORTING
     IV_PAREAID              = <Planning Area  ID>
     IV_VERSIONID            = <Version ID>
     IV_START_DATE           = <Start Date>
     IV_END_DATE             = <End Date>
EXPORTING
     EV_DIFFERENT_HORIZONS   = <KeyFigure Horizon>
```

/SAPAPO/TS_PAREA_VERSIO_CREATE: Used to create planning version for planning area.

FUNCTION /SAPAPO/TS_PAREA_VERSIO_CREATE.

```
*"----------------------------------------
*"*"Lokale Schnittstelle:
*"  IMPORTING
```

```
*"      VALUE(IV_PAREAID) TYPE /SAPAPO/TS_PAREAID
*"      VALUE(IV_VRSIOID) TYPE /SAPAPO/VRSIOID
*"      VALUE(IV_TSTRID_GENER) TYPE /SAPAPO/TSTRGUID
*"      VALUE(IV_FROMDATE) TYPE /SAPAPO/TSTR_STARTDATE
*"      VALUE(IV_TODATE) TYPE /SAPAPO/TSTR_TODATE
*"      VALUE(IV_FLG_UPDATE) TYPE /SAPAPO/AS400FLAG DEFAULT SPACE
*"   EXCEPTIONS
*"      VERSION_ALREADY_EXIST
*"      ERROR
*"-----------------------------------------
```

Explanation

```
IMPORTING
     IV_PAREAID     = <Planning Area  ID>
     IV_VERSIONID   = <Version ID>
     IV_FROMDATE    = <Start Date>
     IV_TODATE      = <End Date>
```

/SAPAPO/TS_LCM_INIT_MASTERDATA: It is used to create required master data based on planning area id and version id.

FUNCTION /sapapo/ts_lcm_init_masterdata.

```
*"-----------------------------------------
*"*"Lokale Schnittstelle:
*"   IMPORTING
*"      REFERENCE(IV_PAREAID) TYPE /SAPAPO/TS_PAREAID
*"      REFERENCE(IV_VERSION) TYPE /SAPAPO/VRSIOID
*"      REFERENCE(IS_PAR_PROFILE) TYPE /SAPAPO/SDP_PAR_STR OPTIONAL
*"   EXCEPTIONS
*"      AREA_INVALID
*"      ERROR
*"      BAD_PERFORMANCE
*"-----------------------------------------
```

Explanation

```
IMPORTING
     IV_PAREAID     = <Planning Area  ID>
     IV_VERSIONID   = <Version ID>
```

/SAPAPO/TS_LCM_DELTA_MASTER: It is used to update master data based on planning area id and version id.

FUNCTION /sapapo/ts_lcm_delta_master.

```
*"-----------------------------------------
*"*"Lokale Schnittstelle:
*"   IMPORTING
*"      REFERENCE(IV_PAREAID) TYPE /SAPAPO/TS_PAREAID
*"      REFERENCE(IV_VERSION) TYPE /SAPAPO/VRSIOID
```

```
*"  EXCEPTIONS
*"      AREA_INVALID
*"      ERROR
*"      VERSION_NOT_INITIALIZED
*"      BAD_PERFORMANCE
*"--------------------------------------
```

Explanation

```
IMPORTING
        IV_PAREAID    = <Planning Area  ID>
        IV_VERSIONID  = <Version ID>
```

/SAPAPO/TS_LCM_INIT_GENERAL: This FM is used to create time series, delete queues for aggregates without time series key figures.

FUNCTION /sapapo/ts_lcm_init_general.

```
*"------------------------------------
*"*"Lokale Schnittstelle:
*"  IMPORTING
*"      REFERENCE(IV_PAREAID) TYPE /SAPAPO/TS_PAREAID
*"      REFERENCE(IV_VERSION) TYPE /SAPAPO/VRSIOID
*"      REFERENCE(IV_UPDATE) TYPE /SAPAPO/TS_FLAG_UPDATE_TS DEFAULT
*"        SPACE
*"      REFERENCE(IV_SHOW_LOG) TYPE /SAPAPO/TS_FLAG_SHOW_LOG OPTIONAL
*"      REFERENCE(IV_PAR_PROFILE)TYPE /SAPAPO/SDP_PARALLEL_PROF_NAME
*"        OPTIONAL
*"  EXCEPTIONS
*"      AREA_INVALID
*"      ERROR
*"      LC_CONNECT_FAILED
*"      INVALID_SEASON_ASSIGNMENT
*"--------------------------------------
```

Explanation

```
IMPORTING
        IV_PAREAID    = <Planning Area  ID>
        IV_VERSIONID  = <Version ID>
```

/SAPAPO/TS_LCM_INIT_SNP: This FM is used to create SNP network. Prerequisite for creating SNP network are process production model, resource, transportation lane, location and product.

FUNCTION /sapapo/ts_lcm_init_snp.

```
*"-----------------------------------
*"*"Lokale Schnittstelle:
*"  IMPORTING
*"      REFERENCE(IV_PAREAID) TYPE /SAPAPO/TS_PAREAID
*"      REFERENCE(IV_VERSION) TYPE /SAPAPO/VRSIOID
```

```
*"      REFERENCE(IV_UPDATE) TYPE /SAPAPO/TS_FLAG_UPDATE_TS DEFAULT
*"        SPACE
*"   EXCEPTIONS
*"      AREA_INVALID
*"      ERROR
*"      LC_CONNECT_ERROR
*"------------------------------------
```

Explanation

```
IMPORTING
     IV_PAREAID     = <Planning Area  ID>
     IV_VERSIONID   = <Version ID>
     IV_UPDATE      = 'X'
```

/SAPAPO/TS_LCM_QUEUES_DELETE: FM is used to delete master data queues level 2.

FUNCTION /sapapo/ts_lcm_queues_delete.

```
*"------------------------------------
*"*"Lokale Schnittstelle:
*"   IMPORTING
*"      REFERENCE(IV_PAREAID) TYPE /SAPAPO/TS_PAREAID
*"      REFERENCE(IV_VERSION) TYPE /SAPAPO/VRSIOID OPTIONAL
*"----------------------------------------
```

Explanation

```
IMPORTING
     IV_PAREAID     = <Planning Area  ID>
     IV_VERSIONID   = <Version ID>
```

1. *APO Master Data Change*

   If there is a change in the master data of *SAP Advanced Planning and Optimization (SAP APO)*, the system sends a change notification to SNP, where the changes are lined up in the SNP level one queue (table /SAPAPO/TSQUEUE). The system automatically performs change notification and registration and immediately after the master data change.
2. *SNP Queue Update*

   The system updates SNP queue during planning area initialization, at the start of SNP interactive planning or any other SNP planning application.

   The SNP queue update deletes the entries in the level one queue and by processing them creates entries in the level two queues (in table */SAPAPO/TSQMLO*). Entries in level two queues are more detailed than entries in level one queue, and they also describe the required changes in SNP master data.

   By default the queue update is executed in a background process to speed up the startup of interactive planning. One can change the runtime behavior of queue update in Customizing for *Advanced Planning and Optimization* under -> *Supply Chain Planning* -> *Supply Network Planning (SNP)* -> *Basic*

Settings -> Maintain Global SNP Settings. Change the runtime behavior in the *Que. Proc.* field. The queue update process can also be executed manually with the *report /SAPAPO/TS_LCM_QUEUE_UPDATE.*

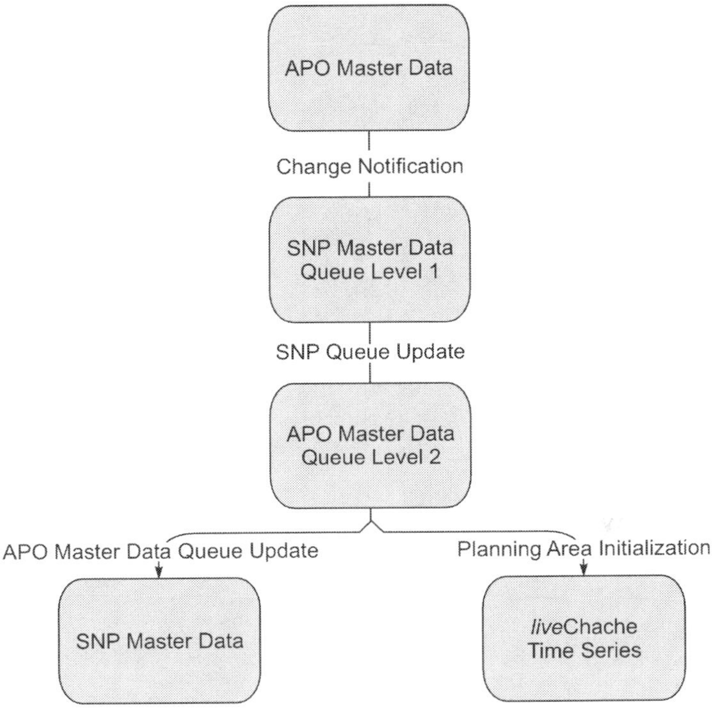

Figure 8.4 Data update process in SCM-APO

3. *SNP Master Data Update*
   At the start of an SNP application (for example, SNP heuristic), the system updates SNP master data based on the entries of the level two queue. SNP master data update is also performed as a part of planning area initialization or at the start of SNP planning applications. SNP interactive planning performs the master data update when load a selection to the shuffler.
4. *Delta Initialization of Planning Areas*
   The system updates the time series every time planning area initialization is carried out.

/SAPAPO/OM_ORDER_GET_DATA: Used to fetch order data from LiveCache. In many cases only part of order data is required. If certain export table is not required, exclude it while calling the module or use exclude structures to instruct LiveCache not to fill it.

FUNCTION /sapapo/om_order_get_data.

```
*"--------------------------------------
*"*"Lokale Schnittstelle:
*"  IMPORTING
*"     REFERENCE(IS_GEN_PARAMS) TYPE /SAPAPO/OM_GEN_PARAMS
*"     VALUE(IV_SIMSESSION) TYPE /SAPAPO/OM_SIMSESSION
*"     REFERENCE(IT_ORDER) TYPE /SAPAPO/OM_ORDID_TAB
*"     VALUE(IV_GET_FIX_PEG_ONLY) TYPE /SAPAPO/OM_BOOL OPTIONAL
*"     REFERENCE(IS_EXCLUDE_EXPORTS)TYPE/SAPAPO/OM_GETDATA_OPTIONS
*"      OPTIONAL
*"     REFERENCE(IS_EXCLUDE_FIELDS) TYPE /SAPAPO/OM_EXCLUDE_FIELDS
*"      OPTIONAL
*"  EXPORTING
*"     REFERENCE(ET_ORDKEYS) TYPE /SAPAPO/OM_ORDKEY_TAB
*"     REFERENCE(ET_ORDMAPS) TYPE /SAPAPO/OM_ORDMAP_TAB
*"     REFERENCE(ET_ORDERS) TYPE /SAPAPO/OM_ORDER_EXT_TAB
*"     REFERENCE(ET_ACTIVITIES) TYPE /SAPAPO/OM_TAB_ACT
*"     REFERENCE(ET_MODES) TYPE /SAPAPO/OM_MODE_TAB
*"     REFERENCE(ET_CAP_REQS) TYPE /SAPAPO/OM_CAP_REQ_TAB
*"     REFERENCE(ET_BUCKETVECTOR_CHARACTS) TYPE
*"      /SAPAPO/OM_ORD_BUC_CHARACT_TAB
*"     REFERENCE(ET_POSITIONS) TYPE /SAPAPO/OM_ORDER_POSITION_TAB
*"     REFERENCE(ET_INPUTS) TYPE /SAPAPO/OM_IO_TAB
*"     REFERENCE(ET_OUTPUTS) TYPE /SAPAPO/OM_IO_TAB
*"     REFERENCE(ET_EXT_INPUTS) TYPE /SAPAPO/OM_IO_PP_TAB
*"     REFERENCE(ET_EXT_OUTPUTS) TYPE /SAPAPO/OM_IO_PP_TAB
*"     REFERENCE(ET_CONTI_IO) TYPE /SAPAPO/OM_IO_CONTI_DATA_TAB
*"     REFERENCE(ET_PRODFLOW) TYPE /SAPAPO/OM_PRODFLOW_TAB
*"     REFERENCE(ET_INTERN_CONSTRAINTS) TYPE /SAPAPO/OM_CONSTRAINT_
       TAB
*"     REFERENCE(ET_EXTERN_CONSTRAINTS) TYPE /SAPAPO/OM_CONSTRAINT_
       TAB
*"     REFERENCE(ET_INTERN_CONSTRAINTS_EXT) TYPE
*"      /SAPAPO/OM_CONSTRAINT_EXT_TAB
*"     REFERENCE(ET_EXTERN_CONSTRAINTS_EXT) TYPE
*"      /SAPAPO/OM_CONSTRAINT_EXT_TAB
*"     REFERENCE(ET_CHARACT_VAL_ACTS) TYPE /SAPAPO/OM_CHARACT_VAL_
       TAB
*"     REFERENCE(ET_CHARACT_REQ_INPNODE) TYPE
*"      /SAPAPO/OM_CHARACT_REQ_TAB
*"     REFERENCE(ET_CHARACT_VAL_OUTNODE) TYPE
*"      /SAPAPO/OM_CHARACT_VAL_TAB
*"     REFERENCE(ET_PEG_INPNODE) TYPE /SAPAPO/OM_TAB_PEGGING
*"     REFERENCE(ET_PEG_OUTNODE) TYPE /SAPAPO/OM_TAB_PEGGING
*"     REFERENCE(ET_RC) TYPE /SAPAPO/OM_LC_RC_TAB
```

```
*"   EXCEPTIONS
*"      LC_CONNECT_FAILED
*"      LC_COM_ERROR
*"      LC_APPL_ERROR
*"----------------------------------------------
```

Explanation

```
IMPORTING
     IS_GEN_PARAMS      = <General Parameter like SIM version>
     IV_SIMSESSION      = <SIM version>
     IT_ORDER-ORDID     = <Order ID>
EXPORTING
     ET_ORDKEYS         = <Order Key Data>
     ET_ORDMAPS         = <Order Mapping Info>
     ET_ORDERS          = <Orders Details>
```

Sample source code by using this function module.

Example

Source of supply is required to be determined for the specified order.

Note: I am not covering data declaration part here.

```
* Get the source of Supply
      CALL FUNCTION '/SAPAPO/RRP_LC_ORDER_GET_DATA'
        EXPORTING
          iv_order  = p_ordid
        IMPORTING
          es_supply = lw_supply.

* Get all source of supply with pegid ID give PPM SOS
      CALL FUNCTION '/SAPAPO/RRP_SOURCES_GET'
        EXPORTING
          iv_pegid         = lw_supply-pegid
          iv_quantity      = lw_supply-quantity
          iv_reqdat        = lw_supply-io_time
        IMPORTING
          et_source        = li_source
        EXCEPTIONS
          user_canceled = 1
          not_qualified  = 2
          unknown_error = 3
          OTHERS         = 4.

      LOOP AT li_source INTO lw_source.
        lw_sos_tab-ordid       = p_ordid.
        lw_sos_tab-matid       = lw_supply-source matid.
```

```
        lw_sos_tab-locid    = lw_supply-source-locto.
        lw_sos_tab-tgt_trpid = lw_source-trpid.
        lw_sos_tab-cur_trpid = lw_supply-source-trpid.
        APPEND lw_sos_tab TO li_sos_tab.
        CLEAR : lw_source, lw_sos_tab.
      ENDLOOP.
```

BAPI_PBSRVAPS_GETDETAIL2: Used to read key figure values from one data view for a planning book. The parameters key figure, key figure value and characteristic combination serve as return parameters.

The key figure details are contained in Key Figure. These entries use the field CharComId to refer to the characteristics combinations in parameter Characteristics Combination for which they are valid. The key figure values for the individual periods of time are contained in parameter Key Figure Value.

By default, no macros are executed for DP planning books. If, however, to execute macros for the planning book or the data view, the field Macro Execution Flag must be set in parameter read options. In the case of SNP planning books on the other hand, macros are always executed.

If no macros are executed, the key figure selection and the time selection are a pre selection, that is, internally only those key figure values that are really required are read. If, on the other hand, macros are to be executed, these selections are a subsequent selection, since all key figure values must be available when the macros are being processed. This can result in a significant increase in the method runtime. If, on the other hand, ensure that only the selected key figure values are required in the macros to be executed, set the corresponding indicator in parameter read options to specify that the relevant selection also be used as a pre-selection.

FUNCTION BAPI_PBSRVAPS_GETDETAIL2.

```
*"-------------------------------------------
*"*"Lokale Schnittstelle:
*"  IMPORTING
*"     VALUE(PLANNINGBOOK) LIKE BAPI10030GENFIELDS-PLANNING_BOOK
*"     VALUE(DATA_VIEW) LIKE BAPI10030GENFIELDS-DATA_VIEW
*"     VALUE(PLANNING_VERSION) LIKE BAPI10030GENFIELDS-VRSIOEX
*"      OPTIONAL
*"     VALUE(SELECTION_ID) LIKE BAPI10030GENFIELDS-SELECTION_ID
*"      OPTIONAL
*"     VALUE(READ_OPTIONS) LIKE BAPI10030PBREADOPTIONS2 STRUCTURE
*"      BAPI10030PBREADOPTIONS2 OPTIONAL
*"     VALUE(PERIOD_TYPE) LIKE BAPI10030GENFIELDS-PERIOD_TYPE2
*"      OPTIONAL
*"     VALUE(DATE_FROM) LIKE BAPI10030GENFIELDS-DATE_FROM2 OPTIONAL
*"     VALUE(DATE_TO) LIKE BAPI10030GENFIELDS-DATE_TO2 OPTIONAL
```

```
*"  EXPORTING
*"      VALUE(NUMBER_OF_CHAR_COMBS) LIKE
*"       BAPI10030GENFIELDS-NO_OF_CHAR_COMBS
*"  TABLES
*"      SELECTION STRUCTURE BAPI10030PBSELECTION OPTIONAL
*"      GROUP_BY STRUCTURE BAPI10030PBGROUPBY OPTIONAL
*"      KEY_FIGURE_SELECTION STRUCTURE BAPI10030KEYFIGURE OPTIONAL
*"      KEY_FIGURE STRUCTURE BAPI10030PBTIMESERIES2O OPTIONAL
*"      KEY_FIGURE_VALUE STRUCTURE BAPI10030PBTIMESERIESITEM2O
*"       OPTIONAL
*"      CHARACTERISTICS_COMBINATION STRUCTURE BAPI10030PBCHARCOMB2O
*"       OPTIONAL
*"      RETURN STRUCTURE BAPIRET2 OPTIONAL
*"      EXTENSION_IN STRUCTURE BAPIPAREX OPTIONAL
*"      EXTENSION_OUT STRUCTURE BAPIPAREX OPTIONAL
*"----------------------------------------------
```

Explanation

```
IMPORTING
     PLANNINGBOOK          = <Planning Book>
     DATA_VIEW             = <Data View>
     PLANNING_VERSION      = <Planning Version>
     SELECTION_ID          = <Selection ID>
     READ_OPTIONS          = <In case of Macro Execution>
     DATE_FROM             = <Start Date>
     DATE_TO               = <End Date>
EXPORTING
     KEY_FIGURE STRUCTURE          = <Key Figures>
     KEY_FIGURE VALUE              = <Key Figures Values>
     CHARACTERISTICS_COMBINATION = <CVC>
```

Example

Code to read the Key Figure's data from the LiveCache.

```
DATA : gt_selection TYPE TABLE OF bapi10030pbselection INITIAL SIZE 0,
       gt_group_by  TYPE TABLE OF bapi10030pbgroupby INITIAL SIZE 0,
       gt_key_figure TYPE TABLE OF bapi10030keyfigure INITIAL SIZE 0,
       gt_key_figure_value TYPE TABLE OF bapi10030pbtimeseriesitem2o INI-
       TIAL SIZE 0,
       gt_return1     TYPE TABLE OF  bapiret2 INITIAL SIZE 0.

gs_selection-characteristic_name = cf_9alocno.   "Characteristic name
gs_selection-char_val_sign     = cf_i.           "Sign
gs_selection-char_val_option   = cf_eq.          "Option
gs_selection-char_val_low      = gs_/sapapo/matkey-matnr. "s_matnr-low.
APPEND gs_selection TO gt selection.
```

```
gs_selection-characteristic_name = cf_9amatnr.  "Characteristic name
gs_selection-char_val_sign    = cf_i.           "Sign
gs_selection-char_val_option = cf_eq.           "Option
gs_selection-char_val_low     = gs_/sapapo/matkey-matnr. "s_matnr-low.
APPEND gs_selection TO gt_selection.

gs_group_by-characteristic_name = cf_9alocno.
APPEND gs_group_by TO gt_group_by.
CLEAR : gs_group_by.

gs_group_by-characteristic_name = cf_9amatnr.
APPEND gs_group_by TO gt_group_by.

*Read Key Figure Values
CALL FUNCTION 'BAPI_PBSRVAPS_GETDETAIL2'
  EXPORTING
    planningbook       = gf_planningbook
    data_view          = p_dview          ' from the selection screen
    planning_version = gf_planning_version
    read_options       = gs_read_options
    period_type        = 'A'
    date_from          = pct_date_from
    date_to            = pct_date_to
  TABLES
    selection          = gt_selection
    group_by           = gt_group_by
    key_figure         = gt_key_figure
    key_figure_value   = gt_key_figure_value
    return             = gt_return1.
```

BAPI_POSRVAPS_GETLIST3: Use this method to read procurement orders for specific selection criteria. There are the following options for selecting orders. Combinations of the alternatives are not possible or will be ignored.

FUNCTION bapi_posrvaps_getlist3.

```
*"------------------------------------------
*"*"Lokale Schnittstelle:
*"  IMPORTING
*"      VALUE(LOGICAL_SYSTEM) LIKE BAPIGENFIELDS-LOGSYSTEM
*"      VALUE(START_TIME) LIKE BAPIGENFIELDS-START_T OPTIONAL
*"      VALUE(END_TIME) LIKE BAPIGENFIELDS-END_T OPTIONAL
*"      VALUE(EXCLUDE_EXPORT_FLAGS) LIKE BAPI10502SELRETFLAGS2
*"       STRUCTURE  BAPI10502SELRETFLAGS2 OPTIONAL
*"      VALUE(MAX_NUMBER_OF_ORDERS) LIKE BAPIF4A-MAX_ROWS OPTIONAL
*"      VALUE(TRANSFER_MODE) LIKE BAPIGENFIELDS-TRANSMODE OPTIONAL
*"      VALUE(PLNG_VERSION) LIKE BAPIGENFIELDS-VRSIOEX DEFAULT '000'
*"      VALUE(IO_NODE_SELECTION) LIKE BAPI10502GENFIELDS-IO_NODE_SEL
```

```
*"       DEFAULT 'O'
*"   EXPORTING
*"       VALUE(NUMBER_OF_ORDERS) LIKE BAPIGENFIELDS-SEL_ROWS
*"   TABLES
*"       PRODUCT_SELECTION STRUCTURE BAPIPRODUCTRANGE OPTIONAL
*"       LOCATION_SELECTION STRUCTURE BAPILOCRANGE OPTIONAL
*"       LOCTYPE_SELECTION STRUCTURE BAPILOCTYPERANGE OPTIONAL
*"       ORDER_SELECTION STRUCTURE BAPIORDERRANGE OPTIONAL
*"       ORDERTYPE_SELECTION STRUCTURE BAPI10502R3OBJSEL_STR OPTIONAL
*"       PRODUCT_LOCATION_KEYS STRUCTURE BAPI_PRODLOC_KEY OPTIONAL
*"       ATPCAT_SELECTION STRUCTURE BAPIAPOATPCAT OPTIONAL
*"       ORDER_GUIDS STRUCTURE BAPIAPOORDID OPTIONAL
*"       ORDER_KEYS STRUCTURE BAPI10502ORDERKEY OPTIONAL
*"       CFG_SELECTION STRUCTURE BAPI10502CONFCLSEL OPTIONAL
*"       RECEIPTS STRUCTURE BAPI10502POOUTO OPTIONAL
*"       REQUIREMENTS STRUCTURE BAPI10502POINO OPTIONAL
*"       PEGGING_INPUT_NODES STRUCTURE BAPI10502ORDINPUTPEGOUT OPTIONAL
*"       PEGGING_OUTPUT_NODES STRUCTURE BAPI10502ORDOUTPUTPEGOUT
*"        OPTIONAL
*"       VENDOR_SELECTION STRUCTURE BAPI10502VENDSELI OPTIONAL
*"       CFG_HEADERS STRUCTURE BAPIAPOCUCFG OPTIONAL
*"       CFG_INSTANCES STRUCTURE BAPIAPOCUINS OPTIONAL
*"       CFG_PART_OF STRUCTURE BAPIAPOCUPRT OPTIONAL
*"       CFG_VALUES STRUCTURE BAPIAPOCUVAL OPTIONAL
*"       CFG_VAR_KEYS STRUCTURE BAPIAPOCUVK OPTIONAL
*"       CFG_BLOB STRUCTURE BAPIAPOCUBLB OPTIONAL
*"       RETURN STRUCTURE BAPIRET2 OPTIONAL
*"       EXTENSION_IN STRUCTURE BAPIPAREX OPTIONAL
*"       EXTENSION_OUT STRUCTURE BAPIPAREX OPTIONAL
*"-----------------------------------------
```

Selection using product and/or location the following combinations can be used for this:

PRODUCT_SELECTION + LOCATION_SELECTION + LOCTYPE_SELECTION (optional) + ATPCAT_SELECTION (optional) + ORDERTYPE_SELECTION (optional) + CHARACTERISTICS_SELECTION (optional) + VENDOR_SELECTION (optional)

PRODUCT_LOCATION_KEYS + ATPCAT_SELECTION (optional) + ORDERTYPE_SELECTION (optional) + CFG_SELECTION (optional) + VENDOR_SELECTION (optional)

Selection using order numbers if one of the following tables is filled, exactly these orders are transferred. In each case, only one table may be filled. The VENDOR_SELECTION may be used here optionally.

ORDER_KEYS + ORDERTYPE_SELECTION

ORDER_SELECTION + ORDERTYPE_SELECTION (optional)

ORDER_GUIDS

The parameters START_TIME and END_TIME are only taken into account when parameter ORDER_SELECTION is used.

Note that the VENDOR_SELECTION parameter may only be used if the procurement order does not possess INPUT and OUTPUT nodes.

In this case, use the IO_NODE_SELECTION parameter.

/SAPAPO/MSDP_DEP_MULTI_SOURCE: Used to run deployment heuristic for multiple source location based on selection criteria SNP timestamp, real time deployment indicator, version id, location id, alerts, spool list, matmod table containing model assignment with material and location, source location, destination location.

FUNCTION /sapapo/msdp_dep_multi_source.

```
*»-------------------------------------------
*»*»Local Interface:
*»   IMPORTING
*»      REFERENCE(IV_STARTAT) TYPE /SAPAPO/SNPTSTMP
*»      REFERENCE(IV_DEPLOY_TO_TARGET) TYPE /SAPAPO/DEPREALTIME
*»      REFERENCE(IV_VERSION) TYPE /SAPAPO/VRSIOID
*»      REFERENCE(IV_LOCTAR) TYPE /SAPAPO/LOCID
*»      REFERENCE(IV_REALTIME) TYPE /SAPAPO/DEPREALTIME
*»      REFERENCE(IV_ALERTS) TYPE BOOLEAN
*»      REFERENCE(IV_SPOOLLST) TYPE BOOLEAN
*»      REFERENCE(IV_SY_BATCH) TYPE SYBATCH OPTIONAL
*»      REFERENCE(IT_MATMOD) TYPE /SAPAPO/MSNP_MATMOD_TAB
*»      REFERENCE(IT_LOC) TYPE /SAPAPO/MSNP_LOC_TAB
*»      REFERENCE(IT_LOC_SOURCE) TYPE /SAPAPO/MSNP_LOC_TAB
*»      REFERENCE(IT_COLS) TYPE /SAPAPO/TS_COLS_EXT_TAB
*»      REFERENCE(IV_NERRTG) TYPE /SAPAPO/MSG_FOR_NO_TARG OPTIONAL
*»   CHANGING
*»      REFERENCE(CV_DATA_EXIST) TYPE  BOOLEAN
*»      REFERENCE(CS_CTRL) TYPE /SAPAPO/MSNP_CTRL
*»      REFERENCE(CS_DEPP) TYPE /SAPAPO/MSNP_DEPP
*»      REFERENCE(CT_LOG) TYPE /SAPAPO/MSNP_DEPLOG_TAB
*»      REFERENCE(CT_MATERIAL) TYPE /SAPAPO/MSNP_MATERIAL_TAB
*»   EXCEPTIONS
*»       ERROR_LOCMAT_LOCKED
*»-------------------------------------------
```

Explanation

```
Importing
     IV_STARTAT             = <Time stam>
     IV_DEPLOY_TO_TARGET    = <Target System>
     IV_VERSION             = <Version ID>
Changing
     CV_DATA_EXIST     = <CV exists or not>
     CS_CTRL           = <Control Data>
```

/SAPAPO/MSDP_SNPHEU_LLC_GET: This FM determines information for MRP level. It helps to determine low level code based on selection criteria material and location id.

FUNCTION /sapapo/msdp_snpheu_llc_get.

```
*"-------------------------------------------
*"*"Local Interface:
*"  IMPORTING
*"     REFERENCE(IS_CTRL) TYPE /SAPAPO/MSNP_CTRL
*"     REFERENCE(IT_MATMOD) TYPE /SAPAPO/MATMOD_TAB
*"     REFERENCE(IT_R_DISST) TYPE /SAPAPO/R_DISST_TAB OPTIONAL
*"  EXPORTING
*"     REFERENCE(ET_SEQ_LLC) TYPE /SAPAPO/SNPHEU_LLC_TAB
*"  EXCEPTIONS
*"     ERROR_INTERFACE
*"     LLC_NOT_FOUND
*"-------------------------------------------
```

Explanation

```
Importing
     IS_CTRL      = <control parameter>
     IT_MATMOD    = <material id , location id>
Exporting
     ET_SEQ_LLC   = <Low level code table>
```

/SAPAPO/MSDP_SUBST_CONS_CHK: It determines consistency check for interchangeability group

FUNCTION /sapapo/msdp_subst_cons_chk.

```
*"-------------------------------------------
*"*"Local Interface:
*"  IMPORTING
*"     REFERENCE(IV_MODELID) TYPE /SAPAPO/C_MODELID OPTIONAL
*"     REFERENCE(IS_VERSION) TYPE /SAPAPO/S_MVM_CHK_VERS OPTIONAL
*"     REFERENCE(IV_CHKDATE) TYPE /SAPAPO/MVM_CHK_DATE OPTIONAL
*"     REFERENCE(IV_CONS_CHK_FLG) TYPE /SAPAPO/CONS_CHK_FLG
*"     REFERENCE(IV_MVIEW) TYPE /SAPAPO/PB_MVIEW OPTIONAL
*"     REFERENCE(IT_OBJ_CONS_CHK_TAB) TYPE /SAPAPO/OBJ_CONS_CHK_TAB
```

```
*"      REFERENCE(IT_CHKID_TAB) TYPE /SAPAPO/MVM_CHK_IDS_TAB OPTIONAL
*"      REFERENCE(IV_SNPDATE) TYPE /SAPAPO/SNPDAT00 OPTIONAL
*"   EXPORTING
*"      REFERENCE(ET_CONS_CHK_MESS_TAB) TYPE /SAPAPO/MVM_CHK_MESS_TAB
*"   CHANGING
*"      REFERENCE(CT_INC_ACTIVE) TYPE /SAPAPO/DM_MATLOC_IDS_TAB
*"       OPTIONAL
*"----------------------------------------------------------------------
```

Explanation

```
Importing
      IV_MODELID   = <Model Id>
      IS_VERSION   = <Version>
      IV_MVIEW     = <data view>
      IT_OBJ_CONS_CHK_TAB  = <object for consistency check matid, locid>
Exporting
      ET_CONS_CHK_MESS_TAB = <message table of consistency check>
```

/SAPAPO/TS_DM_SIMSESSION_GET: It returns the current simsession.

FUNCTION /sapapo/ts_dm_simsession_get.

```
*"----------------------------------------------------------------------
*"*"Lokale Schnittstelle:
*"  EXPORTING
*"      VALUE(EV_SIMSESSION_ORDERS) TYPE /SAPAPO/OM_SIMSESSION
*"      VALUE(EV_SIMSESSION_TS) TYPE /SAPAPO/OM_SIMSESSION
*"      VALUE(EV_SIM_VERSION) TYPE /SAPAPO/VRSIOID
*"      VALUE(EV_SIM_PAREAID) TYPE /SAPAPO/TS_PAREAID
*"----------------------------------------------------------------------
```

Explanation

```
Exporting
      EV_SIMSESSION_ORDERS = <Simession id>
      EV_SIM_VERSION       = <Version id>
      EV_SIM_PAREAID       = <planning area id>
```

/SAPAPO/TS_DM_SIMSESSION_OPEN: This FM is used to create new simsession. Whenever we want to read some LiveCache data, we need to open a “session” first, for it is a required parameter to most of APO functions reading data from or writing to LiveCache. Exceptions are of course BAPIs, that are dedicated to be called easily from outside.

FUNCTION /sapapo/ts_dm_simsession_open.

```
*"----------------------------------------------------------------------
*"*"Lokale Schnittstelle:
*"  IMPORTING
*"      REFERENCE(IV_PAREAID) TYPE /SAPAPO/TS_PAREAID
*"      REFERENCE(IV_VRSIOID) TYPE /SAPAPO/VRSIOID
```

```
*"      VALUE(IV_BATCH) TYPE  SYBATCH OPTIONAL
*"      REFERENCE(IV_ORDERS) TYPE /SAPAPO/BOOLEAN OPTIONAL
*"      REFERENCE(IV_TIMESERIES) TYPE /SAPAPO/BOOLEAN OPTIONAL
*"  CHANGING
*"      REFERENCE(CT_RC) TYPE /SAPAPO/OM_LC_RC_TAB OPTIONAL
*"  EXCEPTIONS
*"      LC_CONNECT_FAILED
*"      LC_COM_ERROR
*"      LC_APPL_ERROR
*"      MULTI_TASIM_REGISTRATION
*"      CUSTOMIZING_ERROR
*"----------------------------------------
```

Explanation

```
Importing
     IV_PAREAID  = <Planning area id>
     IV_VRSIOID  = <Version ID>
```

/SAPAPO/TS_DM_SIMSESSION_CLOSE: This FM is used to close simsession.

FUNCTION /sapapo/ts_dm_simsession_close.

```
*"----------------------------------------
*"*"Lokale Schnittstelle:
*"  IMPORTING
*"      REFERENCE(IV_PAREAID) TYPE /SAPAPO/TS_PAREAID
*"      REFERENCE(IV_SIMSESSION_METHOD) TYPE
*"                 /SAPAPO/OM_SIMSESSION_METHOD
*"      VALUE(IV_BATCH) TYPE  SYBATCH OPTIONAL
*"      VALUE(IV_MERGE_AND_DELETE) TYPE  BOOLEAN OPTIONAL
*"      VALUE(IV_COMMIT_WORK) TYPE  BOOLEAN DEFAULT 'X'
*"      VALUE(IV_ESA_SE) TYPE /SAPAPO/BOOLEAN OPTIONAL
*"  CHANGING
*"      REFERENCE(CT_RC) TYPE /SAPAPO/OM_LC_RC_TAB OPTIONAL
*"  EXCEPTIONS
*"      LC_CONNECT_FAILED
*"      LC_COM_ERROR
*"      LC_APPL_ERROR
*"      MULTI_TASIM_REGISTRATION
*"      MERGE_FAILED
*"      DELETE_FAILED
*"----------------------------------------
```

Explanation

```
Importing
     IV_PAREAID            = <Planning area id>
     IV_SIMESSION_METHOD   = <Simsession method>
```

/SAPAPO/MSDP_CALL_DEPLOYMENT: This FM is used to call deployment based on source location and product.

FUNCTION /sapapo/msdp_call_deployment.

```
*"----------------------------------------------------------
*"*"Local Interface:
*"  IMPORTING
*"     REFERENCE(IS_MATERIAL) TYPE /SAPAPO/MSNP_MATERIAL
*"     REFERENCE(IV_LOCID) TYPE /SAPAPO/LOCID
*"     REFERENCE(IV_INTAKT_FLG) TYPE /SAPAPO/INTAKTFLG
*"     REFERENCE(IV_REALT) TYPE  BOOLEAN
*"     REFERENCE(IT_LOC) TYPE /SAPAPO/MSNP_LOC_TAB OPTIONAL
*"     REFERENCE(IV_OM_SIMSESSION) TYPE /SAPAPO/OM_SIMSESSION
*"     REFERENCE(IV_NO_ALERTS) TYPE  BOOLEAN OPTIONAL
*"     REFERENCE(IV_STARTAT) TYPE /SAPAPO/SNPTSTMP OPTIONAL
*"     REFERENCE(IT_COLS) TYPE /SAPAPO/TS_COLS_EXT_TAB OPTIONAL
*"     REFERENCE(IV_KF_RESQ_EXIST) TYPE  CHAR01 OPTIONAL
*"     REFERENCE(IT_ATD_SUBST)TYPE/SAPAPO/MSDP_ATD_STR_TAB OPTIONAL
*"     REFERENCE(IV_MATID_SUBST_FROM) TYPE /SAPAPO/MATID OPTIONAL
*"     REFERENCE(IT_PEGID) TYPE /SAPAPO/PEGID_TAB OPTIONAL
*"  CHANGING
*"     REFERENCE(CT_LOG) TYPE /SAPAPO/MSNP_DEPLOG_TAB
*"     REFERENCE(CS_DEPP) TYPE /SAPAPO/MSNP_DEPP
*"     REFERENCE(CS_CTRL) TYPE /SAPAPO/MSNP_CTRL
*"     REFERENCE(CT_SELECTION) TYPE /SAPAPO/TS_IOBJ_SELECTION_TAB
*"     REFERENCE(CT_GROUP_BY) TYPE /SAPAPO/TS_GROUP_BY_TAB
*"  EXCEPTIONS
*"     ERROR_READING_DATA
*"     ERROR_WITH_RC
*"     ERROR_CALCULATE_DEPLOYMENT
*"     ERROR_CALCULATE_SNP
*"     NO_TARGET_LOCATIONS
*"     NO_LANE_FOUND
*"     LC_CONNECT_FAILED
*"     ERROR_SAVING_PPDS_ORDERS
*"----------------------------------------------------------
```

Explanation

```
Importing
    IS_MATERIAL         = <Material>
    IV_LOCID            = <Location>
    IV_INTAKT_FLG       = <Interactive mode or not>
    IV_REALT            = <Real time deployment or not>
    IV_OM_SIMSESSION    = <Simsession>
```

```
Changing
     CS_DEPP              = <Deployment parameter>
     CS_CTRL              = <Control parameter>
     CT_SELECTION         = <Selection with infoobject>
     CT_GROUP_BY          = <Group by based on info object>
```

/SAPAPO/MSDP_TD_TRANSFER_SET: It is used to set transfer indicator and order status for snp order changes.

FUNCTION /SAPAPO/MSDP_TD_TRANSFER_SET.

```
*"----------------------------------------------------------------
*"*"Lokale Schnittstelle:
*"  IMPORTING
*"     REFERENCE(IV_APPL) TYPE /SAPAPO/C_APKZ
*"     REFERENCE(IV_IS_INITIAL_LOAD) OPTIONAL
*"     REFERENCE(IV_PAREAID) TYPE /SAPAPO/TS_PAREAID OPTIONAL
*"  CHANGING
*"     REFERENCE(CT_POCO) TYPE /SAPAPO/MSNP_POCO_TAB OPTIONAL
*"     REFERENCE(CT_PROD) TYPE /SAPAPO/MSNP_PROD_TAB OPTIONAL
*"----------------------------------------------------------------
```

Explanation

```
Importing
     IV_APPL      = <application indicator for APO application>
     IV_PAREAID   = <planning area id>
Changing
     CT_POCO      = <table for stock transfer update>
```

/SAPAPO/TS_DM_TRANS_SET: This FM is used to create, update and delete shipment quantities.

FUNCTION /sapapo/ts_dm_trans_set.

```
*"----------------------------------------------------------------
*"*"Local Interface:
*"  IMPORTING
*"     VALUE(IV_PAREAID) TYPE /SAPAPO/TS_PAREAID
*"     REFERENCE(IT_COLS) TYPE /SAPAPO/TS_COLS_EXT_TAB
*"     REFERENCE(IS_WRITE_OPTIONS) TYPE /SAPAPO/TS_WRITE_OPTIONS
*"     REFERENCE(IT_CHARACT_VAL) TYPE /SAPAPO/OM_CHARACT_VAL_TAB
*"      OPTIONAL
*"  EXPORTING
*"     REFERENCE(ET_RC) TYPE /SAPAPO/OM_LC_RC_TAB
*"     REFERENCE(ET_MESSAGES) TYPE /SAPAPO/TBL_BAPIRET2
*"  CHANGING
*"     REFERENCE(CT_POCO) TYPE /SAPAPO/MSNP_POCO_TAB
*"  EXCEPTIONS
*"     AREA_INVALID
```

```
*"        INVALID_INTERFACE
*"        NO_MASTER_DATA
*"        CUSTOMIZING_ERROR
*"        PEGID_PROBLEM
*"        LC_CONNECT_FAILED
*"        LC_COM_ERROR
*"        LC_APPL_ERROR
*"        LC_UNKNOWN_ERROR
*"        PROBLEM_READING_PAPLOB
*"-----------------------------------------------
```

Explanation

```
Importing
     IV_PAREAID          = <planning area id>
     IT_CHARACT_VAL      = <column index planning metrix>
Changing
     CT_POCO             = <table for stock transfer update>
```

/SAPAPO/MSDP_SNPHEU_DRPFROMDEP: This FM is used to run SNP heuristics fro deployment.

FUNCTION /sapapo/msdp_snpheu_drpfromdep.

```
*"-----------------------------------------------
*"*"Local Interface:
*"  IMPORTING
*"       REFERENCE(IV_MVIEW) TYPE /SAPAPO/PB_MVIEW
*"       REFERENCE(IV_DVIEW) TYPE /SAPAPO/PB_DVIEW
*"       REFERENCE(IV_VERSION) TYPE /SAPAPO/VRSIOID
*"       REFERENCE(IV_SIMSESSION) TYPE /SAPAPO/OM_SIMSESSION
*"       REFERENCE(IS_MATID_LOCID) TYPE /SAPAPO/MSNP_MATID_LOCID
*"       REFERENCE(IT_LOCID) TYPE /SAPAPO/MSNP_LOCID_TAB
*"       REFERENCE(IT_SELECTION_EXT) TYPE /SAPAPO/TS_IOBJ_SELECTION_
         TAB
*"       REFERENCE(IT_GROUP_BY_EXT) TYPE /SAPAPO/TS_GROUP_BY_TAB
*"       REFERENCE(IV_STARTDATE) TYPE  D
*"       REFERENCE(IV_ENDDATE) TYPE  D
*"       REFERENCE(IV_MODELID) TYPE /SAPAPO/C_MODELID
*"       REFERENCE(IV_PLANMODE) TYPE /SAPAPO/PLANMODE DEFAULT SPACE
*"  EXPORTING
*"       REFERENCE(ET_POCO) TYPE /SAPAPO/MSNP_POCO_TAB
*"       REFERENCE(ET_SUBST) TYPE /SAPAPO/MSNP_SUBST_TAB
*"       REFERENCE(EV_NR_OF_PRODUCTS) TYPE  INT4
*"  EXCEPTIONS
*"       LC_POCO_ERROR
*"       TIMESTREAM_ERROR
*"-----------------------------------------------
```

Explanation

```
Importing
    IV_DVIEW           = <Data View>
    IV_VERSION         = <Version>
    IV_SIMSESSION      = <Simsession>
    IS_MATID_LOCID     = <Material Location ID>
    IT_SELECTION_EXT   = <Selection table containing info object>
    IT_GROUP_BY_EXT    = <Group info object>
    IV_STARTDATE       = <Start Date>
    IV_ENDDATE         = <End Date>
    IV_MODELID         = <Model id>
Exporting
    ET_POCO            = <Stock transfer table>
```

SAP SCM deployment is more over a back ground program, user can create an interactive deployment like planning book using above described Function Modules. Also refer the chapter "Programming using LiveCache" to check the use of Function Modules.

9

ALERT PROGRAMMING

9.1 ALERTS

Alerts notify the planner about situations which require his attention or interference to look into the situation and take the necessary action. A shortage situation caused by higher demand due to increased sales or caused by production shortfall due to increased scrap is a typical example where an alert (in this case of the type "*order has under coverage*") helps the planner to act as early as possible.

Alert Management (ALM) comes into play, when business-critical problems occur. Within ALM, conditions for critical situations are predefined. When an alert is triggered in ALM that meets these conditions, responsible or interested parties are determined and informed immediately. One more example of critical situations might be an important customer terminating a contract or a budget being exceeded. Conditions should be pre-defined during the configuration settings of the Alerts, this is done considering the business scenarios.

Alerts are displayed either in the alert monitor as a stand alone application or are integrated into other planning functionalities. The alert monitor is called with the *transaction code /SAPAPO/AMON1.*

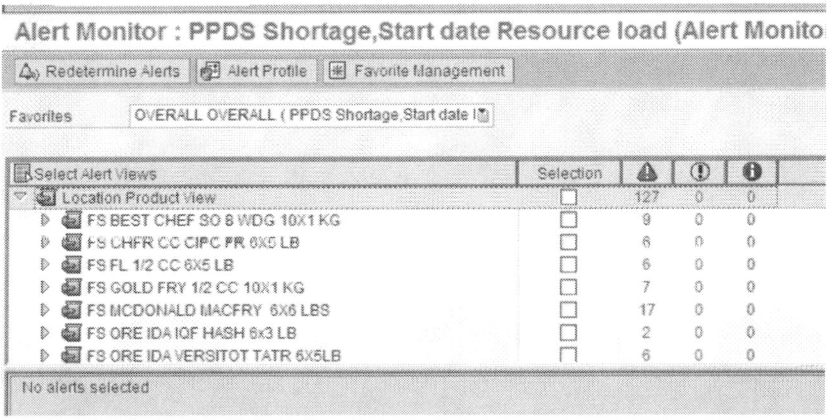

Figure 9.1 Alert monitor

9.2 ALERT MONITORING

The alert monitor is structured into two parts: In the area above the objects for the alerts are selected. In the alert view below only those alerts for the objects are shown, which had been selected in the alert profiles and for which current alerts exist. The navigation becomes clearer after regarding the structure of the alert monitor configuration (with the *transaction code /SAPAPO/AMON_SETTING*).

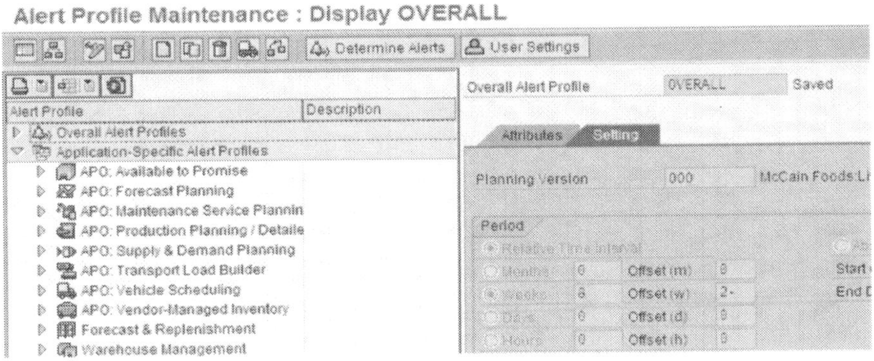

Figure 9.2 Alert profile maintenance

There are additional profiles for VS (vehicle scheduling), VMI (vendor managed inventory) and MSP (maintenance and service planning). In the alert profiles the alert types and the objects for which the alerts should be displayed are selected. Depending on the application different alert types and selection criteria are used. Generally it is recommended not to be too generous in the choice of alert types since performance will be an issue in alert monitoring. In the '*alert monitor settings*' the version and the horizon for the alert display is defined. To apply these settings in the alert monitor they have to be assigned for each user as favorites.

These favorites are selected in the alert monitor. Still there is a small catch defining the alert monitor settings: define the name of a new setting, make the respective changes and save, the system asks to save the changes. The right answer here is no, else the old settings will be changed.

To each alert there are lots of information – *alert priority, alert type, product, location, target and actual value* are only a few of them. The selection of the displayed information and their sequence are configured using the '*select layout*' button in the header of the alert display box. In the menu bar of '*select layout*' a new layout is created, in '*manage layout*' it is set as a default. Non-default layouts have to be applied manually. In the alert monitor those alerts are displayed that were valid at the time the alert monitor was called. If the planning situation has changed in the meantime a refresh is necessary.

9.3 ALERT TYPES

APO provides some standard alert types and allows for supply and demand planning to define own alert types. The alert types are selected per application area for the according profile.

Forecast Alerts

The alert types in the forecast alert profile are all related to the trespassing of forecast error limits. Therefore the prerequisites to use forecast errors are the selection of the errors in the forecast profile and the definition of the limits for the errors in the respective diagnosis groups.

SDP Alerts

SDP alerts are based on the planning book structure and the time series. These alerts are calculated using macros. Technically there are two types of alerts, *dynamic alerts* and *database alerts*. In SNP and DP both dynamic and database alerts can be used, but especially for a huge data amount it is not recommended to use dynamic alerts because of performance disadvantages.

Database alerts are usually calculated by planning jobs (with the structure) and relate to the planning situation at the point in time of the planning job. Database alerts are stored in the database. Therefore it is recommended first to delete the existing alerts before creating new ones.

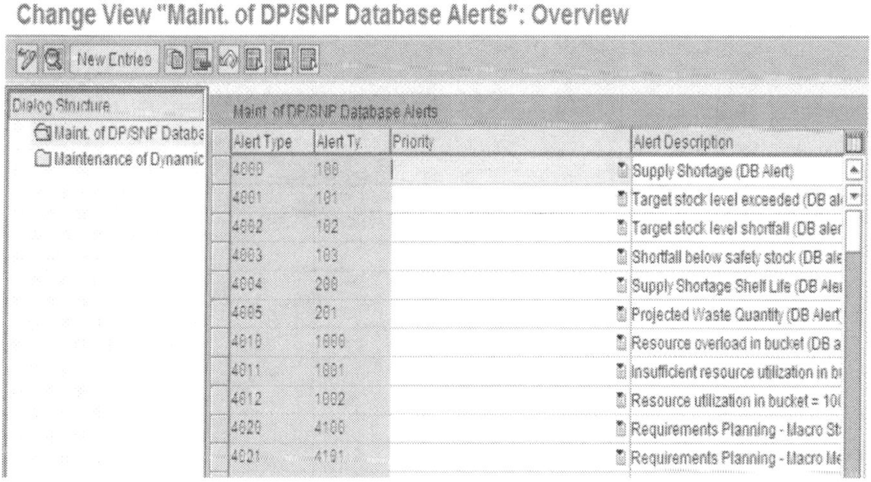

Figure 9.3 Maintain DP/SNP database alerts

9.4 EXCEPTION REPORTING

As an example to apply database alerts syntactically correct. The syntax for the same semantic using a dynamic alert is shown for comparison.

Note that the alert semantic is defined in the macro itself and the alert type are only used for organizational purposes. All alert types of the SDP alert profile can be used in the macro builder, but most of the alert types are used in standard macros in the SNP planning book *9ASNP94*. It is possible to define alert types with the *transaction code /SAPAPO/ATYPES_SDP* including the definition of their priority and their thresholds. With the syntax as shown in figure actual values are appended from the assigned rows to the alert text.

9.5 ALERT DEFINITION

Alert Text

Syntax to Append Information to the Alert Text is possible to define alert types which change their priority according to the deviation of the assigned parameters by defining a relational operator (usually '*greater than*') in the alert type. The ratio of parameter one divided by parameter two is used. It is possible to call the alert monitor with the according button from the header of the planning book as well. The alerts can be restricted to the version, the planning book or the data selection, but not to the displayed data after drill down. The small icon to the right of the alert button closes the alert monitor within the planning book.

Another macro functionality which is used to attract the attention to deviations in the interactive planning is the coloring of the concerned cells. When adding the row to be changed, make sure that the scope of the row is changed from '*values*' to '*attributes*'.

TLB Alerts

The alerts in the TLB profile relate to both deployment and TLB. Regarding deployment there are alerts for shortages after fair share, for TLB there are alerts for minimum and maximum load violations.

PPDS Alerts

There is a large variety of PPDS alerts concerning *shortage and surplus, lateness, pegging constraints, order relationship, resource overload, characteristics and others*. In contrast to the SDP alerts the logic is predefined.

The alerts for shortage and surplus are calculated depending on the pegging between nodes. If a supply node is too late for the demand node, no pegging exists any more between the nodes. In this case the system creates a shortage alert and a surplus alert, even though no real shortage exists. If backward pegging is allowed (a setting in the product master), the pegging is kept and a lateness alert is created instead. Another example shows the possible lateness alerts during the order life cycle of in-house production.

The first delay refers to the opening date – when a planned order has to be converted into a production order. Consequently this alert only applies to planned orders.

After the first operation has slipped into the past, the alert '*confirmation date in the past*' is created – accordingly only for production orders. If the last operation lies in the past, the system creates the alert '*receipt date in the past*', which applies for both planned order and production order. For all delays alerts it is possible – and advisable – to define offsets.

The PPDS applications product view, planning board and product planning table allow to call the alert monitor within the respective transaction. Since the PPDS applications work with transactional simulations, the alert monitor reflects the planning positions of this transactional simulation which is not necessary identical with the current situation in the active version.

If the alert monitor is called from the planning board, network alerts are automatically displayed although they are rather performance consuming.

ATP Alerts

A prerequisite to get ATP alerts at all is to flag the checkbox in the check instructions.

Available alert types are shortages in the availability check, in the forecast check and in the allocations check. The suggestion of what is considered as a shortage in ATP alert monitoring needs an explanation. Neither a partial confirmation nor no confirmation at all is regarded as a shortage.

ATP alerts are saved to the data base without the link to the order and are therefore not automatically updated. Due to these restrictions ATP alerts are not used very frequently.

Alert Handling

In order to help the planner to keep an track of the alert situation it is possible to sort the alerts according to any column in ascending or descending order, confirm the alert, that is to mark it as *checked* (for example because its resolving is already triggered), *hide an alert*, for example because it is due to some exceptional constraints which are not defined in the system and display hidden alerts again.

Another feature to support the planner in resolving the alert situations is the functionality to freeze the alerts. In this case any change is marked in the status column.

This feature is particularly helpful when calling the alert monitor in the transactional simulation mode from a PPDS application. This way it is possible to experiment with actions and to test their impact on the alert situation.

Depending on this impact it is possible to decide whether to save or not. With right mouse click on the alerts it is possible to branch into an application to rectify the alert. This functionality depends on the alert type. It is not recommended to use this functionality from a transactional simulation since in that case the application may represent a different planning situation.

There are three priorities for alerts – '*information*' (priority 3), '*warning*' (priority 2) and '*error*' (priority 1). For some alert types it is possible to set the priority depending on thresholds. Additionally the general priority of some alert types can be changed in customizing.

9.6 ALERT CALCULATION IN THE BACKGROUND

It is possible to send alerts regularly per batch job either to the SAP office or to a specified e-mail address. These settings are maintained in the automatic messaging profile with the *transaction code /SAPAPO/AMONMSG*. The actual sending of the alerts is triggered with the *transaction code /SAPAPO/AMONMSG_SEND.*

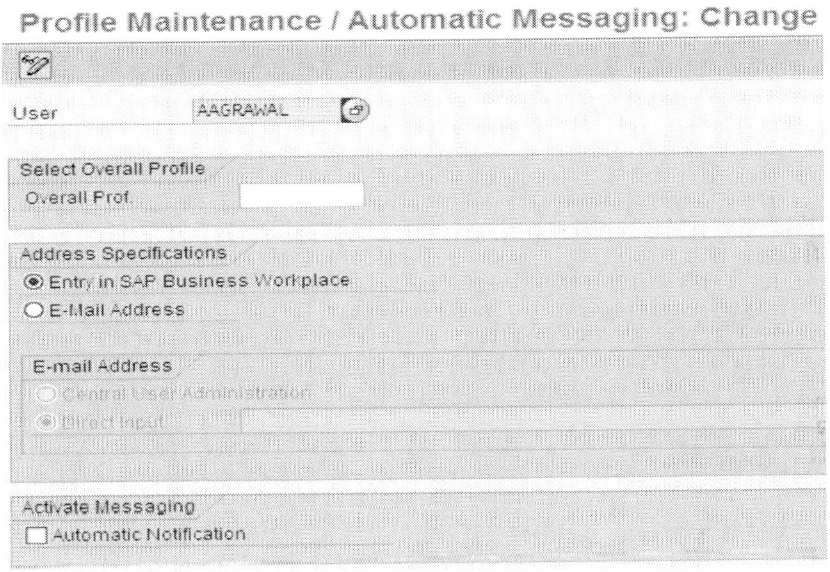

Figure 9.4 Alert message sending options

- **Send Alert Monitor mails** with *report /SAPAPO/AMON_MAIL_BROADCAST*. Depending on user profiles, mails are sent with an overview over existing alerts. The responsible persons should then call the APO Alert Monitor, investigate the reasons for the alerts, and take corrective actions in order to keep the production plan close to the needs of the organization.
- **Delete Alert Monitor alerts** with *report /SAPAPO/AMON_REORG* deletes alerts being older than a specified age.

To track the R/3 MRP alerts in APO, one must maintain the **R/3 MRP Alert Profile**. MRP alerts refer to the results of materials requirements planning run. In the Alert Monitor, check a frozen display of the latest MRP run. This profile contains an automatically generated list of R/3 Systems connected to APO system. In order to see the alerts in APO, create a user view in the R/3 System in which one want to track MRP alerts.

To support the Alert Monitor's function as a tool for exception-based management, send messages via email to other planners to inform them of the alert situation. Can also have messages sent automatically to own inbox to get information of alerts in specific area.

Maintain a list of favorite Alert Monitor profiles so to switch back and forth easily between various profiles.

For example, one may have an alert profile for his own area of responsibility, but may also want to look at alerts in other areas.

9.7 SUPPLY CHAIN COCKPIT

The supply chain cockpit provides an overview about the supply chain structure, both graphical in the right window and listed per elements (locations, products, resources, production and transport lanes) in the object view in the left window. The objects for display are selected with the selection functionality and saved into the work area when leaving the transaction.

The supply chain cockpit is called with the *transaction code /SAPAPO/SCC02*. The benefit of the supply chain cockpit is that it links the supply chain structure with an overview of the alerts. In the bottom line the existence of current alerts is displayed per application and priority. In the object view the number and priority of related alerts is displayed per object.

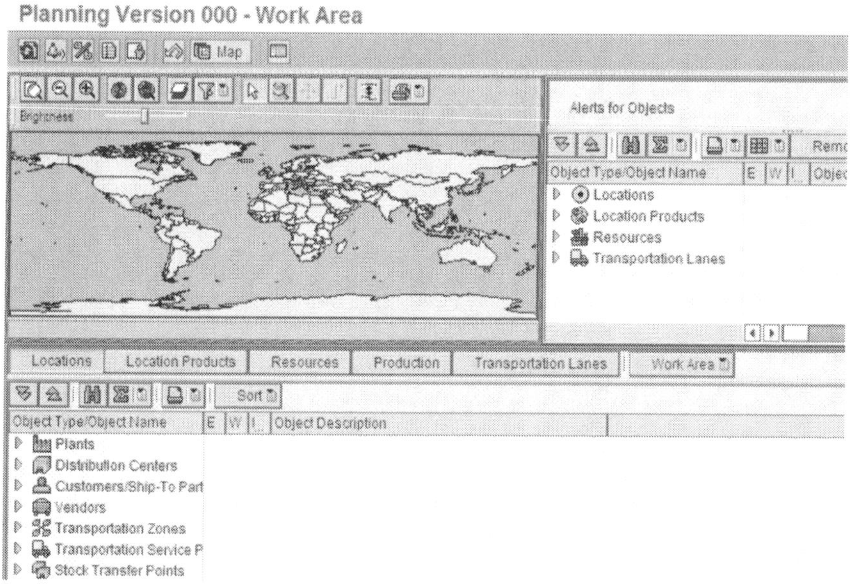

Figure 9.5 Planning work area

Implementing the Alert Monitor Functionality Using Macro Alerts to Highlight Custom Alert Situations in APO DP

In this section, I will provide a detailed step by step procedure for implementing the Alert Monitor and Macro Alerts for highlighting custom alert situations in APO DP. Any given alert situation in APO DP, for example, forecast deviating from average sales history by a given percentage can be highlighted and monitored using the Alert Monitor. It demonstrates all the steps involved in setting up of an Alert Monitor and Macros in APO DP and its implications, along with useful implementation tips.

Procedure in this chapter, describes the setting-up an Alert Monitor and the Macro alerts to highlight the 'alert' situations in APO DP. Also I will cover some of the definitions which will help readers to understand the subject.

Alert Types

The first step involves in defining an alert type. There are two types of alert types available:

- Database Alert Type
- Dynamic Alert Type

Dynamic alert reflects the '*current*' situation that exists in the LiveCache. It is performance intensive and should be avoided if dealing with large number of alerts.

Database alert types are recommended to highlight planning situations as it was during the last Macro run or planning run. For performance reasons, database alert types are recommended when dealing with large number of alerts and data volume. We shall define a database alert type for our example. The database alert type needs to be defined using the following configuration:

MySAP SCM -> Implementation Guide -> SCM Basis -> Alert Monitor -> Maintain Database Alert Types for Demand Planning and SNP

One can define a separate database alert type for APO DP macro alerts. This enables the demand planners to view only relevant DP alerts and also enables to setup a process for proper maintenance of Alerts on a periodic basis. This is particularly useful while setting up alert profiles and differentiating the alerts generated by other modules such as SNP or PPDS. Separate alert profiles can be defined for demand planners and the DP database alert type defined can be assigned to the alert profiles which ensure that Demand Planners see only alerts relevant to them and not any other alerts, some of the settings are covered in configuration which also require transport request while some settings are just as per daily or changing business requirement that is just as data change in the system.

9.8 MACROS

The second step would be to define the Macro in the relevant planning book/data view for highlighting the alert situation. We will consider an example where an alert situation is highlighted when forecast for the current month varies from the average of past three months sales history by more than 20%. Similarly, any other similar situation can also be highlighted by configuring a relevant macro.

Database Alert Type defined in above step, is assigned to the alert step ('*Update in Context: Standard status alert*' shown below) in the macro. Execution of this macro, results in generation of an alert whenever forecast for the current month varies from the average of past three months sales history by more than 20%. These alerts can be viewed in Interactive Planning or Alert Monitor. However to view these alerts, we need to define an Alert Profile and assign the alert type, planning book, data view and relevant selection ID. This will be explained in detail in following steps.

Alert Macros can then be assigned to '*Start*' event which will ensure that the macro executes whenever the demand planners load the selection and will get highlighted in the Interactive Planning. Else, the alert will not get highlighted in Interactive Planning unless the demand planners manually execute the Macro. The macros need to be executed in change mode in Interactive Planning for the alerts to be visible. Please also note that, the alerts can be generated by scheduling the Macro run in DP background jobs and viewed in Alert Monitor.

A sample code for defining the above mentioned Macro is given below. A different logic can also be applied to further simplify the code in the macro below. The following transaction / menu path can be used for defining the macros.

SAP Menu -> Demand Planning -> Environment -> Current Settings -> Macro Workbench

Transaction Code /SAPAPO/ADVM

The following macro generates an alert whenever the final forecast figure (Consensus Forecast) of current month varies from the three month average sales history (Shipped Quantity) by more than 20%. Similarly, any other logic can also be built in the macro accordingly to highlight a given alert situation.

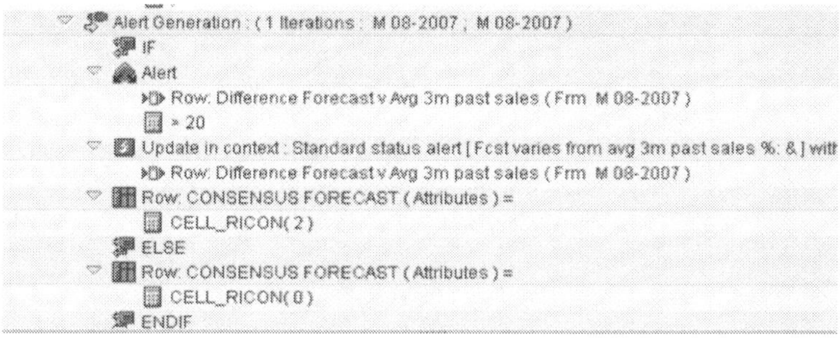

Figure 9.6 Writing alert

Overall Alert Profiles and SDP Profiles

The third step involves creating an Overall Alert Profile and a Supply Demand Planning (SDP) profile. This enables the demand planners to view the alerts created by the above macros. The following transaction / menu path is used to create alert profiles. If no SDP alert profile and Overall Profile are created, then the users will not be able to see the alerts generated by the macros. Also users should be careful for all settings related changes.

SAP menu -> Supply Chain Monitoring -> /SAPAPO/AMON1 - Alert Monitor.

The Relative Time Interval controls the '*time horizon*' over which the alerts are displayed in Alert Monitor. This controls which alerts the users will see in the Alert Monitor. Once the horizon is defined, if a macro generates an alert which is outside this horizon then that alert can only be viewed in Interactive Planning but will not be displayed in the Alert Monitor. This enables the users to control to view only the relevant period alerts in Alert Monitor, making it more significant rather than cluttering with too many irrelevant alerts.

Enter a 12 month horizon in our example which will display any alerts generated 12 months into the future horizon, in the screen shot we used 29 weeks but in current example we will go with 12 months to make. This setting ensures a '*rolling*' horizon. If a fixed absolute horizon is needed then the '*Absolute Time Interval*' needs to be defined and dates specified which will display any alerts generated within those dates.

Next, an SDP profile is defined within the Overall Profile. Database Alert Type defined earlier and used in our Macro is assigned to this SDP profile.

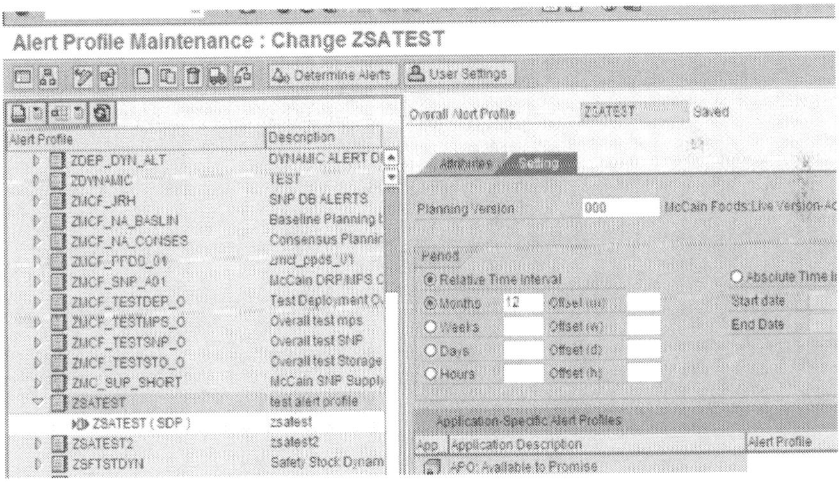

Figure 9.7 Settings in alert profile

The planning book in which the above macro is created is assigned to this SDP profile. Data view which contains the macro created above is also assigned to the SDP profile. Selection IDs can be additionally defined and assigned to the SDP profile thus enabling the viewing alerts for relevant data.

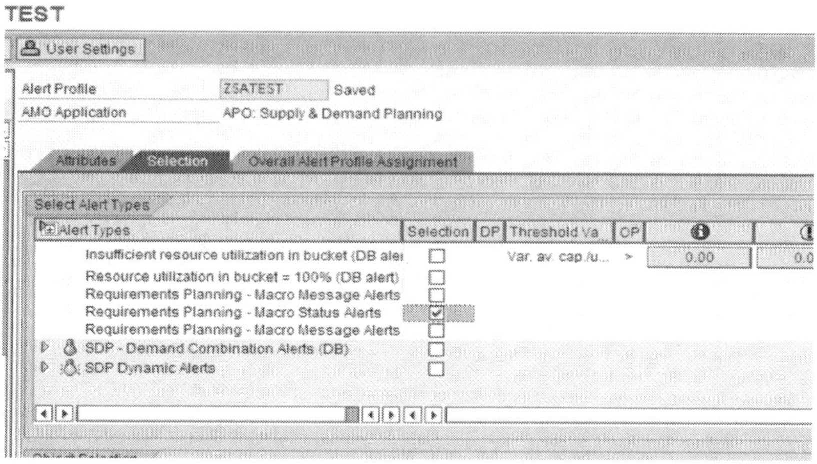

Figure 9.8 Setting database alert in alert profile

If we have more than one demand planner managing different product groups or geographies out of a single planning book/data view, then the user can create different Overall Profiles for each of the demand planners, assign the alert type, planning book, data view and then assign specific selection IDs for each of the planners. When the users login to the Alert Monitor, only alerts generated for the data within that selection ID is displayed. This ensures that the planners will see alerts relevant only to their set of data.

Alert Profile Assignment

The next step is to assign the above created SDP profile to the demand planner's SAP user IDs, enabling them to view alerts in Interactive Planning. Please note that the planners will not be able to see any alerts in Interactive Planning unless their SAP user ID is assigned to an alert profile. They can see the alerts in Alert Monitor though, provided their SDP alert profile is assigned to the Overall Profile.

SAP menu -> Demand Planning -> Environment -> Current Settings -> /SAPAPO/SDPALPR – Assign Planners to Alert Profiles

Database Alert Deletion and Maintenance

Once the demand planners view the alerts and rectify the situation in Interactive planning, the 'old' or 'viewed' alerts need to be deleted from the system. For database alert types, the alerts will not disappear automatically once the situation is rectified in Interactive Planning. The alerts need to be either deleted manually or using a scheduled program. This is recommended in order to avoid the 'irrelevant' alerts from accumulating and keep the alert monitor meaningful.

Program /SAPAPO/AMON_REORG needs to be scheduled to run on periodic basis to delete the alerts. Relevant alert types and time intervals can be specified thus ensuring only the relevant DP alerts are deleted. When the alerts are re-determined the next time, only the relevant alerts will be displayed in the alert monitor. If the alert situation of a previous alert has been rectified by the planners, then that alert will not re-appear again, thus ensuring the users do not see any '*obsolete*' alerts.

Schedule this program to be run before the alert macro background job is executed. This ensures that database alerts of any alert situation already rectified by planners is deleted and will not re-appear when alerts are generated afresh by the macro and re-determined in alert monitor. This prevents '*obsolete*' alerts from accumulating in alert monitor and keeps them meaningful.

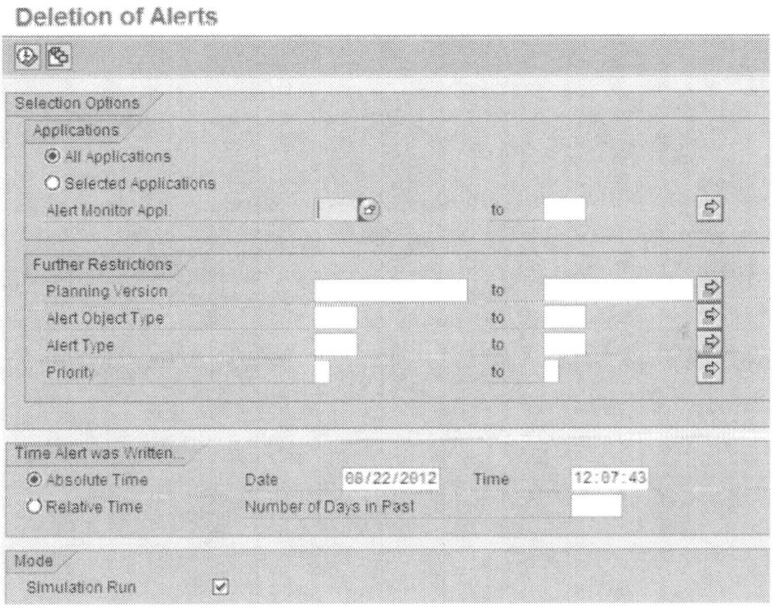

Figure 9.9 Deletion of alerts

9.9 ALERT GENERATION AND VIEWING

The alerts are generated by executing the relevant Macros in the background jobs. They can also be generated by manually executing Macros in Interactive Planning.

There are two methods of viewing the alerts generated by the above macros:

- Alert Monitor
- Interactive Planning

Please note that the Overall Profile and SDP profile needs to be created and assigned before viewing alerts using either of the methods also certain steps required in particular sequence only.

Viewing Alerts in Alert Monitor

Alert monitor is called using the *transaction code /SAPAPO/AMON1* - Alert Monitor. The demand planners can view alerts in the alert monitor. The relevant Overall Profile is assigned to the '*Favorite Management*'. This ensures that the relevant Overall Profile is prompted whenever the planner launches the alert monitor.

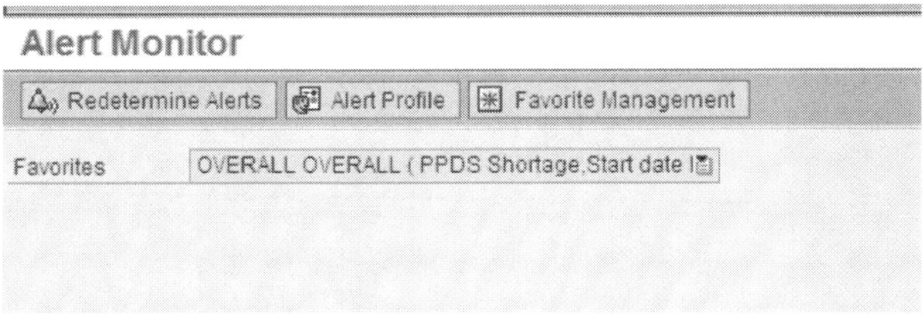

Figure 9.10 Set alert profile in favorites

Press the '*Re determine Alerts*' button to display the alerts. All alerts in the data views assigned to the given SDP profile are displayed.

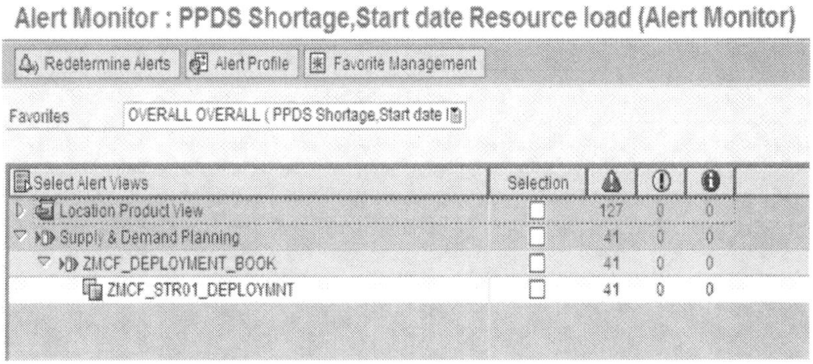

Figure 9.11 Display of alerts defined

Demand Planners can view alerts of more than one planning book by creating different Overall Profiles/SDP Profiles for different planning books and adding them to '*Favorite Management*'. Alert Monitor also enables to limit the horizon over which the alerts are to be displayed thus helping demand planners to see only the relevant alerts unlike Interactive Planning, where all alerts across the horizon are displayed and may result in cluttering, making it difficult to browse through.

Thus, the alert monitor makes it easy for the planners to monitor all alert situations in different planning books and take necessary action accordingly. Also to keep in mind that the planners will not be able to rectify the alert situation from the Alert Monitor itself, but will have to log into the respective planning books and to correct the raised alert from there. Once the alert situation is rectified in Interactive Planning, the database alert needs to be deleted either manually or using the deletion report. When alerts are re-determined the next time, this rectified situation will not show up as alert in the alert monitor.

Viewing Alerts in Interactive Planning

Only alerts generated for the respective planning book can be viewed. When the selection is loaded in Interactive Planning, if the Macros are put in event '*Start*' or '*Default*', the Alerts get highlighted for the given period / key figure.

To view the generated alerts in Interactive Planning, the button needs to be clicked. The generated alerts are displayed at the bottom of the screen. Please note that the user ID should be assigned to the SDP profile. Else, the alerts cannot be displayed. Planners can control whether to see all alerts for the planning book or only alerts relevant to loaded selection by choosing accordingly, i.e. planner can filter the generated alerts.

The planners can then analyze and rectify the alert situation in Interactive Planning. The database alerts should be deleted once the alert situation is rectified which ensures the alert is not displayed the next time the alert macro executes.

9.10 PROCEDURE TO EXTRACT DATA FROM SAPAPO/AM_ALERT

Alert in APO are saved in table *SAPAPO/AM_ALERT*, one can follow the below steps for creating the generic extractor in APO to get the alerts details.

1. In Source System, go to *transaction code SE11* and create a table, then go to RSO2 to create Data Source.
2. Specify the name of the Data Source in the field of RSO2 and hit Create.
3. Give the Application component and description.

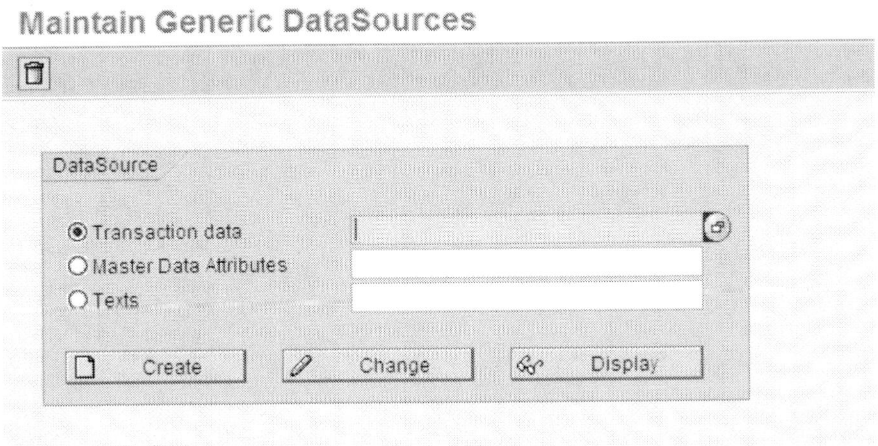

Figure 9.12 Maintain dataSource

4. In View/Table field specify the "Z" custom table name.
5. Then click Save.
6. It will take to the extract structure screen.
7. If need to hide/select any of the field can be done here, otherwise press enter.
8. Change the package of the Data Source and specify the transport request number to it and test the extractor in *RSA3*.

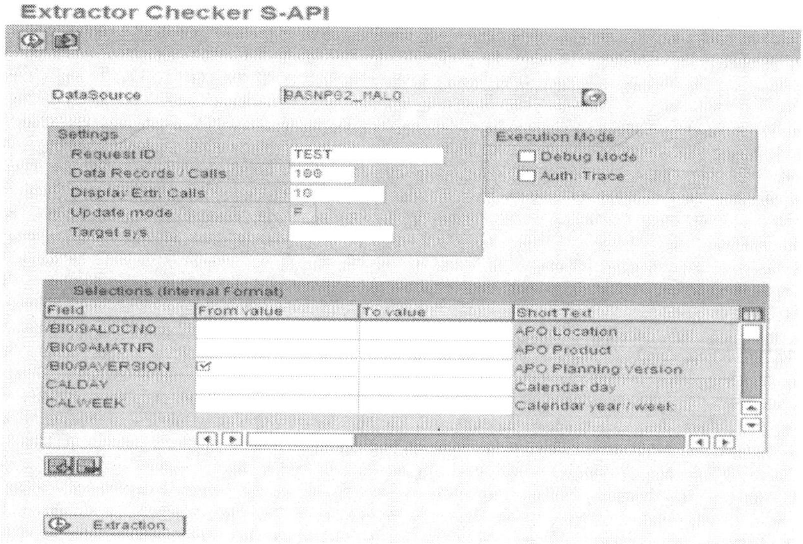

Figure 9.13 DataSource settings

One can also read the alerts using program, sample code for extraction is given here.

```
DATA :  l_plver             TYPE /sapapo/amoplver,
        l_vfrom             TYPE /sapapo/c_vfrom,
        l_vto               TYPE /sapapo/c_vto,
        lt_amoappl_profid   TYPE /sapapo/amoappl_profid_tab,
        ls_profid           LIKE LINE OF lt_amoappl_profid,
        l_alert_manager     TYPE REF TO /sapapo/alert_manager.
        gt_alert_tab        TYPE /sapapo/alert_tab.

* Assign the version, from and to date

l_plver         = '000'.
l_vfrom         = '20100101000010'.
l_vto           = '20201231235949'.
```

```
* Assign the profile id's

ls_profid-applid  = 'SD'.
ls_profid-profid  = 'PN_SNP_ALERT'.
APPEND ls_profid TO lt_amoappl_profid.

* Create the alert object

CREATE OBJECT l_alert_manager.

REFRESH gt_alert_tab.

* Call the method using the parameters and
* read the alerts from the data base

CALL METHOD l_alert_manager->read_alerts
  EXPORTING
    plver             = l_plver
    vfrom             = l_vfrom
    vto               = l_vto
    t_appl_profid     = lt_amoappl_profid
    pllp_switch       = 'X'
  IMPORTING
    t_alerts          = gt_alert_tab
  EXCEPTIONS
    profile_not_found = 1.

IF sy-subrc = 1.
  RAISE profile_not_found.
ENDIF.
```

Function Module to get the alerts saved in LiveCache.

```
CALL FUNCTION '/SAPAPO/OM_ALERTS_GET_DATA'
  EXPORTING
    is_gen_params                =
    iv_simsession                =
*   IT_PEGLIST                   =
*   IT_ORDLIST                   =
*   IT_RESLIST                   =
*   IT_PCMLIST                   =
*   IT_ALERTID                   =
*   IT_CATEGORY                  =
*   IV_REP_RES_ALERTS_DET        = IF_LCA_CONFIG=>FALSE
*   IV_START_TIME                = GC_MINTIME
*   IV_END_TIME                  = GC_MAXTIME
```

```
*    IV_ACTUAL_TIME                     = GC_MINTIME
*    IV_RPM_GET_VIRTUAL_INPUTS          =
* IMPORTING
*    ET_ALERTS                          =
*    ET_RC                              =
* EXCEPTIONS
*    LC_CONNECT_FAILED                  = 1
*    LC_COM_ERROR                       = 2
*    LC_APPL_ERROR                      = 3
*    OTHERS                             = 4.
IF sy-subrc <> 0.
* MESSAGE ID SY-MSGID TYPE SY-MSGTY NUMBER SY-MSGNO
*         WITH SY-MSGV1 SY-MSGV2 SY-MSGV3 SY-MSGV4.
ENDIF.
```

Functionality

This function call returns the exceptions for the objects specified in IT_XXXLIST. If these tables are empty, no exceptions are returned for objects of this type. The IT_XXXALL flags are used to control whether all exceptions for objects of this type are returned. These flags override any entries that may be in the tables.

The return tables contain an entry for each alert. Only those data fields are filled that are appropriate for the type of the specified alert. For this reason, a separate transfer structure exists for each alert object type.

If no exceptions are required for an alert object type, no return table is specified when the function is called.

The parameter iv_rep_res_alerts_det determines whether resource alerts are extracted in detail.

Example

Return codes (see table ET_XXX_RC):

- om_invalid_order: Order does not exist
- om_invalid_activity: Activity does not exist
- om_invalid_pegarea: Pegging area does not exist
- om_invalid_resource: Resource does not exist

Sample report using this function module to read the alerts from LiveCache

```
DATA:  ls_gen_params    TYPE /sapapo/om_gen_params,
       lt_pegid         TYPE /sapapo/om_pegid_tab,
       lt_alertid       TYPE /sapapo/om_alert_type_tab,
       lt_alerts        TYPE /sapapo/om_tab_alertinfo,
       lt_rc            TYPE /sapapo/om_lc_rc_tab,
       lv_simsession    TYPE /sapapo/om_simsession.
```

```
ls_gen_params-simversion = '000'.
APPEND 21 TO lt_alertid. " IoNodeAvailable
APPEND 22 TO lt_alertid. " IoNodeDeficit
APPEND 27 TO lt_alertid. " IoNodeDynPeggingTooLong
```

One can get the simsession using the following function module and also read the pegid, various function modules available, I am not exploring that here.

```
CALL FUNCTION '/SAPAPO/TS_DM_SIMSESSION_GET'
* IMPORTING
*    EV_SIMSESSION_ORDERS          =
*    EV_SIMSESSION_TS              =
*    EV_SIM_VERSION                =
*    EV_SIM_PAREAID                = .

CALL FUNCTION '/SAPAPO/OM_ALERTS_GET_DATA'
    EXPORTING
      is_gen_params      = ls_gen_params
      iv_simsession      = lv_simsession
      it_peglist         = lt_pegid
      it_alertid         = lt_alertid
    IMPORTING
      et_alerts          = lt_alerts
      et_rc              - lt_rc
    EXCEPTIONS
      lc_connect_failed = 1
      lc_com_error       = 2
      lc_appl_error      = 3
      OTHERS             = 4.
  IF sy-subrc NE 0.
    EXIT.
  ENDIF.
```

Various Business Add-Ins (BAdIs) are available for enhancements with reference to the Alerts without having to perform a modification. Some of the BADIs are explained here.

BAdI ALERT_XML

Method ENHANCE_XML_DOCUMENT

If the central alert server is configured to send alerts to an external alert system, an XML document is created and sent to the external system. The BAdI method is called in the final stage of the creation of the XML document.

```
Parameters
  II_DOCUMENT    = <Reference to the XML document>
  II_CONTAINER   = <Container with parameters passed by the
                   application>
  IP_CAT         = <Alert category>
  IP_LOGHANDLE   = <Current log>
```

BAdI ALERT_EXP_DATE

Method GET_EXP_DATE

This method is used to determine the expiry date of an alert. It is provided with the alert category as filter value. The method is called if the application does not pass any expiry date in the container.

```
Parameter
  FLT_VAL        = <Filter value of BAdI>
  II_CONTAINER   = <Container with parameters passed by the
                   application>
  IP_LOGHANDLE   = < Current log>
  RP_EXP_DATE    = <Desired expiry date as time stamp>
```

BAdI ALERT_EXIT

Method TO_BE_DELETED

This method is called immediately before an alert is deleted, and enables the application to react at this point in time.

```
Parameter
FLT_VAL         =     <Filter value of BAdI>
IO_ALERT        =     <Alert to be deleted>
IP_LOGHANDLE    =     <Current log>
```

BAdI ALERT_DELIVERY

Method DECIDE

This method enables the application to override the standard implementation for time dependent delivery (personalization).

```
Parameter
IO_ALERT        =     <Alert>
IS_PERS         =     <Personalization data>
IP_UNAME        =     <User name>
IP_PROTOCOL     =     <Log handle>
PE_PAG          =     <Dispatch by SMS>
PE_INT          =     <Dispatch by Internet mail>
PE_FAX          =     <Dispatch by fax>
```

BAdI ALERT_EXIT

Method WAS_CONFIRMED

This method enables the application to react after an alert has been confirmed.

```
Parameter
FLT_VAL        =    <Filter value of BAdI>
IO_ALERT       =    <Alert that was confirmed>
IP_UNAME       =    < User who confirmed the alert (optional)>
IP_LOGHANDLE   =    < Current log>
```

There are lots more enhancements available for the Alerts but I have stated some of the examples here as it is not possible to write all here, basically I have explained the concept which makes the reader understand how to work in Alerts.

10

APO MACROS

10.1 MACRO OVERVIEW

Macros in APO support the data processing from a simple addition of rows to further complex calculations using a set of standard functions. Even own coding can be incorporated in user function macros. The macros are defined specifically for each data view in the macro builder. The macro builder is accessed via the macro workbench with the *transaction code /SAPAPO/ADVM*.

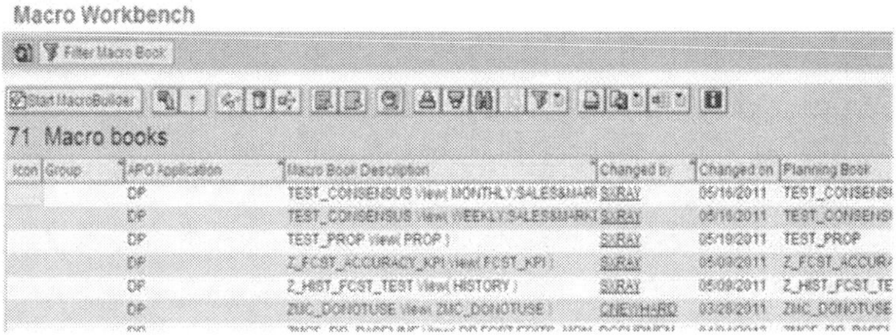

Figure 10.1 Macro workbench

To avoid the tedious search for one's own data views, it is recommend to assign a group to the data views and set a filter for this group as shown in figure.

To create and assign group press (Ctrl + F6).

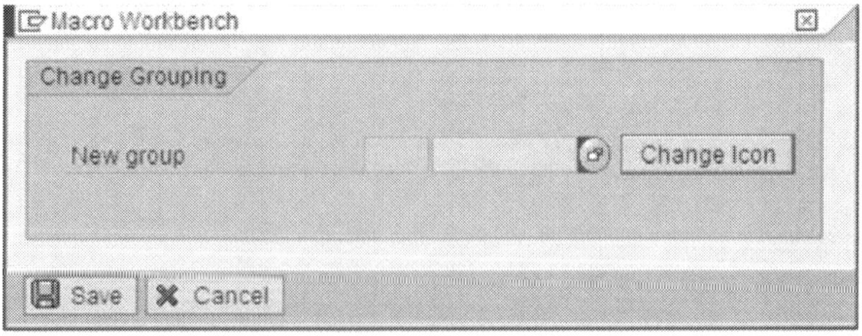

Figure 10.2 Assign group in macro workbench

10.2 TYPES OF MACROS

Standard Macros

A standard macro is a macro that is executed automatically, its execution is not triggered manually by the planner.

A standard macro is one of the following types:

- *Default* – A default macro is executed when the planner opens the planning desktop and loads data, regenerates the screen (for example, by choosing Enter or Tab), or saves the plan. If other types of standard macros can be executed, these are executed before the default macros.
- *Level change* – A level change macro is executed when the planner drills up or down in interactive planning.
- *Start* – A start macro is executed when the system loads data. This is for instance when a planner selects characteristic values in the shuffler and loads the data. The system always reloads data after the user saves the data. This means that start macros are also carried out after saving.
- *Exit* – An exit macro is executed when the planner saves the plan.

To Define a Macro as a Standard Macro

Drag and drop the macro from the macro tree to the appropriate standard macro icon in the Events section of the Macro Builder (top right corner).

Set the attribute "*No direct execution*" for the macro. Since these macros are automatically executed, it's better to prevent users from executing them manually. One major use of standard macros in DP is to calculate the difference between forecasts of different periods.

Sequence

One can specify in which sequence the standard macros should execute. This is the order in which the macros are listed under the requisite heading in the Events screen section. This sequence is also displayed in the Macros screen section of the Macro Workbench. To change the order use drag and drop functionality.

Example

One has defined start, end and default macros. Enter or change data in interactive and now save the planning book. The system first executes the end macro and saves the data in LiveCache. Since it reloads the data, the start macro is executed followed by the default macro. Important point to be noted that the data changed by the start and default macros has not been saved.

Advance Macros

An advanced macro consists of one or more macro steps. To define the conditions under which individual macro steps are carried out, use the control structures. Each macro step consists of one or more calculations. To define these calculations in the macro tree, user has to use calculation structures.

Advanced macros are used to perform complex calculations quickly and easily. Macros are executed either directly or by the user or automatically at a predefined point of time.

The definition of macros is optional. The macros for aggregation and disaggregation come predefined with the system. No need to write them separately. Some stock level and days supply macros are also delivered with the standard SNP planning books. One can create its own planning book for SNP using one of the existing books as a template, and copy the standard macros to the new book.

Integration

An advanced macro can be created either when creating or changing a planning book in Customizing, or in design mode of interactive demand planning. One can define a macro either for an entire planning book or for a specific data view.

Prerequisites

- Planning area has been created.
- Planning buckets profile has been created.
- Planning book with at least one data view has been created.

Features

One can:

- Control how macro steps are processed through control instructions and conditions.
- Build a macro consisting of one or more steps.
- Control how macro results are calculated through control instructions and conditions.

Control Structures

As mentioned above, use control structures at either step level or result level. In the first case one can control structures to decide which step to execute depending on which conditions are satisfied. Its like the same logical expression which we used to perform in any programming language.

The statements that are available here are based on the corresponding ABAP terminologies, such as IF, DO, CASE, WHILE and are similar in most programming languages.

There are more options when working at the step level than the result level. For instance, one can use CASE WHEN structures to branch to different steps depending on the value of a variable or key figure.

The following is an example of a macro that makes extensive use of control structures where multiple logical conditions are used. Note the level of the various objects.

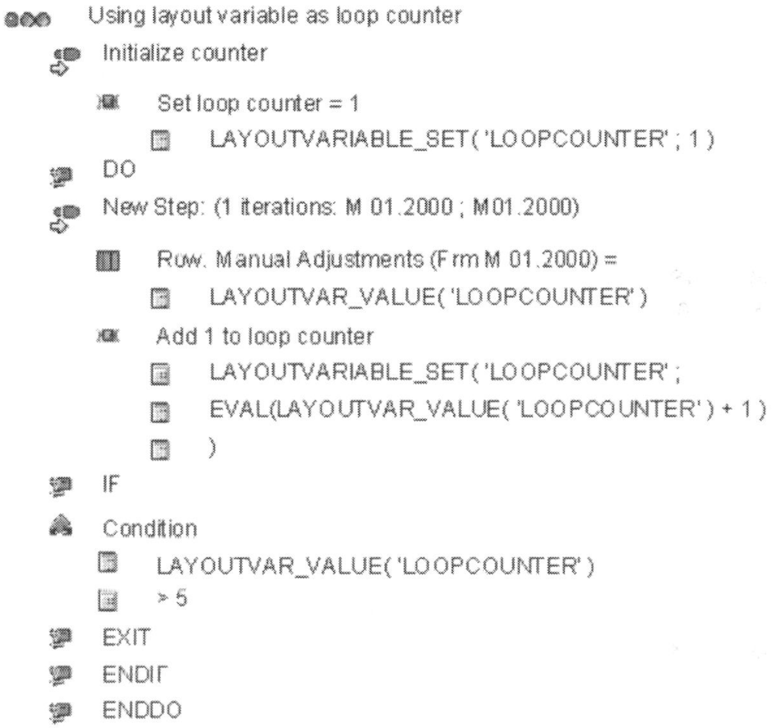

Figure 10.3 Macro example

Calculation Structures

Use calculation structures not only to execute calculations but also to carry out other actions in which a value is not directly assigned to a key figure or variable. Examples of such actions are:

- Triggering an alert
- Displaying a message or dialog box
- Sending an e-mail

Calculation structures always consist of at least one step. In general a calculation step consists of a macro element at the result level followed by one or more elements at the argument level. A simple example is the graphic below.

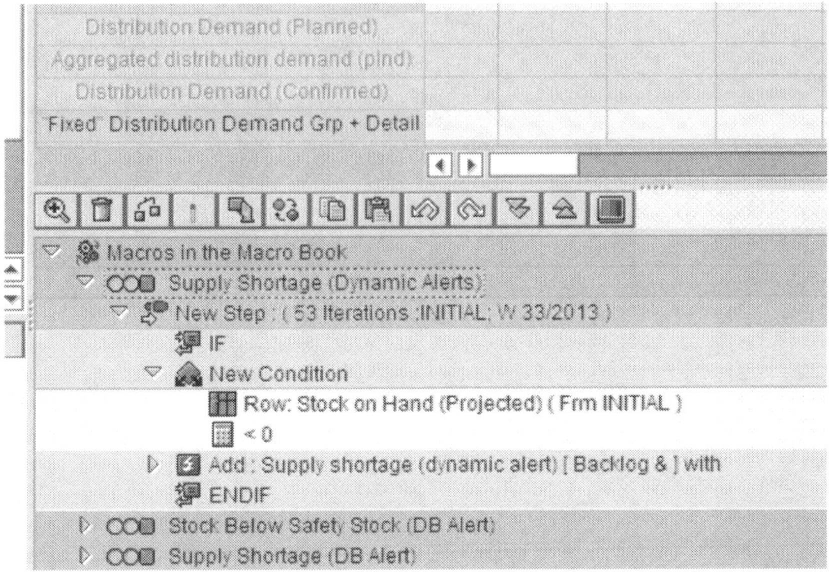

Figure 10.4 Macro definition

10.3 MACRO WORKBENCH

The macro workbench is a tool for administrating macro books and individual macros. It enables to quickly find macro books and perform the functions. One can program the macros themselves in the Macro Builder.

Features

The macro workbench consists primarily of two work areas: The tool area that contains buttons with which can start various functions, and the macro book area where the macro books are displayed. If necessary, separate screens are opened in which the individual macros of a macro book are displayed. Contents of two macro books can be displayed simultaneously.

The macro book area is the center of the function. Here select the macro books one want to work with. The list viewer in which the macro books are displayed offers several features for finding and sorting entries. In the macro book area, one or more macro books can be selected and then perform the following activities:

- Copy the macro books
- Start the macro builder
- Display the macros in the macro books
- Display the coding
- Change the grouping of the macro books

- Generate (activate) all the macros in a macro book
- Start semantic checking for the macro books
- Delete macro books
- Transport macro books to another system

One can also call up a where-used-list without selecting a macro book. The macro workbench consists primarily of two work areas: The *tool area* that contains buttons with which one can start various functions, and the *macro book area* where the macro books are displayed.

If necessary, separate screens are opened in which the individual macros of a macro book are displayed. The list viewer in which the macro books are displayed offers several features for finding and sorting entries. Users can play with the tool as per their choice and requirement, not required to follow any specific set of procedure, user should explore all the functionalities.

Macro Groups

Use macro groups to restrict the selections in the macro workbench. One can select macro books in the SAP List Viewer either manually or by using the filter and sorting functions in the SAP List Viewer.

Where-Used-Lists

Use this function to find macros books and individual macros that contain the following:

- A specific key figure
- A specific macro function
- A particular macro element (alert/status, process message, or document)

The system first displays the macro books in which the object is used, then display the macros in the macro book, the macros in which the object is used are marked with where-used-list icon .

In general, to carry out a function on a macro book, choose the macro book in the macro book window and then select the relevant button in the toolbar or use the context menu.

10.4 STARTING THE MACRO BUILDER

Macro Builder can be started in various ways.

From the macro book screen area:

Select the macro book.

- Choose  from the toolbar.
- Double-click the macro book anywhere except on the Description or the Changed by columns.
- Choose Start Macro Builder from the context menu.

From the macro screen area:

- Choose from the toolbar from the screen area.
- Choose Start Macro Builder from the context menu.

Where-Used Lists

Choose "*Where-used-list*" from the toolbar. A dialog box appears. Now select the indicator next to the required option. An input help is available for each option (the Copy from field) in which choose available objects.

For instance, if want to see the macro books in which the FIX_CALC() function is used, select the Macro function indicator and choose FIX_CALC() from the input help. When FIX_CALC clicked, the function is automatically transferred to the upper line. Now add text (for example, an argument) for the function.

When one choose , the system finds the macro books that are currently in the macro book work area and that contain the search object. Now open the macro book and display the macros in the macro workbench, the macros that contain the search object are flagged with a instead of a traffic light. If then open the Macro Builder, these macros are also adopted automatically in the processing area. To return to the previous display in the macro book work area, choose .

Transporting and Copying Macro Books

Use these functions to transport macro books to other systems.

To be able to use macro books in another system, need to have already exported other objects such as the relevant planning object structures and planning areas to the target system. This can be done in Customizing for *Demand Planning or Supply Network Planning under Basic Settings → Maintain Manual Transport Link for DP/SNP.* Use this activity to transport macro books. If the planning area does not exist in the target system, one can transport the macro book, but one cannot open the macro book or use the macros.

There are two methods of copying entire macro books.

Both of these functions are intended primarily for system administrators. Necessary authorizations are required to execute them.

Using Transport Requests

One can add macro books to a transport request so that they are transported to the target system when the request is released and transported. When transport a macro book, one must also transport notes. This means that notes must exist for at least one macro in the macro book.

To transport a macro book, select the macro book and choose *Transport Request* or, from the menu, choose *Tools → Transport Macro Books.* In the dialog box that appears, enter an existing transport request or create a new one. (In some

Organizations, creating of transport request is restricted to some particular group of people.) The transport request determines to which system the macro book is transported. Choose .

Copy Macro Books Externally

This function uses an RFC connection to copy a selected macro book directly to another SAP APO system.

One must have previously made the necessary settings for the target system. For information about the necessary RFC settings, To transport a macro book via an RFC connection, select one or more macro books and choose *Tools → Copy Macro Book Externally*. In the dialog box that appears, enter the name of the system and the target macro book.

Syntax Check for Macro

The syntax checker in the Macro Builder checks the formal correctness of the macro coding. There were however some situations that cannot be checked, but cause problems when using the macro. These are often performance issues, where setting an indicator can drastically accelerate the execution of a macro. (In an extreme case a macro could contain a never-ending loop that is not detected by the syntax check.) This function has been conceived so that new checks can be added as necessary.

Features

One can start the semantic check at the following levels:

- Macro book
  The check runs for all the macros in the book.
- Macro
  One or more macros are checked
- Step
  A macro step is checked
- Result
  The individual calculation or process is checked. A semantic check at more detailed level is superfluous.

At the moment the following checks are available:

- *'Do not initialize aux. table'*
  The system checks whether this indicator at the macro level has been set. If not a warning is displayed.
  If the auxiliary table is not initialized when the macro is called, any values that are in the table from the execution of previous macros remain in the table and can be used in the current macro. All entries in the auxiliary table are lost when leave the planning book.

- *Layout*

  The system checks that the correct *Change scope* has been assigned to a results element in the attributes. If the function that is called changes the attributes of a cell, for instance by changing the background color or setting an icon, the *Change scope* should be Attributes, otherwise Values or Fixed values.

- *'Do not display initial values'*

  This indicator at macro level affects performance. If it is not set initial values, that is cells that have no entry, are converted to '0', and are taken into consideration during calculations.

- *Parenthesis count*

  The system checks that there are even number of parentheses or not. It also checks that the parentheses match up, that there is an opening parenthesis for each closing parenthesis and vice-versa (and).

- *Parenthesis and space*

  The system checks that there is a space before and after every parenthesis.

- *Semicolon and space*

  Similarly the system checks that there is a space before and after every semicolon.

- *Single inverted comma count*

  As with parentheses there must an even number of these delimiters (') for character values. The system checks this.

One can start the semantic check from either the Macro Workbench or the Macro Builder. In both cases start the checks by selecting the relevant object and choosing .

A log in table form appears listing any irregularities. All messages are classed either as information or warning messages. Since it is usually not clear whether a particular situation is intentional, no error messages are used.

In the Macro Workbench one can see an overview of the messages for one or more macro book. If double-click on an entry, the macro book is opened in the Macro Builder. More detailed information is available here. Choose  for more information. This can be the screen on which settings can be made or a more detailed message. One can correct the situation by choosing . The tool id designed as fully interactive tool, user choose any of the functionality and can move back and forward on the screen using any of the selections.

Macro Elements

Use macro elements in combination with macro tools and drag and drop techniques to define macros.

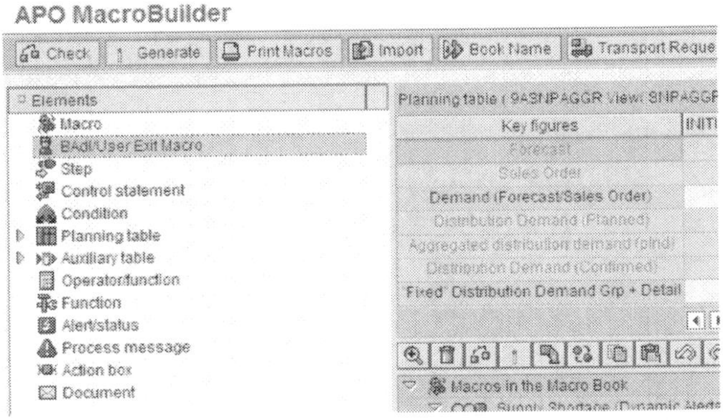

Figure 10.5 Macro builder

Macro Tools

Use macro tools in combination with macro elements and drag and drop techniques to define macros.

Macro Builder

When defining advanced macros, one works in a special desktop environment known as the Macro Builder.

There are two methods of accessing the Macro Builder:

- Via the Macro Workbench from the SAP Easy Access menu, choose *Demand Planning -> Macro Workbench -> Current Settings -> Environment.*
- From design mode of interactive demand planning, choose *Macro Builder -> Planning book* or *Macro Builder -> Data view*

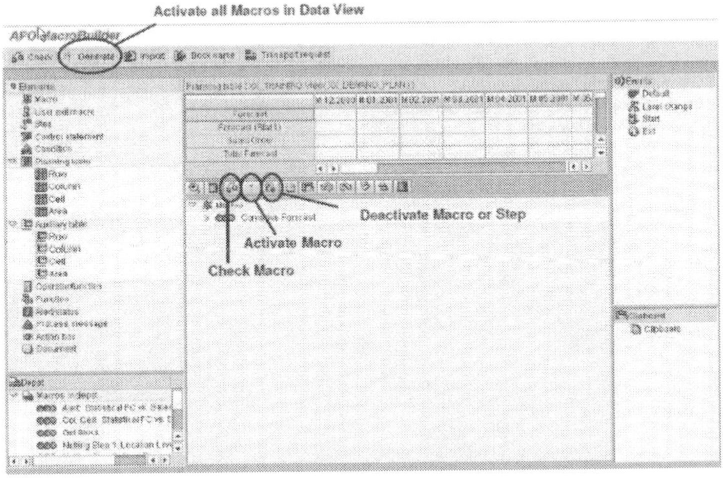

Figure 10.6 Macro builder-components

Layout - The Macro Builder consists of the several screen areas:

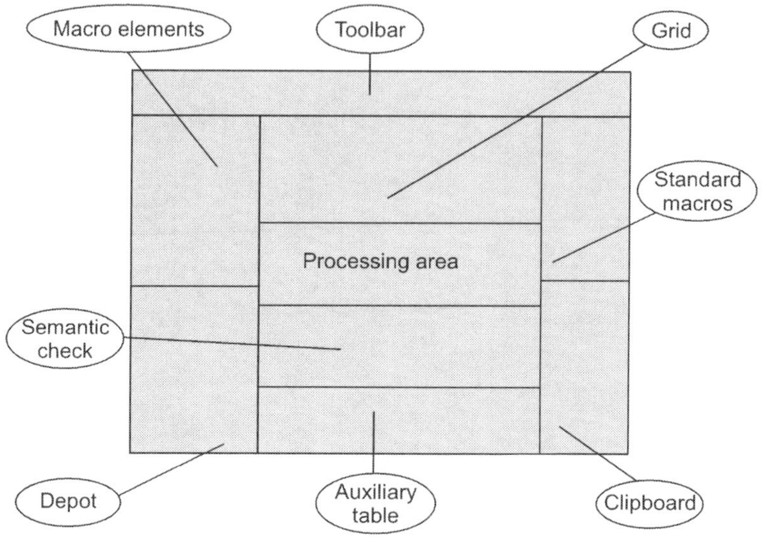

Figure 10.7 Macro builder-layout

- Macro elements in a tree on the top left
- Depot with parked macros on the bottom left

Keep all macros that are not currently editing in the depot. This has performance advantages: the macros tree containing the macros that are currently editing works faster.

- Demand planning table in the top center
- Processing area where macros are edited
- Macro tree with the macro tools in the bottom center

  To see the attributes of any item in the tree, double-click on the item.
- Standard macros on the top right
- Clipboard on the bottom right
- Results area for semantic checks
- Auxiliary table

The last two screen areas are hidden when the Macro Builder is opened. Make them visible by dragging the lower edge of the processing area upwards. Similarly then drag the lower edge of the semantic check area upwards.

10.5 DEFINING MACROS IN THE MACRO BUILDER

There are two basic methods of working in the Macro Builder:

- The context menu
- Drag and Drop techniques

Define macros in planning books in combination with macro elements and macro tools.

Context Menu

Use the context menu primarily in the macro tree section. If select an existing macro element (this can even be at the *Macro* level), the system displays a menu with all the available options for this element at the current position in the macro. Each macro element is listed separately.

Insert - Enter the new element before the selected element

Attach - Enter the new element after the selected element at the same level

Add - Enter the new element after the selected element at the next level

The context menu offers two options that are not available with Drag & Drop:

- Active/inactive - Activate/deactivate an element in the macro tree as in the macro toolbar.
- Stopping point on/off sets a stopping point. This means that during execution of the macro the macro stops at this element. A dialog box appears in which the value of the element is displayed. Continue processing by choosing .

These two options are for use when creating macros, particularly for debugging complex macros.

Drag and Drop

Use Drag and Drop to do any of the following:

- Add or insert any macro element in the macro tree
  When drop the element, the system offers a choice of options if more than option is available.
- Move elements within the macro tree
- Drag a macro from the macro tree to the standard macros screen area
- Remove a macro from a standard macro sequence by dragging the macro downwards to the blank space in the standard macros screen area
- Change the sequence of the standard macros
- Copy a part of the macro tree to the clipboard

The appearance of the icon means that the action is not possible for this element. The appearance of the + icon means that the action is possible for this element, in which case one can let go of the left mouse button.

Operators and Functions in Macros

Macro functions are entered in the following manner:

1. Drag and drop the operator/function icon to the relevant line in the macro work area. A dialog box appears.

2. On the bottom line choose the function to insert by using the pull-down box or *F4* help. The function automatically appears in both lines. On the top line add alpha-numeric arguments to the functions.

For more details of individual function one can refer SAP help as there are large number of operators and functions available for mathematical, date, general, planning table functions, SNP functions etc.

Menu Functions for Macros

Three functions are available to in the Macro Builder as a stand-alone application (*Demand Planning/Supply Network Planning -> Environment -> Current Settings -> Macro Builder*) as opposed to through interactive planning. These functions are in the *Edit* menu.

Entry Conventions

An argument is an input parameter, an independent variable, in a function. Enter character values of an argument in single inverted commas. Enter numerical values of an argument without single inverted commas.

Use a semicolon as a separator between the arguments of a function. Leave no space between a function operator and a parenthesis, but insert blanks before and after arguments in the parentheses, these are the syntax of coding the macro and one has to follow that, for example,

- ROUND(X ; Y)
- ROUND(SUM (X ; Z) ; Y)

$ represents a fixed coordinate.

Changing Attributes

Most of the functions available are value functions, controlling the numbers or values stored within APO. However, there is another class of functions in APO, the attribute functions, that control the properties of the data view instead of the stored values. For instance, these functions change the color of a cell or row, hide or unhide cells or rows, or changes the availability for input.

To use one of these functions, change the scope field on the attributes of the result (row, column, or element) to Attributes.

The results of attribute functions are not persistent in APO. In other words, if turned a row's background color green, this change is not stored permanently by the system. So when a new selection is made in interactive planning or leaving and re-enter the planning view, that green color change will be lost. Therefore, if want to see the results of the attribute change next time, enter the selection, one need to re-run the relevant macros again. In some circumstances may also need an additional key figure to save the results of actions from previous sessions or selections. It is not possible to modify the same result row with two or more attribute functions at the same time. The example below would lead to an error during the check. Result row for each attribute function must be repeated again.

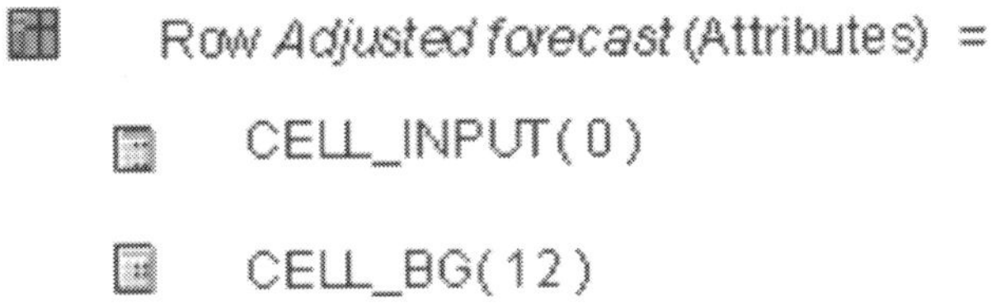

Figure 10.8 Macro-writing logic

Similarly to use the attribute of a cell, column, or row in a calculation, change the Data Source field in the attributes of the argument to Row attributes or Column attributes.

Multilevel Functions in the Supply Chain Network

These four functions enable to determine statistical values for use with multilevel scenarios.

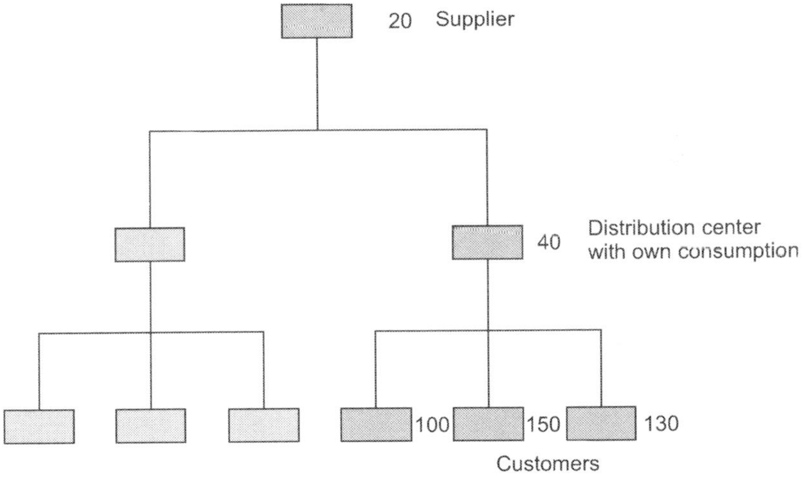

Figure 10.9 Macro logic-Case 1

In the above graphic example, the figures represent the planned consumption of a product at different levels in the supply chain for one particular period in one supply chain. As well as aggregating the demand from the lower levels the locations also have their own consumption.

The function *MULTILEVEL_DEMAND_MEAN* forms the sum of these planned demands, in this case 100 + 150 + 130 + 40 + 20 = 440.

The function *MULTILEVEL_DEMAND_VAR* determines the error variance between the planned and actual values for the whole specified period or if no period specified, then the complete past.

(Error variance = $\Sigma(Xp_i - Xa_i)^2$ where Xp_i and Xa_i are the planned and actual values respectively.)

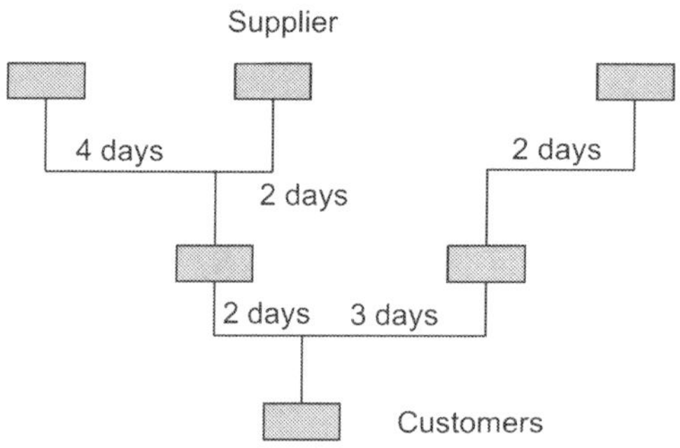

Figure 10.10 Macro logic–Case 2

Similarly, the function *MULTILEVEL_LEAD_MEAN* calculates the planned lead time for a customer to receive a product in the period. The system always uses the longest lead time, that is the values from the critical path. The system considers the time from the customer back to the next location that has safety stock. In the above graphic the value would be 6 days.

The function *MULTILEVEL_LEAD_VAR* determines the error variance between the planned and actual values for the whole specified period or if no period is specified, then the complete past.

(Error variance = $\Sigma(Xp_i - Xa_i)^2$ where Xp_i and Xa_i are the planned and actual values respectively.)

Attributes of Macro Elements

One can change the attributes of the various macro elements (macros, steps, conditions etc.). The attributes that can be edited vary with the element type and include the periods for which the element is valid and additional functions.

Macro Execution

Here the user can specify:

- Whether the macro can be executed directly
- Whether a confirmation prompt appears when the macro is executed.
- Whether the auxiliary table is initialized when the macro is called.

  If the auxiliary table is not initialized when the macro are called-up, any values that are in the table from the execution of previous macros remain in the table and can be used in the current macro. All entries in the auxiliary table are lost when leave the planning book.

- The level at which the macro operates
  The level is defined by the current drill-down situation. This means in interactive planning that the aggregate level is the level at which one enter the planning book by making a selection. If drill-down on characteristic A, this is level 1. If subsequently drill-down on a further characteristic B, this is level 2. In batch mode the drill-down situation is controlled by the macro functions DRILL_DOWN() and DRILL_UP().
- Whether cells that have no entries (initial) are left blank or receive the value "0". To improve performance, it is recommend to set this indicator.

One can also assign the macro an icon that appears in the planning table. Then execute the macro by clicking on this icon.

Check whether the macro is used as a standard macro and if so, which type and at which position the macro appears in the list for the relevant type (start, exit, level change, or default).

Also define collective macros that consist of other macros in the planning book. These macros are then performed automatically in the given order.

One can define a macro as a collective macro when creating it, by setting the *Macro type* field to *Collective macro*. If already assigned other elements (steps, conditions etc.) to it, no changes are possible to a collective macro.

Steps

In the step attributes, primarily define the time period to which the step applies. It applies to:

- The whole period
- The past
- The future
- Freely definable. Here existing time buckets or columns can be entered. This means that the position of the column in the table remains constant, the dates may move. For example, the macro applies to the second time bucket in the future to the tenth time bucket in the future.
- Date dependent. Here the time buckets are selected that contain the specified dates. The dates remain constant and the time bucket may change.
- Whether the columns at the start and end are adjusted automatically.

When creating a new macro element the attribute dialog box appears automatically. Can access it later via the context menu, or by double-clicking on the element in the work area.

Several of these functions are only available in expert mode. One can switch the export on or off by choosing *Settings -> Expert Mode On/Off*. This reverts to the default the next time enter in the Macro Builder. To save the setting user-specifically choose *Settings -> Save Mode Setting*.

Since the macro syntax is a bit tricky in some cases, the use of the 'check' function is helpful. Especially for the search of errors the deactivation of macro steps is another useful feature. In total macros created in the Demand Planning building block. They are all defined for the planning book DP_001. Create macros for forecast calculation according to the following instruction.

EXAMPLE

Requirement

In the *DP_STANDARD* view of the planning book *DP_001*, create two macros:

The first macro is used for the standard and consensus-based planning. The system calculates the arithmetic average of *Statistical Forecast, Sales Forecast* and *Logistics Forecast,* the result of average forecast data plus *Promotion* Data is inserted in the *Final Forecast* cell. It enables the user to consider the forecast input and the promotion plan from different departments within the organization. The planner can make manual adjustments and enter the final agreed forecast into the *Final Forecast* cell. All of this information can be shown in the planning book screen.

The second macro multiplies the *Final forecast* data with the *Planned price* to calculate the sales volume. The third macro is an alert macro used for highlighting exceptional situations in consensus-based planning.

In the DP_SALES view of the planning book DP_001, create the fourth macro. This macro multiplies the *Final forecast* data with the *Planned price* to calculate the sales volume, which is the same as the one in the standard view.

Solution

Here it is described how to create the alert macro for consensus-based planning.

Creating Macros for the Standard View

1. Access the activity using one of the following navigation options:

   Advanced Planning and Optimization -> Demand Planning -> Environment -> Current settings -> Define Planning Book

   Transaction Code - /SAPAPO/SDP8B
2. Enter the name of the planning book: *DP_001*
3. Select *Data view* DP_standard.
4. Choose *Edit.*
5. Choose *Macro Builder Data view.*

Creating the Macro for Consensus-Based Planning

1. Right-click the macro node below the planning table and choose *Create New Macro-> Add macro.* In the *APO Macro Builder* dialog box, enter a descriptive text for the macro, for example, *Forecast + Promotion -> Final Forecast.* Choose *Continue.*
2. Right-click the macro and choose *Add macro Element-> Step.*

   In the *APO Macro Builder* dialog box, in the descriptive text section, enter a name for the macro step, for example, *First Step* and choose *Continue.*

3. Right-click the macro step and choose *Add Element (Result Level)* -> Add *results row*. In the *APO Macro Builder* dialog box, choose *Final Forecast* in the *Row* field. Choose *Adopt*.
4. Right-click the result row which was just created and choose *Add Element (Argument Level) -> Add Operator/Function*. In the *APO Macro Builder* dialog box, choose "(".
5. Right-click the operator/function and choose *Add Element (Argument Level) -> Planning Table Element -> Append argument row*.

   In the *APO Macro Builder* dialog box, choose *Statistical Forecast* in the *Row* field.
6. Right-click the argument row which was just created and choose *Add Element (Argument Level) -> Append Operator/Function*. In the *APO Macro Builder* dialog box, choose "+".
7. Right-click the operator/function and choose *Add Element (Argument Level) -> Planning Table Element -> Append argument row*. In the *APO Macro Builder* dialog box, choose *Sales Forecast* in the *Row* field.
8. Right-click the argument row and choose *Add Element (Argument Element) -> Append Operator/Function*. In the *APO Macro Builder* dialog box, choose "+".
9. Right-click the operator/function and choose *Add Element (Argument Level) -> Planning Table Element -> Append argument row*. In the *APO Macro Builder* dialog box choose *Logistics Forecast* in the *Row* field.
10. Right-click the argument row and choose *Add Element (Argument Element) -> Append Operator/Function*. In the *APO Macro Builder* dialog box, choose ")".
11. Right-click the operator/function and choose *Add Element (Argument Element) -> Append Operator/Function*. In the *APO Macro Builder* dialog box, choose "/".
12. Right-click the operator/function and choose *Add Element (Argument Element) -> Append Operator/Function*. In the *APO Macro Builder* dialog box, enter "(".
13. Right-click the operator/function and choose *Add Element (Argument Element) -> Append Operator/Function*. In the *APO Macro Builder* dialog box, choose "SIGN()" and change it to "SIGN(".
14. Right-click the operator/function and choose *Add Element (Argument Level) -> Planning Table Element -> Append argument row*. In the *APO Macro Builder* dialog box, choose *Statistical Forecast* in the *Row* field.
15. Right-click the argument row and choose *Add Element (Argument Element)-> Append Operator/Function*. In the *APO Macro Builder* dialog box, choose ")".
16. Right-click the operator/function and choose *Append Operator/Function*. In the *APO Macro Builder* dialog box, choose "+".

17. Right-click the operator/function and choose *Add Element (Argument Element) -> Append Operator/Function.* In the *APO Macro Builder* dialog box, choose *"SIGN()"* and change it to *"SIGN("*.
18. Right-click the operator/function and choose *Add Element (Argument Level) -> Planning Table Element -> Append argument row.* In the *APO Macro Builder* dialog box, choose *Sales Forecast* in the *Row* field.
19. Right-click the argument row and choose *Add Element (Argument Element) -> Append Operator/Function.* In the *APO Macro Builder* dialog box, choose *")"*.
20. Right-click the operator/function and choose *Add Element (Argument Element) -> Append Operator/Function.* In the *APO Macro Builder* dialog box, choose *"+"*.
21. Right-click the operator/function and choose *Add Element (Argument Element) -> Append Operator/Function.* In the *APO Macro Builder* dialog box choose the character *"SIGN()" and change to "SIGN("*.
22. Right-click the operator/function and choose *Append argument row.* In the *APO Macro Builder* dialog box, choose *Logistics Forecast* in the *Row* field.
23. Right-click the operator/function and choose *Add Element (Argument Element) -> Append Operator/Function.* In the *APO Macro Builder* dialog box, choose *")"*.
24. Right-click the operator/function and choose *Add Element (Argument Element) -> Append Operator/Function.* In the *APO Macro Builder* dialog box, choose *")"*.
25. Right-click the operator/function and choose *Add Element (Argument Element) -> Append Operator/Function.* In the *APO Macro Builder* dialog box, enter *"+"*.
26. Right-click the operator/function and choose *Append argument row.* In the *APO Macro Builder* dialog box, choose *Promotion* in the *Row* field.
27. Select the macro and choose *Check* to check it. Generate the macro by choosing *Generate*.
28. Move the macro by using drag and drop to the *Events* section and to the *Default* folder in the upper right screen area.
29. If want to continue with the configuration, proceed with the next activity to create the *Sales Volume Macro*.

If want to discontinue the configuration at this point, its recommend to save settings. To do this, go back to the *Planning Book Design* screen and choose *Save*. Choose

Creating the Sales Volume Macro

1. Right-click the macro node below the planning table and choose *Create New Macro -> Add macro.* In the *APO Macro Builder* dialog box, enter a

descriptive text for the macro, for example, *Sales Revenue Forecast.* Choose *Continue.*

2. Right-click the macro and choose *Add Macro Element -> Step.* In the *APO Macro Builder* dialog box, in the descriptive text section, enter name for the macro step for example, *First Step.*
3. Right-click the macro step and choose *Add Element (Result Level) -> Add results row.* In the *APO Macro Builder* dialog box, choose *Sales Revenue Forecast* in the *Row* field.
4. Right-click the results row and choose *Add Element (Argument Level) -> Planning Table Element -> Add argument row.* In the *APO Macro Builder* dialog box, choose *Final Forecast* in the *Row* field.
5. Right-click the argument table row and choose *Add Element (Argument Level) -> Append operator/function.* In the *APO Macro Builder* dialog box, enter *.
6. Right-click the operator/function and choose *Add Element (Argument Level) -> Planning Table Element -> Append argument row.* In the *APO Macro Builder* dialog box, choose *Planning Price* in the *Row* field.
7. Select the macro and choose *Check* to check it. Choose *Generate* to generate the macro.
8. Using drag and drop, move the macro to the *Events* section and to the *Default* folder in the upper right corner screen area.
9. Go back to the *Planning book design* screen and choose *Save.*
10. Choose *All Functional Areas* when the confirmation prompt appears and go back to the main menu path.

10.6 CREATING AN ALERT MACRO

In this section, we will create an alert macro. The alert is used to highlight exceptional situations in the consensus-based planning. In this case, the alert macro compares the figure of the *Logistics Forecast* data with that of *Sales Forecast* data. If the deviation is more than 10 percent, an alert is generated.

Procedure

1. Access the activity using one of the following navigation options:
2. Enter the name of the planning book: *DP_001.*
3. Select the *DP_Standard* data view. Choose *Edit.* The *Planning Book: Design Demand Planning Book / Demand_Planner* screen is displayed.
4. Select the *Forecast Deviation* row, right-click it and choose *Selected rows -> Hide.*
5. Choose  *Macro Builder -> Data view.*
6. Right-click the macro node below the planning table and choose *Create a New Macro -> Add macro.* In the *APO Macro Builder* dialog box, in the *Descrip-*

tion section, enter a name for the macro, for example, *Forecast Deviation,* and choose *Continue.*

7. Right-click the macro and choose *Add macro element -> Step.* In the *APO Macro Builder* dialog box, in the *Description* section, enter a name for the macro step, for example, *Calculate Difference,* and choose *Continue.*
8. Right-click the macro step and choose *Add Element (Result Level) -> Add results row.* In the *APO Macro Builder* dialog box, in the *Row* field, choose *Forecast Deviation* and choose *Continue.* Right-click the result row and choose *Add Element (Argument Level) -> Append operator/function.* In the *APO Macro Builder* dialog box, choose an open bracket " (" and choose *Continue.*
9. Right-click the operator/function and choose *Add Element (Argument Level) -> Planning Table Element -> Append argument row.*

   In the *APO Macro Builder* dialog box, in the *Row* field, choose *Sales Forecast* and choose *Continue.* Right-click the argument row and choose *Add Element (Argument Level) -> Append operator/function.* In the *APO Macro Builder* dialog box, choose a minus - and choose *Continue.*
10. Right-click the operator/function and choose *Add Element (Argument Level) -> Planning Table Element -> Append argument row.* In the *APO Macro Builder* dialog box, in the *Row* field, choose *Logistics Forecast* and choose *Continue.* Right-click the argument row and choose *Add Element (Argument Level) -> Append operator/function.* In the *APO Macro Builder* dialog box, enter ") * 100 / " *(separated by blanks)* and choose *Continue.*
11. Right-click the operator/function and choose *Add Element (Argument Level) -> Planning Table Element -> Append argument row.* In the *APO Macro Builder* dialog box, in the *Row* field, choose *Logistics Forecast* and choose *Continue.*
11. Right-click the operator/function and choose *Add Element (Argument Level) -> Planning Table Element -> Append argument row.* In the *APO Macro Builder* dialog box, in the *Row* field, choose *Logistics Forecast* and choose *Continue.*
12. Right-click the macro and choose *Add macro element -> Step.* In the *APO Macro Builder* dialog box, in the *Description* section, enter a name for the macro step, for example, *Alert,* and choose *Continue.*
13. Right-click the macro step and choose *Add Element (Result Level) -> Add Control Statement.* In the *APO Macro Builder* dialog box, in the *Statement* field, choose *IF* and choose *Continue.*
14. Right-click the control statement row and choose *Add Element (Result Level) -> Append Condition.* In the *APO Macro Builder* dialog box, enter *"Condition: Forecast Deviation > 10%"* and choose *Continue.*
15. Right-click the condition row and choose *Add Element (Argument Level) -> Planning Table Element -> Append argument row.* In the *APO Macro Builder* dialog box, in the *Row* field, choose *Forecast Deviation* and choose *Continue.*

Right-click the argument row and choose *Add Element (Argument Level) -> Append operator/function*. In the *APO Macro Builder* dialog box, enter > 10 *(separated by blanks)* and choose *Continue*.

16. Right-click the IF control statement which was created in step 13 and choose *Add Element (Result Level) -> Planning Table Element -> Append results row*. In the *APO Macro Builder* dialog box, in the *Row* field, choose *Sales Forecast* in the *Row* field *and Attribute change* in the *Change mode* field. Choose *Continue*. Right-click the result row and choose *Add Element (Argument Level) -> Add operator/function*. In the *APO Macro Builder* dialog box, enter CELL_BG(6) *(with a blank before and after the figure "6")* and choose *Continue*.
17. Right-click the result row and choose *Add Element (Result Level) -> Append Control Statement*. In the *APO Macro Builder* dialog box, choose *ELSE* in the *Statement* field and choose *Continue*.
18. Right-click the control statement and choose *Add Element (Result Level) -> Planning Table Element -> Append result row*. In the *APO Macro Builder* dialog box, choose *Sales Forecast* in the *Row* field *and Attribute change* in the *Change mode* field.
19. Right-click the result row and choose *Add Element (Argument Level) -> Add operator/function*. In the *APO Macro Builder* dialog box, enter CELL_BG(2) *(with a blank before and after the figure "2"* and choose *Continue*.
20. Right-click the result row and choose *Add Element (Result Level) -> Append Control Statement*. In the *APO Macro Builder* dialog box, in the *Row* field, choose ENDIF and choose *Continue*.
21. Select the macro and choose *Check* to check it. Choose *Generate* to generate the macro.
22. Move the macro to the right upper corner of the screen to the *Events* section and into the *Default* folder by using drag and drop.
23. Go back to the *Planning Book Design* screen and choose *Save*.

Creating the Sales Volume Macro for the Sales View

1. Access the activity using one of the following navigation options:
2. Enter the name of the planning book: *DP_001*
3. Choose *Data view DP_Sales*.
4. Choose *Edit*.
5. Choose *Macro Builder*.
6. Choose *Macro Builder -> Data view*.

To create the macro, perform the following steps:

7. Right-click the macro node below the planning table and choose *Add macro*.
8. In the *APO Macro Builder* dialog box, in the descriptive text section, enter a name for the macro, for example, *Sales Revenue Forecast*

9. Choose *Continue.*
10. Right-click the macro and choose *Add macro element -> Step.*
11. In the *APO Macro Builder* dialog box, in the descriptive text section, enter a name for the macro step, for example, *First Step.*
12. Right-click the macro step and choose *Add results row*. In the *APO Macro Builder* dialog box, choose *Sales Revenue Forecast* in the *Row* field.
13. Right-click the results row and choose *Add element (Argument Element) -> Planning Table Elements -> Add argument row.* In the *APO Macro Builder* dialog box, choose *Final Forecast* in the *Row* field.
14. Right-click the argument table row and choose *Append operator/function.* In the *APO Macro Builder* dialog box, enter *.
15. Right-click the operator/function and choose *Append argument row.* In the *APO Macro Builder* dialog box, choose *Planning Price* in the *Row* field.
16. Select the macro and use the *Check* pushbutton to check it. Choose *Generate* to generate the macro.
17. Move the macro by using drag and drop to the *Events* section and to the *Default* folder in the upper right screen area.
18. Go back to the *Planning book design* screen and choose *Save.*
19. Choose *Save All* and go back to the main menu.

10.7 TRIGGER AN EVENT USING APO PLANNING BOOK MACRO

There are some instances when we want to be able to raise an event using an APO Planning Book Macro. For example, there may be a need to allow the users to execute a certain background job or process chain by just running a macro in the Interactive Planning screen. The background job or process chain can be set to run after a certain event. The user can then execute a Planning Book macro which triggers the needed event. Here it describes the steps to implement this kind of functionality.

Implementing the User Function in SE37

- Create *function module ZTEST_TRIGGER_EVENT* in *transaction code SE37.*

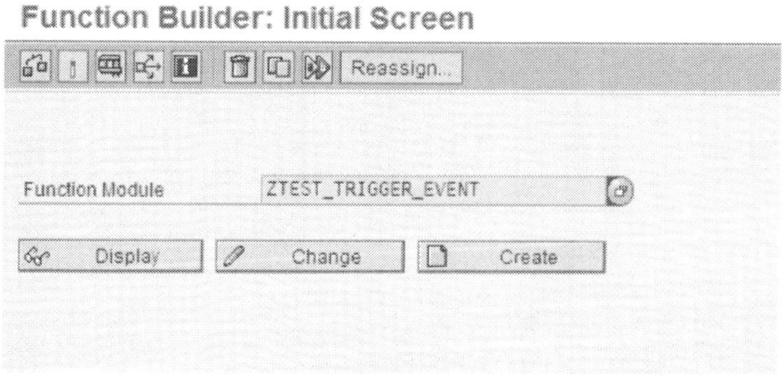

Figure 10.11 Function builder

- Specify the parameters in the "CHANGING" tab.

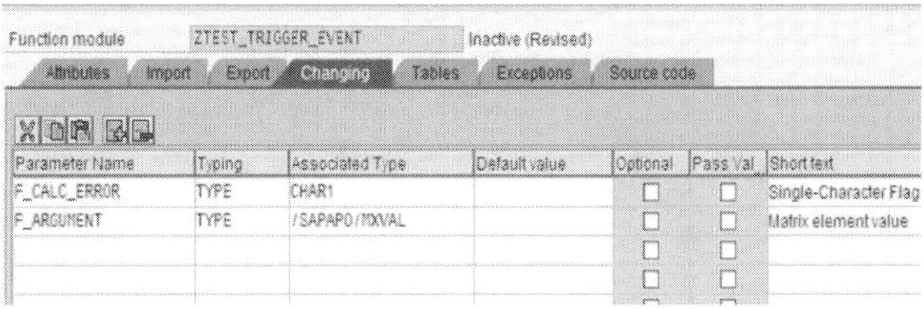

Figure 10.12 Import/Export parameters in function builder

- Specify the parameters in the "TABLES" tab.

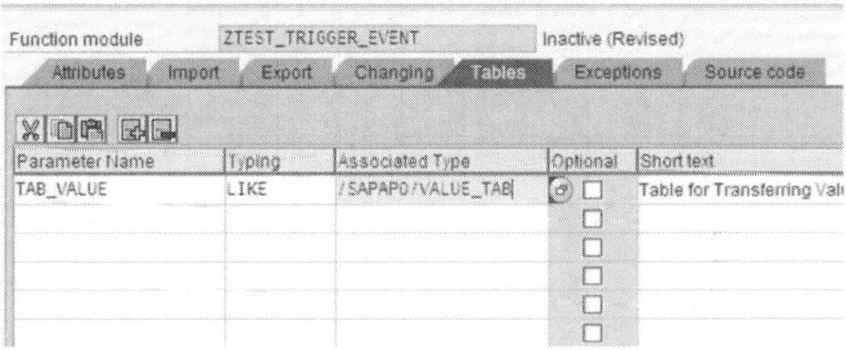

Figure 10.13 Table parameters in function builder

- Write the source code in the "SOURCE CODE" tab.

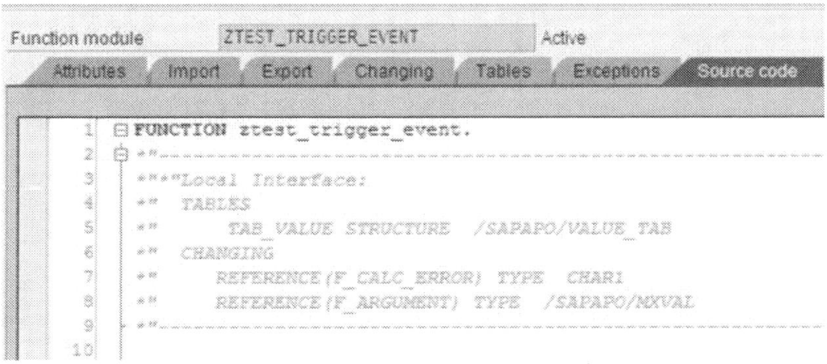

Figure 10.14 Source code in function builder

Write the following code:

```
CONSTANTS: c_error(1) TYPE c VALUE 'X'.
DATA:  l_value_tab TYPE /sapapo/value_tab,
       l_event TYPE /sapapo/funstring.
CLEAR f_calc_error.
READ TABLE tab_value INTO l_value_tab INDEX 1.
IF sy-subrc NE 0.
   f_calc_error = c_error.
   EXIT.
ENDIF.
l_event = l_value_tab-string.
CALL FUNCTION 'BP_EVENT_RAISE'
    EXPORTING
      eventid                 = l_event
    EXCEPTIONS
      bad_eventid             = 1
      eventid_does_not_exist = 2
      eventid_missing         = 3
      raise_failed            = 4
      OTHERS                  = 5.
IF sy-subrc <> 0.
    f_calc_error = c_error.
ENDIF.
```

Using the User Function in the Macro Workbench

Go to the Macro Workbench and enter the name of the planning book and then do the following steps:

- Add your user function to the list of available user functions by proceeding to the *Edit -> Edit User function Menu.*

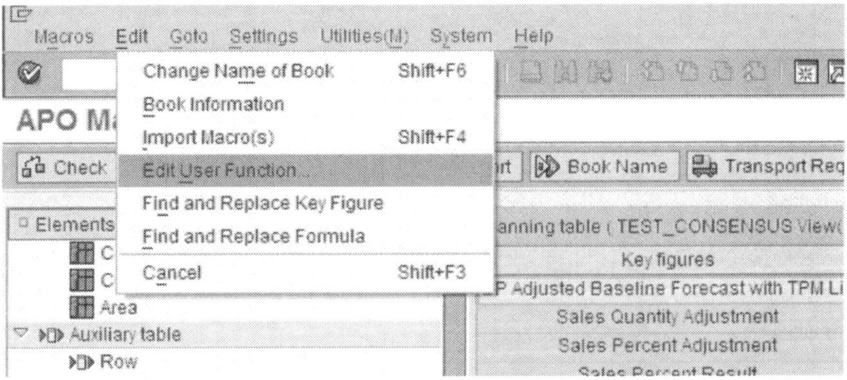

Figure 10.15 Associate the FM in macro workbench

- Enter the name of function and specify the parameter settings (default is OK), in most of the cases these value tab and result covers the requirements of the organizations.

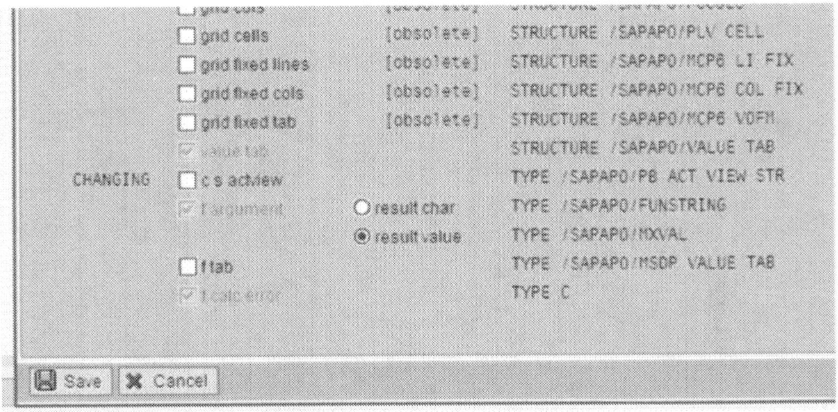

Figure 10.16 FM parameters in macro workbench

- Construct your Macro by following the macro steps (covered above in this chapter), Macro workbench is more over a drag and drop tool which provides options for selections i.e. no need to write coding for normal Macros.

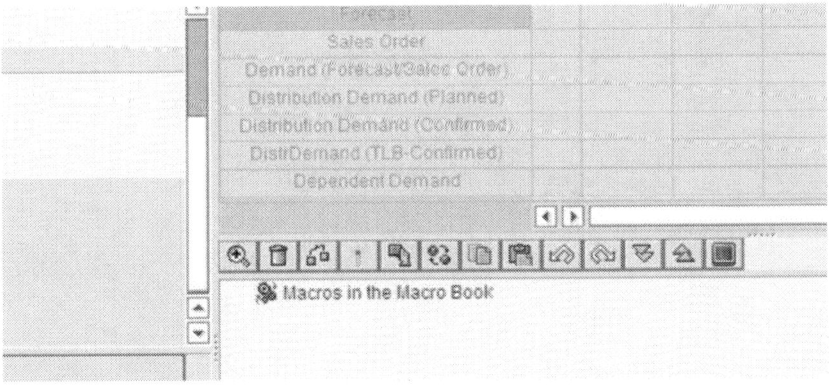

Figure 10.17 Macro workbench–macro construction

We covered here what is macro and how it can be advantageous while creating planning views/planning book. Various functions/features of planning table were covered technically in other chapters also.

11

APO InfoCubes

11.1 OVERVIEW OF InfoCubes

An InfoCube is a set of relational tables with a fact table in the middle and which is in accordance with the star schema. An InfoCube is the primary object used to provide historical data to APO DP (Demand Planning). The goals are to design a warehouse to ensure that most queries initially target this type of database object. They are designed to store summarized and aggregated data for long periods of time.

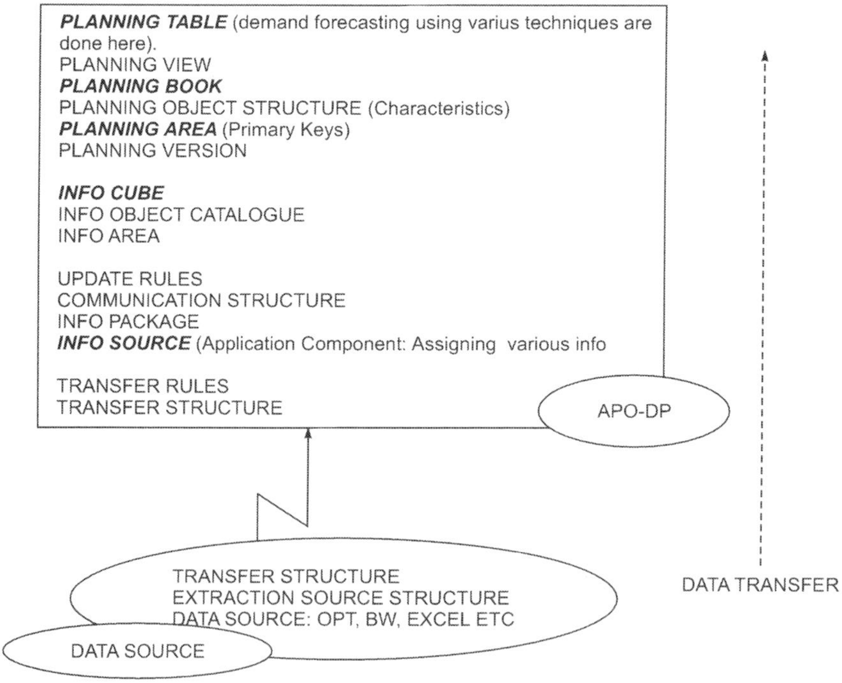

Figure 11.1 Data transfer stages

A Basic Cube is the main InfoProvider used in conjunction with APO DP. An InfoCube consists of one fact table in which key figure values are stored. An InfoCube has a minimum of 4 dimension tables and a maximum of 16. Although SID tables are also part of a characteristics InfoObject master data, they are only important from a technical perspective.

The InfoCubes basically deals with Historical data transfer from various data source, for demand planning to APO.

Historical data is captured from various sources (BW, Excel, R/3, Non-SAP System) and demand forecast is created using various forecasting tools like Statistical and causal analysis techniques, Collaborative forecasting and Promotions.

Once the product has been identified for which demand is to be forecasted, next step is to transfer historical data from data source (BW, Excel, R/3, non-SAP Systems) to APO-DP (Demand Planning module of APO).

Various stages of data transfer are shown below in the figure. (DP reads data only using InfoCubes, hence the focus of the chapter is only on InfoCubes, just to explore little about other terms.)

Star Schema

InfoCubes are made up of a number of InfoObjects. All InfoObjects (characteristics and key figures) are available InfoCube independently. Characteristics relate to master data with their attributes and text descriptions.

An InfoCube fact table only contains key figures, in contrast to an ODS object, whose data part can also contain characteristics. The characteristics of an InfoCube are stored in its dimensions.

An InfoCube consists of several InfoObjects and is structured according to the star schema. This means there is a (large) fact table that contains the key figures for the InfoCube as well as several (smaller) dimension tables which surround it. The characteristics of the InfoCube are stored in these dimensions.

The dimensions and the fact table are linked to each other via abstract identification numbers (dimension IDs), which are in the key part of the specific database table. As a result, the key figures of the InfoCube relate to the characteristics of the dimension. The characteristics determine the granularity (the degree of detail) at which the key figures are kept in the InfoCube.

Characteristics that logically belong together (district and area, for example, belong to the regional dimension) are grouped together in a dimensions, grouping of characteristics are defined by users as per their business requirements. By adhering to this design criterion, dimensions are to a large extent independent of each other and treated independently, and dimension tables remain small with regards to data volume, which is desirable for reasons of performance. This InfoCube structure is optimized for Reporting.

There are various types of InfoCube:

- Physical data stores:
  - Basic InfoCubes
  - Transactional InfoCubes
- Virtual data stores:
  - Remote Cube
  - SAP Remote Cube
  - Virtual InfoCube with Services

Basic InfoCubes

A Basic InfoCube is a type of InfoCube that physically stores data. It is filled with data using BW Staging. Afterwards, it can be used as an InfoProvider in BEx Reporting. As with other InfoCube types, the structure of a Basic InfoCube corresponds to the Star Schema.

Transaction InfoCubes

Transactional InfoCubes differ from Basic InfoCubes in their ability to support parallel write accesses. Basic InfoCubes are technically optimized for read accesses to the detriment of write accesses.

Transactional InfoCubes are used in connection with the entry of planning data. The data from this kind of InfoCube is accessed via transactions, meaning data is written to the InfoCube (possibly by several users at the same time). Basic InfoCubes are not suitable for this. Use Basic InfoCubes for read-only access (for example, when reading reference data).

Remote Cube

A Remote Cube is an InfoCube whose transaction data is not managed in the Business Information Warehouse but externally. Only the structure of the Remote Cube is defined in BW. The data is read for reporting using a BAPI from another system.

Using a Remote Cube, carry out reporting using data in external systems without having to physically store transaction data in the BW. For example, include an external system from market data providers using a Remote Cube.

SAP Remote Cube

An SAP Remote Cube is a Remote Cube that allows the definition of queries with direct access to transaction data in other SAP systems.

SAP Remote Cubes are used for:

- Very up-to-date data from an SAP source system
- To access a small amount of data from time to time

- Only a few users execute queries simultaneously on the database.

Virtual InfoCube with Services

A virtual InfoCube with services is an InfoCube that does not have its own physical data storage in BW. A user-defined function module is used as a data source in the system. The properties of the data source can be defined more precisely using a number of options. Depending on these properties, the Data Manager provides services for converting the parameters and data.

Use a virtual InfoCube with services if want to display data from non-BW data sources in BW without having to copy the data set into the BW structures. The data can be either local or remote (as defined). One can also use his own custom calculations to change the data before it is passed to the OLAP processor.

This function is used primarily in the SAP Strategic Enterprise Management (SEM) application. In comparison to the Remote Cube, the virtual InfoCube with services is more generic. It offers more liberty, but also takes more effort to implement.

Other Definitions

Virtual Provider

A Virtual Provider is a data provider for which the transaction data is not saved. A Multi-Provider is a type of data provider that combines data from several InfoProvider and makes it available for reporting Data Store Object is an object that stores consolidated and cleaned transaction data on the document level (basic level). Data Store Objects often describes and displays a consolidated data set from one or more InfoSources.

DataSource

A DataSource is an infrastructure, which allows information to be transported between OLTP systems and the APO Data Mart. This infrastructure consists of various DDIC structures, which have specific transformation rules between one another. DataSources thus regulate the data flow from the extraction source structure in the source system to the communication structure in the SAP BW, which then provides the data for further analysis.

DataSources can provide both transaction data (this data is stored in InfoCubes), and master data (attributes, texts, and hierarchies - this data is stored in separate transparent tables). DataSources for transaction data and master data have almost an identical structure.

DataSources describe how many pieces of information is available concerning a particular business transaction or transaction type (such as Cost Center Accounting). There are therefore many DataSources in an operative SAP BW environment that describe the individual activities within the applications to be analyzed.

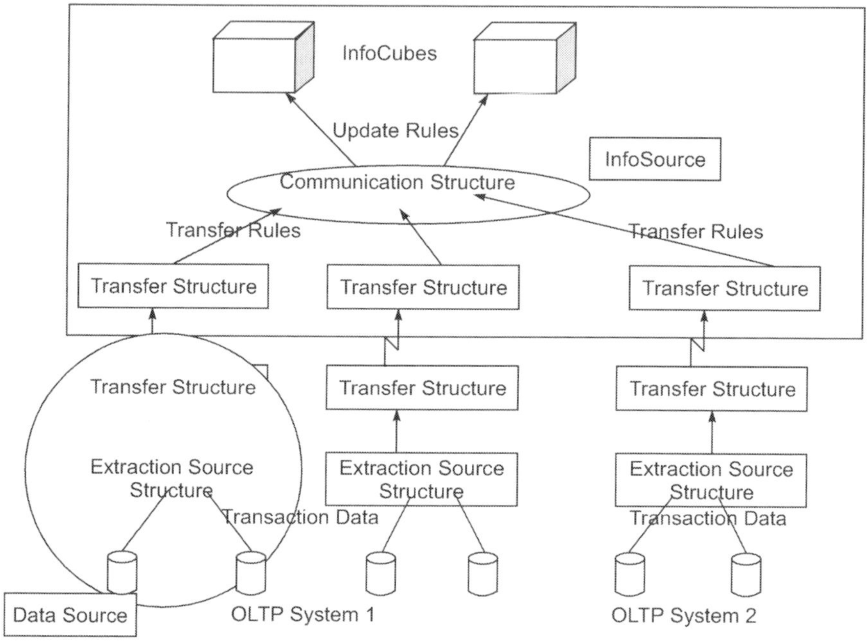

Figure 11.2 Data integration

When a DataSource is generated, the transfer structure, and communication structure are generated in the APO Data Mart system. Transfer structures always exist as a pair in both a source system, and the associated APO Data Mart system. Data is transported in its original application format from a source system into an APO Data Mart, via the transfer structure. From there transformation rules are used to transfer the data to the communication structure of the InfoSource.

The communication structure is independent of the source system and contains all the InfoSource fields that it represents in the APO Data Mart.

InfoSet

This is a semantic view of a DataStore object. Source systems provide data to the BI. (ECC, BIW, APO LiveCache, flat files, legacy). DataSource further divides the available data into a source system. The DataSource are used to transfer master data and transaction data. Once the transfer structure has been replicated to APO, one need to create an InfoSource. An InfoSource is a quantity of InfoObjects that belong together and that contain all the information on a business process. Transfer rules connect the transfer structure to the communication structure (can be in multiple systems). The structure where the InfoObjects are stored is called a communication structure.

InfoSource

Once a transfer structure has been replicated to SAP APO, one need to create an InfoSource. An InfoSource is a quantity of InfoObjects that belong together and that contain all the information on a business process.

There are two types of InfoSource:

- InfoSource with flexible update
- InfoSource with direct update

The InfoSource may contain both transactional and master data.

Update Rules

Connect the communication structure to the Basic Cube. The update rules specify how the data (key figures, time character, characteristics) is updated from the communication structure in an InfoSource to a data target. Update Rules are specific to the data target, not the source system.

Normalization

The process of removing repeated data from the table to auxiliary connected tables, there by making the original tables much smaller. The problems with OLTP's normalization design preclude it being used to support complex, ad hoc data analysis. The classic star schema, is the most frequently used multidimensional model for the relational database. This database schema classified two groups of data: facts, dimension attributes. Facts, sometimes called measures are the focus of the analysis for a business process.

InfoPackage

This is the APO object that contains all the settings directing how this data should be uploaded from the source system. The target of the InfoPackage is the PSA table tied to the specific DataSource associated with the InfoPackage. The InfoPackage sits between the Source System and the DataSource, the transformation occurs after the DataSource.

In a complex APO solution, implementation need many InfoPackage to load your master data and transaction data.

The design of the data flow uses metadata objects such as DataSource, Transformations, InfoSource, and InfoProvider. Once the data flow is designed, the InfoPackage and Data Transfer Processes take over to actually manage the execution and scheduling of the actual data transfer.

11.2 BW AND APO

There are different ways of approaching the production plan of a company. One approach is to use historical information about customer demands and to use these figures to forecast possible future sales volumes.

Since planners want to be flexible in selecting the levels of detail (Material Group instead of Material or Country instead of Customer) a multidimensional model are necessary to provide this kind of flexibility.

Therefore it has been beneficial to use the same kind of methods already developed for reporting again for the planning cycle. The only thing which was missing is the ability to write forecasted, i.e. newly created, figures back to the InfoCube. Usually required an InfoSource to bring the data back to the InfoCube but with some additional functions purely developed for APO this is not necessary for the demand planning.

Because this APO-Interface has been developed on the BW Standard Platform no additional BW-functions are available in the APO environment, i.e. the entire BW Administrator Workbench is delivered with the APO.

However it is necessary to perform certain actions before utilize an InfoCube for planning purposes, consultants should be very careful in defining the InfoCube, prime reason is the performance as might be repeated data is fetched again and again, also it should be data consistency checks.

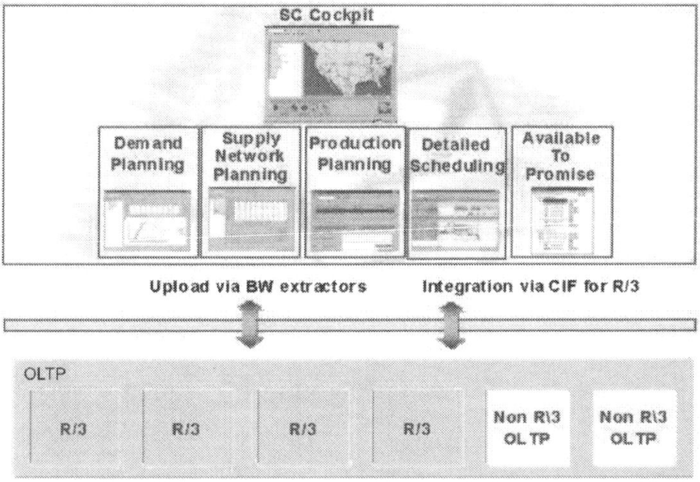

Figure 11.3 BW and APO integration

The ***SAP Business Information Warehouse (SAP BW)***, a pre-configured data warehouse ideal for SAP environments, provides access to both internal and external information from multiple sources (primary will be SAP R/3 and there can be multiple legacy systems also, where different interfaces are defined), as well providing sophisticated reporting and analysis tools SAP BW can now interact with the APO-system in two different ways:

- As a external data provider which supplies consolidated information from different ERP-systems
- As one APO-Component which provides certain functions to simulate and store different planning cycles based on the information coming either from a data warehouse or from different ERP-systems

11.3 INTERFACE BETWEEN APO AND BW

As shown in the picture below the APO and BW currently provide two standard interfaces:

- Data Mart for Demand Planning (also from LiveCache)
- Key Performance Indicators in the Supply Chain Cockpit
- Extractor for Standard Business Content for APO
  - PPDS (Production Planning, Detailed Scheduling)
  - Network Design

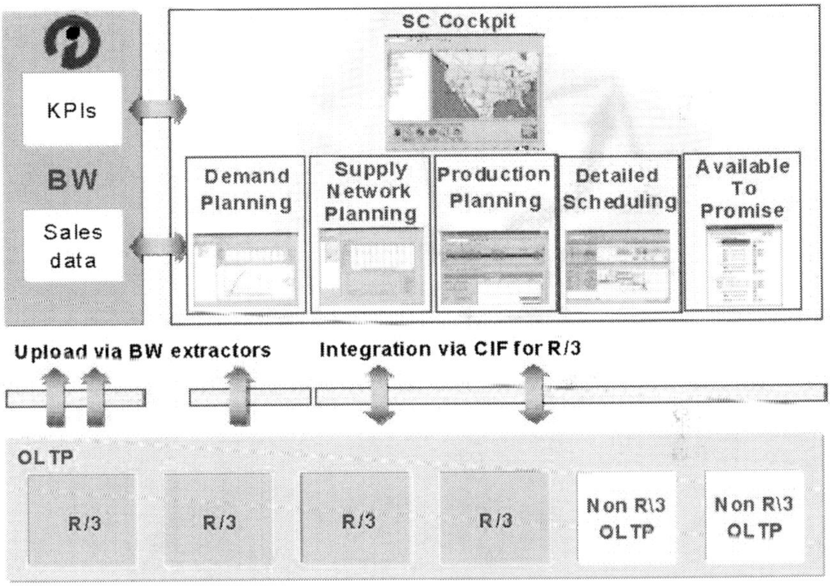

Figure 11.4 BW and APO integration via CIF

Additionally both products can be linked to the same OLTP which provides basic information for the different functions on both systems.

BW extracts transactional and master data from an R/3 system for reporting purposes using functions on the R/3 system which have to be implemented with a Plug-In.

The APO can utilize the same Plug-In functions on the R/3 to extract data for the demand planning. Additionally the Core Interface (CIF) provides master data as well as production and inventory information which are crucial for the live-cache features on the APO-system.

Both systems also provide interfaces to non-R/3 systems to incorporate their data for the respective functions.

11.4 INTERFACES MOSTLY USED

R/3

Since APO includes the same functions as a BW-system it can also use the same extractors which are provided with the Plug In (Plug In-A) on the R/3 system. These extractors can be used for APO purposes, historical sales data for Demand Planning, as well as for BW purposes, i.e. using the embedded BW as a reporting tool rather than just a planning component.

Extraction of LIS-Data

With the new Plug-In it is possible to feed many different systems with the same information, even delta-information. Thus extraction of LIS-Data does not have any impact on any other system so that the same data source can be used for as many systems.

Extraction of Master Data

APO uses two different types of master data:

- BW (DATA MART)
- Core Interface (CIF)

Master Data from BW

With the DATA MART BW does not only provide generated extractors for transactional data but also for all characteristics included in the respective InfoCube.

Example

InfoCube (SalesCube) contains the following InfoObjects

Characteristics	-	SOLD_TO, MATERIAL, SALESORG, DIVISION
Key Figures	-	REVENUE, QUANTITY
Generated InfoSources		
SalesCube	-	SOLD_TO, MATERIAL, SALESORG, DIVISION

Consequently all generated DATA MART-InfoSources use '8' as a prefix. The master data InfoSources do include the same attributes as they were defined on the BW system. This data is going to be extracted on a regular but asynchronous basis. With APO not only master data but also their navigational attributes can be used for planning. With this background the definition, proper loading and extraction of master data from BW becomes quite important for the APO-Demand Planning.

Since demand planning is different from the other APO-functions in its master data utilization it is necessary to ensure that the planning data can be matched to the existing APO-master data later on in Supply Network Planning (SNP). If necessary matching rules can be programmed in an user exit.

Master Data from the Core Interface (CIF)

The master data which is extracted via the CIF contains pure planning relevant information. Data is extracted synchronously. APO differentiates between central master data, like weight or size, and location specific master data, like planning strategy.

Interdependencies between both Techniques

Additional Master data extraction from OLTP to BW does not conflict with APO's CIF (Core Interface) for R/3.

- CIF for R/3 establishes the integration between R/3 systems and APO meaning the exchange of master and transactional data as well as planning results.
- Master data for APO Demand Planning are uploaded via DP immanent extractors, which are similar to BW extractors. Both do not conflict which each other.
- Deltas for BW and Demand Planning do not conflict which each other either.

Demand-Planning

The following scenario is based on the concept that a BW-system keeps historical sales data for reporting purposes. The same data can, of course, also be used as a starting point for future sales planning. Consequently the data does not have to be extracted a second time from the underlying OLTP but can directly be retrieved from the BW-system.

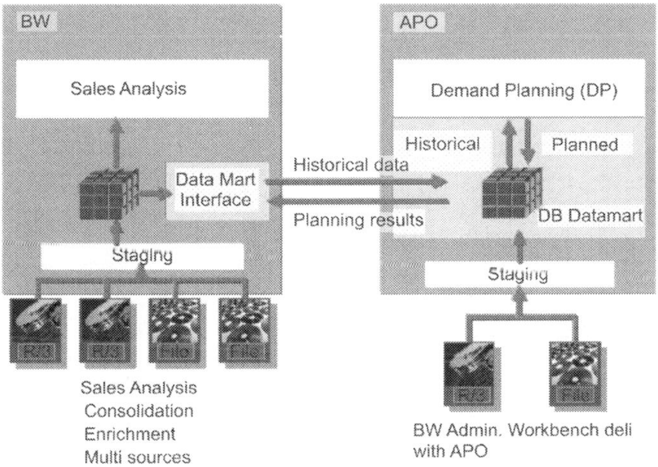

Figure 11.5 BW and APO closely coupled

BW supports this process with the so called DATA MART interface. A DATA MART in this case is a single InfoCube which can be used as a DataSource; i.e. all the data which is kept in the InfoCube can be extracted and delivered to the APO-system if required. If a subset of this DATA MART is sufficient selection criteria on the APO-request can delimit the number of records.

Since APO includes all the functions of a BW-system the extraction procedure works in the same way as it is known from the BW; i.e. the administrator requests data from a source system based on a data source (InfoSource), the InfoPackage defines what subset of data shell be extracted at what time using a certain transfer technique (IDOC, PSA) and one or several data targets InfoCube.

The common case is to have just one DATA MART on the BW (Sales InfoCube) which acts as a data source for the APO. APO extracts the data on a regular basis for the planning process. The historical data will be stored in an InfoCube and the planned data will be calculated and stored in the LiveCache. This technique is used for performance reasons.

11.5 CUSTOMIZING ON InfoCube FOR PLANNING

Technically the APO-InfoCube matches exactly with the BW-InfoCube, i.e. it consists of dimensions, and a fact table. Since the APO-InfoCube has to support additional functions it is necessary to perform some more customizing.

Transaction : RSA1 – Data Warehousing workbench: Modeling

DataSource : Configure the data source for the system.

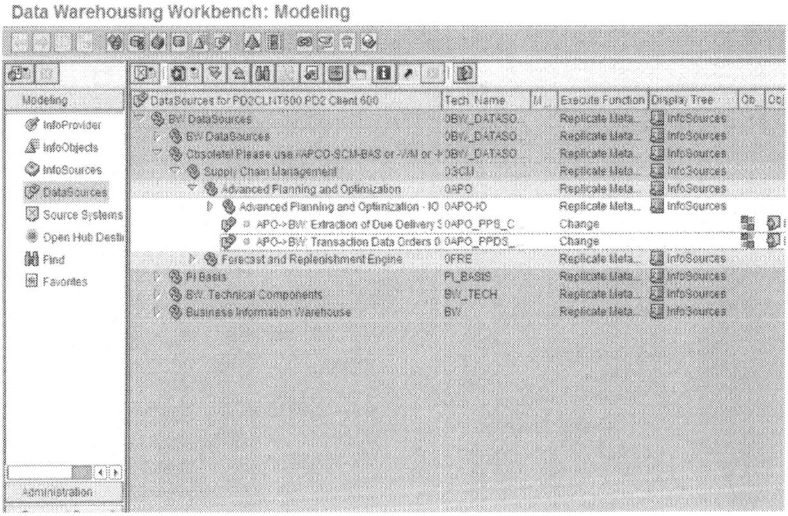

Figure 11.6 Data warehouse workbench

1. In the left screen area of the Data Warehousing Workbench: Modeling screen, choose Source Systems.

2. In the right screen area, right-click Source Systems and choose Create.
3. In the Select Source System Type dialog box, select the File System (Manual Metadata, Data using file interface) option and choose Transfer. The Create Source System dialog box is displayed.
4. Enter Excel in both rows (Logical System Name and Source System Name) and choose Enter.

   If "*No entry for BW_USER in table RSADMIN available*" appears. In this case, choose Help and double-click on Proposal for Users in Source System in the Performance Assistant.
5. Choose the Customizing activity (*transaction code RSCUSTV3*).
6. Enter RFCUSER in field SS user ALE.
7. Choose Save and choose or create a workbench request.
8. Go back and leave (!) the Data Warehousing Workbench.
9. Try again to create the source system.

InfoSource : Configure the InfoSource for the System

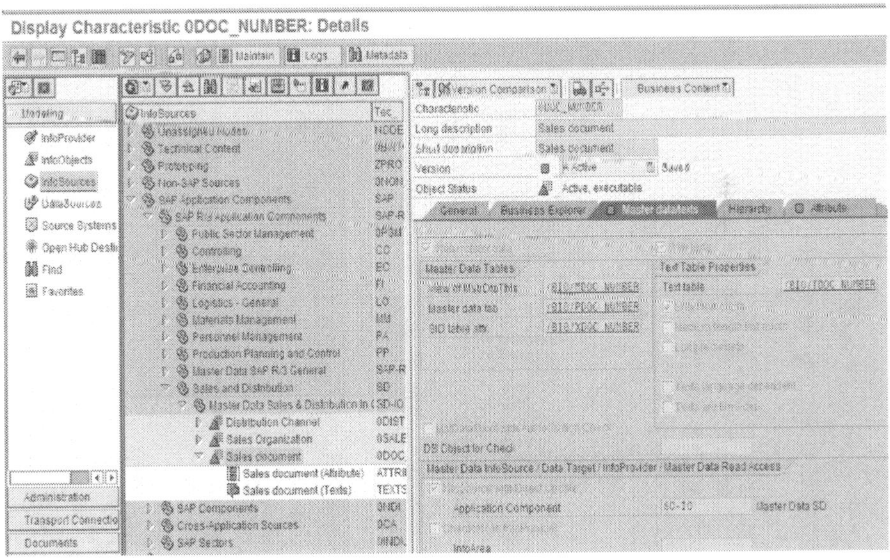

Fiqure 11.7 Characteristic display in data warehouse workbench

1. In the Modeling section of the Data Warehousing Workbench screen, choose InfoSource.
2. In the Modeling screen area on the left, choose InfoSource.
3. Right-click the InfoSource node and choose Create Application Component.
4. Make the following entries:

Field name	User action and values	Comment
Application comp.	DP_APPL_COMP	The systems add the prefix "z" · zdp_APPL_COMP
Long description	Demand Planning Application Component	

Figure 11.8 Settings for InfoSource

5. Choose Continue.
6. Right-click the Demand Planning Application component you have created, and choose Additional Functions -> Create InfoSource 3x.
7. In the Create InfoSource dialog box, select Flexible Update in any Data Target and enter the following values:

Field	User action and values
InfoSource	DP_IS
Long description	Demand planning infoSource
Template-info Source	Leave empty

Figure 11.9 Settings for InfoSource

8. Choose Transfer.
9. Right-click the new info source and choose Additional Functions -> Create Transfer rules.
10. In the dialog box that appears, enter the source system EXCEL using the input help.
11. Choose Transfer.
12. Confirm the system prompt to save your changes
13. In the right screen area, choose Communication Structure to expand the structure.
14. Enter the following InfoObjects in the InfoObject column:

InfoObjects	Description
9ALOCNO	APO Location
9AMATNR	APO Product
9ABRAND	Brand
9ALOCTO	APO Destination Loc.
9AVKORG	Sales Organization
0CALMONTH	Cal.year/month
9AMHISTORY	History
0UNIT	Unit of measure

Figure 11.10 Further settings for InfoSource

15. To expand the transfer structure entry screen, choose "Transfer_structure / Transfer_rules".
16. In the drop down menu in the Source System field, choose the source system Excel. The system then automatically proposes the data source in the DataSource field, on the DataSource/Trans. structure tab and also on the Transfer rules tab.
17. Save the InfoSource.
18. Choose Activate on the menu bar to activate the InfoSource.
19. Go back to the Data Warehousing Workbench.

InfoArea : Configure InfoArea for the System

1. On the left side, in the Modeling screen area of the Data Warehousing Workbench, choose InfoProvider.
2. In the right screen area, right-click InfoProvider and choose Create InfoArea.
3. Enter the following data:

Field name	Description	User action and values	Comment
Info Area		DP_INFOAREA	
Long Description		Demand Plannign info Area	

Figure 11.11 Settings for InfoArea

4. Choose Continue.

InfoCubes: Configure the InfoCubes for the System

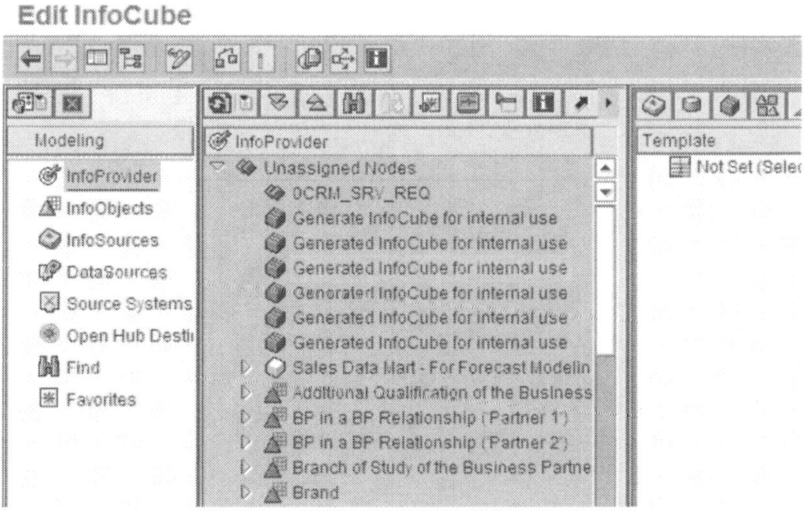

Figure 11.12 InfoCube creation

1. In the left screen area of the Data Warehousing Workbench, choose InfoProvider.
2. Right-click the new InfoArea and choose Create InfoCube.
3. In the Edit InfoCube dialog box, make the following entries:

Field name	User action and values	Comment
InfoCube	DP_ IC	
Description	Demand planning infoCube	
InforProvider Type	Select the ratio button Standard InfoCube	

Figure 11.13 Settings for InfoCube creation

4. Choose Create.
   The choice of BW Application dialog box is displayed.
5. Double-click BW.
   The Edit InfoCube screen is now divided into four columns:
   - Navigation area (Modeling or other) on the left
   - InfoProvider area
   - Template area
   - InfoCube area

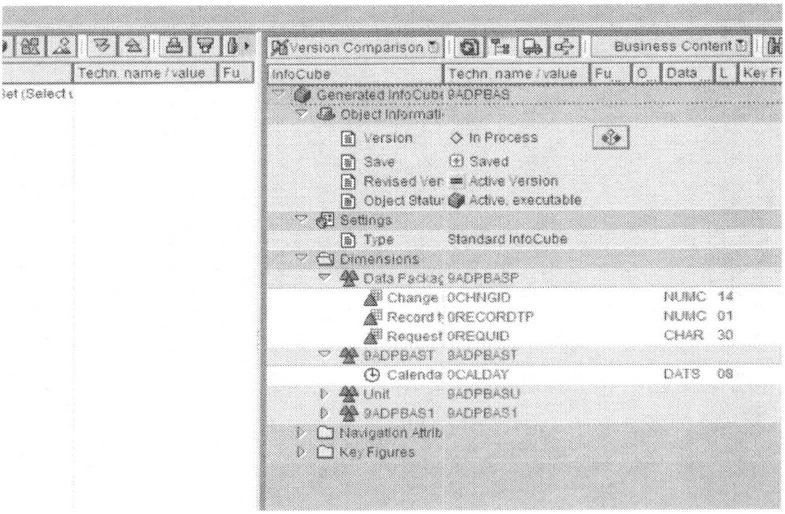

Figure 11.14 InfoCube creation

6. In the Template area, choose with the quick info text Info Source 3.x to display the InfoSource table.
7. In the Select Info Source window, choose All Applications, then click on *DP_ IS* Demand Planning Info Source in the InfoSource table. *Choose Continue.*

The InfoSource template is now displayed in the template area.

8. Expand all folders of the InfoSource template.
9. Select the following characteristics from the template area (in the Characteristics folder):
   - APO Location
   - APO Product
   - Brand
   - APO Destination Location
   - Sales Organization
10. Using drag and drop, move these characteristics to the Dimension 1 element under the Dimensions folder in the InfoCube area on the right side of the screen.
11. Likewise, assign the time characteristics Calendar year/month to the dimension Time of the InfoCube. As a result, the InfoObject Unit of measure is automatically assigned to the InfoCube.
12. Assign the key figure History to the Key Figures folder of the InfoCube.
13. To assign the APO Planning Version (*9AVERSION*) characteristics to this InfoCube, right click the InfoCube dimension Dimension 1 and choose InfoObject Direct Input.
14. In the Insert InfoObjects dialog box, enter 9AVERSION and choose Continue. You have assigned all relevant characteristics to the InfoCube.
15. Save the InfoCube, activate the InfoCube and go back to the Data Warehousing Workbench.

11.6 CREATING THE UPDATE RULES

1. Right-click the Demand Planning InfoCube and choose *Additional Functions -> Create update rules.*
2. In the Info Source field, select the Demand Planning InfoSource and choose *Continue.*
3. In the Update Rules create: Rules screen, default update rules are generated from the InfoCube. Update rules must be created for all key figures and characteristics in the InfoCube.
4. Double-click key figure History or choose Detail. The Update Rule: Detail dialog box is displayed.
5. On the Key Figure tab, choose Addition n the Update Type section. A key figure can be updated according to different rules (Addition or No update option). No update means that the InfoCube is not updated. In other words, no data records are written to the InfoCube during the initial data transfer, or the data records that are already available remains with subsequent transfers.

   Addition means that new values are added where the primary key is the same.
6. In the Update Method section, choose History as a Source Key Fig (Source Key Figure).

7. Go to the Characteristics tab.
8. Choose method blank of the characteristic APO-Planning Version.
9. Choose Constant and enter the value *"000"*.
10. *Choose Transfer*.
    In the Update Rules table, the status must be green for the next step.
11. *Choose Update Rules -> Activate* from the menu bar and go back to the Data Warehousing Workbench.

11.7 CREATING THE InfoPackage

1. In the left part of the Data Warehousing Workbench, in the Modeling section, choose InfoSources.
2. Look for the relevant InfoSource, for example, *DP_IS* Demand Planning InfoSource.
3. Expand the InfoSource *DP_IS* and right-click the second sub node and choose Create InfoPackage.
4. In the Create InfoPackage dialog box, enter the InfoPackage description (e.g. Demand Planning Info Package). *Choose Save*.
5. The Scheduler (Maintain InfoPackage) screen is displayed.
6. Choose the External Data tab page. In the Load external data from section, select Client Workstation.
7. In the File Type section, select the CSV file radio button. In the Data separator field, enter ";". In the Escape sign field.
8. In the Name of file field, enter the path to the Excel file which contains the data to be uploaded.
9. Choose the Processing tab page and select the radio button PSA and then into Data Targets (Package by Package).
10. Choose the Data targets tab page and select the radio button Select Data Targets.
11. Choose your InfoCube and set the indicator Updating the data target. Do not set the indicator Delete entire content of data target.
12. Choose the Update tab and select the radio button Full update and always update data, even if no master data exists for the data.
13. On the Schedule tab page, specify when the data is to be uploaded (either immediately, or as a batch job).
14. Save the InfoPackage.

I tried to cover most of the concepts of InfoCubes, more on the concept is described in chapter 12 "Integrating APO with BI" also.

12

INTEGRATION OF APO WITH BI (BUSINESS INTELLIGENCE)

12.1 APO AND BI

APO implementation is always done on a different hardware and a different landscape to that of R/3. The APO server would communicate with R/3 as well as with BW. The interaction with R/3 is through CIF which is was transferring master as well as transaction data (viz. stock , orders) which is needed to deploy the planning books in the planning areas, CIF we already discussed in other chapters.

APO has a BW implementation of its own which interacts with the BW for import/export of data i.e. APO imports master data as well as historical sales and delivery data from BW. This integration is identical to the integration between two data targets/info providers. Connection between APO server and the BW server is stabilized (just as to connect R/3 with BW). The data sources are replicated in APO and then follow the same steps as in BW i.e. creating InfoPackage to load data till PSA followed by DTP creation to load data till the data targets in APO.

The APO data which is usually available in planning area (with respect to Demand Planning) is available to BW in the form of a DataSource. i.e. each planning area can be converted into a DataSource. This data source can be replicated in BW (just as to replicate the R/3 data source) and the next steps are absolutely similar to any other implementation i.e. PSA, info package, transformations, DTP etc. only need to decide the data flow whether full-init / delta.

For other modules in APO i.e. SNP and PPDS the data integration with BW can be through DP i.e. SNP transfers data to DP and then the steps from DP to BW are as explained above.

BW Info Providers

Definition

Objects for which the queries in SAP BW can be created or executed. There are two types of InfoProviders. One type includes objects that contain physical data. These are known as data targets, such as InfoCubes, ODS objects, and InfoObjects (characteristics with attributes, texts, or hierarchies). The other type includes objects that display no physical data storage, such as InfoSets, RemoteCubes, SAP RemoteCubes, and MultiProviders. InfoProviders are the objects or views that are relevant for reporting.

Use

Connecting to an InfoProvider furnishes the data routing / data mapping of BW in all implementations. The following are brief definitions of the various types of InfoProviders that can be used in SAP BW implementations. For detailed information, user can check SAP Business Information Warehouse documentation.

- **InfoCube**

  An InfoCube is a central data store for reports and evaluations that enables multi-dimensional analysis. It refers to how data is structured within BW tables. Each InfoCube consists of several InfoObjects, which create the dimensions and characteristics of the cube. Each query references a single InfoCube. InfoCubes we discussed in detail in Chapter 11.

  Query: A query represents a particular view of a specific InfoCube. Queries are predefined and users cannot add more parameters to them. All the queries that a user is allowed to see become part of the user's toolbar as defined in the BW system.

- **ODS**

  An ODS is an Operational Data Store where it is possible to combine information from several data sources before storing it in InfoCubes. An ODS provides a query with access to more detailed data than that which is available in an InfoCube, which is often necessary for a proper business analysis.

InfoObject

Each of the InfoProvider types described above consists of InfoObjects. An InfoObject is the basic unit of information in the BW environment. It is a generic term for business evaluation objects such as customer, product, region, revenue, and so on. An InfoObject represents a unit of metadata in the BW repository, containing both technical information and business logic. An InfoObject can have attributes, each of which in itself is an InfoObject as well.

In Demand Planning and Supply Network Planning, data can be stored in three different ways:

- In LiveCache time series objects
- In LiveCache orders
- In an InfoCube

Each key figure in a planning area has its own storage method.

12.2 DataStore OBJECT

Definition

A DataStore object serves as a storage location for consolidated and cleansed transaction data or master data on a lowest level. This data can be evaluated using a BEx query.

A DataStore object contains key fields (such as document number, document item) and data fields that, in addition to the key figures, can also enclosed with character fields (such as order status, customer). The data from a DataStore object can be updated with a delta update into InfoCubes (standard) or other DataStore objects or master data tables (attributes or texts) in the same system or across different systems.

Unlike multidimensional data storage using InfoCubes, the data in DataStore objects is stored in transparent, flat database tables. The system does not create fact tables or dimension tables.

Table 12.1 Data Maintenance Table

Overview of DataStore Object Types Type	*Structure*	*Data Supply*	*SID Generation*
Standard DataStore Object	Consists of three tables: activation queue, table of active data, change log	From data transfer process	Yes
Write-Optimized DataStore Objects	Consists of the table of active data only	From data transfer process	No
DataStore Objects for Direct Update	Consists of the table of active data only	From APIs	No

A DataSource is a source of data residing in the source system. It contains fields that are offered to be transferred to the BW system from the source system. Data is transferred from the DataSource in the form of transfer structure and is dependent of the source system (design in the source system). A DataSource contains the following attributes:

- Extract structure
- Extraction method
- Extractor

As per requirement sometimes transaction data from R/3 system is required to be fetched directly, there are various methods for interfaces also but here we will discuss about the Extractor only. This is nothing but the Extraction of data from R/3 system. Here Extract structure means a structure containing all the fields that are available for Extraction.

Extraction method signifies the type of extraction whether Full or Delta. *Extractor* will have the required logic for extraction purpose. The Extractors can be categorized into the following:

- Standard Extractor
- Generic Extractor

Generic Extractor

There are many cases in BW installation when there is a requirement where custom fields are needed from the source system, here in our case its R/3 and these fields are not present in the standard extractor provided by SAP. In such cases to make the fields available in BW; a new data source need to be created which will extract data. This custom made data source is called *Generic extractor*.

Generic extractors are of 3 types:

- Created based on View/table
- Created based on InfoSet query
- Created based on Function module

The BW Service API (SAPI) is a technology package in the SAP source system that enables the tight integration of data transfer from SAP source systems into the BW system. The Service API allows to

- Make available SAP application extractors as a basis for data transfer into BW
- Carry out generic data extraction
- Implement intelligent delta methods
- Access data in the source system directly from BW (Remote Cube support).

Customizing extractors comprises all activities required for extracting and transferring data between an SAP source system and BW.

A distinction is made between data transfer from OLTP- / R/3 systems, BW systems as source systems and other SAP source systems.

Irrespective of the type of source system, Customizing for extractors comprises activities that belong to the scope of SAPI:

- General settings for data transfer from source systems into BW.
- The option of installing Business Content delivered by SAP.
- The option of maintaining generic DataSources
- The option of post-processing the application component hierarchy and DataSources on a source system level

Customizing for extractors is done from the context menu for any source system in the Administrator Workbench (*transaction code SBIW*).

Integration

Along with the activities that belong within the scope of SAPI, Customizing for extractors contains settings for OLTP and other SAP source systems / source-system specific settings for application-based DataSources.

Functions

General Settings

These include the following:

- Maintaining Control Parameters for Data Transfer

- Restricting Authorizations for the Extraction
- Checking the Delta Queue

Installing Business Content Delivered by SAP

DataSources delivered within Business Content and those delivered by partners appear in a delivery version. If to use a partner or Business Content DataSource to transfer data from a source system into a BW, one needs to transfer this DataSource from the D- into the active (A-) version.

In the source system, the DataSources are assigned to a particular application component. If want to display these DataSources in the source system view within BW Administrator Workbench modeling as a part of this application component hierarchy, to transfer them from the D version into the A version.

The following section of Customizing for extractors explains, how to transfer the application component hierarchy and DataSources delivered with BW Business Content / Partner Content into the active version.

Transferring Data from an OLTP System or Other SAP Source Systems

Some settings in advance to be made for some Business Content DataSources before transfer data into a BW happens. These settings are available in the section *Settings for Application-Specific DataSources* within Customizing for extractors. (For only those SAP source systems for which it has pertinence.)

The following activities are associated with the transfer of Business Content:

- Transferring the Application Component Hierarchy
- Installing Business Content DataSources

Generic DataSources

Regardless of the specific application, use generic data extraction to extract data from any transparent tables, database views or SAP query InfoSets. No need to program in ABAP. Function Modules can also be used for generic data extraction.

In this way, DataSources for transaction data, master data attributes or texts can be used for the specific requirement. The data for such DataSources are read generically and then transferred into the BW.

Generic DataSources allow extracting data which cannot be supplied to the BW either with the DataSources delivered within Business Content or with customer-defined DataSources of the application.

12.3 EXTRACTION PROCESS

The Function Module is called up again and again during an extraction process:

1. *Initialization call:* Only the request parameters are transferred to the module here. The module is as yet unable to transfer data.

2. *First read call:* The extractor returns the data typified with the extract structure in an interface table. The number of rows the system expected is determined in the request parameter (I_MAXSIZE).
3. *Second read call:* The extractor returns the data enclosed within the first data package in a separate package with I_MAXSIZE rows.
4. The system calls up the function module again and again until the module returns the exception *NO_MORE_DATA*. Data cannot be transferred in the call in which this exception is called up.

Example

An example of a function module that fulfills this requirement is *RSAX_BIW_GET_DATA_SIMPLE*. A simple way of creating a syntactically correct module is to copy it into its own function group and then to copy the rows of the top-include of *function group RSAX (LRSAXTOP)* into the top-include of its own function group. Afterwards, the copied function module must be adjusted to the individual requests.

The following update modes are available in the BW Scheduler:

- Full Update
  A Full Update requests all data that meet the selection criteria set in the Scheduler.
- Delta Update
  A Delta Update only requests data that has appeared in the source system since the last load.
- Initializing the Delta Process
  Initialize a delta method before it can work. The initialization selections are taken for the loading of delta records, with large data volumes, a performance-friendly extraction of data from the source system is only possible using a delta method.

In the maintenance of the generic DataSource, one can set up a delta for master data attributes and texts. One can also set up a generic delta using a (delta-relevant) field with a value increasing monotonously.

Extraction using SAP Query

The SAP query is a comprehensive tool to define reports. It uses many different forms of reporting. It allows users to define and execute their own evaluations of data in the SAP system without knowing anything about ABAP.

To determine the structure of evaluations, texts are entered in the SAP query, field and options are also selected. The selection of relevant fields is made easier by using InfoSets and functional groups.

An InfoSet is a special view on a set of data (logical database, table join, table, sequential file). It serves as a data source in the SAP query. An InfoSet determines the tables and fields of these tables are included within an evaluation. InfoSets are usually based on logical databases.

The maintenance of InfoSets represents a component of the SAP query. When an InfoSet is created, a data source is selected in an application system. As the number of fields of a data source can be very high, fields can be combined into logical units, the functional groups. Functional groups are groups of different fields for a logical unit within an InfoSet. Fields that is to be used in an extract structure must be assigned to a functional group. All fields of all functional groups for this InfoSet are available for generic data extraction.

SAP Query is important for the Business Information Warehouse in the definition of the extract structure by selecting fields of a logical database, a table join or other datasets in an InfoSet. Use generic data extraction for master or transaction data from any InfoSet. A query is generated for an InfoSet that gets data and transfers this data to the generic extractor.

Thus, InfoSets are additional and manageable data source for generic data extraction. InfoSets allows using logical databases of all SAP applications, table joins, and further datasets as data sources for BI.

In the following section, the terms SAP Query and InfoSet are used independently of the source system release. SAP Query is the same as an ABAP Query, dependent on the source system release. The InfoSet is also called a functional area in some source system releases.

Function module RSDRI_INFOPROV_READ

FUNCTION rsdri_infoprov_read .

```
*"----------------------------------------------------------------------
*"*"Lokale Schnittstelle:
*"  IMPORTING
*"     REFERENCE(I_INFOPROV) TYPE RSINFOPROV
*"     REFERENCE(I_TH_SFC) TYPE RSDRI_TH_SFC
*"     REFERENCE(I_TH_SFK) TYPE RSDRI_TH_SFK
*"     REFERENCE(I_T_RANGE) TYPE RSDRI_T_RANGE OPTIONAL
*"     REFERENCE(I_TH_TABLESEL) TYPE RSDRI_TH_SELT OPTIONAL
*"     REFERENCE(I_T_RTIME) TYPE RSDRI_T_RTIME OPTIONAL
*"     VALUE(I_REFERENCE_DATE) TYPE RSDRI_REFDATE DEFAULT SY-DATUM
*"     VALUE(I_ROLLUP_ONLY) TYPE RS_BOOL DEFAULT RS_C_TRUE
*"     REFERENCE(I_T_REQUID) TYPE RSDR0_T_REQUID OPTIONAL
*"     VALUE(I_SAVE_IN_TABLE) TYPE RSDRI_SAVE_IN_TABLE DEFAULT SPACE
*"     VALUE(I_TABLENAME) TYPE RSDRI_TABLENAME OPTIONAL
*"     VALUE(I_SAVE_IN_FILE) TYPE RSDRI_SAVE_IN_FILE DEFAULT SPACE
*"     VALUE(I_FILENAME) TYPE RSDRI_FILENAME OPTIONAL
*"     VALUE(I_PACKAGESIZE) TYPE I DEFAULT 1000
*"     VALUE(I_MAXROWS) TYPE I DEFAULT 0
*"     VALUE(I_AUTHORITY_CHECK) TYPE RSDRI_AUTHCHK DEFAULT
*"       RSDRC_C_AUTHCHK-READ
*"     VALUE(I_CURRENCY_CONVERSION) TYPE RSDR0_CURR_CONV DEFAULT 'X'
*"     VALUE(I_USE_DB_AGGREGATION) TYPE RS_BOOL DEFAULT RS_C_TRUE
*"     VALUE(I_USE_AGGREGATES) TYPE RS_BOOL DEFAULT RS_C_TRUE
```

```
*"      VALUE(I_READ_ODS_DELTA) TYPE RSDRI_CHANGELOG_EXTRACTION DEFAULT
*"        RS_C_FALSE
*"      VALUE(I_CALLER) TYPE RSDRS_CALLER DEFAULT RSDRS_C_CALLER-RSDRI
*"      VALUE(I_DEBUG) TYPE RS_BOOL DEFAULT RS_C_FALSE
*"      VALUE(I_CLEAR) TYPE RS_BOOL DEFAULT RS_C_FALSE
*"  EXPORTING
*"      REFERENCE(E_T_DATA) TYPE STANDARD TABLE
*"      VALUE(E_END_OF_DATA) TYPE RS_BOOL
*"      VALUE(E_AGGREGATE) TYPE RSINFOCUBE
*"      VALUE(E_SPLIT_OCCURRED) TYPE RSDR0_SPLIT_OCCURRED
*"      REFERENCE(E_T_MSG) TYPE RS_T_MSG
*"      REFERENCE(E_STEPUID) TYPE SYSUUID_25
*"  CHANGING
*"      REFERENCE(C_FIRST_CALL) TYPE RS_BOOL
*"  EXCEPTIONS
*"      ILLEGAL_INPUT
*"      ILLEGAL_INPUT_SFC
*"      ILLEGAL_INPUT_SFK
*"      ILLEGAL_INPUT_RANGE
*"      ILLEGAL_INPUT_TABLESEL
*"      NO_AUTHORIZATION
*"      ILLEGAL_DOWNLOAD
*"      ILLEGAL_TABLENAME
*"      TRANS_NO_WRITE_MODE
*"      INHERITED_ERROR
*"      X_MESSAGE
*"----------------------------------------
```

Import Parameters:

I_INFOPROV: Technical name of InfoProvider (InfoCubes, DSOs, MultiProviders)

I_TH_SFC: Characteristics of the InfoProvider which to be returned in the output

I_TH_SFK: Key Figures of the InfoProvider which to be returned in the output

I_T_RANGE: Contains the list of conditions based on which the data is to be fetched

I_REFERENCE_DATE: Specifies the key date for which time-dependent values are to be assessed.

I_ROLLUP_ONLY: Should only data that has been rolled up into the aggregates be considered, or should the most current data be read, which is possibly only located in the fact table of the InfoCube?

If a table of requests was specified (i_t_requid), if i_rollup_only = true, it is truncated at the number of requests already rolled up into the aggregates.

I_T_REQUID: With this parameter, a user can define a restriction using the request for an InfoCube.

I_PACKAGESIZE: Size of Returned Data Package (Default Value:1000)

Export Parameters:

E_T_DATA: Internal Table with Query Result

E_END_OF_DATA: Internal Table with Query Result: Last Data Package Yes/No

Functionality

The function module *RSDRI_INFOPROV_READ* reads data from the InfoProvider whose technical name is specified in I_INFOPROV. Supported InfoProviders are currently InfoCubes, ODS Objects and MultiProviders.

Using the parameters listed below:

- Restrictions can be defined for the data to be read,
- Return types can be determined, and
- General conditions (authorization check, avoidance of program generation, etc.) can be specified.

A logical read access with *RSDRI_INFOPROV_READ* can contain more than one physical read access to the database. This is designated as a *split*. Splits may occur especially with MultiProviders, but multiple accesses through aggregate optimization or access to F- and E fact tables can take place with normal InfoCubes.

Furthermore, results that are not completely aggregates can result in virtual InfoCubes. Therefore, setting the parameter *I_USE_DB_AGGREGATION = 'X'* does not guarantee complete aggregation of the result. Module *RSDRI_AGGREGATE_DATA* is useful to aggregate a table *E_T_DATA*.

Non-cumulative values can also be read using this interface. However, there is the restriction that only the non-cumulative for the specified times (I_T_RTIME) can be calculated; Aggregation over time (such as LAST or AVERAGE, for example) cannot be calculated using this interface. Even when the time-reference characteristic is not explicitly requested, a drilldown is inserted internally according to this time characteristic. Thus it may be that no completely aggregated result table is returned.

Function Module: RSDPL_CUBE_DATA_READ

FUNCTION rsdpl_cube_data_read

```
*"----------------------------------------------------
*"*"Lokale Schnittstelle:
*"  IMPORTING
*"     VALUE(I_INFOCUBE) TYPE RSDPO_INFOCUBE
*"     VALUE(I_REFERENCE_DATE) TYPE RSDPO_REFDATE
*"     VALUE(I_S_RFCMODE) TYPE RSDPO_S_RFCMODE
*"     VALUE(I_S_DELTAMODE) TYPE RSDPO_S_DELTAMODE
*"  EXPORTING
*"     VALUE(E_TABLENAME) TYPE RSDPO_TABLENAME
*"  TABLES
*"     I_T_CHA TYPE RSDPO_T_CHA
*"     I_T_KYF TYPE RSDPO_T_KYF
```

```
*"      I_T_RANGE TYPE RSDP0_T_RANGE
*"      E_T_COLUMN TYPE RSDP0_T_COLUMN
*"   EXCEPTIONS
*"      INFOCUBE_ERROR
*"      DELTAMODE_ERROR
*"      DELTA_EMPTY
*"      INHERITED_ERROR
*"----------------------------------------
```

Exporting

i_infocube	=	rsdp0_infocube InfoCube
i_reference_date	=	rsdp0_refdate Key Date
i_s_rfcmode	=	rsdp0_s_rfcmode DM API: RFC Mode
i_s_deltamode	=	rsdp0_s_deltamode DM API: Load mode

Importing

e_tablename	=	rsdp0_tablename DM API: Table Name

Tables

i_t_cha	=	rsdp0_t_cha Characteristic Table
i_t_kyf	=	rsdp0_t_kyf Key Figure Table
i_t_range	=	rsdp0_t_range Selection Range Table
e_t_column	=	rsdp0_t_column DM API: DB Table Description

Exceptions

INFOCUBE_ERROR	=	1	" Invalid InfoCube
DELTAMODE_ERROR	=	2	" Error in delta mode specification
DELTA_EMPTY	=	3	" Request Not Executed; Delta is Empty
INHERITED_ERROR	=	4	" Error in Called Routine

Function RSDRI_INFOCUBE_DATA_COPY

```
*"----------------------------------------
*"*"Lokale Schnittstelle:
*"   IMPORTING
*"      REFERENCE(I_INFOPROV_FROM) TYPE RSINFOPROV
*"      REFERENCE(I_INFOCUBE_TO) TYPE RSINFOPROV
*"      REFERENCE(I_T_RANGE) TYPE RSDRI_T_RANGE OPTIONAL
*"      VALUE(I_PACKAGESIZE) TYPE I DEFAULT -1
*"      VALUE(I_ROLLUP_ONLY) TYPE RS_BOOL DEFAULT RS_C_TRUE
*"      REFERENCE(I_EXITNM) TYPE FUNCNAM OPTIONAL
*"      REFERENCE(I_TH_IOBJ_MAP) TYPE RSDRI_TH_IOBJ_MAP OPTIONAL
*"      VALUE(I_DEBUG) TYPE RS_BOOL DEFAULT RS_C_FALSE
*"   EXPORTING
*"      REFERENCE(E_RECORDS) TYPE I
*"      REFERENCE(E_REQUESTS) TYPE I
```

```
*"      REFERENCE(E_REQUID) TYPE RSREQUNR
*"      REFERENCE(E_T_MSG) TYPE RS_T_MSG
*"  EXCEPTIONS
*"      READ_ERROR
*"      WRITE_ERROR
*"--------------------------------------------
```

Function RSDRI_CUBE_WRITE_PACKAGE

```
*"--------------------------------------------
*"*"Lokale Schnittstelle:
*"  IMPORTING
*"      VALUE(I_INFOCUBE) TYPE RSD_INFOCUBE
*"      VALUE(I_CURR_CONVERSION) TYPE RS_BOOL DEFAULT RS_C_TRUE
*"      VALUE(I_NCUM_INIT) TYPE RS_BOOL DEFAULT RS_C_FALSE
*"      VALUE(I_MDATA_CHECK) TYPE RSDRI_MDATA_CHECK DEFAULT RS_C_FALSE
*"      VALUE(I_DELTA) TYPE RS_BOOL DEFAULT RS_C_FALSE
*"  EXPORTING
*"      REFERENCE(E_REQUID) TYPE RSREQUNR
*"      REFERENCE(E_RECORDS) TYPE I
*"      REFERENCE(E_TS_MSG) TYPE RSDRI_TS_MSG
*"  CHANGING
*"      REFERENCE(C_T_DATA) TYPE STANDARD TABLE
*"  EXCEPTIONS
*"      INFOCUBE_NOT_FOUND
*"      ILLEGAL_INPUT
*"      ROLLBACK_ERROR
*"      DUPLICATE_RECORDS
*"      REQUEST_LOCKED
*"      NOT_TRANSACTIONAL
*"      INHERITED_ERROR
*"--------------------------------------------
```

Exporting

```
    i_infocube          =              " rsd_infocube  InfoCube Name
*   i_curr_conversion   = RS_C_TRUE    " rs_bool Convert Cur to DB Format
*   i_ncum_init         = RS_C_FALSE   " rs_bool Initialize Set?
*   i_mdata_check       = RS_C_FALSE   " rsdri_mdata_check Error code
*   i_delta             = RS_C_FALSE   " rs_bool Write Delta Cube content
  IMPORTING
    e_requid            = " rsrequnr Request ID, Inserted Data
    e_records           = " i Number of Records Written
    e_ts_msg            = " rsdri_ts_msg Message Table
  CHANGING
    c_t_data            = " standard table  Data (structure: V2 view)
```

```
EXCEPTIONS
  INFOCUBE_NOT_FOUND    = 1    " InfoCube does not exist
  ILLEGAL_INPUT         = 2    " Incorrect Input Parameter
  ROLLBACK_ERROR        = 3    " Error Deleting Request Cube
  DUPLICATE_RECORDS     = 4    " Duplicates When Writing Cube
  NOT_TRANSACTIONAL     = 6    " No transactions can be written
  INHERITED_ERROR       = 7    " Other Error
```

Functionality

This module enables to write data to an InfoCube. An RFC-compatible version of this module also exists: *RSDRI_CUBE_WRITE_PACKAGE_RFC.*

The class CL_RSDRI_INFOCUBE also allows writing to an InfoCube. The modules RSDRI are also included in this class, explore the class separately also to check the components assigned to the class.

- If the InfoCube is a transactional InfoCube in planning mode, the data is written to an open planning request. This planning request will be used jointly by all write programs that use *RSDRI_CUBE_WRITE_PACKAGE* to write to the InfoCube. The system closes the planning request automatically and opens a new planning request (at any given particular time, only one planning request can be active), if the currently open planning request has reached a certain size. Only one open planning request can exist for each InfoCube.

If a write error occurs that is intended to cause a termination (see parameter i_mdata_check), the current package is not written at all. The open planning request remains in the state it had before it was called. In this case, no further actions from outside are required to roll the data back.

- If the InfoCube is in staging mode, or if the InfoCube is not a transactional InfoCube, *RSDRI_CUBE_WRITE_PACKAGE* opens a new planning request. In this case, only one write program at a time can write to the APO request, since only one planning request can be open at a time. The opened planning request is closed again at the end of the *RSDRI_CUBE_WRITE_PACKAGE* call. This means that each *RSDRI_CUBE_WRITE_PACKAGE* call results in a new planning request, which is closed at the end.

If a write error occurs that is intended to cause a termination (see parameter i_mdata_check), the request that has just been opened has errors and is closed. It is then deleted automatically in the system.

Update Task

In standard it is possible to use an update task-compatible module to call *RSDRI_CUBE_WRITE_PACKAGE* or its RFC-compatible variant *RSDRI_CUBE_WRITE_PACKAGE_RFC*. The following restrictions exist, nevertheless:

- Writes with delta determination are not possible in the update task.
- If the InfoCube has changed in the meantime, the InfoCube write program

must be generated again. In the update task, this possible only without a *COMMIT*, meaning that other write programs have to wait until the update task that has regenerated the write program has executed a *COMMIT*.

- If the structure of an InfoCube for which delta determination has been permitted has changed (check parameter *i_delta*), the staging table must also be regenerated as part of the write program generation. This is not possible in the update task and raises the exception *INHERITED_ERROR*.
- Settings in the InfoCube, such as "*automatic ROLLUP of a request*" or "*automatic COMPRESSION of a request*", are not possible if the transactional request has been closed in the UPDATE task.
- Speedy rollups or compressions can be guaranteed by scheduling a regular background job.

To avoid these generation problems, it is recommended calling the function module ***RSDRI_INFOCUBE_GEN_PROGRAM*** for the InfoCube before the update task is called. This module regenerates the InfoCube write program and if necessary, also regenerates the staging table.

```
CALL FUNCTION 'RSDRI_INFOCUBE_GEN_PROGRAM'
EXPORTING
      I_INFOCUBE = l_infocube
EXCEPTIONS
      OTHERS = 1.
```

Function RSDRI_INFOPROV_DELETE

```
"----------------------------------------------------------------
*"*"Lokale Schnittstelle:
*"  IMPORTING
*"     REFERENCE(I_DATATARGET) TYPE RSDDATATARGET
*"     REFERENCE(I_THX_SEL) TYPE RSDRD_THX_SEL
*"     REFERENCE(I_AUTHORITY_CHECK) TYPE RS_BOOL DEFAULT RS_C_TRUE
*"     REFERENCE(I_MODE) TYPE RS_BOOL DEFAULT RSDRD_C_MODE-CHOOSE
*"     REFERENCE(I_THRESHOLD) TYPE F DEFAULT '0.1'
*"     REFERENCE(I_PARALLEL_DEGREE) TYPE I DEFAULT 1
*"     REFERENCE(I_NO_LOGGING) TYPE RS_BOOL DEFAULT RS_C_FALSE
*"     REFERENCE(I_NO_COMMIT) TYPE RS_BOOL DEFAULT RS_C_FALSE
*"     REFERENCE(I_NO_ENQUEUE) TYPE RS_BOOL DEFAULT RS_C_FALSE
*"     REFERENCE(I_SHOW_REPORT) TYPE RS_BOOL DEFAULT RS_C_FALSE
*"     REFERENCE(I_TRANSACTIONAL_ODS) TYPE RS_BOOL DEFAULT RS_C_FALSE
*"  CHANGING
*"     REFERENCE(C_T_MSG) TYPE RS_T_MSG
*"  EXCEPTIONS
*"     X_MESSAGE
*"     INHERITED_ERROR
*"----------------------------------------------------------------
```

Function rsdri_odso_insert .

```
*"----------------------------------------
*"*"Lokale Schnittstelle:
*"  IMPORTING
*"     REFERENCE(I_ODSOBJECT) TYPE RSDODSOBJECT
*"     REFERENCE(I_T_INSERT) TYPE STANDARD TABLE
*"  EXPORTING
*"     REFERENCE(E_RECORDS) TYPE I
*"  EXCEPTIONS
*"     DATA_TARGET_NOT_ODS
*"     ODS_TYPE_NOT_TRANSACTIONAL
*"     ACTIVE_TABLE_NAME_NOT_FOUND
*"     RECORD_KEY_ALREADY_EXISTS
*"     ARRAY_INSERT_FAILED
*"     INTERNAL_ERROR
*"----------------------------------------
```

Functionality

This function module receives the technical name of the DataStore object as a return parameter. Data transfer is done in a table with the same structure as the active table of the DataStore object.

A check is carried out to check whether the DataStore object is a DataStore object for direct writing. The number of data records inserted is returned (e_numrows). In the event of errors during this process, the relevant exception is returned.

Notes

Data is either accepted in full or rejected in full. For this reason, please ensure that the data is correct and that the structure of the data matches the structure of the DataStore object table exactly. Incorrect data or structures may result in SQL errors, exceptions, or in data being transferred in the wrong format.

Since a DataStore object for direct writing is often supplied with new data, lock management must be implemented in the calling object. For example, it might be implement no lock (except at database level) for quick insertion of a small number of records but implement a lock for lengthy inserts involving a large number of records.

Function rsdri_odso_modify.

```
*"----------------------------------------
*"*"Lokale Schnittstelle:
*"  IMPORTING
*"     REFERENCE(I_ODSOBJECT) TYPE RSDODSOBJECT
*"     REFERENCE(I_T_MODIFY) TYPE STANDARD TABLE
*"  EXPORTING
*"     REFERENCE(E_RECORDS) TYPE I
```

```
*"   EXCEPTIONS
*"       DATA_TARGET_NOT_ODS
*"       ODS_TYPE_NOT_TRANSACTIONAL
*"       ACTIVE_TABLE_NAME_NOT_FOUND
*"       RECORD_KEY_ALREADY_EXISTS
*"       ARRAY_MODIFY_FAILED
*"       INTERNAL_ERROR
*"----------------------------------------
```

Functionality

This function module receives the technical name of the DataStore object as a return parameter. Data is transferred in a table with the same structure as the active table of the DataStore object.

A check is carried out to see whether the DataStore object is a DataStore object for direct writing. The number of data records inserted is returned (e_numrows). In the event of errors during this process, the relevant exception is returned.

Notes

Data is either accepted in full or rejected in full. For the reason, one must ensure that the data is correct and the structure of the data matches the structure of the DataStore object table exactly. Incorrect data or structures may result in SQL errors, exceptions, or in data being transferred in the wrong format.

Since a DataStore object for direct writing is often supplied with new data, lock management must be implemented in the calling object. For example, no lock might be implemented (except at database level) for quick modifications of a small number of records but implement a lock for lengthy modifications involving a large number of records.

Function rsdri_odso_update .

```
*"----------------------------------------
*"*"Lokale Schnittstelle:
*"   IMPORTING
*"       REFERENCE(I_ODSOBJECT) TYPE RSDODSOBJECT
*"       REFERENCE(I_T_UPDATE) TYPE STANDARD TABLE
*"   EXPORTING
*"       REFERENCE(E_RECORDS) TYPE I
*"   EXCEPTIONS
*"       DATA_TARGET_NOT_ODS
*"       ODS_TYPE_NOT_TRANSACTIONAL
*"       ACTIVE_TABLE_NAME_NOT_FOUND
*"       RECORD_KEY_DOES_NOT_EXIST
*"       ARRAY_UPDATE_FAILED
*"       INTERNAL_ERROR
*"----------------------------------------
```

Functionality

This function module receives the technical name of the DataStore object as a return parameter. Data is transferred in a table with the same structure as the active table of the DataStore object.

A check is carried out to see whether the DataStore object is a DataStore object for direct writing. The number of data records inserted is returned (e_numrows). In the event of errors during this process, the relevant exception is returned.

Notes

Data is either accepted in full or rejected in full. Ensure the data is correct and the structure of the data matches the structure of the DataStore object table exactly. Incorrect data or structures may result in SQL errors, exceptions, or in data being transferred in the wrong format.

Example

Step 1: Select the filer condition stored in a different DSO based on 'Customer', 'Chain ID' ,'National Group' . Store those values to internal table t_phsdrbse.

SELECT * FROM/bic/aphsdrbse00 INTO TABLE t_phsdrbse.

Step 2: Store the characteristics whose values are to be fetched from Multiprovider

******** CHARACTERISTIC ********************

```
* For the following characteristics / navigational attributes val-
ues  should be returned:
* 0MATERIAL, 0MATERIAL__0MATL_GROUP, 0DIVISION.

* 0MATERIAL
CLEAR wa_s_sfc.
* --- name of characteristic
wa_s_sfc-chanm      = '0MATERIAL'.
* --- name of corresponding column in G_T_DATA
wa_s_sfc-chaalias = '0MATERIAL'.
* --- no ORDER-BY
wa_s_sfc-orderby   = 0.
* --- include into list of characteristics
INSERT wa_s_sfc INTO TABLE t_th_sfc.

* 0MATERIAL__0MATL_GROUP
CLEAR wa_s_sfc.
* --- name of characteristic
wa_s_sfc-chanm      = '0MATERIAL__0MATL_GROUP'.
* --- name of corresponding column in G_T_DATA
wa_s_sfc-chaalias = 'S003_0MATERIAL'.
* --- no ORDER-BY
```

```
wa_s_sfc-orderby  = 0.
* --- include into list of characteristics
INSERT wa_s_sfc INTO TABLE t_th_sfc.

* 0DIVISION
CLEAR wa_s_sfc.
* --- name of characteristic
wa_s_sfc-chanm    = '0DIVISION'.
* --- name of corresponding column in G_T_DATA
wa_s_sfc-chaalias = '0DIVISION'.
* --- no ORDER-BY
wa_s_sfc-orderby  = 0.
* --- include into list of characteristics
INSERT wa_s_sfc INTO TABLE t_th_sfc.

CLEAR wa_s_sfc.
* --- name of characteristic
wa_s_sfc-chanm     = 'PIPBRAN1'.
* --- name of corresponding column in G_T_DATA
wa_s_sfc-chaalias = '/BIC/PIPBRAN1'.
* --- no ORDER-BY
wa_s_sfc-orderby  = 0.
* --- include into list of characteristics
INSERT wa_s_sfc INTO TABLE t_th_sfc.

CLEAR wa_s_sfc.
* --- name of characteristic
wa_s_sfc-chanm     = 'PIPBRAN2'.
* --- name of corresponding column in G_T_DATA
wa_s_sfc-chaalias = '/BIC/PIPBRAN2'.
* --- no ORDER-BY
wa_s_sfc-orderby  = 0.
* --- include into list of characteristics
INSERT wa_s_sfc INTO TABLE t_th_sfc.
```

Step 3: Store the Key Figures whose values are to be fetched from Multiprovider.

```
CLEAR wa_th_sfk.
* Miscellaneous Fees
wa_th_sfk-kyfnm      = 'PIPMISFEE'.
wa_th_sfk-kyfalias   = '/BIC/PIPMISFEE'.
wa_th_sfk-aggr       = 'SUM'.
INSERT wa_th_sfk INTO TABLE t_th_sfk.

CLEAR wa_th_sfk.
wa_th_sfk-kyfnm    = 'PIPNETWR'.
```

```
wa_th_sfk-kyfalias    = 'SUBTOTAL_1'.
wa_th_sfk-aggr= 'SUM'.
INSERT wa_th_sfk INTO TABLE t_th_sfk.
```

Step 4: Assemble the selection condition which was fetch in Step 1 into an internal table.

```
******** SELECTION CRITERIA ********************
LOOP AT t_phsdrbse INTO wa_phsdrbse.
* Posting Date
CLEAR wa_th_range .
wa_th_range-chanm        = '0PSTNG_DATE'.
wa_th_range-sign         = rs_c_range_sign-including.
wa_th_range-compop       = rs_c_range_opt-between.
wa_th_range-low          = wa_phsdrbse-/bic/phrbfr.
wa_th_range-high         = wa_phsdrbse-/bic/phrbto.
APPEND wa_th_range TO t_th_range.
CLEAR wa_th_range.
* Customer

IF wa_phsdrbse-customer IS NOT INITIAL.
wa_th_range-chanm       = '0SOLD_TO'.
wa_th_range-sign        = rs_c_range_sign-including.
wa_th_range-compop      = rs_c_range_opt-equal.
wa_th_range-low         = wa_phsdrbse-customer.
APPEND wa_th_range TO t_th_range.
CLEAR wa_th_range.
ENDIF.

* Chain ID
IF wa_phsdrbse-/bic/zcustchid IS NOT INITIAL.
wa_th_range-chanm       = 'PIPCUSTCH'.
wa_th_range-sign        = rs_c_range_sign-including.
wa_th_range-compop      = rs_c_range_opt-equal.
wa_th_range-low         = wa_phsdrbse-/bic/zcustchid.
APPEND wa_th_range TO t_th_range.
CLEAR wa_th_range.
ENDIF.

* National Grp
IF wa_phsdrbse-/bic/zcnltgpc IS NOT INITIAL.
wa_th_range-chanm         = 'PIPBRAN1'.
wa_th_range-sign          = rs_c_range_sign-including.
wa_th_range-compop        = rs_c_range_opt-equal.
wa_th_range-low           = wa_phsdrbse-/bic/zcnltgpc.
```

```
APPEND wa_th_range TO t_th_range.
CLEAR: wa_th_range .
ENDIF.
ENDLOOP.
```

Step 5: Call the function module.

```
* --- this variable will be set to TRUE when the last data  pack-
age is read
g_end_of_data = rs_c_false.
* --- this variable indicates whether this is an initial  call to
the reading module or a follow-up
*    call or  simply retrieves already selected data)
g_first_call   = rs_c_true.

WHILE g_end_of_data = rs_c_false.

  CALL FUNCTION 'RSDRI_INFOPROV_READ'
    EXPORTING
      i_infoprov                = 'ZDMG_C17'
      i_th_sfc                  = t_th_sfc
      i_th_sfk                  = t_th_sfk
      i_t_range                 = t_t_range
      i_reference_date          = sy-datum
      i_save_in_table           = rs_c_false
      i_save_in file            = rs_c_false
      i_packagesize             = 10
      i_authority_check         = rsdrc_c_authchk-read
    IMPORTING
      e_t_data                  = g_t_data
      e_end_of_data             = g_end_of_data
    CHANGING
      c_first_call              = g_first_call
    EXCEPTIONS
      illegal_input             = 1
      illegal_input_sfc         = 2
      illegal_input_sfk         = 3
      illegal_input_range       = 4
      illegal_input_tablesel    = 5
      no_authorization          = 6
      illegal_download          = 8
      illegal_tablename         = 9
      OTHERS                    = 11.
ENDWHILE.
```

12.4 EXTRACTING THE DATA FROM APO TO BW

Consider the following business scenario:

A company is using APO Demand Planning (DP) to create a forecast of market demand for its products. The company is using SAP R/3 as a transactional system and SAP BW for reporting.

To monitor the forecasting accuracy, the forecast should be tracked against the actual shipments. We can have such monitory reports in SAP BW. For such reports we would need to load the APO Demand Planning data to the SAP BW and then we can create a report to show the comparison of forecasts against the actual shipments.

Process to Create Data Source in APO

To load data to SAP BW, we need to create a data source in APO system.

Step 1: Login to APO system and open the SAP menu. Go to "Administration of Demand Planning and Supply" as shown below:

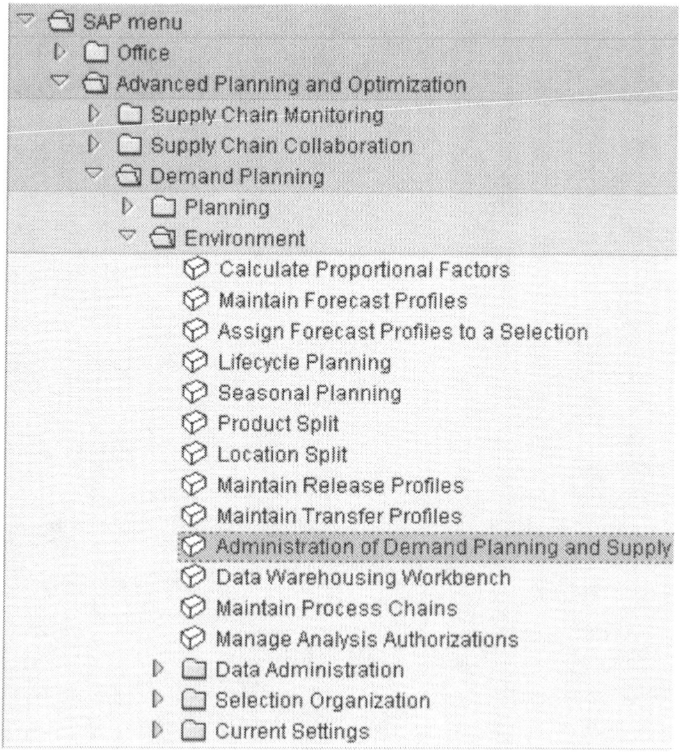

Figure 12.1 Menu path for administration of DP

Step 2: This will take to the S&DP Administration screen (Figure 12.2), it shows all the planning areas and the status of the planning areas is displayed by the lights (red or green) as shown below:

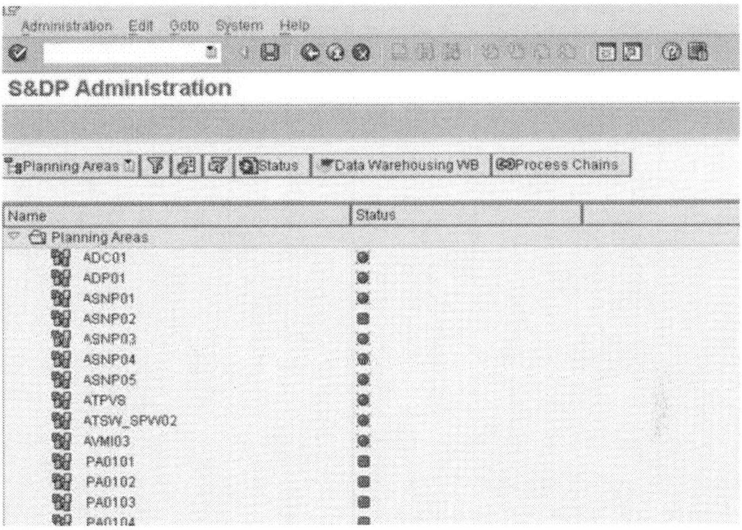

Figure 12.2 Planning area of DP

Here one will find the list of all the planning areas created in the system for Demand Planning. Double click on the Planning Area for which Data Source is to be created.

Step 3: After double clicking on a particular Planning Area, following screen will appear. Here go to

Extras -> Data Extraction Tools

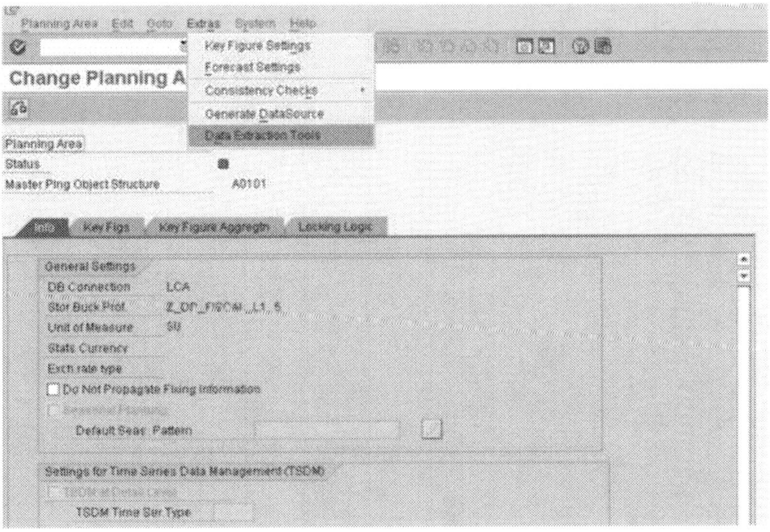

Figure 12.3 Call data extraction tool

Step 4: By selecting above option following screen will appear: The screen below (Figure 12.4) is having multiple options and multiple navigations like a transaction itself, it provides the options to the users to perform actions related to DataSources, Like Generation/Change/Repair etc.

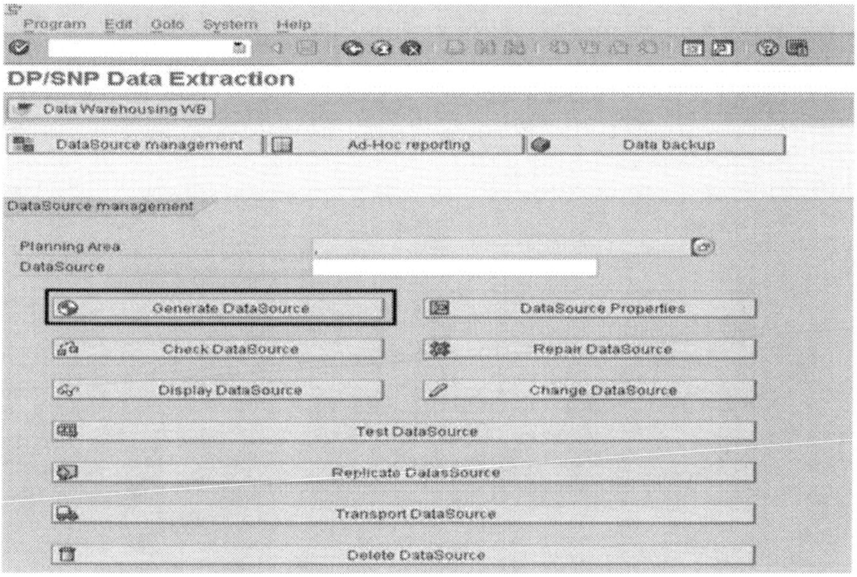

Figure 12.4 Generate DataSource

Here click on the Generate DataSource and then the system will ask for the Data-Source name and other settings.

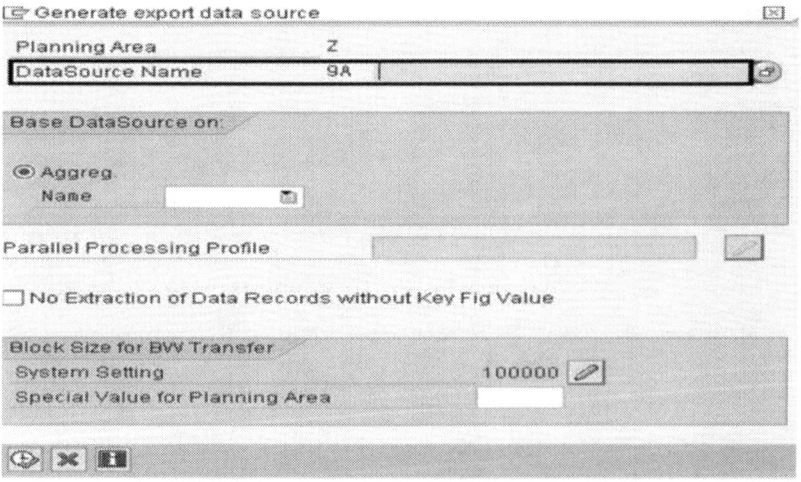

Figure 12.5 DataSource parameters

Note: The DataSource generated will by default have name starting with "9A". This is as per the SAP standard naming conventions. These naming conventions SAP is following to make the system standard. The various settings that we can do on this screen are:

"No Extraction of Data Records without Key Fig Values", this option user can choose from the screen showed below:

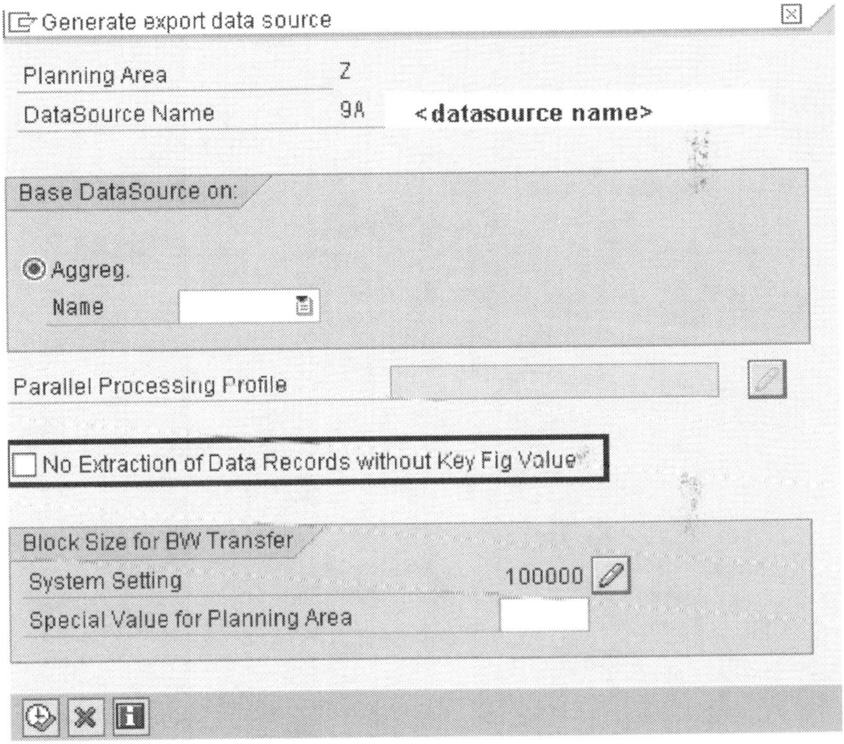

Figure 12.6 DataSource settings

Set this indicator to prevent the system from transferring data records to InfoObjects in the Business Information Warehouse if all key figures in the data record have the value zero. Depending on data this can drastically reduce the volume of information that the system transfers, applying the settings along with other techniques result improvement in the performance.

Package Size:

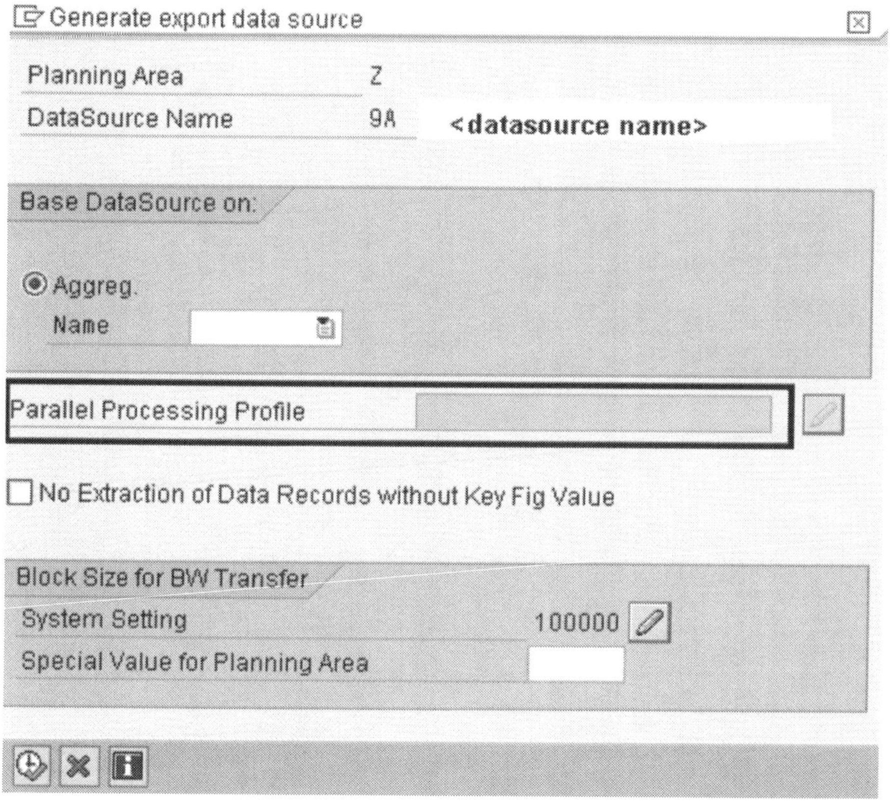

Figure 12.7 DataSource settings

In the lower box, specify how many data records are transferred in one package. When transferring large data volumes it is essential that the data is split into packages to avoid memory problems. When the source system has finished reading the data packages, it is transferred to BW and processed further. In this box it is possible to change the default for all data extraction in the system or just the value for the current planning area.

Parallel Processing Profile

Parallel processing we have discussed in other chapters also, hence not explaining the concept again here and just applying the setting.

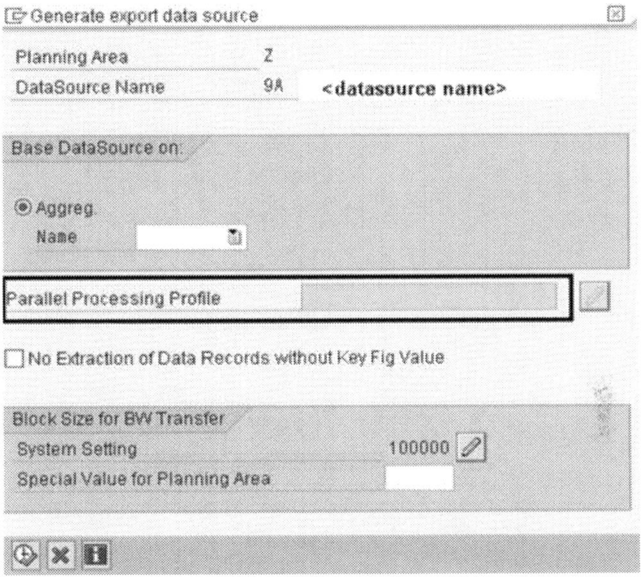

Figure 12.8 DataSource settings for parallel processing

Enter a parallel processing profile that has previously created in Customizing (*Demand Planning -> Profiles -> Maintain Parallel Processing Profile*). This determines how and if the reading and transfer of the packages is split into parallel processes. As such the block sizes that entered in the parallel processing profile should be significantly smaller than the package sizes above.

Step 5: With the following options we can test, transport or replicate the DataSource.

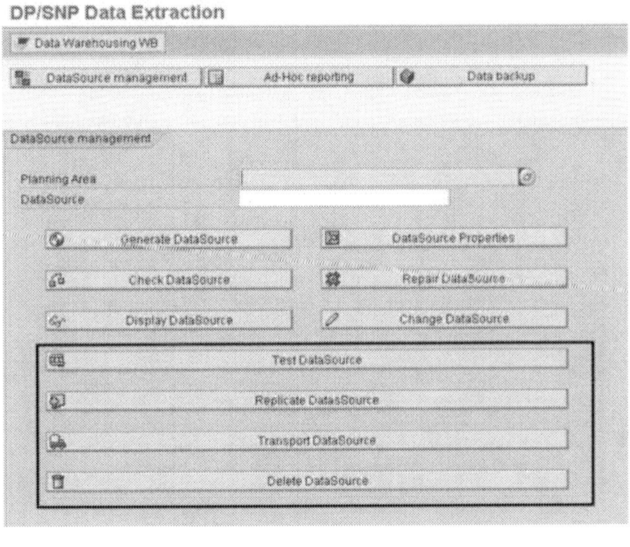

Figure 12.9 DataSource testing

12.5 EXTRACTING THE DATA FROM BW TO APO

Data Flow

Data flow diagram from BW to APO

The diagram below (Figure 12.10) shows the flow of data from BW to APO, it shown the basic architecture how data should flow and there are always exceptions in the the requirements exists and new design or customized design is always has scope to be implemented in the system.

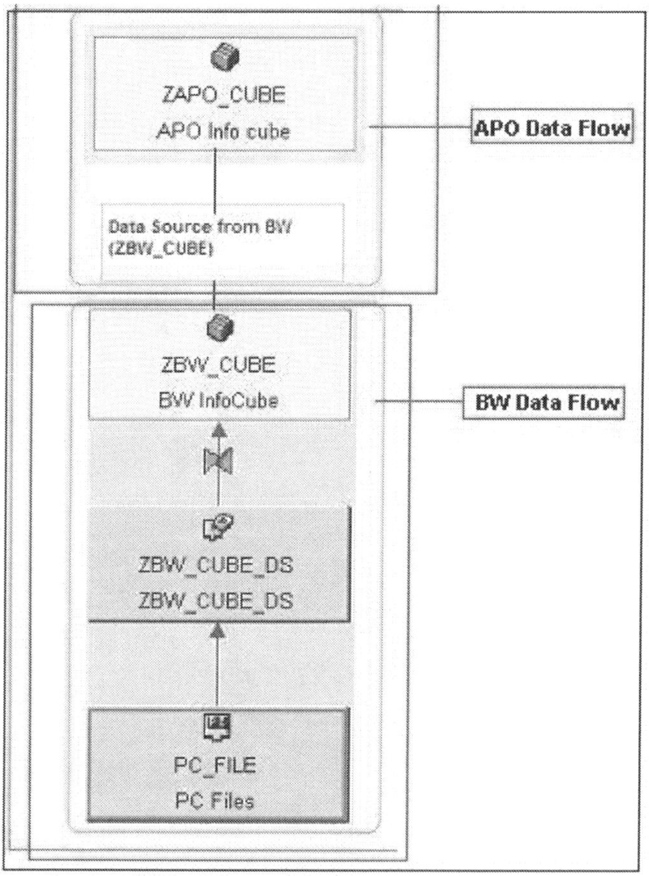

Figure 12.10 DataSource testing

Steps

Step 1: We need to replicate the DataSource from BW to APO.

Note: Before replicating the data source, we need to ***Generate Export data source*** on BW cube (to act as a Data source to APO).

Generating Export Data Source

Login to BW system with your login credentials.

Select the Data target --> Right click and select Generate Export Data source (as shown in Figure 12.11).

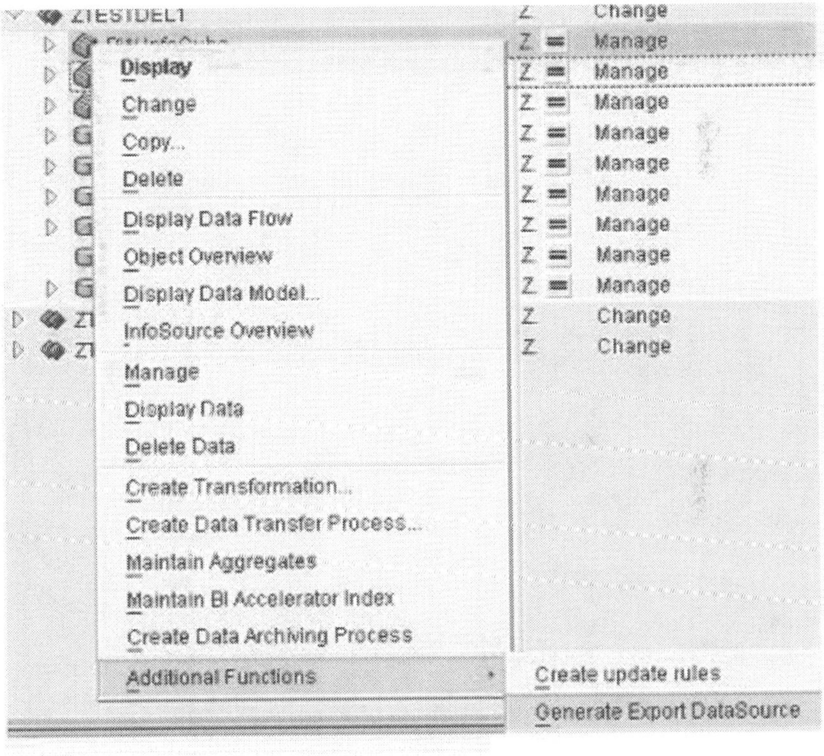

Figure 12.11 Generate export of DataSource

Check message in the task bar for the successful generation of DataSource (as it always shows the status of the action performed).

Step 2: Now Logon to *APO system* RSA1 -> Data source -> *BW Data sources* -> Business Ware house -> *Select Data Mart -> Right click and select Replicate Meta Data.*

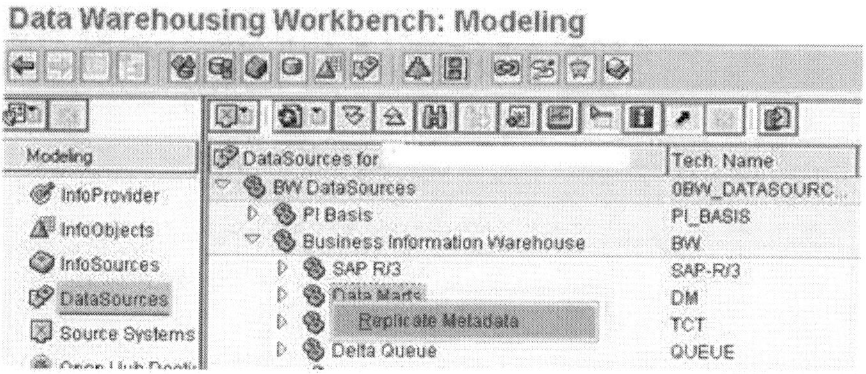

Figure 12.12 DataSource workbench

Check the new Pop-up message:

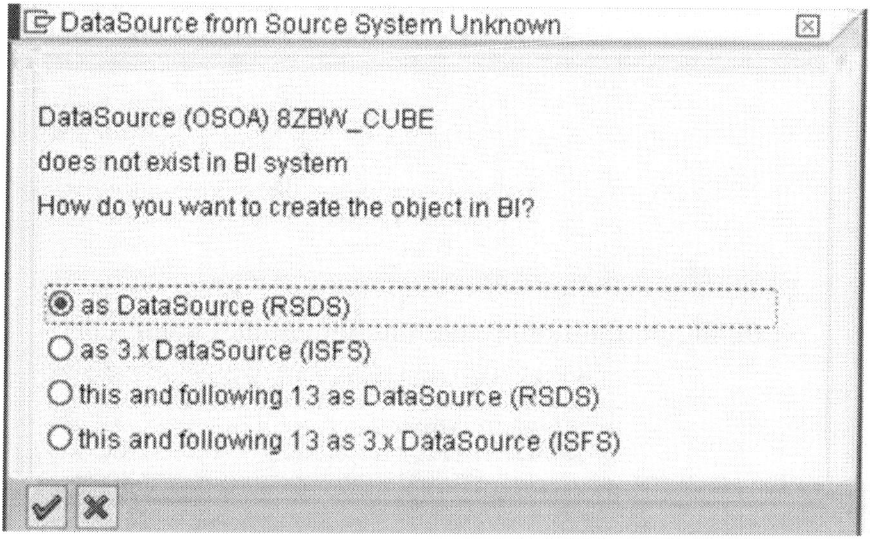

Figure 12.13 DataSource replication

Click on Continue, the data source will get replicated now, but it will be in Delivered (D) version initially, so need to *activate the data source.*

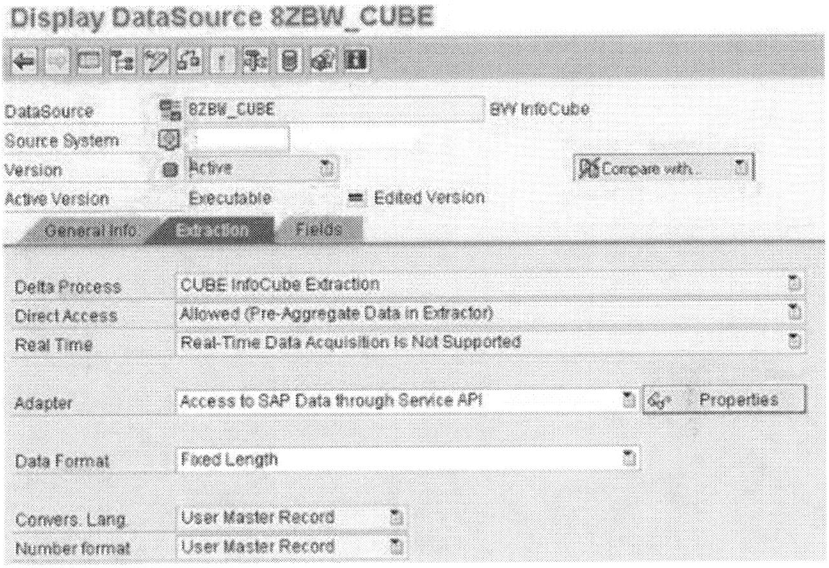

Figure 12.14 Activate DataSource

Step 3: Now data source has been replicated to APO, We need to Map this Data source to the existing APO cube ZAPO_CUBE.

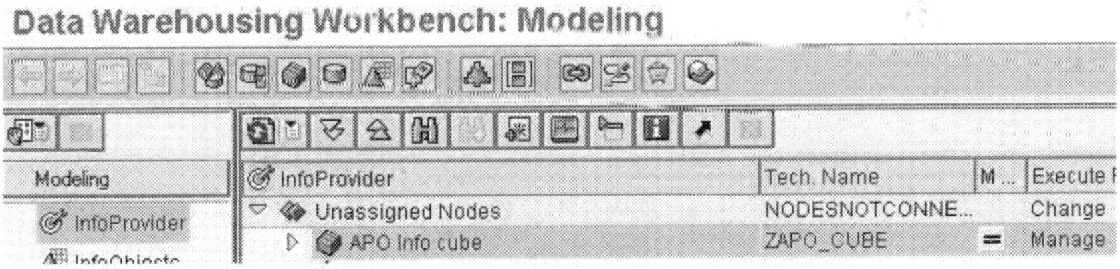

Figure 12.15 DataSource mapping

Create **Transformation, Data Transfer Process (D.T.P.), Info Package (IP)**

Figure 12.16 Data transfer process of DataSource

Execute *InfoPackage* (which will extract data from BW cube to till PSA), then execute *D.T.P* (which will extract the records from PSA to APO cube).

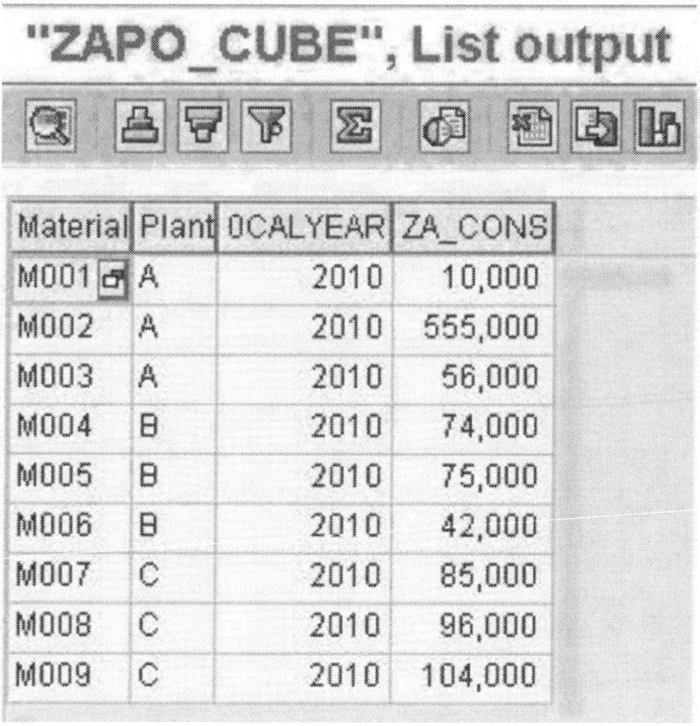
"ZAPO_CUBE", List output

Material	Plant	0CALYEAR	ZA_CONS
M001	A	2010	10,000
M002	A	2010	555,000
M003	A	2010	56,000
M004	B	2010	74,000
M005	B	2010	75,000
M006	B	2010	42,000
M007	C	2010	85,000
M008	C	2010	96,000
M009	C	2010	104,000

Figure 12.17 Data transferred in the InfoCube

Now we have enough discussed about DataSources, InfoCubes, etc. and how to move data between various systems. The more the readers explore the subject helps them to gain experience and knowledge of the subject.

Appendix

TRANSACTION CODES OF APO

/SAPAPO/AASP_PR_G_D	Set Standard Service Profile
/SAPAPO/AC03	Product Availability
/SAPAPO/AC04	ATP Simulation
/SAPAPO/AC05	Time Series
/SAPAPO/AC06	Temporary Quantity Assignments
/SAPAPO/AC07	Exclusive Lock Records
/SAPAPO/AC08	Generate Safety Stock Requirement
/SAPAPO/AC09	Execute ATP Check With Stored Data
/SAPAPO/AC10	Call Alert Monitor (ATP)
/SAPAPO/AC11	Call ATP Alert Monitor
/SAPAPO/AC12	Simulation Rounding in ATP
/SAPAPO/AC42	Display Product Allocation Situation
/SAPAPO/ACTTYPECUST	Maintain PPM Activity Types
/SAPAPO/ACTVERCREATE	Creation of Active Model/Version
/SAPAPO/ADVM	Macro Workbench
/SAPAPO/ADVR	Start Report
/SAPAPO/ADVRR	Evaluation results
/SAPAPO/AHC1	Action Handler Settings
/SAPAPO/AHTS1	Start-up of Action Handler
/SAPAPO/ALRT_CUST_PP	Maintain Alert Monitor Profile
/SAPAPO/AMOCFG	Alert Monitor Configuration
/SAPAPO/AMON0	Alert Monitor Grid for ITS
/SAPAPO/AMON1	Alert Monitor
/SAPAPO/AMON1_OLD	Alert Monitor (obsolete)
/SAPAPO/AMON2	Internal call for problem solution
/SAPAPO/AMON3	Alert Monitor-Alert Overview
/SAPAPO/AMONMSG	Settings 'Automatic Sending'
/SAPAPO/AMONMSG_SEND	Sending Alerts
/SAPAPO/AMON_AT_DESC	Descriptive Texts for Alert Types
/SAPAPO/AMON_REORG	Delete Database Alerts

/SAPAPO/AMON_SETTING	Alert Monitor Settings
/SAPAPO/AMON_SET_DC	Define Double-Click Event per AOT
/SAPAPO/AMO_BATCH	Alert Determination in Background
/SAPAPO/AP	APO VMI Maintenance
/SAPAPO/APNTYP_MAINT	Maintenance of APN Type
/SAPAPO/APO	
/SAPAPO/ATP2PPDS	ATP -> PP/DS Conv. in Background
/SAPAPO/ATPC	Maintain availability check
/SAPAPO/ATPC00	Global Settings
/SAPAPO/ATPC01	ATP Group
/SAPAPO/ATPC02	Business Event
/SAPAPO/ATPC03	Maintain Categories
/SAPAPO/ATPC04_05	Maintain ATP Check Control
/SAPAPO/ATPC06	Maintain Check Mode
/SAPAPO/ATPC07	Maintain Check Instructions
/SAPAPO/ATPC08	Maintain Requirements Profile
/SAPAPO/ATPC09	Maintain: ChkMode & Bus.Trans.Deter.
/SAPAPO/ATPC10	Maintain Correlation Profile
/SAPAPO/ATPCH01	Maintain ATP Characteristic View
/SAPAPO/ATPCLEAN01	Clean up PAR service structures
/SAPAPO/ATPCLEAN02	Cleanup old TQA
/SAPAPO/ATPCLEAN03	Remove old ATP trees
/SAPAPO/ATPCLOG_DEL	ATP: Delete C Log Files
/SAPAPO/ATPCQ	Maintain Product Allocations
/SAPAPO/ATPCQ_AREA	Maintain Plng Area Assignments
/SAPAPO/ATPCQ_CHECK	Check Prod. Allocations Customizing
/SAPAPO/ATPCQ_CUBE	Maintain InfoCube Assignment
/SAPAPO/ATPCQ_GENER	Generate Objects
/SAPAPO/ATPCQ_GRP	Maintain Product Allocation Group
/SAPAPO/ATPCQ_LST	Maintain Seq. of Prod. Alloc.Proced.
/SAPAPO/ATPCQ_MOD	Maintain Check Mode
/SAPAPO/ATPCQ_OBJ	Maintain Product Allocations Object
/SAPAPO/ATPCQ_PRO	Maintain Product Alloc. Procedure
/SAPAPO/ATPCQ_RESET	Reset Time Stamp
/SAPAPO/ATPCQ_TSTMP	APO: Generation Status, Transfer
/SAPAPO/ATPEX	Global ATP
/SAPAPO/ATPLOG	Activate ATP Application Log
/SAPAPO/ATPLOG_DEL	ATP: Delete Application Log
/SAPAPO/ATPLOG_DSP	ATP: Display Application Log
/SAPAPO/ATPQ_ALERT	APO: Product Allocations, Shortage
/SAPAPO/ATPQ_CHKCHAR	Check Characteristics Combinations
/SAPAPO/ATPQ_CHKCUST	Product Alloc. Assgmt, Sales Order

/SAPAPO/ATPQ_CHKUSG	Check Product Allocation Assignment
/SAPAPO/ATPQ_COLLECT	Generate Coll. Prod. Alloc. Charact.
/SAPAPO/ATPQ_KCGRP_U	Product Allocations: Update Assgmt
/SAPAPO/ATPQ_PAREA_C	Copy Characteristics Combinations
/SAPAPO/ATPQ_PAREA_K	Copy Characteristics Combination
/SAPAPO/ATPQ_PAREA_R	Product Allocations from Plan. Area
/SAPAPO/ATPQ_PAREA_W	Product Allocations in Plan. Area
/SAPAPO/ATPTUBE_DISP	Display Parameter Buffers
/SAPAPO/ATP_FC	Availability Check-Field Catalog
/SAPAPO/ATP_GCM	Condition Maintenance ATP
/SAPAPO/ATP_VC_GROUP	Condition Maintenance Group ATP
/SAPAPO/ATREE_DSP	ATP: Display ATP Tree Structures
/SAPAPO/ATYPES_SDP	Maintenance of Dynamic DP/SNP Alerts
/SAPAPO/ATYPES_VS	Maintenance of Cust.-Spcf. VS Alerts
/SAPAPO/A_ASS_SP	Autom. Ass. of Ant. Dem. Cov. Prof.
/SAPAPO/A_ASS_SP_BAD	Autom. Ass. of Ant. Dem. Cov. Prof.
/SAPAPO/BID1	Request processes
/SAPAPO/BLRG01	Generation of Reqmnts from Blocks
/SAPAPO/BOD001	Maintain BOD
/SAPAPO/BODMASS	Mass Assignment of BOD to future BOD
/SAPAPO/BOP	ATP: Batch Backorder Processing
/SAPAPO/BOPC_CATMODE	Mainten.: Check at Sched. Line Level
/SAPAPO/BOPC_ELSE	Parameters
/SAPAPO/BOPC_FILTER	Filter Type
/SAPAPO/BOPC_GENER	Filter Type, Generate Sort Profile
/SAPAPO/BOPC_ORDER	Special Sorting
/SAPAPO/BOPC_PARA	Parallelization
/SAPAPO/BOPC_SORT	Sort Profile
/SAPAPO/BOPI	Backorder Processing (Interactive)
/SAPAPO/BOPIN	Backorder Processing (Interactive)
/SAPAPO/BOP_COMPARE	Backorder Processing: Comparison
/SAPAPO/BOP_DELETE	Delete Backorder Processing
/SAPAPO/BOP_MONITOR	Monitor Backorder Processing
/SAPAPO/BOP_PARAINFO	Info BOP, Parallel Processing
/SAPAPO/BOP_PARAMNTR	Monitor BOP, Parallel Processing
/SAPAPO/BOP_PARASTAT	Parallelizing BOP, Statistics
/SAPAPO/BOP_RESULT	Backorder Processing Results
/SAPAPO/BOP_RUNTIME	Backorder Processing: Runtimes
/SAPAPO/BOP_UPDATE	Backorder Processing: Update
/SAPAPO/BOP_VARMAINT	Display and Delete PVAR Data
/SAPAPO/BOP_VARSPLIT	Variant Split Based Parallelization
/SAPAPO/BOP_VS	ATP: Backorder Processing for VS

/SAPAPO/BOP_WORKLIST	ATP, BOP: Worklist
/SAPAPO/BOUND	SNP: Optimization Limit Profile
/SAPAPO/BP1	Send Transaction Data
/SAPAPO/BP2	Delete Transaction Data
/SAPAPO/BP3	Send Master Data
/SAPAPO/C1	Create Business System Group
/SAPAPO/C2	Assign Logical System to BSG
/SAPAPO/C3	Display Application Log
/SAPAPO/C4	Maintenance of global parameters
/SAPAPO/C41	Activate/Deactivate Login
/SAPAPO/C5	Send Planning Results to OLTP
/SAPAPO/C6	Delete Application Log
/SAPAPO/C7	Find Entries
/SAPAPO/C91	Activate/Deactivate bgRFC for CIF
/SAPAPO/CALENDAR	Calendar
/SAPAPO/CAPREV_REL	Capacity reservation Release Report
/SAPAPO/CAPRIO	Priority Maintenance
/SAPAPO/CBCLPCONF	Remove Configuration from Orders
/SAPAPO/CBMM	Maintain Versions (Batches)
/SAPAPO/CC	Core Interface Cockpit
/SAPAPO/CCR	CIF_DELTAREPORT3
/SAPAPO/CCRR	CIF Compare/Reconcile Reorganization
/SAPAPO/CCR_PAR	Profile Maint. for Parallel Process.
/SAPAPO/CC_PERF_SAVE	Saving Performance Data
/SAPAPO/CDICHKCONF	CDI check service configuration
/SAPAPO/CDORDGDL	Transport Guideline Change Documents
/SAPAPO/CDPRTCAT	Partner Prod. Category Change Docs
/SAPAPO/CDPRTLOC	Change Docs Partner Location
/SAPAPO/CDPRTPROD	Partner Product Change Docs
/SAPAPO/CDPS0	DPS Variable View
/SAPAPO/CDPS0_HTML	Display DPS Variable View
/SAPAPO/CDPS1	DPS View 1
/SAPAPO/CDPS2	DPS View 2
/SAPAPO/CDPS3	DPS View 3
/SAPAPO/CDPSB0	Production Planning Run
/SAPAPO/CDPSB1	Prod. Planning Run in the Background
/SAPAPO/CDPSB2	Display Logs
/SAPAPO/CDPSB3	Delete Logs
/SAPAPO/CDPSC0	Customizing: Maint Overall Profile
/SAPAPO/CDPSC1	Customizing: Maint. Strategy Profile
/SAPAPO/CDPSC10	Customizing: Maint. of Setup Matrix
/SAPAPO/CDPSC11	Customizing: Heuristic Maintenance

/SAPAPO/CDPSC12	System Table for Background Sched.
/SAPAPO/CDPSC13	Customizing: Maintain Heuristic Pfle
/SAPAPO/CDPSC2	Customizing: Maint.Plan. Table Prof.
/SAPAPO/CDPSC3	Customizing: Maintain Work Area
/SAPAPO/CDPSC4	Customizing: Maintain Time Profile
/SAPAPO/CDPSC5	Customizing: Maintain Optimizr Prfl.
/SAPAPO/CDPSC6	Setup Group Maintenance
/SAPAPO/CDPSC7	Maintenance of Setup Matrices
/SAPAPO/CDPSC8	Cust.: Maint. of Propagation Range
/SAPAPO/CDPSC9	Customizing: Maint. of Setup Group
/SAPAPO/CDPSS0	Simulation Version
/SAPAPO/CDPSS0_HTML	Display Simulation Version
/SAPAPO/CDPS_CHARMAT	Maintain Char. Value Matrices
/SAPAPO/CDPS_GRPRULE	Rules for Setup Group Generation
/SAPAPO/CDPS_MATGEN	Generation of Setup Matrices
/SAPAPO/CDPS_MATRULE	Rules for Setup Matrix Generation
/SAPAPO/CDPS_NOTMAT	Display Flagged Setup Matrices
/SAPAPO/CDPS_REPT	Evaluations
/SAPAPO/CDPS_SETUP	List Output for Setup Matrix
/SAPAPO/CFMINCR	CIF Incremental Data Transfer
/SAPAPO/CFM_ANALYSIS	Schedulable Forecast Analysis Report
/SAPAPO/CFM_FC_REL	Schedulable forecast release report
/SAPAPO/CFM_POWL	CFM POWL
/SAPAPO/CFM_PROFILES	CFM Profiles Maintenance
/SAPAPO/CFM_PROF_MAI	CFM-Profile Maintenance
/SAPAPO/CFM_WFALL	Waterfall Analysis
/SAPAPO/CHECK_CUST	Check Country-Specific Settings
/SAPAPO/CIFPUCUST02	CIF External Procurement Orders
/SAPAPO/CL02CDP	Classes
/SAPAPO/CLP01	Create/Change Collaboration Partner
/SAPAPO/CLP02	Display Collaboration Partner
/SAPAPO/CLPBID	Col. Planning-RFQs
/SAPAPO/CLPBID1	CLP do not use: Outgoing RFQ
/SAPAPO/CLPBID2	CLP do not use: Incoming RFQ
/SAPAPO/CLPBIDCLEAR	CLP: Do not Use
/SAPAPO/CLPEPCAL	Coll. Promotion Planning (ITS)
/SAPAPO/CLPESDP	Collab. Supply/Demand Planning (ITS)
/SAPAPO/CLPETPL	Collaborative Transp. Planning (ITS)
/SAPAPO/CLPIPCAL	Collaborative Promotion Planning
/SAPAPO/CLPISDP	Collab. Supply and Demand Planning
/SAPAPO/CLPITPL	Collaborative Transport. Planning

/SAPAPO/CLPRPATPPUBL	CLP: Publish ATP Categories
/SAPAPO/CLPRPBPRF01	Create/Change RFQ Process Profile
/SAPAPO/CLPRPBPRF02	Display RFQ Process Profile
/SAPAPO/CLPRPCHECK	CLP RFQs Consistency Check
/SAPAPO/CLPRPDEL	CLP: Delete RFQs
/SAPAPO/CLPRPIN	Incoming RFQ Processes
/SAPAPO/CLPRPINCALL	Incoming RFQ Processes
/SAPAPO/CLPRPOUT	Outgoing RFQ Processes
/SAPAPO/CLPRPOUTCALL	Outgoing RFQ Processes
/SAPAPO/CLPRPSTART	CLP: Publish RFQs
/SAPAPO/CLPSDP_USER	User Settings for CLPSDP
/SAPAPO/CLP_PBPULL	Read Time Series
/SAPAPO/CLP_PBPUSH	Send Time Series
/SAPAPO/CLP_PBSEND	Send Time Series
/SAPAPO/CLP_SETTINGS	Collaboration Partners
/SAPAPO/CLX_DEX	CLX: Display Exchange Table
/SAPAPO/CMDS_CHKFEA	Feasibility Check
/SAPAPO/CMDS_CUST1	Maintenance of Control Profiles
/SAPAPO/CMDS_CUST11	Maint. of DelSched. Splitting Rule
/SAPAPO/CMDS_CUST12	Maint. of DelSched. Splitt. Profile
/SAPAPO/CMDS_CUST13	Assignment of DelSchd Splitting Rule
/SAPAPO/CMDS_CUST2	Maintenance of Confirmation Profiles
/SAPAPO/CMDS_CUST6	Maintenance of Tolerance Profiles
/SAPAPO/CMDS_CUST7	Maintain Conf. Profile Procurement
/SAPAPO/CMDS_CUST8	Procedures for Tolerance Check
/SAPAPO/CMDS_DEFCNF	Maintain Default Confirm. Profiles
/SAPAPO/CMDS_DEFCNTR	Maintain Default Control Profiles
/SAPAPO/CMDS_DEL	Delete Releases and Confirmations
/SAPAPO/CMDS_SCO1	Maintain Sales Scheduling Agreements
/SAPAPO/CMDS_SCO2	Delete Sales Scheduling Agreements
/SAPAPO/CMDS_SCO4	Manage Fiscal Year
/SAPAPO/CMDS_STPD	Define Sold-To Party Determination
/SAPAPO/CMDS_STPSR	Define Inbound Release Processing
/SAPAPO/CNDP	Cost Maintenance: Network Design
/SAPAPO/CODEPAR	maintenance of table /SAPAPO/CODEPAR
/SAPAPO/COMP_VARIANT	Comparison of Product Variants
/SAPAPO/CONFR_CFGREL	Convert Configuration Relevance
/SAPAPO/CONSCHK	Model Consistency Check
/SAPAPO/CONSPRF	Model Consistency Check: Profile
/SAPAPO/CONSSHOW	Read log from database
/SAPAPO/COPT00	RCCF Settings

/SAPAPO/COPT00_OLD	Opt. Global Customizing
/SAPAPO/COPT01	RCCF Settings
/SAPAPO/COPT01_OLD	Table Maintenance for /sapapo/optsvr
/SAPAPO/COPT10	RCCF Extra Parameter
/SAPAPO/COPT10_OLD	Maintain Special Parameter for Opt.
/SAPAPO/COPT11	Maintain Special Data for Optimizer
/SAPAPO/CP1	Maintenance of Distribution Criteria
/SAPAPO/CP2	Generation of Distribution Definitns
/SAPAPO/CP3	Runtime Information for Publishing
/SAPAPO/CPP	CIF Postprocessing
/SAPAPO/CPP1	CIF Postprocessing: Multiple Call
/SAPAPO/CPP2	Display CIF Postprocessing Records
/SAPAPO/CPPA	CIF Error Handling: Alert
/SAPAPO/CPPR	Reorg. CIF Postprocessing Records
/SAPAPO/CQ	SCM Queue Manager
/SAPAPO/CQ1	Check CIF Outbound Queues
/SAPAPO/CQ2	Check CIF Inbound Queues
/SAPAPO/CQINW	qRFC Monitoring for Inbound Queues
/SAPAPO/CSNP	Cost Maintenance: SNP
/SAPAPO/CSP1	Maintain consumption group
/SAPAPO/CSP2	CSP Reorganization
/SAPAPO/CSPRF	Maintain TSP Profile
/SAPAPO/CT	Compartment Type
/SAPAPO/CT04CDP	Characteristics
/SAPAPO/CTHU	Number Range Maintenance: /SAPAPO/CT
/SAPAPO/CTM	Capable-to-Match: Main Screen
/SAPAPO/CTM01	CTM: Consistency Check
/SAPAPO/CTM02	CTM: Stock Limits
/SAPAPO/CTM10	CTM: Distribute Receipt Objects
/SAPAPO/CTMAPLOG	CTM Logs
/SAPAPO/CTMB	Execute CTM in Background
/SAPAPO/CTMCRIT	Maintain supported sort criteria
/SAPAPO/CTMCTPR	Order Category Priorities
/SAPAPO/CTMCUST	CTM: Global Customizing
/SAPAPO/CTMEXPL	Explanation Profile for CTM
/SAPAPO/CTMMSEL	Selection of CTM Master Data
/SAPAPO/CTMORDSEL	CTM: Maintain Order Selection
/SAPAPO/CTMPAR	CTM: Parallel Processing Profiles
/SAPAPO/CTMPARCOMP	CTM: Determine Submodels
/SAPAPO/CTMPARPROC	CTM: Available Process Resources
/SAPAPO/CTMSCPR	Profile Maint. Supply Categorization

/SAPAPO/CTMSSTRAT	Define CTM Search Strategy
/SAPAPO/CTMTEST	Create CTM Test Data
/SAPAPO/CTMTP	Transport CTM Profile
/SAPAPO/CTMTSTR	Define CTM Time Stream
/SAPAPO/CTMVIEWER	CTM: Call Viewer
/SAPAPO/CTRP	Cost Maintenance - Vehicle Sched.
/SAPAPO/CTSW00	TSW Control Global Customizing
/SAPAPO/CTSW_NOMTK	
/SAPAPO/CTVEH	Mapping Table for Veh./Compart. Type
/SAPAPO/CTVTY	Transportation mode maintenance
/SAPAPO/CUCDP_REFMAP	Map Reference Characteristics
/SAPAPO/CULL_RTO_DEL	Delete Production Data Structure
/SAPAPO/CURTO_GEN_DP	Generate DP PDS
/SAPAPO/CURTO_SIMU	Display Production Data Structures
/SAPAPO/CUTABLEINFO	Configuration Storage
/SAPAPO/CW	qRFC Monitoring
/SAPAPO/DBOR_REORG	Delete Order Headers Without Items
/SAPAPO/DCHAR_PRIO	Descriptive Chars: Prioritization
/SAPAPO/DC_DM	Data Maint. Demand Combination
/SAPAPO/DC_REORG	Reorganization Results Table
/SAPAPO/DEPLCUST	SPP Deployment Customizing
/SAPAPO/DEPLODL	Deployment: Order Due List
/SAPAPO/DEPLSPRF	SPP Deployment: Service Profil
/SAPAPO/DEPL_HAZ	Ex. M. of T. Exp- Ship. of Dang. Gds
/SAPAPO/DEPL_IND_DEF	Maintain Deployment Indicator Rules
/SAPAPO/DFCT	Maintain Distribution Function
/SAPAPO/DISPLAY_CONF	Display of DelSched and Confirmation
/SAPAPO/DMP1	Display Consumption Situation
/SAPAPO/DMP2	Generate Planned Independent Reqmts
/SAPAPO/DMST	Requirements Strategy Maintenance
/SAPAPO/DM_PEGCHECK	Consistency Check Pegging Areas
/SAPAPO/DP00	DP00
/SAPAPO/DPC1	Maintain Planning Profile
/SAPAPO/DPC3	Change Overview
/SAPAPO/DPC4	Create Planning Table (Structure)
/SAPAPO/DPC5	Maintain Planning Table (Structure)
/SAPAPO/DPC6	Display Planning Table (Structure)
/SAPAPO/DPC7	Maintain Planning Table (Content)
/SAPAPO/DPLSPLIT	Deployment Stk Transfer Prioritizatn
/SAPAPO/DPL_OPTPR_CU	SNP Optimizer Maintenance
/SAPAPO/DRPAPPRSET	Release Rule Settings
/SAPAPO/DRPCONF	Repl Service Profile Configuration

/SAPAPO/DRPC_EP	Profile: DRP Approval Maximum Values
/SAPAPO/DRPDELPRFL	Repl Deletion Service Profile Config
/SAPAPO/DRPEOALIM	User Limits for Management Approval
/SAPAPO/DRPNO	Number Ranges: Plan. Replen. Orders
/SAPAPO/DRPSSP	VMI DRP safety stock planning
/SAPAPO/DRP_APPRRLS	Maintenance of DRP Release Rules
/SAPAPO/EDQA	EDQA Processes
/SAPAPO/EDQA_DEL	Delete EDQA Process Data
/SAPAPO/EDQA_EC	Display EDQA Event Linkage
/SAPAPO/EDQA_ED	Process-Dependent Results Determin.
/SAPAPO/EDQA_HI	Stock History for Process Category
/SAPAPO/EDQA_OS	EDQA: Overview and Simulation
/SAPAPO/EDQA_PD	Maint. EDQA Process Type Customizing
/SAPAPO/FATT	Activation of Additional Attributes
/SAPAPO/FCSTOUTL	Outlier Correction Settings
/SAPAPO/GATP	Global ATP
/SAPAPO/GATPC	ATP Settings
/SAPAPO/GENART	Display Generic Product
/SAPAPO/GEN_CHK_PDS	Generate iPPE Check PDS
/SAPAPO/GEN_PDS	Generation of iPPE PDS
/SAPAPO/GRPVAL_MAINT	Values Product Groups
/SAPAPO/HEUR1	Execute Heuristic
/SAPAPO/HEUR2	Define Planning Package
/SAPAPO/ICH_PROMTEST	Test Run for Promotion
/SAPAPO/ICTOPA	Generate Planning Area from IC
/SAPAPO/INBND_STATUS	Inb. Delivery Monitor: Tech. Status
/SAPAPO/INCMD_MODEL	Model Assignment
/SAPAPO/IPM01	integrated profile management
/SAPAPO/LCDEL	Deletion of Orders in LiveCache
/SAPAPO/LCIN	Release External Data to LiveCache
/SAPAPO/LCOUT	Release from SNP -> DP
/SAPAPO/LOC3	Master Data: Locations
/SAPAPO/LOCALI	Location Alias
/SAPAPO/LOCPRF_DEF	Define Fixed Costs Profile for Loc.
/SAPAPO/LOCTZCALC	Calculate Transp. Zone Coordinates
/SAPAPO/LOC_CD_READ	Change Documents for Location
/SAPAPO/LOC_DEL_LOG	Location: Delete Application Log
/SAPAPO/LOC_DISP_LOG	Location: Display Application Log
/SAPAPO/LOGMANAGE	Transaction for TS_RLG_CPY_LOG_M..
/SAPAPO/LO_CDC_LOC	Curr. Change Doc. Location
/SAPAPO/LTTYPE	Maintain Location Resources
/SAPAPO/LTTYPE_C	Maintain Location Resources

/SAPAPO/LTTYPE_D	Maintain Location Resources
/SAPAPO/MAABCD	Maintain ABC Indicators
/SAPAPO/MAP_TSER	Map Time Series to Planning Area
/SAPAPO/MASSGEOCODE	Location: Mass-Geocoding
/SAPAPO/MAT1	Product
/SAPAPO/MAT2	Maintain Penalty Costs for Products
/SAPAPO/MAT3	Maintain Penalty Costs Loc. Product
/SAPAPO/MATLREF1	Maintain Values for Inheritance
/SAPAPO/MAT_CDC_PROD	Current Change Document: Product
/SAPAPO/MAT_CI_GEN	Generation of Maintenance for CIs
/SAPAPO/MAXSTORAGE	Generate Storage Capacity Alerts
/SAPAPO/MC01_BBD	Block Basis Definitions
/SAPAPO/MC01_CLCH_RM	Remove Char. from Class (CDP)
/SAPAPO/MC62	Maintain Characteristic Values
/SAPAPO/MC77	Change Selection
/SAPAPO/MC7A	Location Split
/SAPAPO/MC7B	Product Split
/SAPAPO/MC8D	Mass Processing: Create Planning
/SAPAPO/MC8E	Mass Processing: Change Planning
/SAPAPO/MC8F	Delete Planning Job
/SAPAPO/MC8G	Schedule Mass Processing
/SAPAPO/MC8I	Mass Processing: Check Planning
/SAPAPO/MC8J	Copy Mass Processing Jobs
/SAPAPO/MC8K	Logs
/SAPAPO/MC8S	Transfer Profiles
/SAPAPO/MC8T	Activity
/SAPAPO/MC8U	Transfer Profile
/SAPAPO/MC8V	Calculate Proportional Factors
/SAPAPO/MC90	Release to Supply Network Planning
/SAPAPO/MC96B	Maintain Forecast Profile
/SAPAPO/MCPGUIDEL	Delete all GUID Profiles
/SAPAPO/MCPSELDEL	Delete selections
/SAPAPO/MC_VRSIO2	Compare Forecast Versions
/SAPAPO/MD74	Reorganization: Adapt Indep.Reqmts
/SAPAPO/MDP6	Modeling
/SAPAPO/MMLS	Versions for Header Products
/SAPAPO/MNTPROF01	Maintain Display Profile
/SAPAPO/MODEL	Maintain Model
/SAPAPO/MOIGRC	Create MOI Groups
/SAPAPO/MP31	Maintain Promotion Attribute Types
/SAPAPO/MP32	Maintain Cannibalization Group
/SAPAPO/MP33	Maintain Promotion Key Figures

/SAPAPO/MP34	Supply & Demand Planner: Init.Screen
/SAPAPO/MP39	Promotion Reporting
/SAPAPO/MP40	Maintain Promotion Bases
/SAPAPO/MP41	Promotion Reporting
/SAPAPO/MP41A	Maintain Settings for Report
/SAPAPO/MP41B	Promotion Reports
/SAPAPO/MP42	Promotion Management
/SAPAPO/MP43	Delete Promotion
/SAPAPO/MP44	Show Overlaps
/SAPAPO/MP45	Promotion Log Management
/SAPAPO/MP46	Activate Promotions
/SAPAPO/MP47	Update for consistencies
/SAPAPO/MP48	Change Promotions
/SAPAPO/MP49	Promotionen kopieren
/SAPAPO/MP_CBPF	Maintain Cannibalization Profile
/SAPAPO/MRPACUST01	Customizing for MRP Areas
/SAPAPO/MSDP_ADMIN	SNP and DP Administration
/SAPAPO/MSDP_BAPI1	External Start Promotion Update
/SAPAPO/MSDP_FCST1	Lifecycle Settings
/SAPAPO/MSDP_FCST2	Assign Forecast Profiles
/SAPAPO/MSDP_SB	Safety Stock Calculation
/SAPAPO/MSGTSTP_TR	/SAPAPO/MSGTSTP_ID Mapping
/SAPAPO/MSP01	Maint. and Service Planning Board
/SAPAPO/MSP_CUST	MSP Customization (Prerequisite)
/SAPAPO/MSP_CYCMAINT	Cycle Maintenance
/SAPAPO/MSP_DNO	Number range maintenance: /SAPAPO/DM
/SAPAPO/MSP_ESIM	MSP Easy Simulation
/SAPAPO/MSP_MCNO	Number Range Maint.: Maint. Cycles
/SAPAPO/MSP_MITN	Number Range Maint.: Maint. Items
/SAPAPO/MSP_MNO	Number range maintenance: /SAPAPO/MO
/SAPAPO/MSP_MOBJ	Maintenance of one Maint. Object
/SAPAPO/MSP_PERFPROF	Maintenance of Performance Profile
/SAPAPO/MSP_SNO	Number range maintenance: /SAPAPO/SL
/SAPAPO/MTI	Maintainance of TPSRC for ICH
/SAPAPO/MTI2	Ext. Proc. Relationship (SAP SNC)
/SAPAPO/MTL01	Maintenance Task List
/SAPAPO/MTRCOMB	Means-of-Transport Combination
/SAPAPO/MVM	Model/Planning version
/SAPAPO/MVSEL	Selection of Material Versions
/SAPAPO/ND	Network Design: Main Screen
/SAPAPO/NDFCTYP	Create Fixed Cost Elements for Loc.

/SAPAPO/ND_DEMAND	Maintain Demand in ND (Tabular Form)
/SAPAPO/ND_MSG_SCR	Log File Display ND
/SAPAPO/ND_RESULT	Network Design Results Display
/SAPAPO/ND_RUN	Planning Run Network Design
/SAPAPO/OCURTOGEN	Customizing for PDS Generation
/SAPAPO/ODL	Display Order Due Lists
/SAPAPO/ODLC	Create Order Due Lists
/SAPAPO/ODLR	Reorganize ODL
/SAPAPO/ODL_LOG	ODL: Display Change Log
/SAPAPO/OM00	Overview of LCA Transactions
/SAPAPO/OM01	Display LCA Trace File
/SAPAPO/OM02	Tracing LCA Object
/SAPAPO/OM03	Test Program for LiveCache and LCA
/SAPAPO/OM03A	Test Program for LiveCache and LCA
/SAPAPO/OM04	Display of Current LCA Version
/SAPAPO/OM10	Display Meaning of Return Code
/SAPAPO/OM11	LiveCache Application Log
/SAPAPO/OM13	Analyze LiveCache and LCA Builds
/SAPAPO/OM14	Test Cockpit
/SAPAPO/OM15	Evaluation of Performance Verifier
/SAPAPO/OM16	Data Viewer
/SAPAPO/OM17	Data Reconciliation
/SAPAPO/OM18	LiveCache Inspector
/SAPAPO/OM19	LiveCache Browser
/SAPAPO/OM20	Profiling
/SAPAPO/OM21	Read Log for OM Modules
/SAPAPO/OM22	Set Log for OM Modules
/SAPAPO/OM24	Memory Consumption in LiveCache
/SAPAPO/OM25	Daily Reorganization of APO
/SAPAPO/OM26	Statistics for Persistent Data
/SAPAPO/OMSL	Output Format for Products
/SAPAPO/OMSL2	Output Format for Products
/SAPAPO/OMTS_BROWSE	SAPTS Data Browser
/SAPAPO/OMTS_DPLOG	DP Test Framework Log
/SAPAPO/OMTS_DPTF	DP Test Framework
/SAPAPO/OO_PPM_CONV	Maint. Mode Comb. for PPM Conversion
/SAPAPO/OPRESULT	SNP Optimizer: Display Results
/SAPAPO/OPT00	PP/DS Optimizer
/SAPAPO/OPT01	Session Display of Engines in RCCF
/SAPAPO/OPT01_OLD	DPS Optimizer User Display
/SAPAPO/OPT03	Session Display of Engines in RCCF

/SAPAPO/OPT03_OLD	Optimizer User Display
/SAPAPO/OPT09	Version Display of External Engines
/SAPAPO/OPT09_OLD	Optimization Version Display
/SAPAPO/OPT10	Optimization Internal Settings
/SAPAPO/OPT11	Main Log Display in RCCF
/SAPAPO/OPT11_OLD	Log Display
/SAPAPO/OPT12	Session Display of Engines in RCCF
/SAPAPO/OPT12_OLD	Opt. Server Process Overview
/SAPAPO/OPTB1	PP/DS optimizer background run
/SAPAPO/OPTDBG0	Optimization of Debug Indicators
/SAPAPO/OPTDBG1	Optimization of Debug Indicators
/SAPAPO/OPTEXPLAIN	Explanation of Optimization Events
/SAPAPO/OPT_DPL	DPL Optimizer GUI: Initial Screen
/SAPAPO/OPT_EXP	PP/DS Explanation Log
/SAPAPO/OPT_INST	RCCF Settings
/SAPAPO/OPT_INST_OLD	Optimizer Installation Test
/SAPAPO/OPT_PRIOPROF	SNP Opt.: Priority Profile
/SAPAPO/OPT_SEQ	SEQ Optimizer GUI: Initial Screen
/SAPAPO/OPT_SNP	SNP Optimizer GUI Initial Screen
/SAPAPO/OPT_STOP	Session Display of Engines in RCCF
/SAPAPO/OPT_STOP_OLD	Terminate Optimization Runs
/SAPAPO/OPT_VSR	VSR-Optimizer GUI: Initial Screen
/SAPAPO/ORSP	Customizing for Reservation Planning
/SAPAPO/PBDVWTBT	Maintain Toolbar Texts
/SAPAPO/PBKEYFUN	Functions for PlArea, PlOb, KeyFig
/SAPAPO/PBMLKEYT	Assign User-Def. Texts to Key Fig.
/SAPAPO/PBSTDOBJ	Maintain Standard Functions
/SAPAPO/PCMP	Customizing: PCM Profile Maintenance
/SAPAPO/PCMT	Production Campaign
/SAPAPO/PCM_DELETE	Deletion Report for Empty Campaigns
/SAPAPO/PDEMCUST	General Settings for Demand History
/SAPAPO/PDEM_RLGSTEP	Maintain Data Realignment Steps
/SAPAPO/PDEM_RLG_INI	Check Realignment Profile
/SAPAPO/PDEM_SRV_V	Maint. Service Profile for Realign.
/SAPAPO/PDRP_GLB_DFT	Set DRP Standard Service Profile
/SAPAPO/PDSLOG	PDS Generation Logs
/SAPAPO/PEG1	Pegging Overview
/SAPAPO/PERFMON	APO Application Monitor
/SAPAPO/PE_CFG	Define Planning Profile
/SAPAPO/PE_CFG2	Define Storage Service Profile
/SAPAPO/PE_CFG3	Define Process Profile

/SAPAPO/PE_CFG4	Vers.-Dep. Std.-Service Profile
/SAPAPO/PE_LOG_DISP	Display PSM Application Log
/SAPAPO/PE_PERF_LOG	Display PSM Performance Log
/SAPAPO/PE_RUN	Execute Planning Service Manager
/SAPAPO/PE_SEL	Define Selections
/SAPAPO/PE_SEL_RR	Define Selections (RR)
/SAPAPO/PE_SEL_SPP	Define Selections (SPP)
/SAPAPO/PE_SLG1	Display PSM Application Logs
/SAPAPO/PE_SRV_CFG	Planning Service Manager Config.
/SAPAPO/PFCS_SEM	Semantic Maintenance for LI
/SAPAPO/PFL2	Product Flow Logic
/SAPAPO/PFRCUSTGEN	PFR Scenario Customizing Generator
/SAPAPO/PHASESRV	PSM Service Prof. Phase In/Out Fcst
/SAPAPO/PHINGR	Maintain Phase-In Group
/SAPAPO/PHOUTGR	Maintain Phase-Out Group
/SAPAPO/PINV_DT_MAIN	Inventory Planning: Decision Tables
/SAPAPO/PINV_EX_MAIN	Maintain Location Exclusion Table
/SAPAPO/PINV_FMAP	Fcst Strat. Inv. Pl. Pr. Type Assign
/SAPAPO/PINV_MS_MAIN	EOQ/SFT Model Determination Rules
/SAPAPO/PINV_TL_MAIN	Maintain Target Safety Stock Values
/SAPAPO/PLANNER	Maintain Planner
/SAPAPO/PLN_GRP	Assignment Analyst to Supp. + PrGrp.
/SAPAPO/PMON	Plan Monitor
/SAPAPO/PMONDEF	Definition: Key figure schema
/SAPAPO/POM1	Planned Order Management
/SAPAPO/POV1	Product Overview Transaction
/SAPAPO/PPC1	Confirmation Entry
/SAPAPO/PPC2	Display Confirmation
/SAPAPO/PPCCU1	Maintain Confirmation Settings
/SAPAPO/PPCCU2	Maintain Confirmation Settings
/SAPAPO/PPCCU3	Maintain Confirmation Settings
/SAPAPO/PPDS00	Product Planning/Detailed Scheduling
/SAPAPO/PPE	iPPE Workbench Professional
/SAPAPO/PPELUI	iPPE Workbench Express
/SAPAPO/PPFSCO	Output of Confirmations
/SAPAPO/PPL1	Production List
/SAPAPO/PPM_CONV	Conversion of PP/DS PPMs to SNP PPMs
/SAPAPO/PPM_CONV_310	Report for Generating SNP PPMs
/SAPAPO/PPM_CONV_LOG	Log of SNP-PPM generation
/SAPAPO/PPM_DEL	Mass Deletion of Plans and PPMs
/SAPAPO/PPS0	Production Planning/Detailed Sched.

/SAPAPO/PPT1	Product Planning Table
/SAPAPO/PRJ1	Select Project Orders
/SAPAPO/PROD2BODDISP	Display Assignment-> Products to BOD
/SAPAPO/PROD2BOD_M	Assign and Unassign Product to BOD
/SAPAPO/PROD2RGPDISP	Display Assignment-> Products to RGP
/SAPAPO/PROD2RGP_M	Assign and Unassign Product to Regpt
/SAPAPO/PROD_CD_READ	Change Documents for Product
/SAPAPO/PROD_DISP	Display Products Assigned to a BOD
/SAPAPO/PROMMR	Promotion Parameters
/SAPAPO/PROM_EVENT	Maintain Promotion Event Type
/SAPAPO/PROM_OFFSET	Maintain Promotion Offset Profile
/SAPAPO/PROM_PATT	Promotion Pattern
/SAPAPO/PROM_PROF	Maintain Promotion Profile
/SAPAPO/PRT_LOCATION	Maintain Partner-Dep. Location Data
/SAPAPO/PRT_LOCPROD	Maintain Partner-Dep. Location Prod
/SAPAPO/PRT_PRODUCT	Maintain Partner-Dep. Product Data
/SAPAPO/PRT_PURGROUP	Maintain Partner-Dep. Purch. Group
/SAPAPO/PSTRUCONS	Plng Obj. Struct. Consistency Check
/SAPAPO/PUSH	Transaction for Push Production
/SAPAPO/PVB	Display Production Supply Area
/SAPAPO/PWBSCH1	Create SA Release(s)
/SAPAPO/PWBSCH2	Release Output
/SAPAPO/PWBSCH3	Process Sched. Agreement Releases
/SAPAPO/PWBSCH4	Enter Confirmation
/SAPAPO/PWBSRC1	Maintain Ext. Proc. Relationships
/SAPAPO/PWBSRC2	Delete External Proc. Relationships
/SAPAPO/PWB_CM1	Define Release Creation Profile(s)
/SAPAPO/QTA1	Quota Arrangements
/SAPAPO/QTA2	Quota Arrangements
/SAPAPO/QUAN	Maintenance for Qty-Based Penalty
/SAPAPO/RBA04	Integrated Rule Maintenance
/SAPAPO/RBAC01	Maintain Rule Strategy Determination
/SAPAPO/RBAC02	Define Rule Strategy Sequence
/SAPAPO/RBAC20_O	Field Mapping for /SAPAPO/KOMGO
/SAPAPO/RBAC20_U	Field Mapping for /SAPAPO/KOMGU
/SAPAPO/RDPLCUST	Inventory Balancing Customizing
/SAPAPO/RDPLPRF	Inventory Balancing Parameter Prof.
/SAPAPO/RDPLPRFA	Inventory Planning Profile-Area
/SAPAPO/RDPLSPRF	Inventory Planning Service Profile
/SAPAPO/RDPLWSSPRF	Inventory Balancing WSS Profile
/SAPAPO/RDPLWSTPLIMP	Import WSS Storage Type per Location
/SAPAPO/RDPLWSTYPE	Inventory Balancing WSS Storage Type

/SAPAPO/RDPLWSTYPLOC	Inv. Balanc. WSS Storage Type/Loc.
/SAPAPO/RELHDELETE	Delete Hierarchy
/SAPAPO/RELHSHOW	Hierarchy Maintenance
/SAPAPO/REL_TO_OLTP	Direct Release InfoProvider to ERP
/SAPAPO/REL_TO_SNP	Direct Release InfoProvider to SNP
/SAPAPO/REORG_WUL	Reorg. of Where-Used-Lists in LC
/SAPAPO/REO_MATLOCTD	Reorganization of MATLOCTD
/SAPAPO/REPDUE_STAT	Overdue Schedue Lines Status
/SAPAPO/REPLCTRL	Maintain VMI forecast control data
/SAPAPO/RES00	Resources
/SAPAPO/RES01	Change Resources
/SAPAPO/RESC01	Capacity Variants
/SAPAPO/RESC02	Grouping by Resource Type
/SAPAPO/RESNET	Resource Network
/SAPAPO/REST01	Call Up Tools for Resource
/SAPAPO/REST02	LC Resources
/SAPAPO/RET1	Restriction Maintenance - Display
/SAPAPO/RET2	Restrictions Maint.- Create & Change
/SAPAPO/RET_CHECK	Check Restrictions Used
/SAPAPO/RET_CLEAN_DB	Clean Up Restriction Database
/SAPAPO/RET_CU01	Object Characteristic for Restrictns
/SAPAPO/RET_EVAL	Restriction Evaluation
/SAPAPO/RET_REFRESH	Refresh all Restriction DB Tables
/SAPAPO/RET_RP	Restrictions & Reservation Planning
/SAPAPO/RET_VIEW	DB tables joint in view in ret
/SAPAPO/RFCDEST	Maintain RFC Destinations
/SAPAPO/RGPAT01	Maintain Regional Pattern
/SAPAPO/RLCDEL	Delete Orders from Livecache
/SAPAPO/RLGCOPY	Realignment
/SAPAPO/RLGSTEP_IDS	Number range maintenance: /SAPAPO/RG
/SAPAPO/RNWDEL	Resource network delete
/SAPAPO/ROUNDINGPROF	Rounding Profile
/SAPAPO/ROUNDPRF	Maintain Rounding Profiles
/SAPAPO/RPT	Resource Planning Table
/SAPAPO/RP_ACC_SEQ	Maintenance RP Access Sequence
/SAPAPO/RP_COND_TYPE	Maintenance RP Condition Types
/SAPAPO/RP_CT	Maintenance RP Condition Tables
/SAPAPO/RP_DET_PROC	Maintenance Determination Procedure
/SAPAPO/RRP1	Requirements View
/SAPAPO/RRP2	Process Order
/SAPAPO/RRP3	Product View
/SAPAPO/RRP4	Receipts view

/SAPAPO/RRP5	Create Order
/SAPAPO/RRP7	Mass Conversion of Orders
/SAPAPO/RRP8	ATP Check for REM Planned Orders
/SAPAPO/RRPC1	Number Range Maintenance: /SAPAPO/PP
/SAPAPO/RRPC2	Number Range Maintenance: /SAPAPO/PK
/SAPAPO/RRPCUST1	Global Customizing PP
/SAPAPO/RRPCUST2	Maintain Planning Package Types
/SAPAPO/RRPC_GENER	Generate Sort Profile for PP/DS
/SAPAPO/RRPDEBUG	Recording PP/DS Planning Tasks
/SAPAPO/RRPEVAL	Log for Last Planning Run
/SAPAPO/RRPLOG1	Display Logs
/SAPAPO/RRPLOG2	Delete Logs
/SAPAPO/RRP_ATP2PPDS	ATP Tree Structure Conversion
/SAPAPO/RRP_CONF_QTY	Convert Pegging-Relevant Quantity
/SAPAPO/RRP_CVTYP	Maintain Days' Supply Types
/SAPAPO/RRP_NETCH	Planning File Entries
/SAPAPO/RRP_SET_RRPT	Change Planning Procedure f. Product
/SAPAPO/RRP_SNP2PPDS	Conversion SNP -> PP/DS
/SAPAPO/RSA1	Remote Call Admin Workbench
/SAPAPO/RSP01	Activation of Reservation Planning
/SAPAPO/RSP_BINI	Basic Initialization
/SAPAPO/RSP_CHPTRDEL	Delete Change Pointers
/SAPAPO/RSP_CLOSE	Delete Time Series
/SAPAPO/RSP_CONSIS	Cons. Check RSC + Per.-Slot Creation
/SAPAPO/RSP_DBORSHOW	Display Configuration for Orders
/SAPAPO/RSP_DCR	Releasing Daily Packages
/SAPAPO/RSP_DICP	Daily Package Creation
/SAPAPO/RSP_DPND	Sub Processes - Dependencies
/SAPAPO/RSP_D_DEL	Delete Delta Records
/SAPAPO/RSP_EXPLAIN	Explanation Facility
/SAPAPO/RSP_G1	Planning Table
/SAPAPO/RSP_G1CU	Customizing Interactive RSP
/SAPAPO/RSP_GC	Customizing Restriction Check
/SAPAPO/RSP_INFO	Information Center RP
/SAPAPO/RSP_LC01	Initialize Time Series
/SAPAPO/RSP_LC03	Update Time Series
/SAPAPO/RSP_LC04	Restore Time Series
/SAPAPO/RSP_LOGDEL	Delete Logs from Planning Table
/SAPAPO/RSP_LOGSHOW	Display Logs from Planning Table
/SAPAPO/RSP_MCSC	Manuf.Compl. Proposed Orders f.Stock
/SAPAPO/RSP_MON	Process Monitor Reservation Planning
/SAPAPO/RSP_MON_CLR	Process Monitor Reorganisation

/SAPAPO/RSP_P1	Copy Orders
/SAPAPO/RSP_P2	Start Medium-Term Planning
/SAPAPO/RSP_P3	Reset Result of Medium-term Planning
/SAPAPO/RSP_P4	Copying Proposed Orders
/SAPAPO/RSP_PAPRO	Assignment Processes - Server Groups
/SAPAPO/RSP_PLNVERS	Disply Planning Version Time Series
/SAPAPO/RSP_PROV	Processes in Reservation Planning
/SAPAPO/RSP_RD_SIMU	Simulation of Restriction Explosion
/SAPAPO/RSP_REQ	Standard Requirements Profile
/SAPAPO/RSP_REVERT	Delete Open Transactions
/SAPAPO/RSP_RSC	Rescheduling
/SAPAPO/RTO_ORD_COMP	Compare PP/DS PDS (ERP)
/SAPAPO/RULESCUST	Determination of Rule Strategy
/SAPAPO/S002	APO system administration
/SAPAPO/SAPAPO	
/SAPAPO/SAPAPO00	ATP
/SAPAPO/SBC_XML	Deletion of XML Documents
/SAPAPO/SBC_XML1	Restart of XML Documents
/SAPAPO/SCC02	Supply Chain Cockpit
/SAPAPO/SCC03	PPM Maintenance
/SAPAPO/SCC05	PPM Maintenance
/SAPAPO/SCC07	Supply Chain Engineer
/SAPAPO/SCC_COL	Colors in Supply Chain Cockpit
/SAPAPO/SCC_CON_MENU	Context Menu Profile
/SAPAPO/SCC_MAP	Maps in Supply Chain Cockpit
/SAPAPO/SCC_MAPL	Map layers in SCC
/SAPAPO/SCC_SEL_SCR	Selection Screen for SCC/SCE
/SAPAPO/SCC_TB1	Request processes
/SAPAPO/SCC_TL1	Transportation Lanes
/SAPAPO/SCC_TL2	Mass Creation of Transport Rltnships
/SAPAPO/SCC_TL5	TP/VS Transportation Lanes for TSP
/SAPAPO/SCC_TQ1	Quota Arrangements
/SAPAPO/SCC_TQ2	Quota Arrangements
/SAPAPO/SCC_USR_PROF	SCC Cockpit User Settings
/SAPAPO/SCEVERSCOMP	Compare Planning Versions
/SAPAPO/SCE_QTA	Quota Arrangement Maintenance
/SAPAPO/SCE_USR_PROF	SCC Engineer User Settings
/SAPAPO/SCHED_CHECK	Consistency check - scheduling
/SAPAPO/SCHED_CND	Test Condition Technique Scheduling
/SAPAPO/SCHED_TEST	Simul. Transp. & Shipment Scheduling
/SAPAPO/SCH_ACC_SEQ	Access Sequence for Scheduling

/SAPAPO/SCH_COND_TYP	Condition Types for Scheduling
/SAPAPO/SCH_CT	Condition Tables for Scheduling
/SAPAPO/SCH_DET_PROC	Determination Proced. f. Scheduling
/SAPAPO/SCH_FC	Field Catalog for Scheduling
/SAPAPO/SCH_GCM	Condition Maintenance for Scheduling
/SAPAPO/SCMB_MP32	Maintain Cannibalization Group
/SAPAPO/SCNCTRL	Define Scenario Control Keys
/SAPAPO/SDORDER_DEL	Deletion Report for SD DB Data
/SAPAPO/SDORDER_DISP	Display S&D Document Data
/SAPAPO/SDP	Create/Change SNP/DP Planning Book
/SAPAPO/SDP08	Customizing in SDP
/SAPAPO/SDP110	Transfer to OLTP Systems
/SAPAPO/SDP20	Initial Cust. for Spec. SDP Transac.
/SAPAPO/SDP21	Planning Books and Views (Delivery)
/SAPAPO/SDP8B	Define Planning Book
/SAPAPO/SDP94	Supply & Demand Planner: Init.Screen
/SAPAPO/SDPALPR	Assign Planners to Alert Profiles
/SAPAPO/SDPDIS	DISAGGREGATION
/SAPAPO/SDPPLBK	Assign User to Planning Book
/SAPAPO/SDPSDP	Planning Run: Propagation
/SAPAPO/SDPT	SD Sched. Agrmt. Prod.Planning Table
/SAPAPO/SDPTBFX	Define Fixed Time Buckets Profile
/SAPAPO/SDPUSET	SDP User Settings
/SAPAPO/SDP_EXTR	DP/SNP Data Extraction
/SAPAPO/SDP_NOTES	Note Overview
/SAPAPO/SDP_PAR	DP/SNP Parallel Processg Prfl.Maint.
/SAPAPO/SDP_PARB	Block Size DP/SNP Parallel Processng
/SAPAPO/SDP_SEASON	Settings for Seasonal Planning
/SAPAPO/SDP_SEL	Selection Mgmt for Planning Area
/SAPAPO/SDP_SPLIT	Maintain Period Split Profile
/SAPAPO/SDRQCR21	Correction Report /sapapo/sdrqcr21
/SAPAPO/SEQ1	Interactive Sequencing
/SAPAPO/SEQ2	Model Mix Planning Run
/SAPAPO/SEQC1	Model Mix Proc. Pckges Customizing
/SAPAPO/SEQC10	Sequencing Order Specification Cust.
/SAPAPO/SEQC11	Sequencing: Line-Specific Profiles
/SAPAPO/SEQC2	Model Mix Single Proc. Customizing
/SAPAPO/SEQC3	Model Mix EDP Parameters Customizing
/SAPAPO/SEQC4	Model Mix GA Parameters Customizing
/SAPAPO/SEQC5	Model Mix Char. Views Customizing
/SAPAPO/SEQC6	Model Mix LP Paramter Customizing

/SAPAPO/SEQC7	Modell Mix PG Parameter Customizing
/SAPAPO/SEQC8	Model Mix SH Parameters Customizing
/SAPAPO/SEQC9	ALV Grid Variants: User Maintenance
/SAPAPO/SHPEDI	EDI Transfer of Planned Shipments
/SAPAPO/SIMUVMI	Simulation report for VMI Indound
/SAPAPO/SNP0	Supply Network Planning
/SAPAPO/SNP00	Supply Network Planning
/SAPAPO/SNP01	SNP Run
/SAPAPO/SNP02	Deployment
/SAPAPO/SNP03	Call Deployment Optimizer
/SAPAPO/SNP04	Transport Load Builder
/SAPAPO/SNP041	Call Old TLB Mass Processing
/SAPAPO/SNP042	Access Mass Processing of New TLB
/SAPAPO/SNP05	Capacity leveling
/SAPAPO/SNP06	Hierarchical Planning Disaggregation
/SAPAPO/SNP07	SNP Order Aggregation
/SAPAPO/SNP08	SNP Single-Level Mapping
/SAPAPO/SNP09	SNP Resource Disaggregation
/SAPAPO/SNP10	SNP Shelf Life Propagation
/SAPAPO/SNP101	Maintain SNP Demand Profile
/SAPAPO/SNP102	Maintain SNP Supply Profile
/SAPAPO/SNP103	Maintain TLB Profile
/SAPAPO/SNP104	Maintain SNP Demand Profile
/SAPAPO/SNP106	Display of Costs
/SAPAPO/SNP107	Cost Multipliers for Optimizer
/SAPAPO/SNP109	Key Figures - Category Groups
/SAPAPO/SNP110	SNP: VMI Category Settings
/SAPAPO/SNP111	Maintain SNP Deployment Profile
/SAPAPO/SNP112	Maintain SNP Lt Size Prof.-TransLane
/SAPAPO/SNP113	SNP: Maintain Costs
/SAPAPO/SNP2PPDS	SNP -> PP/DS Conv. in Background
/SAPAPO/SNP94	SNP: Interactive Planning
/SAPAPO/SNPAPLOG	Application Logs
/SAPAPO/SNPCG	Maintain Category Groups
/SAPAPO/SNPCOSF	SNP Optimizer: Cost Function
/SAPAPO/SNPCOSMAIN	Maintenance for SNP Cost Function
/SAPAPO/SNPDRP	DRP: Interactive Planning
/SAPAPO/SNPFCST	Release SNP Forecast
/SAPAPO/SNPGRP	Maitanence for Penality Cost Group
/SAPAPO/SNPLLC	Low-Level Code Determination
/SAPAPO/SNPMVAP	Schedule a Background Job
/SAPAPO/SNPOP	Call Up SNP Optimizer

/SAPAPO/SNPOPLOG	SNP Optimizer Log Data
/SAPAPO/SNPSA	Sched. Agreemt: Interactive Planning
/SAPAPO/SNPSOP	SOP: Interactive Planning
/SAPAPO/SNPSRC	Call: Sourcing of Forecast in SNP
/SAPAPO/SNPTLB	TLB: Interactive Planning
/SAPAPO/SNPVMI	SNP: Interactive Planning with VMI
/SAPAPO/SNP_OPTPR_CU	SNP Optimizer Maintenance
/SAPAPO/SNP_PENGRP	Penalty Cost Grp Profile Maintenance
/SAPAPO/SNP_SFT_PROF	Define SFT Planning Profiles
/SAPAPO/SNP_SHLFPROF	Define SNP Shelf Life Profiles
/SAPAPO/SNP_USR_PROF	SCC_SNP User Settings
/SAPAPO/SORCUST	Gen. Settings Surp. and Obsol. Serv.
/SAPAPO/SORDECCODE	Surplus Decision Code
/SAPAPO/SORREASON	Surplus Decision Code for Surp. Dec.
/SAPAPO/SORRETGRP	Retention Strategy Group
/SAPAPO/SORRETGRPSEL	Selection of Retention Strat. Groups
/SAPAPO/SORRETQTYDET	Retention Qty Determination Table
/SAPAPO/SORSCRAPORD	Display Scrapping Orders
/SAPAPO/SORSELMOD	Modification of Product Selection
/SAPAPO/SORSELMODIMP	Import Product Selection Modif.
/SAPAPO/SORSPRF	Surplus and Obsol. Service Profile
/SAPAPO/SORSVALAPPRL	Surplus Value Approval Limits
/SAPAPO/SORSVALRESET	Reset Surplus Value Approval Check
/SAPAPO/SPP	SPP
/SAPAPO/SPPDEPL	SPP Deployment
/SAPAPO/SPPDMDH	SPP Demand History
/SAPAPO/SPPDMRD	SPP Raw Data Adjustment
/SAPAPO/SPPDRPAPPR	SPP DRP Mass Approval
/SAPAPO/SPPDRPM	SPP DRP Matrix
/SAPAPO/SPPDRPMR	SPP DRP Release Filter
/SAPAPO/SPPDRPPR	SPP DRP Planning Lock
/SAPAPO/SPPDRPSB	Ext. Procurement - Schedule Maint.
/SAPAPO/SPPFCST	SPP Forecast
/SAPAPO/SPPFCSTAPPR	SPP: Approve Forecast
/SAPAPO/SPPFCSTPRF	SPP Forecast Profile
/SAPAPO/SPPFCSTTRACK	SPP Historical Forecast
/SAPAPO/SPPFIXREQ	SPP Fixed Demands and Fixed Receipts
/SAPAPO/SPPINBD	SPP Inbound Monitor Standard Time
/SAPAPO/SPPINVAPPR	SPP Stocking / Destocking Approval
/SAPAPO/SPPINVP	SPP Inventory Planning
/SAPAPO/SPPINVPDEC	SPP Decision Tables

/SAPAPO/SPPLONGFCST	SPP Long-Term Forecasting
/SAPAPO/SPPMSP	Processing of Manual Surplus Qty
/SAPAPO/SPPNEWFCST	SPP Forecast for New Products
/SAPAPO/SPPREPSTRAT	Customizing Replacement Strategies
/SAPAPO/SPPSIM	SPP Simulation
/SAPAPO/SPPSIMCUST	General Settings SPP Simulation
/SAPAPO/SPPSIMSTODEL	Delete Stock Transport Order in SimV
/SAPAPO/SPPSIMVERPRF	SPP Simulation: Version Profile
/SAPAPO/SPPSNAPSHDEL	SPP Simulation: Delete Snapshots
/SAPAPO/SPPSNAPSHOT	SPP Simulation: Create Snapshots
/SAPAPO/SPPSOR	Surplus and Obsolescence Approval
/SAPAPO/SPPSRVLOSS	SPP Change Service Loss Reason
/SAPAPO/SPP_CNA_ACT	Activate Obj. for Autom. Forwarding
/SAPAPO/SPP_CUSTOMER	SPP Planner View
/SAPAPO/SPP_DEALER	SPP Dealer View
/SAPAPO/SPP_DLR_LIST	Customer's Worklist
/SAPAPO/SPP_EP_RO_CP	Reorg ext proc docs (CP change)
/SAPAPO/SPP_IBUN_PPA	Inv. Balancing Unsrv. Area-ParPrf
/SAPAPO/SPP_IBUN_PRP	Inventory Balancing Unsrv. Par. Prf.
/SAPAPO/SPP_KSD	SPP Kit-to-Stock Shutdown
/SAPAPO/SPP_NOTE_DEL	Delete Analyst Note
/SAPAPO/SPP_PDBP	Hide Product Detail Tab (Partner)
/SAPAPO/SPP_PDPL	Hide Product Detail Tab (Planner)
/SAPAPO/SPP_PLN_LIST	Planner's Worklist
/SAPAPO/SPP_SCHD_EXP	Explanation Prog. for SPP Scheduler
/SAPAPO/SPP_SSD	SPP Supplier Shutdown
/SAPAPO/SPP_SUPPLIER	SPP Supplier View
/SAPAPO/SPP_TG_ACT	Activate Triggers for SPP
/SAPAPO/SPRSCUST	Supersession Customizing
/SAPAPO/SPRSSPRF	Supersession Service Profile
/SAPAPO/SPRS_OBS_UPD	Update Supersession Obsolescence
/SAPAPO/SP_ACC_SEQ	Maintenance Access Sequence Use SP
/SAPAPO/SP_COND_TYPE	Maintenance Condition Types Use SP
/SAPAPO/SP_CT	Maintenance Condition Tables Use SP
/SAPAPO/SP_DET_PROC	Maintenance Determination Procedure
/SAPAPO/SRVF_STATUS	Status
/SAPAPO/SR_KOKR_MURX	Scheduling Agreement Monitor
/SAPAPO/STEST	Maintain Scheduler Test Profiles
/SAPAPO/STORDEF	Product Storage definition
/SAPAPO/STYPES_DP	Maintain Customer-Specific DP Status
/SAPAPO/SUPCAT	CTM Supply Category Maintenance
/SAPAPO/TCATTR	MTr Comb./Compartment Attributes

/SAPAPO/TCLSYS	Set Configuration Relevance
/SAPAPO/TDLCAPA_CORR	Correct Transportation Allocations
/SAPAPO/TDLCAPA_INIT	Initialize Capacities for TSP
/SAPAPO/TDL_APO_SEM	TDL: Semantic Mapping
/SAPAPO/TDL_EQ_TEST	TDL: Equipment Data Browser
/SAPAPO/TDL_INV_TEST	TDL: Stock Data Browser
/SAPAPO/TDL_ORD_TEST	TDL: Order Data Browser
/SAPAPO/TDL_TS_HTEST	TDL: Time Series Hist. Data Browser
/SAPAPO/TDL_TS_TEST	TDL: Time Series Data Browser
/SAPAPO/TI01	Evaluation of Production Tracking
/SAPAPO/TIERDEF	Priority Tier Hierarchy Definition
/SAPAPO/TL1	Transportation Lanes
/SAPAPO/TL2	Mass Creation of Transport Rltnships
/SAPAPO/TL3	Transportation Lanes
/SAPAPO/TLBPARAM	TLB Parameter Maintenance
/SAPAPO/TLBPRF	TLB Profile Maintenance
/SAPAPO/TMREF	Changeable Time Reference
/SAPAPO/TMS_CAL	Departure Calendar
/SAPAPO/TPK	Route Det.: Maintain Cost Profile
/SAPAPO/TPOP_ASSIGN	Product Supplier Assignments
/SAPAPO/TPOP_POREL	Convert Planned Purchase Orders
/SAPAPO/TR30	Maintain DP/SNP Time Buckets Profile
/SAPAPO/TR32	Periodicities for Planning Area
/SAPAPO/TRCOUPTM	Loading/Unload. Duration for Trailer
/SAPAPO/TRIGDPRF	Service Profile for Trigger Deletion
/SAPAPO/TRIGGER	Trigger
/SAPAPO/TR_CDC_QUOTA	Change Doc. Activation for Quotas
/SAPAPO/TR_CDC_TLANE	Change Doc. Activation Transp. Lanes
/SAPAPO/TR_CD_QUOTA	Change Docs for Quota Arrangements
/SAPAPO/TR_CD_TLANE	Change Docs for Transportation Lanes
/SAPAPO/TR_DELTRPR	Delete Product-Specific Trnsp. Lane
/SAPAPO/TR_GDELTRPR	Schedule Transportatn Lane Deletion
/SAPAPO/TR_IGS_BPSEL	Scheduling of GIS Preselection
/SAPAPO/TR_IGS_BUTRM	Update of GIS Data
/SAPAPO/TR_IGS_RPSEL	Reorganization of GIS Preselection
/SAPAPO/TSCONS	Time Ser. Network Consistency Check
/SAPAPO/TSCOPY	Copy/Version Management
/SAPAPO/TSCUBE	Load Planning Area Version
/SAPAPO/TSKEYFMAIN	Mass Maint. for Time Series Key Fig.
/SAPAPO/TSLCREORG	Check LC Time Series Master Data
/SAPAPO/TSLPAR	SPP Deployment: TSL Parameters
/SAPAPO/TSLPARIMP	Mass Maintenance of TSL Parameters

/SAPAPO/TSOBJ	Transport Connection DP/SNP
/SAPAPO/TSPSTRU	Toolbox for Planning Object Struct.
/SAPAPO/TSW_MDC_PR	APO-TSW: Partner Roles Maintenance
/SAPAPO/TTC1	Schedule Maintenance
/SAPAPO/TTV1	Maintain Validity Area
/SAPAPO/TTW1	Itinerary Maintenance
/SAPAPO/TZONE01	Maintain Transportation Zone
/SAPAPO/TZONE03	Display Transportation Zone
/SAPAPO/USRPLN	Assignment of Users to Planners
/SAPAPO/VASOSORT	Variant-Dependent Special Sorting
/SAPAPO/VC_GROUP	Condition Maintenance Group
/SAPAPO/VERCOP	Copy Version
/SAPAPO/VERCREATE	Create a Planning Version
/SAPAPO/VERDELLD	Delete a planning version
/SAPAPO/VERMER	Merge Planning Versions (SNP)
/SAPAPO/VERMRM	Merge Versions: Messages
/SAPAPO/VM_SPP	Merge into active version for SPP MD
/SAPAPO/VS01	VS Interactive Planning
/SAPAPO/VS021	Maintain Optimization Profile
/SAPAPO/VS022	Change Optimization Profile
/SAPAPO/VS023	Display Optimization Profile
/SAPAPO/VS05	Schedule optimization run
/SAPAPO/VS06	Relevant Optimization Dimension/Unit
/SAPAPO/VS08	Schedule Optimization Run
/SAPAPO/VS09	Upgrade TSP Strategies
/SAPAPO/VS10	Transportation Service Provider Sel.
/SAPAPO/VS11	TPVS: Define Delivery/Pickup Windows
/SAPAPO/VS12	TP/VS: Define Compatibilities
/SAPAPO/VS14	Maintain Split Rules
/SAPAPO/VS15	Maintain Conditions
/SAPAPO/VS16	Define Route Determination Profile
/SAPAPO/VS17	Number Range Maintenance: /SAPAPO/OT
/SAPAPO/VS18	Interactive Routing Guide
/SAPAPO/VS50	Orders for Delivery Generation
/SAPAPO/VS501	Schedule Delivery Generation
/SAPAPO/VS51	Change Plan. Shipments to Shipments
/SAPAPO/VS511	Transfer Planned Shipments to OLTP
/SAPAPO/VS52	Check Release of Planned Shipments
/SAPAPO/VS521	Check Release of Planned Shipments
/SAPAPO/VS53	Deleting deliveries
/SAPAPO/VS531	Delete Deliveries

/SAPAPO/VS54	Deleting Shipments
/SAPAPO/VS541	Delete Shipments
/SAPAPO/VS551	Release Shipments in the Background
/SAPAPO/VS60	Monitor for OLTP Publication
/SAPAPO/VS61	Monitor Tenderings
/SAPAPO/VS611	Schedule Monitoring of Tendering
/SAPAPO/VS70	Apply Split Rules
/SAPAPO/VS71	Determine Split Rules
/SAPAPO/VS72	Maintain Access Sequence for Splits
/SAPAPO/VS73	Maintain Split Rules
/SAPAPO/VS80	Control Rules for ext. Order Changes
/SAPAPO/VSCC	Vehicle Scheduling Consistency Check
/SAPAPO/VSHIST	Display the Change History
/SAPAPO/VSSP	Manual Creation of Freight Units
/SAPAPO/VSTLBCONV	Convert TP/VS Shipments to TLB Order
/SAPAPO/VS_03	Means of Transport - Transp. Group
/SAPAPO/VS_04	General Vehicle Scheduling Settings
/SAPAPO/VS_05	Means of Transport - Shipment Type
/SAPAPO/VS_07	Vehicle - Means of Transport
/SAPAPO/VS_08	Number Ranges for Shipments
/SAPAPO/VS_09	Number Ranges for Temporary Shipmts
/SAPAPO/VS_11	Number range maintenance: /SAPAPO/PL
/SAPAPO/VS_ATPA	Activate VS RG in ATP check
/SAPAPO/VS_CST_OP1	Display VS Cost (NO DIRECT CALL !!)
/SAPAPO/VS_HEURSCHED	Schedule Optimization Run
/SAPAPO/VS_OPT2	New VS Optimization Profile
/SAPAPO/V_SNP01	Parameter Transaction IMG Activity
/SAPAPO/V_SNP02	Parameter Transaction IMG Activity
/SAPAPO/V_SNP03	Parameter Transaction IMG Activity
/SAPAPO/V_SNP11	Parameter Transaction IMG Activity
/SAPAPO/V_SNP12	Parameter Transaction IMG Activity
/SAPAPO/V_SNPSFT01	Maintanance View SFT Plan.Profile
/SAPAPO/V_TLB_SH	Display Rule Parameters in TLB
/SAPAPO/WD_START	Start Web Dynpro Application
/SAPAPO/XMLPROMID	Promotion ID customizing

Made in United States
Orlando, FL
04 November 2026

90218960R00186